THE TREATY OF BUKAREST, 1913

The
Troubled
Alliance

Gerard E. Silberstein

The Troubled Alliance

German-Austrian
Relations
1914 to 1917

Lexington, Kentucky

The University
Press of
Kentucky

Standard Book Number 8131–1196–X
Library of Congress Catalog Card Number 77–94072

Copyright © 1970 by The University Press of Kentucky

A statewide cooperative scholarly publishing agency
serving Berea College, Centre College of Kentucky,
Eastern Kentucky University, Kentucky State College,
Morehead State University, Murray State University,
University of Kentucky, University of Louisville,
and Western Kentucky University.

Editorial and Sales Offices: Lexington, Kentucky 40506

*To the memory of my parents
Blanche and Louis Silberstein*

Contents

Preface   xi

Part I   The Background

   1. The Future Allies   3
   2. Diplomatic Disappointments   31
   3. Military Preparedness   59

Part II   Balkan Diplomacy of the Central Powers

   4. Turkey's Declaration of War   73
   5. The Turkish Ally   99
   6. Bulgaria Pursued   129
   7. The Second Link   150
   8. Rumania, Uncertain Neutral   179
   9. Rumania, Point and Counterpoint   198
   10. The Rumanian Link Unforged   226

Part III   The High Commands—Unity and Disunity

   11. Initial Operations   251
   12. A Year of Success, 1915   275
   13. The Setbacks of 1916   302

   14. Conclusions   334
   Selected Bibliography   345
   Index   355

Maps and Illustrations

Maps

The Balkan States following the Treaty of Bukarest, 1913   *Endpapers*

The Turkish Campaign against Russia in the Caucasus, 1915   113

The Balkan Railroads in 1914   115

The Turkish-Bulgarian Border Agreement of 1915   125

The Bulgarian-Serbian Alliance of 1912   159

Areas Promised to Bulgaria, 1915   175

The Disposition of Eastern Armies, August 1914   183

The Gorlice-Tarnow Breakthrough   285

The Serbian Campaign, 1915   295

The Brussilov Offensive, 1916   311

The Campaign of the Central Powers against Rumania, 1916–1917   331

Illustrations   *following page* 242

Theobald von Bethmann-Hollweg and Gottlieb von Jagow in Rome, 1910

Leopold von Berchtold; Stephan von Burian; Stephan Tisza

Franz Conrad von Hötzendorf; Erich von Falkenhayn

Paul von Hindenburg; August von Mackensen

Enver Pasha; Talaat Bey; Djemal Pasha

Hans von Wangenheim; Johann von Pallavicini

King Ferdinand of Bulgaria; Vasil Radoslavov

Adam Tarnowski; Gustav Michahelles

King Ferdinand of Rumania; Ion Bratianu

Ottokar von Czernin; Hilmar von dem Bussche

Heinrich von Tschirschky; Gottfried von Hohenlohe, as a younger man

Preface

It has been a half century since World War I ended. In spite of the vast literature which now exists on the subject, there are still certain gaps in the knowledge of what happened during that war. This is particularly so in the field of diplomatic history where a definitive work covering the entire war period remains to be written. Because of the availability of the complete German and Austrian Foreign Ministry files it is now possible to develop the full story concerning the diplomatic activities of the Central Powers. The present work offers an account of a small part of that diplomatic action.

This monograph does not offer a revolutionary thesis. It is a book of explication, one that attempts a detailed picture of what it was that happened. Herein lies its *raison d'être*, for, while the general outlines of what took place have been known for a long while, the important details have heretofore been woefully absent.

I have restricted the discussion to German and Austrian policies as they pertained to the establishment of a Balkan coalition aligned against the Entente. My aim has been to show what the policies of these allies were, how they diverged or coalesced, and how and why they succeeded or failed.

In examining the diplomacy of the Central Powers it is impossible to exclude the relations between the German and Austrian High Commands, since diplomatic and military decisions were inextricably intermeshed. The health and well-being of the German-Austrian wartime alliance was obviously much affected by the unity or disunity between the two headquarters. Chapters 11, 12, and 13 deal with the matter.

The narrative ends in January, 1917, with the successful completion of the campaign against Rumania. This date constitutes the culmination of German-Austrian efforts to seal off the most important Balkan states from the enemy.

The table of contents attests to the omissions. No detailed account of Greece or Italy is offered, though both have been woven into the narrative where they are essential to understanding negotiations with Turkey, Bulgaria, and Rumania. Since the Central Powers largely dealt with these last three states as a unit, I have considered them as such.

A word seems necessary concerning the sources used for this study. The largest part of my discussion is based on the documentary collections at the Haus-Hof-und Staatsarchiv and Kriegsarchiv in Vienna and the microfilm collections of the German Foreign Ministry Archives available in this country. Since the two groups of materials mesh almost perfectly on a day-to-day basis, a very full account of German-Austrian policy development is possible. The attitudes and positions of Turkish, Bulgarian, and Rumanian statesmen emerge clearly from these same sources. The great quantity of documents available makes it unwise for me to claim exhaustion of the materials germane to my subject, but I hope that in the course of ten years of research I have seen the largest part of the most important groups. I have found the majority of secondary accounts rather disappointing. Many are outdated, fragmentary, or unreliable, and in some cases share all three characteristics equally. The bibliography therefore lists only those works I consider most valuable for investigating the subject at hand.

In the spelling of various names of persons and places, I have used those renditions which are most generally employed. For the purist this may not strike a sympathetic chord but hopefully the reader will find my choices comfortable. The terms Austria, Austria-Hungary, and Monarchy have been used interchangeably. Where something more or less is meant to be conveyed I have relied on the context for clarification.

I owe much to many people without whose help this book could not have been written. Professor William L. Langer of Harvard, now Emeritus, guided me through the initial research on the subject, which was submitted in more limited form as a dissertation. It was he who encouraged me to continue my labors in the direction of a full-length monograph. He has not seen the manuscript, for it seemed to me that his duties as a scholarly shepherd on my behalf were more than fulfilled some years ago. For his kindnesses and attentions as my teacher I offer him my deep gratitude.

I wish to acknowledge my debt to the United States Fulbright Commission in Austria under whose auspices a year's research was made possible in 1958–1959. A brief stay in Vienna in 1966 was made into a successful research trip through the kind and warm efforts of Professor Anton Porhansl, executive secretary of the Austrian Fulbright Commission, and the senior member of his staff, Frau Dr. Eva Schussek.

A special thank you is in order for Archivist Herr A. Nemeth, whose knowledge of the Austrian Foreign Office files saved me many an hour of precious time. Certainly, a warm acknowledgment must be made of the great help given me by Dr. Allmayer Beck who originally made me aware of the Conrad-Falkenhayn Korrespondenz and allowed me to see and microfilm large segments of these papers. Without the cooperation of Dr. Peball and Herr Peschek, both of the Kriegsarchiv, I would not have seen certain crucial collections.

My sincere appreciation is extended for the assistance given me by the State University of New York, which financed a summer's research at the University of California and Stanford University libraries in 1963. The University of Kentucky and the Kentucky Research Foundation have been more than generous in providing me with three summer grants and an overseas stipend needed to complete the research and writing of this book.

I must indeed acknowledge the efficient and patient aid tendered me by the staffs of the National Archives, the Congressional Library, the Austrian National Bibliothek, Harvard's Widener Library, the Doe Library at the University of California in Berkeley, the Hoover Library at Stanford, and the Margaret King Library at the University of Kentucky.

Grateful acknowledgment is made for permission to reproduce those photographs supplied by the Bildarchiv, Osterreichische Nationalbibliothek; Deutsche Staatsbibliothek; and the Historisches Bildarchiv, Handke.

For my history department colleagues at Kentucky, scholars and great gentlemen, who have so tactfully pushed me on, I would hope the results are not disappointing.

Mrs. Eula Hardy Moore, who has painstakingly typed the manuscript over long months, has intelligently waded her way through my messy corrections.

Last, but certainly not least, I wish to thank my wife, Ruth Grun Silberstein, who so painstakingly rendered the initial map drafts. A professional historian in her own right, she has somehow managed, between lecturing and the demands of child-rearing, to play devil's advocate, to offer objective criticism when she did not feel objective, and always to provide her most gracious understanding.

Part I

The Background

Chapter 1

The Future Allies

When the holocaust began in the hot summer days of 1914 Europe exuded excitement and confidence. In highest German and Austro-Hungarian governmental circles the optimism stemmed from a good deal more than the patriotic masses upon whom they could count, from more than an acute awareness of well-oiled military machines and carefully conceived military plans and strategems. The leaders of both empires had agreed upon a common diplomatic policy which they believed would substantially contribute to final victory. Their diplomatic goal on the European continent was to establish a powerful Balkan coalition comprising Turkey, Bulgaria, and Rumania, which would actively engage in the war on the side of the Central Powers. The implications of such a fighting coalition were obvious—the control of the Balkan peninsula and the addition of considerable armed might which could be turned loose upon the enemy with telling, perhaps even crucial, effect.

This unity of diplomatic purpose was a most recent development, for it had been achieved a mere month before the conflict began. Prior to this time and particularly since the Balkan Wars of 1912–1913, Germany and Austria-Hungary had not at all agreed on how the situation in the Balkans might best be handled.[1] Their differences were based on disparate points of view concerning each of the three Balkan states involved.

Negotiations for a Turkish Alliance

In the case of Turkey and the policy to be employed there, German and Austrian agreement came only at the last moment. In spite of this, efforts to obtain Turkish participation in the war met with rapid success, a success rooted in certain economic, political, and military conditions which did not obtain in the case of Bulgaria or Rumania.

Within the Ottoman Empire, both Germany and Austria-Hungary had developed large economic interests, particularly after 1900, although of the two powers it was Germany which held the predominant position at Constantinople by 1914. Aside from developing a lively

3

export trade with Turkey, Germany controlled the Turkish railroads and ranked second only to France in the size of financial investments. Germany's economic strength in Turkey was based not only on the daring of German bankers, but also on the close cooperation which they established with German industrialists and merchants who were interested in developing a Turkish market and who were eagerly supported in such an enterprise by the German government itself.[2]

In addition to its economic activities, Germany had acquired in Turkey a military predominance, the foundations of which had been laid by the work of General Colmar von der Goltz, who had been sent to Turkey in an advisory capacity in 1909. The predominance was assured when General Otto Liman von Sanders arrived in Constantinople in 1913 to enlarge upon Turkish military reforms already instituted under German leadership.[3]

In their diplomatic relations with Constantinople the Germans were in a strong position well before the assassination of Archduke Franz Ferdinand in June 1914. That position was largely the result of the efficiency and knowledgeability of the men who had been chosen to represent the Kaiser at the Turkish court: Marschall von Bieberstein and his successor Hans von Wangenheim. Upon Ambassador von Wangenheim's shoulders lay the major burden for the successful implementation of German policy with the Sublime Porte in 1913–1914. An imposing figure of a man, with an intense face enhanced by piercing eyes, Wangenheim came to Turkey with twenty-five years of experience as a professional diplomat. He spoke German, French, and English equally well, and since he had already served as chargé d'affaires for several years before taking over the ambassadorial post, he was no stranger to Turkish habits and methods. Somewhat high-strung and destined to crack under the strain of his obligations, he was nevertheless capable of great control and proved able to vary his approach according to what was needed, whether tact or an almost brutal frankness.

Wangenheim's job was made easier by those surrounding him. He could rely, for example, on the naval attaché, Hans Humann, who had

---

[1] Carl Mühlmann, *Deutschland und die Türkei, 1913–1914*, pp. 36–39.

[2] Harry Howard, *The Partition of Turkey, 1913–23*, pp. 48–50. German investments in Turkish securities stood at 1.4 billion francs by 1914. By 1911 Germany already had 30 million Turkish pounds invested in railroads and, since 1903, controlled the Bagdad Railway; René Pinon, "La Rivalité des Grandes Puissances dans l'Empire Ottoman," *Revue des Deux Mondes*, 42 (1907): 346–48.

[3] Robert J. Kerner, "Mission of Liman von Sanders," *Slavonic Review*, 6 (June 1927): 17; Maurice Larcher, *La Guerre Turque dans la Guerre Mondiale*, p. 34.

been born in Smyrna, spent most of his life in Turkey, knew every language of the East, and had close personal connections with leading Turkish statesmen. There was also the well-informed correspondent for the *Frankfurter Zeitung*, Paul Weitz, a person who had access to any of the Turkish government leaders at almost any time.[4]

While Austria did not enjoy so strong a position in Turkey as did Germany, it hardly lacked interest in developing Ottoman connections. By 1911 Austrian exports to Turkey already totalled over 100 million kronen. To further its economic position there, the Austrian government had fixed its eyes on controlling areas within the Turkish Empire, including the Gulf of Adalia, the port of Haifa, and the hinterland south of the French sphere in Syria. When it came to military affairs, Austria had made no attempt to place itself in a commanding position, but diplomacy was quite another matter. To serve as Austrian ambassador, Vienna made sure it sent one of its best men, Margraf Johann Pallavicini. Taking over his duties in 1906, Pallavicini held his office until the end of the war. He was astute, capable, and highly respected by Turkish officialdom, and became dean of the diplomatic corps in Constantinople.[5]

Despite Pallavicini's eminence, however, the Young Turk leaders tended to center thinking on Germany rather than on Austria-Hungary. These men were convinced that the multinational character of the Habsburg Empire and the existing internal dissensions reflected decay and meant the eventual death of the Dual Monarchy. Germany, on the other hand, seemed to them the epitome of the modern power state. Therefore, as negotiations between Turkey and the Central Powers went on in the summer of 1914, the Turks made their strongest representations to Berlin. For this reason, as well as for others that will become clear, Austria, in the final stages of the pourparlers, allowed Germany to take the lead in tying Turkey to the camp of the Triple Alliance.[6]

After the Balkan Wars, Turkey found itself in a difficult position. The defeat of the Turks by the Balkan states very clearly demonstrated the need for reforms within Turkey in financial, administrative, mili-

[4] Henry Morgenthau, *Ambassador Morgenthau's Story*, pp. 4–8, 29–30, 90; Lewis Einstein, *Inside Constantinople*, pp. 24–25, 92–93; Herman Christern, ed., *Deutsches Biographisches Jahrbuch, 1914–16*, p. 343.

[5] Geza Lukacs, *Die Handelspolitische Interressengemeinschaft Zwischen dem Deutschen Reiche und Österreich-Ungarn*, p. 43; Howard, *Partition of Turkey*, pp. 52–53; W. W. Gottlieb, *Studies in Secret Diplomacy During the First World War*, p. 21; Morgenthau, *Ambassador Morgenthau's Story*, p. 10.

[6] Maurice Bompard, "L'Entrée en Guerre de la Turquie," *La Revue de Paris* 13 (1 July 1921): 69; see pp. 12 ff. for details.

tary, and naval affairs.[7] But aside from this, Constantinople had emerged from the wars diplomatically isolated, and government leaders were now painfully aware of Turkey's weak international position. The Ottomans had lost almost all their territory on the Balkan peninsula and had become estranged from the successor states. It was believed that England and France desired even further partition and viewed with equanimity the ambitions of Russia, which posed the greatest threat of all to Turkish existence. It was this Russian danger which led the Turks to consider the possibilities and advisability of allying with one or more of the very Balkan countries against whom they had just fought. Bulgaria and Rumania were the two obvious partners, not only because both countries opposed the idea of Russia's controlling the Dardanelles, but also because a coalition of Turkey, Bulgaria, and Rumania would constitute the most powerful military combination possible.[8] Unfortunately, the attempts made in this direction by July, 1914, had produced negligible results because the Balkan states had refused to commit themselves to binding obligations.[9]

What then was the key to Turkey's dilemma? The solution clearly lay in attachment to the Triple Alliance. Of the great powers only Germany had made no attempt to obtain Turkish possessions and it was on Germany that Turkish officials turned their sights in July.[10] The situation, however, was complicated by the fact that within the Turkish cabinet there was by no means total agreement that an approach to Germany and Austria constituted the best diplomatic line. The cabinet itself was divided between an extremist Germanophile and a moderate Francophile wing. The latter believed that since Germany and Austria did not constitute a threat to Turkish territorial integrity, Turkey's interests would best be served by establishing concrete understandings with those powers who were dangerous, the Entente.[11] Such negotiations had indeed been attempted during the tenure of Mahmoud Shevket Pasha as grand vizier, but had come to no conclusion. Because of this failure and because Germanophiles had come to hold the significant posts in the cabinet, Turkey turned to Germany and Austria. The pro-German element included the grand vizier, Said Halim Pasha, the minister of war, Enver Pasha, and the minister of

---

[7] Howard, *Partition of Turkey*, p. 32; Mühlmann, *Deutschland und die Türkei*, pp. 28–29; Ahmed Emin, *Turkey in the World War*, p. 65.

[8] Mühlmann, *Deutschland und die Türkei*, p. 32; Luigi Albertini, *Origins of the War of 1914*, 3:608.

[9] Mühlmann, *Deutschland und die Türkei*, p. 34.

[10] Djemal Pasha, *Memories of a Turkish Statesman*, pp. 112–13.

[11] Emin, *Turkey in the World War*, pp. 66, 68; Mühlmann, *Deutschland und die Türkei*, pp. 29–31.

interior, Talaat Bey.[12] These three recognized that it was not to Germany's benefit to ignore Turkey's plight, for the Turks constituted a large factor in German commercial ventures in the Near East. Equally important was the fact that the Ottoman lands constituted a gap in what the Germans saw as an otherwise solid iron ring of encirclement, and Berlin's advantage clearly lay in maintaining the passageway.[13] Moreover, the Germanophiles realized that from the standpoint of self-interest a strong attachment to the Triple Alliance constituted Turkey's salvation. Once the Turks were aligned with such powerful allies, the Entente powers would hesitate to attempt partition for fear of causing a general conflict, and the Balkan states would not have the courage to risk further intrusions on Turkish territory.[14]

The decision by the Turkish government to court the Central Powers was based on further astute reasoning. Of the Balkan nations, it was Bulgaria in which the Turks took a particular diplomatic interest. An alliance with Sofia would constitute insurance against Greece. Neither Bulgaria nor Turkey was on good terms with Greece as a result of the Treaty of Bukarest, which in ending the Balkan Wars had enhanced Greek territorial holdings to a considerable degree at the expense of both those states. Even more significant was the counterweight such an alliance would offer against Russia, whose relationship with Bulgaria was now strained. If Constantinople could ally itself with Rumania as well, it would be in a strong position should Russia decide to attack the Ottoman Empire.[15] Toward this end, negotiations had been going on with the Bulgarians since September, 1913, but by the following July nothing definite had been arranged. Now, because Sofia during this time had swung in the direction of the Triple Alliance, and because the Rumanians had been formally connected to Germany and Austria since 1883, it seemed clear to the Turks that the solution to their whole Balkan problem would be found by reaching these states through Berlin and Vienna.[16] Then, too, there was the question of Pan-Turanism, which in recent years had been fostered by the Young Turks. This program could not help but lead toward the Central Powers, for if the desired union with those of the same race, language, and religion was to be accomplished it could be done only at the expense of England in Egypt, France in Syria, and Russia in Persia.[17]

[12] Emin, *Turkey in the World War*, pp. 66, 68; Mühlmann, *Deutschländ und die Türkei*, p. 31.
[13] Djemal Pasha, *Memories of a Turkish Statesman*, p. 113.
[14] Ibid.
[15] Mühlmann, *Deutschland und die Türkei*, pp. 33-34.
[16] Albertini, *Origins of the War of 1914*, 3:608-9.
[17] Emin, *Turkey in the World War*, pp. 64-66.

In light of all these factors, the course of action was quite clear to the Germanophile wing of Turkish governmental circles. These were the officials who established policy and who completed the negotiations resulting in the German-Turkish Alliance, to which Austria gave its endorsement.

Turkish overtures to the two imperial governments were initially neither accepted nor rejected. Neither Germany nor Austria suffered any illusions whatsoever concerning the military strength of Turkey. It was apparent to them that as an ally this nation would constitute a military liability rather than an asset. General Liman, upon his arrival at Constantinople, still found conditions in the army deplorable, to say the least. As late as May 12, 1914, the German chief of staff, von Moltke, had expressed to his Austrian counterpart, Conrad von Hötzendorf, his opinion that the Turkish forces were "absolutely worthless."[18]

But Germany's hesitancy was based on something much deeper than merely military considerations. Germany took a position calculated to give itself the best possible advantage no matter what the fate of Turkey might be. In the year preceding the war Germany had negotiated with Austria, Italy, France, and Great Britain concerning future partition of the Ottoman Empire should it collapse. Germany sought its share if such partition should indeed take place. But in case Turkey did not collapse, the Germans would need no specific diplomatic alliance there since domination could be effected by economic means.[19]

In the question of a Turkish alliance with the Balkans the goal for Berlin was to make sure Turkey joined no Balkan coalition which would lean in the direction of the Entente, placing Germany and her allies at a disadvantage.[20] With this in mind, and in accordance with the Kaiser's pro-Greek inclinations, Berlin had for some time advised that Turkey negotiate its differences with Greece to clear the way for a possible Greek-Rumanian-Turkish grouping.[21]

In the final analysis Berlin's position was to maintain a connection with Constantinople but await the development of events. If Turkey became a crucial factor, such a connection would be useful. Should Turkey collapse, Germany could, being uncommitted, turn a deaf ear without embarrassment.[22]

---

[18] Otto Liman von Sanders, *Five Years in Turkey*, p. 10; Franz Conrad von Hötzendorf, *Aus Meiner Dienstzeit, 1906–1918*, 3:672.

[19] Howard, *Partition of Turkey*, p. 60; Moukhtar Pasha, *La Turquie, l'Allemagne et l'Europe*, pp. 255–56.

[20] Mühlmann, *Deutschland und die Türkei*, pp. 35–36.

[21] Ibid., pp. 36–37.

As late as July 22, 1914, Germany held to this position. On July 14, Foreign Secretary Gottlieb von Jagow had recapitulated in a telegram to the ambassador in Vienna his own remarks as made to Ladislaus Szögyény, the Austrian representative in Berlin. He had told Szögyény that both he and Wangenheim felt Turkey constituted a "passive factor" at this time, that it would be unable to counter any aggressive action by Russia, and that an alliance would merely obligate Germany to meet Turkish demands with nothing being gained in exchange. Jagow considered it useless and hazardous to engage in a démarche "because of inevitable demands, incapable of fulfillment, for counter-performance on our part."[23]

The German Foreign Office had been much influenced by the opinions of Wangenheim in Constantinople. On July 18, three days after he had returned to Turkey from a trip to Berlin for conversations with his superiors, he cabled that he strongly disagreed with Austria's desire to win Turkish support against the Serbs. He declared, "Without doubt, Turkey today is totally incapable of carrying out an alliance." The development of a Turkish-Bulgarian bond, something which Austria fostered, would not be beneficial and would only end by provoking Russian action. He concluded, "For the present, Turkey can only be advised to remain aloof from any political adventure and to maintain good relations with all countries."[24]

The position of Austria-Hungary by this time had come to differ considerably from that of Germany. The Austrians were now definitely in favor of establishing some sort of alliance with the Turks which would rank them alongside the Dreibund. Pallavicini had suggested to Vienna that everything be done to eliminate the possibility of Turkey's joining the Entente.[25] He did not necessarily want a direct and specific agreement between Turkey and the Central Powers, for he concurred with Wangenheim in thinking that such an agreement would place too heavy a load on the Triple Alliance, which could "not defend Turkey against everybody."[26] What he sought was a link between Turkey and Bulgaria, which would necessarily tie Turkey to

---

[22] Moukhtar Pasha, *La Turquie*, p. 255; German Foreign Ministry Archives, University of California Microfilm Collection, ser. 1, reel 13, no. 349, Ambassador Wangenheim to Berlin, 18 July 1914 (hereafter cited as GFMA).

[23] GFMA, ser. 1, reel 13, no. 910, von Jagow to Tschirschky in Vienna, 14 July 1914; Karl Kautsky, ed., *Die Deutschen Dokumente zum Kriegsausbruch*, vol. 1, no. 45, Jagow to ambassadors in Vienna and Constantinople, 14 July 1914.

[24] GFMA, ser. 1, reel 13, no. 349, Wangenheim to Berlin, 18 July 1914.

[25] Albertini, *Origins of the War of 1914*, 3:610.

[26] Kautsky, *Deutschen Dokumente*, vol. 1, no. 149, Wangenheim to Berlin, 23 July 1914.

the Central Powers. Basic to his thinking was the fact that since the end of the Balkan Wars the relationship between Vienna and Sofia had become a close one.[27] With Bulgaria presenting a pro-Austrian attitude, a diplomatic agreement between Sofia and Constantinople could only mean an assurance of Turkish friendship. Relations between Austria and Serbia were now very much strained as a result of Archduke Franz Ferdinand's assassination, and therefore a Bulgarian-Turkish coalition would serve Austrian interests if it came to a Serbian showdown.[28]

The Austrians looked askance at the negotiations between Turkey and Greece which, through the insistence of Germany, had proceeded in the spring and summer of 1914. Should these negotiations be successful, Vienna feared they would end in a Turkish-Greek-Rumanian accord which would lead, contrary to the Kaiser's opinion, in but one direction—that of the Entente. Since by July the Serbian issue had reached the explosive stage, such a development was most certainly to be avoided. On July 23, in accordance with instructions from the Ballhausplatz, Pallavicini warned the Turks against concluding an alliance with Greece.[29]

Thus, while Germany and Austria were equally aware of the importance of Turkey, they had come to differ on the precise diplomatic policy to be pursued. But suddenly on July 22 Germany decided on a major change in its position, and from this time took the lead in bringing about an accord with the Turkish government, while Austria proved content merely to second the steps taken in Berlin.

The documents of the German Foreign Office show the reasons for the shift in policy. On the crucial day Wangenheim cabled that he had been approached by Enver Pasha, who had openly asked that Turkey be permitted to join the Triple Alliance. Enver stated that Turkey urgently desired this, and that only if rejected would "she decide with a heavy heart in favor of a pact with the Triple Entente." He pointed out that Turkish internal reforms could be effected only if the nation was secure against external attack, that Turkey needed the support of one of the diplomatic groups, and that the majority of the Committee of Union and Progress—the powerful political party representing the Young Turk Movement—favored the Central Powers, considering them militarily the stronger. He further stated that what his government wanted was the support and patronage of the Dreibund for a secondary alliance with Bulgaria.[30]

[27] Albertini, *Origins of the War of 1914*, 3:610–11.
[28] Ibid.
[29] Kautsky, *Deutschen Dokumente*, vol. 1, no. 149, Wangenheim to Berlin, 23 July 1914; Albertini, *Origins of the War of 1914*, 3:610–11.

Wangenheim remained unconvinced of the wisdom of such a move. In his opinion a connection with the Triplice would hinder Turkish recovery, since neither Russia nor France would then sign economic contracts with Constantinople. Further, as an ally of the Central Powers, Turkey would have to face Russia in any war; this meant that the weakest point in the strategic disposition of the Triple Alliance would be the Turkish borders, which the Russians would attack. Even the addition of Bulgaria would not offer much more in the way of advantages for Germany and Austria unless Rumania could also be brought in, an expectation of which "there seems at present to be little prospect."[31]

In a marginal note to this telegram the Kaiser agreed with Wangenheim, but only on a theoretical level. War clouds were looming, and in the coming conflict between Austria and Serbia the Kaiser sought to offer Germany's ally every advantage. He therefore declared that for "opportunist politics" a Turkish alliance was necessary. Every gun in the Balkans was needed to shoot against the Slavs, "*for* Austria." What the Kaiser now advised was a Turkish-Bulgarian-Rumanian connection to be placed at the disposal of the Habsburg monarchy. This, he said, "is better in any case than driving Turkey into the arms of the Triple Entente by theoretical scruples."[32]

On July 23 the grand vizier, Said Halim, repeated the overtures made by Enver, openly asking for formal entry into the Triple Alliance. Wangenheim's continuing coolness prompted Wilhelm to issue strong and precise instructions. The Turks had offered themselves to the Dreibund. To reject them was to drive them into the Entente camp and eliminate the influence of the Central Powers "once and for all." The Kaiser commanded that "Wangenheim must speak to the Turks concerning a connection with the Triple Alliance with unmistakably plain compliance and obtain their desires and report them. Under no circumstances at all can we afford to turn them away."[33]

Wangenheim did not particularly like these instructions, which he felt were peremptory and which ignored his own analysis, but he nevertheless immediately followed the wishes of his government. On July 27 he reported the development of a Turkish treaty proposal and said that he would "readjust" his own opinion on the capability of Turkey's fulfilling any alliance obligations if the Turkish armies were

[30] Kautsky, *Deutschen Dokumente*, vol. 1, no. 117, Wangenheim to Berlin, 22 July 1914.

[31] Ibid.

[32] Ibid., marginal note by the Kaiser.

[33] Kautsky, *Deutschen Dokumente*, vol. 1, no. 149, Wangenheim to Berlin, 23 July 1914, and marginal note by the Kaiser.

controlled by German officers, a condition which he felt would triple the value of these forces.[34]

The following day Said Halim offered concrete terms. The agreement would be an offensive-defensive alliance against Russia. The *casus foederis* would exist if Russia attacked Turkey, Germany, or Austria, or if a member of the Triple Alliance attacked Russia. Turkey, seeking protection for itself from the Czar, asked that the German military mission remain in case war occurred. Supreme command of the Turkish army and field command of one quarter of it would be given to the military mission if a conflict developed. Certain international questions concerning capitulations and debts were to remain untouched.[35]

Theobald von Bethmann-Hollweg, the German chancellor, promptly telegraphed the Kaiser's general acceptance of these terms, but the stipulations sent along to Wangenheim to use as the basis of an agreement reduced the alliance to a merely defensive vehicle. Both Germany and Turkey were to observe strict neutrality in the conflict between Austria and Serbia. If Russia intervened, bringing a *casus foederis* for Germany in relation to Austria, the same would exist for Turkey. Germany guaranteed Turkey its present territories against Russia and agreed to leave the military mission in Turkey in the event of war. Turkey was to allow the military mission to exercise actual command over Turkish forces. The German chancellor included an additional stipulation, that the treaty would be in force "for the purpose of the present Austro-Hungarian-Serbian conflict and for that of any possible international complications arising therefrom." On the other hand, if no war took place between Germany and Russia as a result of this conflict, the treaty was to become inoperative.[36]

The Turks agreed to all but this last provision. They felt it was impossible to fix the time when war might develop between Germany and Russia as a result of the Austro-Serbian conflict. War might come one or two years later, as an aftereffect. Certainly Germany could not ask Turkey to bind itself now and then leave it to face alone a possible Russian attack stemming from Turkey's friendly feeling toward the Triple Alliance. Said Halim did not want a long-term agreement, for both parties would have to test the value of such a connection; the shortest time he was willing to consider was the expiration of General Liman's contract in 1918.[37]

On July 31 Bethmann wired Wangenheim that Berlin agreed to the

[34] Ibid., no. 256, Wangenheim to Berlin, 27 July 1914.
[35] Ibid., vol. 2, no. 285, Wangenheim to Berlin, 28 July 1914.
[36] Ibid., no. 320, Bethmann-Hollweg to Wangenheim, 28 July 1914.
[37] Ibid., no. 411, Wangenheim to Berlin, 30 July 1914.

Turkish time stipulation and instructed him to sign the alliance as soon as possible. It is significant that even at this late date Germany approached the accord with caution. The chancellor telegraphed that "it should be determined first whether Turkey either can or will undertake any action against Russia worthy of the name. In case she should be unable to do so, the alliance would, of course, be worthless and should not be signed."[38]

Wangenheim was now convinced that Turkey would take worthwhile action, since it had become apparent through Liman von Sanders's estimates and the latter's conversations with Enver Pasha that Turkey really was capable of putting an army in the field against the Czar. Wangenheim now believed that if the Germans wanted to conclude an alliance with Turkey, it was "high time," else they might have 300,000 Turkish troops against them rather than with them. He hurried the negotiations and on August 2 cabled that the alliance had been concluded.

As the negotiations had evolved, Germany found itself accepting an accord which went beyond the present Austro-Serbian conflict and made the Germans responsible to Turkey for unforeseen political repercussions which might develop in the next four years. However, the rapidity of events following the Austrian ultimatum to Serbia on July 23 and the fear of driving Turkey, through hesitation, into the Entente camp led to the German move. Berlin had been forced to make what it saw as a hasty alliance.[39]

In these last days Austria had cooperated in the negotiations although remaining in the background. Pallavicini's feeling that the Triple Alliance would have to support Turkey against possible attacks from Russia, France, and England (in Armenia, Syria, and Arabia respectively), if Turkey was allowed to join, had led him to turn a cool shoulder to the grand vizier's suggestion on July 22 that they talk about an arrangement. The Austrian merely stated that an alliance would have to wait until the Austro-Serbian crisis had been resolved.[40] If Said Halim's word could be taken at face value, Pallavicini was running no risk for in this same conversation the grand vizier had stated flatly that Turkish sympathy in the Serbian crisis lay with

[38] Ibid., vol. 3, no. 508, Bethmann-Hollweg to Wangenheim, 3 July 1914.
[39] Ibid., no. 517, Wangenheim to Berlin, 31 July 1914; Mühlmann, *Deutschland und die Türkei*, pp. 41–43; GFMA, ser. 1, reel 13, nos. 406, 407, 408, Wangenheim to Berlin, 2 August 1914; Kautsky, *Deutschen Dokumente*, vol. 1, no. 144, Jagow to Wangenheim, 24 July 1914.
[40] Austria, *Österreich-Ungarns Aussenpolitik von der Bosnischen Krise 1908 bis zum Kriegsausbruch 1914*, vol. 8, nos. 10489, 10674, Pallavicini to Vienna, 22 and 25 July 1914. (Hereafter cited as *Ö.-U. Aussenpolitik.*)

Austria and that nothing serious would come out of the present Turkish-Greek conversations.[41] On the twenty-sixth the ambassador cabled Vienna that Said Halim had said Turkey would cooperate with the Central Powers, and obviously with Bulgaria as well, if Russia intervened in the Serbian affair.[42] Now that Turkey was leaning this strongly in the direction of the Central Powers, Pallavicini could afford greater diplomatic caution. The next day Wangenheim confidentially disclosed to Pallavicini the terms offered Germany by the grand vizier.[43] These terms were to be communicated to Berlin on the following day, the twenty-eighth, along with the grand vizier's request that negotiations between Berlin and Constantinople be carried out in strictest secrecy, to the point where Wangenheim, at least for the moment, was not to mention them even to his Austrian and Italian counterparts.[44] Bethmann concurred with this suggestion but his aim was not to keep Germany's allies in the dark. Various members of the Turkish cabinet were opposed to the projected alliance and success in establishing the accord hinged on presenting its opponents with a fait accompli. The requisite for this was utmost secrecy.[45]

Wangenheim had reacted negatively to the chancellor's instructions not to inform his Austrian colleague. He and Pallavicini had worked closely together on the alliance, particularly since Constantinople had always negotiated with both of them. Furthermore he did not believe the alliance could be realized without Austria's participation because the Turks would not agree to limit the treaty to the present crisis. As a member of the Triple Alliance, Austria would have to participate in any long-term arrangement. Then, too, if Russia attacked Turkey but not Austria, it would mean that Austria, excluded from the accord, would not consider the *casus foederis* as binding for itself. Finally, the German ambassador certainly wanted no tension between himself and his Austrian colleague; he therefore requested that Berlin allow him to inform the Austrian representative as soon as a working basis was reached with Said Halim.[46]

[41] *Ö.-U. Aussenpolitik*, vol. 8, no. 10489, Pallavicini to Vienna, 22 July 1914.
[42] *Ö.-U. Aussenpolitik*, vol. 8, no. 10730, Pallavicini, 26 July 1914.
[43] *Ö.-U. Aussenpolitik*, vol. 8, no. 10808, Pallavicini to Vienna, 27 July 1914.
[44] Kautsky, *Deutschen Dokumente*, vol. 2, no. 285, Wangenheim to Berlin, 28 July 1914.
[45] Ibid., no. 320, Bethmann-Hollweg to Wangenheim, 28 July 1914; Emin, *Turkey in the World War*, pp. 63–66, 68, 71, 72. Only five persons in Turkey knew of the treaty and of these only three were kept informed of the proceedings: Said Halim, Talaat Bey, and Enver Pasha. The other two who were told of it were Djavid Bey, minister of finance, and Djemal Pasha, minister of marine.
[46] Kautsky, *Deutschen Dokumente*, vol. 2, no. 398, Wangenheim to Berlin, 29 July 1914.

Berlin gave this consent on July 30 but as we have seen Wangenheim had not waited for the approval of the Foreign Office. Pallavicini knew of the terms offered by Turkey a day before Berlin received them. Wangenheim continued to keep him informed and Pallavicini naturally passed on the information to Vienna. On July 29 the Austrian ambassador wrote that Wangenheim felt Germany could carry through the accord only if Austria agreed to a similar arrangement concerning a defense of Turkey against Russia. Pallavicini thought Austria could go along with such a treaty on an analogous basis to that which had been worked out with Rumania, except that in this case the main treaty would be with Germany rather than with Austria.[47]

The Ballhausplatz was not at all loathe to take such a secondary position. The foreign minister, Count Leopold Berchtold, wired his concurrence, at the same time indicating clearly the reason why Austria had to remain the silent and willing diplomatic partner for the moment. In truth Berlin had thus far not made Vienna cognizant of the pourparlers between Wangenheim and the grand vizier, so that Austria was not in a position to express itself officially. Nevertheless, Berchtold placed great value on the treaty and instructed Pallavicini to support his German colleague.[48]

The Austrian representative needed no prompting in the practice of diplomatic discretion. He replied that he did not feel he should at the present time take a direct part in the negotiations but rather should exert the greatest influence possible on Wangenheim's thinking.[49] Berchtold cabled on July 31 that Austria should take up the same commitments as Germany with respect to a Turkish alliance and that for him the major purpose was the same as for Berlin—to support Turkey against Russia.[50]

On the previous day, Berlin had instructed its ambassador in Vienna, Heinrich von Tschirschky, officially to inform the Austrians of the proceedings in Constantinople. Von Tschirschky was to try to arrange that Pallavicini now be ordered to enter into similar negotiations with the Porte. Berchtold offered fullest cooperation, and on August 1 the German was able to wire that Pallavicini would receive such orders "at once."[51]

On August 3 Pallavicini was empowered to submit the following declaration to the Turkish government:

[47] Ibid., no. 431, Jagow to Wangenheim, 30 July 1914; Ö.-U. Aussenpolitik, vol. 8, no. 10969, Pallavicini to Vienna, 29 July 1914.
[48] Ö.-U. Aussenpolitik, vol. 8, no. 11056, Berchtold to Pallavicini, 30 July 1914.
[49] Ö.-U. Aussenpolitik, vol. 8, no. 11153, Pallavicini to Vienna, 31 July 1914.
[50] Ö.-U. Aussenpolitik, vol. 8, no. 11150, Berchtold to Pallavicini, 31 July 1914.
[51] Kautsky, Deutschen Dokumente, vol. 3, no. 586. See his fn. 3.

The Imperial and Royal Government of Austria-Hungary, having taken cognizance of the treaty concluded 2 August 1914 between Turkey and Germany, empowers the undersigned ambassador . . . to declare to the Imperial Ottoman Government the following:

The Imperial and Royal Government adheres formally to the stipulations contained in the treaty mentioned above.

In view of this act of accession the Imperial and Royal Government undertakes toward the Imperial Ottoman Government the same engagements to which the high contracting parties pledged themselves by the stipulations of the said treaty.[52]

The Turkish government was handed this on the fifth and the same day responded with a formal statement that it undertook the same engagements with Austria-Hungary as it had with Germany.[53]

It seemed that the Central Powers were beginning the war with a definite Turkish commitment to their cause. The declarations of war submitted to Russia by Germany and Austria-Hungary, on August 1 and August 6 respectively, clearly meant that Turkey had to meet its treaty obligations and recognize the *casus foederis* as existing. Much to the disappointment of the Central Powers, however, it was to be another three months before Constantinople could be goaded into actual and full participation.

Bulgaria and the Triumph of the Austrian Viewpoint

The negotiations with Turkey were only part of a much larger diplomatic pattern. This pattern had slowly evolved since 1912; but as in the case of Turkey, so also in regard to the more general Balkan plan, Germany and Austria were able to agree on a common policy only in July, 1914. The obstacle to concerted action was basic in nature, involving as it did a disagreement as to whether their diplomacy in the Balkans should center on the wooing of Bulgaria.

The Bulgarians were still oriented in a Russian direction as late as 1913, but the Treaty of Bucharest had left Bulgaria stripped of what it felt was its own by right of conquest. Bulgarian statesmen believed Russia had deserted their nation in its hour of need, and the resultant anti-Russian feeling turned Sofia toward the Central Powers.[54]

Just after the beginning of the Second Balkan War in June, 1913, a letter had been presented to King Ferdinand by the leaders of the

---

[52] Austria, Haus- Hof- und Staatsarchiv, Politisches Archiv, box 521, no. 258, Berchtold to Pallavicini, 3 August 1914. (Hereafter cited as Staatsarchiv, PA.)

[53] Ibid. The Turkish answer is appended to no. 258.

[54] Great Britain, Historical Section of the Foreign Office (hereafter cited as HSFO), *Bulgaria*, p. 59.

Bulgarian liberal parties, Vasil Radoslavov, Nicoll Ghenadiev, and Andreas Tonchev. The opinions which it expressed had already been discussed at a Crown Council in May, namely, that Bulgarian security against any attack from Turkey and Rumania was requisite, and that to obtain this goal Bulgaria must switch its policy in favor of friendship with Austria-Hungary.[55] In the following months a Bulgarian policy evolved which sought to break with Russia, to work against Serbia with the aid of Austria and Albania, and to work against Greece with the aid of Turkey. The most significant factor was the conviction that Bulgaria's best course of action was one which would lead to the closest connection with Vienna.[56]

In June, 1913, the Russophile Bulgarian prime minister, Ivan Geshov, was succeeded by Stojan Danev, who, while leaning toward Russia, began to consider the Austrians more favorably. Within six weeks Danev gave way to Radoslavov, whose policies were pro-German and pro-Austrian, and from this time Bulgaria's affections were directed ever more toward the Central Powers.[57] Having suddenly declared war on the Serbs and Greeks on June 29, Bulgaria quickly found itself pitted against Rumania as well. The resultant disadvantageous Treaty of Bukarest left Sofia in need of a strong friend, and the most beneficial seemed to be the Triplice rather than the Entente group.

After December, 1912, when the Conference of Ambassadors in London met to resolve the differences of the Balkan protagonists, Austria had proceeded to revamp its policy. Berchtold was interested in reducing a Serb threat by destroying the Balkan League. What was needed to serve Austrian interests was a new Balkan alliance, the core to be Bulgaria, with Greece and Turkey as additional members, while Rumania, an ally of the Triplice since 1883, was to be kept friendly.[58] By May, 1913, Vienna was already strongly in favor of advancing Bulgaria to membership in the Triple Alliance. Minister Adam Tarnowski telegraphed from Sofia that leading political circles and army men were dissatisfied with Russophilism, and that, except for a few, all were in favor of concluding an alliance with Rumania and leaning on Austria.[59] The key to the Austrian policy is found in the strained

[55] Dimitri Jotzoff, *Zar Ferdinand von Bulgarien: Sein Lebenswerk im Orient*, p. 271; Stojan Protić [Balkanicus], *The Aspirations of Bulgaria*, pp. 132–33.
[56] Balkanicus, *Aspirations of Bulgaria*, pp. 143–44.
[57] Howard, *Partition of Turkey*, p. 34; Great Britain, HSFO, *Bulgaria*, p. 59; Jotzoff, *Zar Ferdinand von Bulgarien*, p. 271.
[58] Howard, *Partition of Turkey*, p. 34.
[59] Ö.-U. *Aussenpolitik*, vol. 6, nos. 6857, 6858, 6860, Tarnowski to Berchtold, 1 May 1913; E. C. Helmreich, *The Diplomacy of the Balkan Wars, 1912–1913*, p. 345.

relations existing at this time between Serbia and Bulgaria. There was every chance they would mutually declare war and that Serbia would be joined by Greece and perhaps Rumania as well. Against such a combination Bulgaria could not stand, and its defeat would mean victory for an anti-Austrian group. Vienna could not move too boldly since Rumania, though an ally of the Triplice, had already become somewhat estranged,[60] and Austria had no desire to further alienate its affections. Thus, in a summary of his views sent to Berlin on May 2, Berchtold stated that Bulgaria's interests did not collide with Austria's; rather a parallelism existed, aimed at restraining Serbia. What he sought was an accord between Bulgaria and Rumania which, although perhaps not formally, would in fact make Bulgaria a member of the Triple Alliance.[61] Unfortunately the desired Bulgarian-Rumanian agreements were not realized, and with the opening of the Second Balkan War in June, 1913, Rumania sided with Bulgaria's enemies as Vienna had feared. That Austria did not come to Bulgaria's aid prompted the somewhat bitter comment from Radoslavov, "You allow this country to succumb at the very moment when, thanks to its king, the whole nation has at last understood that its enemy is Russia."[62]

Negotiations between Vienna and Sofia nevertheless continued, and on July 22, 1913, the first real approach for an Austro-Bulgarian accord came from Sofia. The Austrian answer was cautious, since any alliance would necessitate consideration by the cabinets of the other Triple Alliance powers. Furthermore, the realization of such a project would come through a full accord with Rumania.[63] At this moment, with the Second Balkan War in full swing, such an accord could not be made. The following November, King Ferdinand visited the Austrian Emperor and offered an alliance once again, and once again the Austrians demurred.[64]

Austrian caution resulted to a large extent from the position taken by Berlin. The two allies strongly disagreed on what was to be done. Germany was in no way interested in establishing a formal connection with Sofia, but rather sought to maintain and strengthen the tie with Bukarest. The Kaiser naturally favored the Rumanian sovereign, Carol, a Hohenzollern, and he had family ties and a firm friendship with the

[60] Helmreich, *Diplomacy of the Balkan Wars*, p. 370; Albertini, *Origins of the War of 1914*, 1:450.
[61] *Ö.-U. Aussenpolitik*, vol. 6, no. 6862, Berchtold to Ambassador Ladislaus Szögyény, 21 May 1913.
[62] Albertini, *Origins of the War of 1914*, 1:460.
[63] *Ö.-U. Aussenpolitik*, vol. 6, nos. 7937, 7964, Tarnowski to Berchtold and Berchtold to Tarnowski, 23 July 1913.
[64] Howard, *Partition of Turkey*, pp. 62–63.

Greek king as well. When the Bulgarian crowned head visited Vienna in November, 1913, Wilhelm remarked that if he came to Berlin he would be told to "keep steam in the locomotive for a speedy departure."[65] German diplomats shared the Kaiser's suspicions, and when Foreign Secretary Jagow was asked his opinion on Bulgarian admittance to the Triplice, he replied that it would be difficult to obtain a sincere Bulgarian adherence. Germany therefore did not shift its orientation and Rumania remained its pivot for any Balkan combination.[66]

The Wilhelmstrasse held no monopoly on its distrust and dislike of Ferdinand, for most European diplomats had learned to proceed cautiously with this strange man. Born to Prince Augustus of Saxe-Coburg-Gotha and Princess Clementine of Orleans, he had excellent familial connections not only on the German but also on the French side. His mother, the daughter of Louis Philippe, the French "citizen king," had great ambitions for her son, and by her persistent representations with Vienna, Paris, and London, was instrumental in his being called to the Bulgarian throne as prince after Alexander of Battenberg had been forced to flee in 1887.[67] By the time Ferdinand took over the reins of state he had already developed a close association with Austria, having been sent as a youth to the Austrian court to acquire polish and further contacts. When World War I broke out he was fifty-three, his personality had long ago been set, and his reputation was based on it. Ferdinand possessed rapierlike wit, particularly when he discussed his own features, including an overly long and large nose. Capable of self-derision, he was not bothered by the backstairs whispers concerning his foppish and effeminate manner, his love for jewels, and his total dislike of sport and athletics. Those admitted to his confidence soon forgot his idiosyncrasies when they discovered that his conversation was stimulating and his knowledge of art, botany, and biology excellent.[68]

On the other hand the man's politics were devoid of saving grace. By the time Bulgaria announced its independence in 1908, when Ferdinand first emerged as king, he had become a master of intrigue and duplicity and was referred to as the "Richelieu of the Balkans." He was interested in two things: the increase of his own domestic political control

[65] Hans Madol, *Ferdinand von Bulgarien*, pp. 154, 157, 171–72, 182; Howard, *Partition of Turkey*, p. 61.

[66] Albertini, *Origins of the War of 1914*, 1:450.

[67] "Tsar Ferdinand: A French Silhouette," *The New Europe* 3, no. 33 (31 May 1917): 220.

[68] Anatole Nekludoff, *Diplomatic Reminiscences before and during the World War, 1911–1917*, p. 7; Marie, Queen of Rumania, *The Story of My Life*, pp. 499–501.

and the unlimited advancement of Bulgaria's stature on the Balkan peninsula. There was in Ferdinand's case no great love between sovereign and people. The relationship was based on the simple realization that one was good for the other. If there was a sizable Russophile element among the population, it did not stop the king from maintaining a strong disposition toward the Austrian Monarchy, something which was rewarded in 1908 when Emperor Franz Joseph agreed to recognize the independence of the Bulgarian state.[69]

Despite the close understanding between Austria and Bulgaria and the Monarchy's well-reasoned desire to include Bulgaria in the Triple Alliance, Germany remained unimpressed. The Kaiser's diplomatic inclinations, seconded by the Wilhelmstrasse and colored by Ferdinand's personality, made a formal tie with Bulgaria seem most undesirable. The disagreement between Berlin and Vienna on the question led to sufficient bitterness to make Berchtold wire Szögyény in Berlin that a continuation of the dispute could endanger the existence of the Triple Alliance itself. The root of Berchtold's impatience was his belief that Germany did not understand that Austria's basic interests were at stake.[70] Yet, in the final analysis, the Austrians were unwilling to take any decisive action on their own and the problem of Bulgaria's relationship remained unresolved.

In the early months of 1914, although Germany and Austria remained at loggerheads on Balkan strategy, the two powers nevertheless established a much closer relationship with Bulgaria on the basis of certain negotiations which, while economic in nature, had definite diplomatic repercussions.

The interest which Germany and Austria had shown in economic intercourse with Bulgaria since 1900 was considerable. Bulgaria was an agricultural nation with 42 percent of its land under cultivation in 1912, heavily devoted to cereal production in which wheat and maize played the largest part. It was also possessed of raw materials such as coal, copper, iron, manganese, and oil, but these deposits remained largely unworked before World War I.[71] In exports, foodstuffs accounted for 68.6 percent while raw materials and semi-manufactured

[69] Nekludoff, *Diplomatic Reminiscences*, pp. 9–14; Jacques Ancel, *L'Unité de la Politique Bulgare, 1870–1919*, p. 12; P. P. de Sokolovitch, "Le Mirage Bulgare et la Guerre Européenne," *Revue d'Histoire Diplomatique* 31 (1917): 11–13.

[70] Albertini, *Origins of the War of 1914*, 1:464–65.

[71] Great Britain, HSFO, *Bulgaria*, pp. 81, 87, 97–101; Ivan Sakazov, *Bulgarische Wirtschaftsgeschichte*, p. 270.

products stood at 24.3 percent of the 1914 totals. While England, Belgium, and Turkey were Bulgaria's largest customers, Germany and Austria took considerable amounts of rye, wheat, and maize in the last years before the war.[72]

It was in Bulgarian imports, however, that the Central Powers played their most significant role. After 1902 the foreign trade of Bulgaria very greatly increased and from 1906 onward both Austria and Germany made a strong bid for control of the import market. With their business concerns carefully choosing commercial representatives who understood the needs of the country, Austria and Germany had taken first and second place, and by 1912 supplied most of Bulgaria's requirements in metals, machinery, railroad cars, and locomotives, and furnished much of its chemical and textile needs.[73]

From these facts one might assume that both were also heavily represented on the Bulgarian financial scene, but this was not the case. In the early 1900s Austria and Germany had established the Banque Balkanique and Bank de Credit through the efforts of the Wiener Bankverein, the Diskonto Gesellschaft, the Norddeutsche Bank, and S. Bleichröder und Sohn. Yet both powers held a secondary position in things financial.[74]

In that decade the Bulgarian government, often finding itself in need of money, sought assistance through a series of foreign loans. German bankers saw Bulgaria as a rather poor financial risk, and since the French offered more attractive terms, the Paris money market became the center for Bulgarian transactions. French banking syndicates were therefore predominant in loan negotiations successfully carried on in 1902, 1904, and 1907. The Austrians, attempting to make inroads and to gain Bulgarian goodwill, successfully floated a loan in 1909 through the Wiener Bankverein. Germany, however, not only refused to participate but, because of fear that a Bulgarian-Russian alliance existed, officially closed the Berlin and Hamburg exchanges to any overtures from Sofia.[75]

After the signing of the Treaty of Bukarest, the Bulgarians found themselves facing a desperate domestic situation. The Balkan Wars had strained the economy to the utmost, revealing the need of a general

---

[72] Milka Dejanova, *Die Warenausfuhr Bulgariens und Ihre Organisation seit dem Jahr 1900*, see table 5; Bulgaria, *Statistique du Royaume de Bulgarie, 1913–22*, part 8, pp. 168–69, 350–52.

[73] Bulgaria, *Statistique*, part 8, pp. 131, 154, 158–59, 160–61, 200; Great Britain, HSFO, *Bulgaria*, pp. 116–17.

[74] Great Britain, HSFO, *Bulgaria*, p. 123; Herbert Feis, *Europe, the World's Banker, 1870–1914*, p. 279.

[75] Feis, *Europe, World's Banker*, pp. 272–75, 279–80.

refurbishing, for which the empty state treasury offered no aid. A debt of over 699 million francs, most of it foreign, already existed, but the only way out lay in the direction of another loan. In late 1913 and early 1914 Sofia turned once again to the Paris bankers.[76]

At this point Bulgarian financial transactions became highly significant for international affairs. When the French were sounded on the question of a new loan, they proved unwilling. Behind this reluctance was the influence of France's ally, Russia, which recognized the shift in Bulgaria's affections toward the Central Powers and sought to reestablish its own predominance.[77] This it now attempted indirectly through the French, who insisted as a condition for completing the loan that the Bulgarians sign a military convention with Russia.[78] The Austrians were quick to see the advantages that might accrue if Austria and Germany combined to grant the needed money. On February 27 Berchtold wired Szögyény in Berlin that he was aware of the Russian pressure which it was clearly in the interests of the Triple Alliance to stop. This could best be done by the German government's using its influence with German banking syndicates to initiate a joint German-Austrian venture. He pointed out that it was not merely a question of granting Bulgaria much-needed finances but, more important, of keeping Bulgaria from inclining towards the Entente.[79]

Szögyény replied on March 1 that Jagow agreed with these comments but felt the loan could not be put through either at the moment or in the near future. He did not mention government opposition but spoke rather of the difficulties which such a loan would face in financial circles.[80] Fortunately, both the Austrian and the German ministers in Sofia realized the consequences of the matter. Through the efforts of the Austrian minister, Tarnowski, a short-term loan of thirty million leva had already been arranged through the Wiener Bankverein and Kreditanstalt, but Bulgaria needed much more. The German representative, Gustav Michahelles, now used his influence with the Diskonto Gesellschaft, which began negotiations. As these proceeded the German government remained aloof. Wilhelm had no desire to mix in the affair and he issued orders to the Foreign Office that while it was to take a benevolent attitude, it was to leave the negotiating banks a free

[76] Vasil Radoslavov, *Bulgarien und die Weltkrise*, pp. 87, 89; Bulgaria, *Statistique*, part 12, p. 38.
[77] Radoslavov, *Bulgarien und die Weltkrise*, p. 89; Feis, *Europe, World's Banker*, p. 277.
[78] Madol, *Ferdinand von Bulgaria*, p. 184.
[79] Ö.-U. *Aussenpolitik*, vol. 7, no. 9422, Berchtold to Szögyény, 27 February 1914.
[80] Ö.-U. *Aussenpolitik*, vol. 7, no. 9428, Szögyény to Berchtold, 1 March 1914.

hand. These orders were issued in May. It was not until July that the loan arrangements were successfully completed; in the interim the Russians and French did everything they could to block the project.[81]

The Russian minister in Sofia pointed to the crux of the matter when he stated that the loan was a question of life or death for the Radoslavov government. If negotiations with Austria and Germany could be stopped, Bulgaria would be forced to turn to the Entente powers. Russia's price for the loan would be the establishment of a coalition ministry of Malinov and Ghenadiev, who, as pro-Russian, would once again reverse Bulgaria's political orientation.[82]

Russia's analysis of the affair was indeed shrewd, but the attempts made to carry out the desired plan were doomed. While the French government gave Paris bankers definite instructions to take no part in the loan, this did not deter the Germans and Austrians from successfully completing it with almost entirely their own capital.[83] Although the French and Russians made a last desperate attempt to block the loan by working through the Bulgarian assembly, the Sobranje, the loan was ratified on July 16.[84]

The loan proved to be the largest Bulgaria had ever made. It was to consist of 500 million francs paid in two equal series with an annual interest of 5 percent. The control of the syndicate handling the operation was in the hands of the Diskonto Gesellschaft, which itself provided sixty-six out of every hundred francs. Austria offered twenty-five, while the rest was split between Dutch, Bulgarian, Belgian, and Swiss concerns.[85] As part of the transaction, three additional contracts were signed at the same time, one of which called for a loan of an additional 120 million francs with Bulgarian treasury bonds as collateral; the other two gave to the Diskonto Gesellschaft control of certain mining operations, along with the right to construct a railroad and port facilities at the terminus of Porto Logos. All materials used for such construction were to be purchased in Germany and Austria, with

[81] Radoslavov, *Bulgarien und die Weltkrise*, p. 89; Jacob Viner, "International Finance and Balance of Power Diplomacy," *Southwestern Political and Social Science Quarterly* 9 (March 1929): 441; *Ö.-U. Aussenpolitik*, vol. 8, no. 9739, Szögyény to Berchtold, 25 May 1914; Richard von Mach, *Aus Bewegter Balkanzeit, 1879–1918*, pp. 184, 219.

[82] Madol, *Ferdinand von Bulgaria*, pp. 186–93; Radoslavov, *Bulgarien und die Weltkrise*, pp. 91, 93–94.

[83] Viner, "International Finance," p. 442; Henri Prost, *La Bulgarie de 1912 à 1930*, pp. 56–57.

[84] Viner, "International Finance," p. 442.

[85] Prost, *La Bulgarie*, pp. 56, 57, 60; Lübomir G. Leschtoff, *Die Staatsschulden und Reparationen Bulgariens, 1878–1927*, p. 61. The Dutch took 3 percent, Bulgarians 3 percent, Belgians 2 percent and the Swiss 1 percent.

German firms filling 75 percent of all orders. In addition, concessions were obtained with respect to other railroads, amounting to some fifty million francs.[86] Bulgaria had received the much-needed funds but not at any bargain.

In the larger context of international affairs Germany and Austria had strengthened their position because the conclusion of the loan meant retention of the Radoslavov cabinet and continuation of a Bulgarian policy oriented toward the Central Powers. The importance of the loan for specific diplomatic negotiations was cogently reflected in Radoslavov's remark to Michahelles that the government was now secure and could "follow a line of conduct of its own, by seeking to become attached to the Triple Alliance."[87]

The impact of this financial affair became much greater when, a little over two weeks before the final arrangements were made, Franz Ferdinand was assassinated at Sarajevo. The assassination broke the diplomatic impasse between Germany and Austria as to Bulgaria, and by the time the Sobranje ratified the loan, both Central Powers had agreed to a positive policy concerning Sofia. The financial agreement, in producing a friendly atmosphere, proved a definite asset for diplomatic negotiations.

The effect of the archduke's death upon Austro-Serbian relations led Emperor Franz Joseph to write what proved to be a most significant letter to Kaiser Wilhelm, accompanied by a long explanatory memorandum from Berchtold, written before the assassination, dealing with the whole Balkan situation. Delivered to the Kaiser on July 5, these documents clearly present the Austrian case. Austria faced a hostile Serbia and a Russia which sought a Balkan alliance aimed against the Dual Monarchy. To check the Russians and to gain support against Serbia, diplomatic counter-moves were necessary, particularly since Rumania could no longer be seen as reliable. The Emperor wrote, "The efforts of my government must in the future be directed toward the isolation and diminution of Serbia. The first stage of this journey should be accomplished by the strengthening of the present position of the Bulgarian government, in order that Bulgaria, whose real interests coincide with our own, may be preserved from a relapse into Russophilism."[88]

Franz Joseph went on to suggest that Bulgaria be taken into the Triple Alliance and this desire was strongly supported by Berchtold in

[86] Prost, *La Bulgarie*, p. 58; Henri Prost, *La Liquidation Financière de la Guerre en Bulgarie*, pp. 35–38.
[87] Kautsky, *Deutschen Dokumente*, vol. 1, no. 162.
[88] Ibid., no. 13.

his memorandum. The foreign minister asserted that the unreliable policy now being pursued by Rumania required Austria to seek support from other quarters for its Balkan policy. The Monarchy must accept the overtures made by the Bulgarians a year ago and enter into what would "practically amount to an alliance."[89] Moreover, Berchtold felt it should be the policy of Austria to foster an alliance between Bulgaria and Turkey, but he also believed the negotiations with Bulgaria should be carried on openly and should not cancel existing Austrian alliance obligations to Rumania.[90] The only thing he saw as crucial to the implementation of these aims was the participation and cooperation of Germany. He declared that "before Austria-Hungary enters upon the measures herein mentioned, she deems it of the greatest importance to come to a full understanding with Germany concerning them, not only from considerations arising from tradition and their close alliance, but particularly for the reason that important interests both of Germany and the Triple Alliance are concerned, and because the successful preservation of those ultimately *common* interests can only be looked for if the equally united action of the Triple Alliance, particularly of Austria-Hungary and the German Empire, is opposed to the united action of France and Russia."[91]

Berchtold concluded by pointing out that Russian military preparations in the west were aimed more against the Germans than against the Austrians and that Russian ambitions in Europe and Asia would necessarily bring German opposition. The allies would have to take joint steps before it became too late to frustrate Russian goals.[92]

The Kaiser's reaction was to call an immediate meeting with Bethmann-Hollweg and Undersecretary for Foreign Affairs Arthur Zimmermann. The seriousness of Austria's position was now manifest, and while Wilhelm thought that Austria must alone solve the Sarajevo crisis, he saw the need for supporting his ally. In giving this support, however, he believed that care must be taken not to alienate Rumania. Bethmann concurred and personally passed on to Szögyény the decision of the German government, which clearly involved a reversal of its former position. Berlin was now ready to support Austrian attempts to gain Bulgaria's adherence to the Triple Alliance.[93] On July 6 Bethmann wired von Tschirschky in Vienna that while the Kaiser felt no "unqualified confidence in Bulgaria and her ruler," he understood the

[89] Ibid., no. 14.
[90] Ibid.
[91] Ibid.
[92] Ibid.
[93] Theobald von Bethmann-Hollweg, *Reflections on the World War*, 1:118–20.

threat posed to Austria and the Triple Alliance by Russia and Serbia. He therefore agreed to support an understanding with Sofia and would proceed to instruct the German representative in Bulgaria to cooperate with his Austrian colleague toward this end.[94]

Thus a mere month before the war opened Germany finally consented to take a diplomatic line which Austria had seen as necessary a year before.

Had the Central Powers been willing to entertain the Bulgarian overtures as they were made by Ferdinand himself in November, 1913, an alliance would have been an easy matter to arrange. It was not so simple now. Bulgaria certainly wanted an alliance, but Ferdinand recognized that if the Serbian crisis should lead to a general war, Bulgaria would be a diplomatic prize sought by both camps, so that any commitment must be made with caution.[95]

Attitudes in Vienna had changed, too. In spite of having conducted serious negotiations, Austria suddenly began dragging its feet. Berchtold's memorandum sent to Berlin on July 5 had just been written when the Sarajevo assassination occurred. While the memo was sent off without alteration, the death of the archduke caused the Austrians to consider with greater subtlety the many facets of the problem facing them. On July 7 at a meeting of the Austrian Council of Joint Ministers, Berchtold appeared rather reserved concerning the whole Bulgarian issue. He talked of the weakness of the pro-Austrian Radoslavov government and thought it might possibly be overturned. Then, too, the Germans had agreed to the alliance only if the connection with Rumania would not be endangered. If negotiations were to proceed profitably, great care would be necessary.[96]

Tarnowski arrived in Vienna for deliberations with Berchtold on July 10, and on the sixteenth he was back in Sofia with an alliance draft. Arranged in seven articles, it called for an agreement between the two parties to make no engagement directed against the other; for a mutual recognition of the *casus foederis* if either was attacked by two states, one of which bordered on the party being attacked; for a mutual, amicable relationship with Rumania and for Bulgaria's recognition of the Treaty of Bukarest as definitive; for an agreement by Austria that it would use its diplomatic influence to make sure that Bulgaria's historic claims were taken into consideration in any future partition of Macedonia; and finally for the drawing up of a military

---

[94] Kautsky, *Deutschen Dokumente*, vol. 1, no. 15.
[95] Albertini, *Origins of the War of 1914*, 3:583.
[96] Ibid., p. 592.

convention providing for cooperation between the armies of the two nations.[97] Tarnowski, however, made no move whatsoever to show the Bulgarians this draft. Asked by Radoslavov what he had brought back from Vienna, he merely answered he brought assurance that "Vienna was disposed toward Bulgaria." In reply to Radoslavov's remark that now was the time for an alliance, he said he was prepared to lay a Bulgarian proposal before Berchtold and therefore wanted concrete terms. Radoslavov now proceeded to confer with Tonchev and Ghenadiev but the final nod for submitting any alliance draft to Vienna rested with King Ferdinand, who did not give his approval until August 2.[98]

Precisely why Austria was now proving to be so shy is explained in the instructions Berchtold had sent to Tarnowski on July 23. The worsening of the Serbian situation had by now led the Ballhausplatz to want an alliance with Bulgaria only under certain conditions. Therefore, Tarnowski was primarily to obtain a guarantee of Bulgarian *neutrality*, since in a war with Serbia, Austria would seek to localize the conflict. If Bulgaria proceeded with troop dispositions, Rumania might conclude that Bulgaria was about to attack her and would retaliate. If an Austro-Serb war led to Russian participation, the Dreibund might still count on Rumania's remaining neutral, assuming that the Bulgarians did not take part. If, however, Rumania became hostile to Austria, then an alliance would be called for, and in this case Tarnowski was to offer Bulgaria the "widest assurances" that the monarchy and its allies would support Bulgarian territorial claims.[99]

The disparity between the Austrian posture of July 5 and that of July 23 is explained by Berchtold's change of attitude towards Serbia after the assassination. He was resolved to make a final disposition of the Serbian problem by means of a localized war. Once it became clear that such localization was not possible—and the trend of events was obvious by August 1—Austria proceeded with an immediate attempt to conclude the Bulgarian accord.[100]

If Austria suddenly took an unexpectedly cautious position in July,

[97] Ö.-U. *Aussenpolitik*, vol. 8, no. 10171, Berchtold to Szögyény, 10 July 1914; no. 10389, Tarnowski to Berchtold, 19 July 1914.

[98] Ibid., no. 10310, Tarnowski to Berchtold, 16 July 1914; Albertini, *Origins of the War of 1914*, 3: 585, 589. For details of the Bulgarian draft see chapter 6 below.

[99] Staatsarchiv, PA, box 512, no. 155, Berchtold to Tarnowski, 23 July 1914; see also Ö.-U. *Aussenpolitik*, vol. 8, no. 10550, Berchtold to Tarnowski, 23 July 1914.

[100] Sidney B. Fay, *The Origins of the World War*, 2:200. For the precise attempts of Austria to conclude the Bulgarian Alliance in the first days of August, see below, chapter 6.

this was not the case with its ally. Once decided on a policy of courting Bulgaria, Germany proceeded with attempts to achieve a strong commitment. By July 25 Michahelles had wired from Sofia that the Bulgarians were in the process of formulating a specific plan for the alliance. Wilhelm commented in the margin, "Hurry it up!" The Germans now worked feverishly to conclude the agreement. This was particularly so in the opening days of August, for by August 2 Germany and Russia were at war and Berlin now believed the only approach was to gain allies as soon as possible.[101] The Bulgarian draft submitted on this day was accepted by Bethmann-Hollweg. Since the Rumanian declaration of neutrality on August 4 seemed to eliminate any danger of Rumania's siding with Russia, and since the fear of losing Rumania for the Triple Alliance was now reduced, the Kaiser sent Michahelles full authorization on August 5 to conclude the alliance. Indeed, Wilhelm went so far as to send a signed ratification.[102]

It now seemed that it would merely be a question of a few days until the formalities would be completed and Bulgaria definitely won. These few days were to stretch into thirteen months, months during which King Ferdinand and his government drove German and Austrian diplomats to the point of desperation with evasions, demands, and counter-demands. Not until September 6, 1915, did Bulgaria join the Central Powers. At the start of the war, and just when Berlin thought it had safely aligned Bulgaria as an ally, Sofia temporized, decided to wait upon events, and backed away from any binding obligations. The Bulgarian government was now well aware that if it attacked Serbia it would face a hostile Rumania and Greece, because Sofia had actually been warned to this effect by those two states. Therefore, the safest course at the moment was to continue neutrality, a precaution which had already been taken through the issuance of a formal declaration on July 28.[103]

In spite of neutrality, Bulgaria was closely oriented toward the Central Powers, an orientation which is explained by more than merely the sympathies of the Radoslavov cabinet coalescing with those of the king. The Bulgarian government had been carrying on serious negotiations for an agreement with Turkey, which itself signed an accord with Germany and Austria on August 2. The idea of a Turco-Bulgarian understanding was nothing new. It had been desired by Sofia and Constantinople for some time and certainly had the backing of the

[101] Kautsky, *Deutschen Dokumente*, vol. 1, no. 162; Albertini, *Origins of the War of 1914*, 3:590.

[102] Albertini, *Origins of the War of 1914*, 3:590–91.

[103] Ibid., pp. 591, 588.

Ballhausplatz, since such an alliance was part of the greater Balkan plan envisaged by Austria.[104]

When, after the cessation of hostilities between them, the Bulgarians and Turks had met in September, 1913, to consider the final disposition of the city of Adrianople, the question of a defensive alliance had been broached. Although they had progressed to a point where both sides had drafted an actual military convention, no formal signature was achieved. Involved in this failure was a whole series of obstacles: changes in the ministries of the two governments, a Bulgarian national election which produced the usual preoccupation with domestic affairs by that government, and disputes between the two states over the fate of nationality groups deeply affected by recent shifts in Turkish and Bulgarian territorial possessions. These obstacles did not make for smooth diplomatic conferences, but they were not insurmountable. More significant in delaying a Bulgarian-Turkish alliance was Sofia's fear that Turkey might rashly attack Greece, leaving Bulgaria to face a Rumanian-Serbian combination which would fly to Greece's rescue. Even this possibility might not have deterred Ferdinand from going ahead had it not been for the fact that Bulgaria in late 1913 and early 1914 was unable to achieve the connection it desired with Austria and Germany through a formal agreement.[105]

Pallavicini in Constantinople accurately assessed the situation when he saw that Sofia's desire to undo the Treaty of Bukarest and Turkey's conflict with Greece over the Aegean Islands would necessarily bring those two powers together. However, Bulgaria refused to make any rash move. Its desire to see itself and Turkey joined to the Triple Alliance was frustrated by German opposition. Berlin continued to press for a Turkish-Greek understanding, and by July, 1914, was still reluctant to back a Turkish-Bulgarian accord.[106]

In spite of Berlin's hesitation, Austria was applying pressure. Pallavicini in Constantinople suggested to the Bulgarian minister there that Turkey and Bulgaria ally and then join Austria if others should come to the aid of Serbia. On July 30 Tarnowski received instructions to talk with Radoslavov about the possibility of renewing attempts at rapprochement with Turkey.[107] This pressure, and the turn of events themselves, changed Germany's approach. On July 6 the Wilhelm-

---

[104] Helmreich, *Diplomacy of the Balkan Wars,* pp. 409–11.

[105] Ibid., pp. 409–10, 412; Howard, *Partition of Turkey,* p. 64.

[106] Helmreich, *Diplomacy of the Balkan Wars,* pp. 409–10, 412, 413; Albertini, *Origins of the War of 1914,* 3:607, 609.

[107] Albertini, *Origins of the War of 1914,* 3:616; Howard, *Partition of Turkey,* p. 87.

strasse had accepted Vienna's plea to seek out Bulgaria as an ally. On July 23 the Kaiser finally decided that the loyalty of Turkey had to be secured. At the same time he came to see the necessity of diplomatically connecting Turkey and Bulgaria to an Austria proceeding against Serbia. Thus, at the eleventh hour, the Central Powers united on a common policy with respect to these two countries.[108]

Radoslavov had told Tarnowski that Bulgaria would sign nothing with Turkey until a Bulgarian agreement was reached with Germany and Austria. When hostilities began no such formal treaty existed, but by now the initiative had passed from Vienna and Berlin to King Ferdinand. The feeling of security produced in Sofia by such a newly won position, along with other factors yet to be discussed, did produce a secret accord signed between Radoslavov and the Turkish representative, Talaat Bey, on August 19.

Hence, by the opening weeks of the war Bulgaria found itself in the interesting position of having delayed formally joining the Triplice while at the same time attaching itself to a new member of this same Triplice—Turkey. Germany and Austria hoped that Bulgaria would soon decide on participation, but Ferdinand and Radoslavov were determined to move in such a direction when—and only when—Bulgarian interests were concretely assured.[109]

[108] Albertini, *Origins of the War of 1914*, 3:612.
[109] Ibid., p. 616. The details of the Bulgarian-Turkish Alliance are considered in detail in chapter 6, below.

Chapter 2

Diplomatic
Disappointments

The refusal of Turkey and Bulgaria to commit themselves immediately may have proved frustrating to Germany and Austria, but the declaration of neutrality by Rumania on August 4 constituted a real diplomatic setback. Rumania had, after all, been an ally of both Central Powers since 1883. King Carol was a Hohenzollern and had remained loyal to the Triplice, while both Berlin and Vienna had used great caution with respect to Rumania so as not to destroy the diplomatic tie. Yet, on August 4 Bukarest refused to honor its alliance obligations.

It was more than just a diplomatic defeat for Germany and Austria. Rumania was a rich and important prize from an economic standpoint. Out of a population of approximately seven and a half million, over 80 percent was rural, and that percentage worked arable land which amounted to the impressive figure of nine million hectares. Before the war Rumania was second only to Russia in the volume of agricultural products supplied to the European continent. It stood as the second largest exporter of corn and the fifth largest of wheat in the world.[1] For handling this produce it could look to an excellent geographical position which gave access to transoceanic markets through the Black Sea and to Central Europe via the Danube, while a relatively good railroad system offered the necessary links between the interior and sea or river ports. In natural resources there were large deposits of iron, copper, coal, and mercury though these still remained largely untapped.[2] There was, however, one resource which *had* been developed and which made Rumania a crucial Balkan state—oil. The fields extended from the Serbian border to the Bukovina, and by 1913 these fields produced close to two million tons a year, making Rumania the fourth largest oil producer of all countries.[3]

In trade relations Rumania did not find its leading customers in Germany or Austria. While each had increased its Rumanian imports after 1911, both were outstripped by Belgium, Holland, Italy, and France. Nevertheless, in millions of marks, the Central Powers imported more from Rumania than from any other Balkan country.[4]

German and Austrian economic activity found its real importance in export to Rumania and in the realm of finance. While as late as 1890 Austria held first place in filling Rumanian import needs, Germany soon took the lead and between 1900 and 1915 controlled the Rumanian import market by meeting approximately 30 percent of Rumanian requirements. Austria, nevertheless, held a strong second place with 25 percent. The Rumanians needed much in the way of metal products, a demand which Germany and Austria could meet with their production of industrial and agricultural machinery, electrical equipment, railroad supplies, and various types of tools.[5]

In finance German preponderance was extreme. By the time the war began Germany held 52 percent of Rumania's foreign debt. Within the country German capital was widely represented in industry, oil, timber, and banks to the extent that, of all German capital investments in the Balkans, approximately half centered in Rumanian ventures. While Austria was not involved to such a degree, its part was by no means inconsiderable.[6]

[1] Great Britain, HSFO, *Rumania*, pp. 12, 97, 100.

[2] George D. Cioriceanu, *La Roumanie Économique et ses Rapports avec l'Étranger de 1860 à 1915*, p. 369. Rumania had 3600 kilometers of railroads and almost all cities were connected to principal arteries; Great Britain, HSFO, *Rumania*, pp. 108–9, 122–23.

[3] Great Britain, HSFO, *Rumania*, pp. 103–4. By December 1915, Germany provided the largest amount of operating capital in Rumanian oil enterprises; Cioriceanu, *Roumanie Économique*, p. 358; Austria, Handelsministerium, *Wirtschaftliche Verhältnisse Rumänien, 1913*, p. 57.

[4] Geza Lukacs, *Die Handelspolitische Interessengemeinschaft Zwischen dem Deutschen Reiche und Österreich-Ungarn*, pp. 34, 43. Lukacs shows that Germany in 1911 imported 107.7 million marks' worth of goods from Rumania while imports from Asiatic Turkey ran a poor second, being only 47.3 million. Austria imported 78.2 millions from Rumania, while the closest competitor, Serbia, sold Austria only 42.6 millions. In spite of this, Germany and Austria by 1911 were taking a mere 3.94 and 6.05 percent of total Rumanian exports; Cioriceanu, *Roumanie Économique*, pp. 405, 401. Cioriceanu points out that from 1911 on, however, Rumanian grain exports, while increasing to some extent for Germany, quadrupled for Austria.

[5] N. Resmiritza, *Essai d'Economie Roumaine Moderne, 1831–1931*, pp. 265–66; Cioriceanu, *Roumanie Économique*, pp. 399, 404–5; Great Britain, HSFO, *Rumania*, p. 126. Aside from machinery, Germany and Austria also met Rumanian orders for textiles, coal, and iron; Germany, Kaiserlichen Statistischen Amte, *Statistik des Deutschen Reichs, Auswärtigen Handel im Jahr 1913, Rumänien*, 4:1. In addition, Germany in 1913 supplied Rumania with over ten million marks' worth of munitions.

[6] Herbert Feis, *Europe, the World's Banker, 1870–1914*, pp. 75, 79, 269, 270. Oil investments were controlled by the Deutsche Bank and the Diskonto Gesellschaft. Germany had founded the Banca General Romana, and Austria, the Banque de Credit Roumain. Both banks helped develop Rumanian industry; Cioriceanu, *Roumanie Économique*, pp. 357, 364–67. German and Austrian capital constituted 27 percent of the total investment in the oil industry. In heavy industry, Germany and Austria contributed 150 million and 65 million marks respectively, of the total 510 million marks invested by foreign interests up to 1914; Great Britain, HSFO, *Rumania*, p. 120. Of the eight biggest banks in Rumania four were established by German and Austrian capital.

Considering that German business agents were adept at understanding Rumania's needs and at dealing with Rumanian customers, that the extensive capital investment in industry was German and Austrian, and that the Central Powers best supplied crucial goods for Rumanian economic improvement, it is not surprising that in the prewar period Rumania should gravitate toward Germany and its ally.[7]

Rumania's Decision for Neutrality

Yet, after the Balkan Wars, Bukarest proved increasingly cool to Berlin and Vienna. The economic welfare of Rumania may have been closely bound up with the Central Powers but Bukarest did not allow that fact to color its political decisions on the international front. The alienation of Rumania from the Triplice was based on two factors. The first of these was closely connected with Rumanian unwillingness to countenance an enlarged Bulgaria—a result of the First Balkan War. When Bulgaria refused to make concessions in the Dobrudja, Rumania sided with Greece and Serbia in the Second Balkan War against the Bulgarians. Out of this conflict came the Treaty of Bukarest, which produced a Bulgarian-Rumanian incompatibility that could not be resolved. Since Austria had not come to Rumania's aid, and since Vienna from this time on took a pro-Bulgarian line of which the Rumanians were well aware, there grew an increasingly greater diplomatic cleft between Vienna and Bukarest.[8] As we have already seen, the Germans were most desirous of maintaining the connection with Rumania and of establishing a Rumanian–Greek-Turkish combination under the aegis of the Triplice. If Austria sought Bulgaria as the core of a new Balkan constellation, it most certainly was not willing to do so at the expense of losing Rumania. Nevertheless, Austria saw more clearly than Germany how great the alienation had become.

In the fall of 1913 the Ballhausplatz dispatched Count Ottokar Czernin as minister to Bukarest. His job was to discover just where Rumania stood and to determine the present strength of the old alliance between the Central Powers and Rumania. Were a conflict to arise between Austria and Serbia, could the Austrians rely on Rumania, which was supporting Serbian ambitions?[9]

Czernin was not long in replying that the alliance with Rumania was not worth the paper it was written on. The difficulty was more than just a question of Austria's looking in the direction of Bulgaria. A

[7] Resmiritza, *Économie Roumaine*, p. 266.

[8] Oswald H. Wedel, *Austro-German Diplomatic Relations, 1908–1914*, pp. 182, 206; Luigi Albertini, *Origins of the War of 1914*, 1:491; 3:549–50.

[9] Ottokar Czernin, *Im Weltkrieg*, p. 103.

second divisive factor constituted a problem difficult to solve: the question of Transylvania and the Rumanians who lived there under Hungarian rule.[10]

The issue of Transylvania and the so-called Hungarian Rumanians was an old problem. Fifty-five percent of this area's population was Rumanian, and this element lay under the heavy domination of the Magyars. For years the Hungarians had attempted to Magyarize this group and for years the Rumanians had fought against such a program and for equality and political autonomy within the Austro-Hungarian Empire.[11] By 1913 sentiment in Rumania had been agitated in favor of fellow nationals in Transylvania, and as a result an anti-Austro-Hungarian attitude was apparent. On December 7 King Carol, discussing the issue with Czernin, declared that any détente between Bukarest and Vienna would require concessions by the Hungarians on the Transylvania problem.[12]

Two camps existed within official Austrian circles. The one was headed by Franz Ferdinand and supported by such men as Czernin and, to some degree, Berchtold himself. This group's viewpoint was pro-Rumanian. Franz Ferdinand denounced the Magyar policy in Transylvania and called for drastic reforms heavily favoring the Rumanians, an idea which Czernin supported even before his appointment as minister. As a matter of fact, even though he recognized it was impossible to achieve, Czernin approved of the plan proposed by Nicholas Filipescu, one of the leaders of the Rumanian Conservative Party, for a Greater Rumania which would include Transylvania, but which by alliance would actually take up a constitutional position within the Austro-Hungarian Empire similar to the status of Bavaria in Germany.[13] Such an idea was, of course, opposed by Count Stephan Tisza, Hungarian prime minister, who headed the second or anti-Rumanian camp. Tisza realized the need for reform but was unwilling to consider more than mild measures. Since he had the backing of Franz Joseph, the pro-Rumanian group was powerless to push through its program. To institute the extensive reforms necessary to bring about amicable relations between Rumania and Austria, what Carol saw as the "arrogant nationalism" of Tisza would have to be much reduced.[14]

[10] Ibid., p. 107.

[11] Robert W. Seton-Watson, *Roumania and the Great War*, Appendix I, p. 73; R. A. Kann, *The Multinational Empire*, 1:304–17. Kann offers a full historical sketch of the Transylvanian issue.

[12] Albertini, *Origins of the War of 1914*, 1:500.

[13] Czernin, *Im Weltkrieg*, p. 107; Robert W. Seton-Watson, *A History of the Roumanians*, pp. 465, 467.

[14] Czernin, *Im Weltkrieg*, p. 108; Seton-Watson, *The Roumanians*, pp. 465–66, 470.

As the result of this impasse, public opinion in Rumania had by the spring of 1914 risen to the point of very strong feeling against Hungarian rule. The Rumanian bourgeoisie, spearheaded by Ion Bratianu's Liberal Party, was now demanding that Transylvania be joined to Rumania. Berlin was much aware of the problem. The Kaiser had himself talked with Tisza in an effort to resolve the issue, for Wilhelm felt that relations with Rumania would depend on what happened in Hungary.[15] Tisza talked only of school and church reforms which he believed would be enough once again to weld Rumania firmly to the Triplice. If this could not be done he was willing to court Bulgaria, and his remarks in a public speech to the effect that if Rumania would not go along, there were other Balkan powers that would, understandably did not sit well with the Bukarest government.[16]

On June 13, 1914, Franz Ferdinand, meeting with the Kaiser at Konipischt, thoroughly denounced Magyar domination of the Rumanian element and charged Tisza with using dictatorial methods. The fact that Franz Ferdinand was the successor to the Habsburg throne had given Rumanians hope that his accession would see something done for their oppressed brothers. His assassination dashed these hopes, and as war approached the anti-Austrian attitude continued strongly in evidence.[17] It was this attitude that made Czernin's task so difficult, for Berchtold wanted to publish the Austro-Rumanian alliance, which had been renewed in February, 1913. Heretofore, the alliance had been a deep secret and the Rumanian public had no idea of its existence. The publication would, Berchtold felt, signify a solidifying of the lines which had previously existed but which by the spring of 1914 had so considerably frayed.[18] Because of the hostile attitude of the Rumanian people, however, King Carol could not risk making the alliance known.

Czernin diagnosed the problem clearly enough when he remarked that Carol was a mediator, a man given to conciliation but not in any way a gambler who would stake everything on one cast of the dice. Carol had personally been pro-German and pro-Austrian. He still was. Born to the house of Hohenzollern-Sigmaringen and sent to Rumania in 1866 as ruling prince, he remained steadfastly Germanophile until his death, shortly after World War I began. In 1914 he could look back on almost fifty years of experience as a ruler. He had long ago learned that

[15] Seton-Watson, *The Roumanians*, pp. 470, 465; Margot Hegemann, "Zum Plan der Abdankung Carols I von Rumänien in September, 1914," *Zeitschrift für Geschichtswissenschaft* 4 (1957): 824. According to Hegemann, Carol was in favor of Filipescu's plan.
[16] Seton-Watson, *The Roumanians*, pp. 466, 470.
[17] Ibid., pp. 471–73.
[18] Albertini, *Origins of the War of 1914*, 1:498–99.

governing and personal bias were incompatible, and although he had a strong will, he recognized the necessity of adjusting to public opinion. So it was that the king, whatever his personal inclinations, would not risk openly committing his country to war on the side of the Triplice in defiance of Rumanian public opinion. In December, 1913, Carol had told Czernin that, as things stood, the idea of Rumanian armed assistance for the Central Powers in case of war was not to be seen as a possibility.[19]

To make matters worse the conservative Majorescu cabinet, which had signed the renewal of Rumania's alliance with Austria and Germany in February, 1913, was replaced at the turn of the year by the liberal Bratianu government, almost unanimously pro-French in attitude. Only Petru Carp, who was a former prime minister, the king, and a few others were pro-German in sympathy.[20]

By April, 1914, Czernin was talking pessimistically about the Rumanian situation. A month before, he had written to the home office that things were getting worse, not better. Now he was of the opinion that a risk had to be taken. If the Central Powers wanted an alliance with Rumania, they had to drop ideas of a connection with Bulgaria, and Austria would somehow have to reach agreement with Serbia.[21] Germany was not at all averse to such an idea, having all along distrusted the Bulgarians. Wilhelm and his advisors had for months been eager for Austria to solve its problem with Belgrade and to win over Tisza for sufficient reforms to ease the Transylvanian difficulty.[22] Unfortunately, neither step was taken.

As war approached, the Central Powers found themselves falling between two stools. They had not won Rumania, and for fear of severing Rumanian ties they had not effected any formal treaty with the Bulgarians. Meanwhile, the Entente powers had hardly been idle, for through the efforts of Russia's Sazonov a rapprochement with Rumania had been made in the spring of 1914, which was clearly reflected by the Constanza meeting between Carol and the Czar in June. Once this meeting occurred, Czernin was convinced that Rumania was going over to the opposition.[23]

[19] Czernin, Im Weltkrieg, p. 124; Albertini, Origins of the War of 1914, 1:500; Marie, Queen of Rumania, The Story of My Life, pp. 213, 431–32, 533–34; Sidney Whitman, Reminiscences of the King of Rumania, pp. xxii–xxiii, 10–11.
[20] Czernin, Im Weltkrieg, pp. 108, 116; Albertini, Origins of the War of 1914, 1:501.
[21] Albertini, Origins of the War of 1914, 1:501, 504.
[22] Robert W. Seton-Watson, "Wilhelm II's Balkan Policy," Slavonic Review 7 (June 1928): 20.
[23] Seton-Watson, The Roumanians, p. 468; Albertini, Origins of the War of 1914, 1:527–30.

It is interesting that not only Czernin but also his German colleague, Julius Waldthausen, was convinced that Rumania could no longer be depended upon. The reports of these two men must have had much to do with the Austrian memorandum sent to Berlin on July 5 and with the subsequent acceptance by Berlin of Austria's desired alliance with Bulgaria.[24]

In the memorandum Berchtold spent much time developing the theme of Rumania's defection. He spoke of the revolution in Rumanian public opinion which fanned the flames for a Greater Rumania. He pointed to Carol's statement that, with the condition of public opinion, Rumania could not be expected to take up its alliance obligations in case of war. He mentioned the Constanza meeting, Bratianu's admission that a rapprochement had been made between Bukarest and St. Petersburg, Rumanian statesmen who now spoke about their foreign policy in terms of using a free hand, and finally the fact that the most they could expect in case of a conflict was Rumanian neutrality, which itself hung only on the pleasure of King Carol.[25] Berchtold did not desire a break with Rumania, but he declared, "These circumstances appear practically to exclude the possibility of Austria-Hungary being able to build up the compact with Rumania so reliably and securely that it might be used as the pivot of the Monarchy's Balkan policy. . . . It would be inexcusable carelessness, seriously endangering the power of self-defense, should the Monarchy . . . fail to enter without delay upon the military preparations and political activities necessary to counteract, or at least to weaken, the effects of the neutrality and the possible hostility of Rumania."[26]

Just before Austria issued its ultimatum to Serbia, Czernin was asked by Franz Joseph whether he could guarantee Rumanian neutrality in the event of war. Czernin could only answer that such a guarantee would be valid for as long as Carol remained alive. Without Carol there would be no guarantee.[27]

Once the ultimatum had been made known, Rumania reacted with further anger against Austria. "Austria has gone mad," was the cry most often heard, and King Carol himself believed the ultimatum was not the solution, that it would lead to war, and that the issue could be solved through peaceful means.[28]

Once Austria had actually declared war upon Serbia, both Vienna

---

[24] Albertini, *Origins of the War of 1914*, 1:506.
[25] Karl Kautsky, ed., *Die Deutschen Dokumente zum Kriegsausbruch*, 1, no. 14, pp. 73–74.
[26] Ibid.
[27] Czernin, *Im Weltkrieg*, p. 18.
[28] Ibid., pp. 115–16.

and Berlin very strongly pressed for Rumanian cooperation. Franz Joseph sent Carol a wire on July 27, declaring that Serbia had provoked a war, that Austria was acting to assure lasting peace, and that, because of the long friendship between himself and Carol, he believed "in these serious hours you will sincerely understand my decisions." Czernin told the Rumanian king "a treaty is a treaty" and honor required that Carol "unsheathe his sword."[29] On July 31, Kaiser Wilhelm wrote, "I trust that as a king and a Hohenzollern you will stand faithfully by your friend and unconditionally fulfill the obligations of your alliance."[30] That same day Jagow sent instructions to Heinrich von Waldburg, the German chargé d'affaires in Bukarest, to guarantee Rumania the possession of Bessarabia in return for its active participation on the side of the Triplice. Waldburg, while reporting that feeling was generally hostile in Rumania, seemed to believe the Rumanians would actually agree. He wired that Bratianu had assured him he would do all he could to carry out the alliance obligations.[31] Waldburg sent this information on August 1, but on August 3 the Rumanian Crown Council met and the result was a declaration of Rumanian neutrality.

Bukarest officials saw where their best interests lay. Public opinion was very hostile to Austria-Hungary, though not yet ready to accept a Russian alliance. The government did not at this time have much faith in the military power of Russia and France, which would both face the German-Austrian juggernaut. On the other hand, if the government honored the alliance it then exposed Rumania to a possible Russian attack. Since Sazonov had, just a few days before the declaration of neutrality, offered Transylvania to Rumania for its participation on Russia's side, Bratianu was in no way inclined to support the Austrians. There was, to be sure, a formal commitment, in existence since 1912, to aid Serbia in case of war, so that to remain on the sidelines meant sacrificing the Serbs. But Rumanian interests came first, and these dictated that the government remain uncommitted.[32]

Only King Carol, supported by Carp, asked for entry into the conflict on the side of the Triplice. A week before, the king had spoken of his wish to fulfill Rumania's diplomatic obligations, but the reply from his own government was that such a weighty decision necessitated the calling of a Great Crown Council. It took seven days

---

[29] Staatsarchiv, PA, box 516, unnumbered draft of Franz Joseph's wire sent to Carol on 27 July, dossier 7-B.

[30] Kautsky, *Deutschen Dokumente*, vol. 2, no. 472, p. 391.

[31] Ibid., vol. 3, nos. 506 and 508.

[32] Seton-Watson, *The Roumanians*, p. 474; Albertini, *Origins of the War of 1914*, 3: 558; C. Jay Smith, Jr., *The Russian Struggle for Power, 1914-1917*, p. 24.

for this council to assemble, since various officials were abroad and general and staff officers were on leave. As Czernin remarked, "In the meantime events precipitated the belief that the government was in a most ticklish position which would be worsened by the uncertain position of the neighboring states."[33]

The council now took the stand that no *casus foederis* existed, pointing to the clause in the formal alliance which called for such to be recognized "if Austria-Hungary was attacked . . . without any provocation on its part." Carol protested vigorously against such an interpretation and even threatened to abdicate, but to no avail. He could not enter a war without the support of a responsible government, nor could he enter a war which the Rumanian people resisted. There was nothing to be done but to accept the council's decision and to take comfort in the fact that he had avoided the declaration of "absolute neutrality" by gaining consent to stipulate that Rumania would protect its borders. Through this clause he hoped Bukarest could keep a free hand and perhaps find a pretext to enter on the side of the Central Powers.[34]

Once again, as in the case of Bulgaria, Berlin and Vienna had failed to achieve their goal. In this case an ally of over thirty years' standing had decided to wait and see how events turned. The only Rumanian concession was a decision on the part of the ministry itself, meeting after the council, to abandon its anti-revisionist posture concerning the stipulations of the Treaty of Bukarest, thus allowing Bulgaria to intervene in Serbia with no fear of Rumanian reprisals.[35] This would give the Germans and Austrians an additional lever to use in their Bulgarian negotiations, but it was small solace in the light of Rumanian neutrality, which meant the loss of 400,000 well-trained Rumanian troops. There was still hope that Rumania could be won over to active participation. The Rumanian chess game, however, was just beginning and in the end it would be won by the Entente.

The Central Powers and the Greek Question

The Entente was destined to win the active support of another Balkan state—Greece. From the time the Greeks revolted against their Turkish overlords in quest of political independence in 1824–25, they had found their mentors in England and France, both of which came

---

[33] Staatsarchiv, PA, box 516, no. 395, Czernin to Berchtold (a resume of the situation sent from Bukarest on 18 August 1914).

[34] Staatsarchiv, PA, box 516, no. 298, Czernin to Berchtold, 18 August 1914; Hegemann, "Plan der Abdankung," p. 824.

[35] GFMA, ser. 2, reel 17, no. 167, Tschirschky to Berlin, 4 August 1914.

to enjoy a favored position with the Greek people. That position did not mean much in the nineteenth century in terms of diplomatic power, for the Greek political renaissance had not brought a concomitant national strength. But it was to mean a great deal by 1914.

Until the turn of the century Greece had remained weak largely because of a consistent lag in economic and financial development. To a large extent the poor economic situation was due to geography. Greece possessed a natural handicap in the rugged mountains covering over half the mainland, making communication difficult and isolating valley communities one from another. A mere 20 percent of the total land area was plain. Thus, in spite of the fact that almost 90 percent of the population was agrarian, the nation had a difficult time satisfying its domestic agricultural needs.[36] Greece grew sizable crops of wheat, barley, oats, and maize, but was still forced to rely on large imports of Russian wheat to feed its population. More than topography was to blame. The Greek peasant was illiterate and conservative and was made indifferent by poor landlord-tenant relationships as well as by government neglect. In many instances agricultural methods and techniques remained two thousand years behind the times.[37]

Industry offered little by way of contrast. Greece had a great variety of ores and minerals, particularly along the eastern coast of the mainland, but the deposits had not, even by 1912, been exploited to any large degree. Throughout the country there were only fifty-one mines and quarries of limited size operating by 1913. Crucial to the lack of heavy industry was the almost complete absence of coal deposits. For its coal Greece depended on imports from England. The expense of such imports and the lack of basic, heavy industry made general industrial development a most difficult task.[38] The great powers did not lack interest in the Greek economy, but though British and French firms, for example, attempted inroads, their success was hampered by a general Greek distrust of foreigners. While the Greeks were delighted to have outside capital invested is their enterprises, they refused to have them supervised by foreign industrialists.[39] The situation in light industry was no better. Flour and cotton mills, tanneries and iron works were to be found in Athens, Salonika, Piraeus, and on a few of

[36] Michail Dorizas, *The Foreign Trade of Greece*, pp. 8–9.
[37] Percy Martin, *Greece of the Twentieth Century*, pp. 241, 246; John Levandis, *The Greek Foreign Debt and the Great Powers, 1821–1898*, pp. 61, 63; Great Britain, HSFO, *Greece with the Cyclades and Northern Sporades*, pp. 94–95.
[38] Arnold Toynbee, *Greek Policy Since 1882*, p. 7; Great Britain, Naval Intelligence Division, *A Handbook of Greece*, pp. 148–49; Dorizas, *Foreign Trade of Greece*, p. 8; Great Britain, HSFO, *Greece with the Cyclades*, pp. 97, 100, 105.
[39] Great Britain, HSFO, *Greece with the Cyclades*, pp. 103–4.

the Greek islands, but the quantities of items produced were small and therefore manufacturing offered little to bolster the economy as a whole.[40]

In spite of these weaknesses, Greece was nevertheless able to maintain a fairly active export trade with European states. Currants, wines, figs, tobacco, oils, emery, and some ores were shipped to England, Austria, Germany, and France. While these four powers controlled some 65 percent of Greek foreign commerce, it was England which significantly took almost two-thirds of that amount. When it came to Greek imports, again it was the British who supplied the largest percentage of Greek needs, namely in coal, textiles, and hardware. The Austrians, whose proximity to Greek markets reduced transportation costs and made Austrian goods attractive from the standpoint of purchase price, supplied Greece with large quantities of lumber, rice, sugar, and paper, and stood second in total value of imports by 1914. France took third place and Germany ranked fourth, supplying textiles, various types of machinery, chemicals, and scientific instruments.[41]

Greece was no exception to the consistent commercial pattern followed by both Austria and Germany in the Balkans. German and Austrian firms studied Greek business habits, Greek needs, the Greek political, social, monetary, and customs structures. They obtained a thorough knowledge of their customers and then met the competition of other nationals by using the Greek language and quoting prices in Greek drachmae. In short, they made it easy for Greek merchants to deal with German and Austrian suppliers. It was this approach which always made the Central Powers something of a threat to others in international trade; yet, in spite of this they were unable to emerge as the dominant powers in this country.[42]

To some extent German and Austrian failure in Greece was due to developments in finance. This was the most significant factor of all, for Greek financial needs and policy do much to explain the general economic weakness of the nation. Moreover, Greek financial dealings with European states had political implications because of the influence which certain powers came to have with the Greek government.

As early as 1824 England first came to the new nation's rescue by granting what was referred to as an independence loan. Throughout the rest of the nineteenth century there followed loan upon loan,

---

[40] Ibid., pp. 100–101.
[41] Dorizas, *Foreign Trade of Greece*, pp. 87–89 and Appendix III.
[42] Ibid., p. 89; Henry Hauser, *Germany's Commercial Grip on the World*, pp. 162, 169; Great Britain, HSFO, *Greece with the Cyclades*, p. 104.

obtained from either English or French bankers. These financiers received exorbitant discount rates of 30 to 40 percent and took an additional 5 to 8 percent in interest charges. The Greek government was in such dire financial straits that it had no choice but to accept extreme terms. In 1869 the Greek debt stood at over 137 million drachmae and by 1893 it had reached the total of 823 million. Half the total state revenues were needed to meet the debt burden. The situation might not have been so bad were it not for the fact that the loans were hastily contracted without thought to future repayment and then were not used to any great extent to increase the productive wealth of the country. Initially, the moneys were spent to repair the ravages of war with the Turks, and later to promote irredentist movements, territorial expansion, and the production of efficient fighting forces to obtain the desired territorial acquisitions. By the early 1890s the government was bankrupt, the victim of eight major loans which since 1833 had snowballed to unmanageable proportions. So it happened that in 1893 Tricoupis, the Greek prime minister, was forced to announce the complete suspension of all international debt payments.[43]

The Central Powers had begun to take an interest in Greek loans in the last quarter of the nineteenth century, and by the time the Greeks declared bankruptcy, German financiers held approximately 20 percent of the burden. When Greece defaulted, the subsequent furor in English, French, and German bondholding circles resulted in strong protests being lodged by these groups with their own governments as well as with Greece. Significantly, it was Germany which took up the cudgels in the financial dispute, and its strong demands produced a negative reaction toward Germany on the part of the Greek public.[44]

Members of an association called the "Free Union of German Retainers of Greek Funds" solicited the aid of the German chancellor, Leo von Caprivi, demanding that an international commission be established to protect their investments by directly controlling Greek finances. Caprivi ended by strongly supporting the group. Berlin declared the Greek default to be a German national question and threatened to recall the German minister, Baron von Plessen, if the Greeks did not meet the problem in a satisfactory manner. The British and

---

[43] Levandis, *Greek Foreign Debt*, pp. ix–x, 14–25, 58, 60–61, 73, 79; Feis, *Europe, World's Banker*, p. 285; Austria, Handelsministerium, *Wirtschaftliche Verhältnisse Griechenland*, pp. 72–73; Martin, *Greece of the Twentieth Century*, pp. 112–13.

[44] E. J. Tsouderos, *Le Relèvement Économique de la Grèce*, pp. 53–54; Levandis, *Greek Foreign Debt*, pp. 79, 82; Nicolas Politis, *La Guerre Grèco-Turque*, p. 122.

French press heaped invective upon Athens, but officially those two countries ended by suggesting that moderation be used in solving the question.

When, in 1897, Greece suffered a military defeat at the hands of the Turks, the major powers mediated the dispute and drew up what was to be the peace treaty. Germany insisted that a special clause be attached to the stipulations which would settle the entire financial issue. In August of that year the German government declared to the Greek minister in Berlin that "before Greece assumes new obligations, it is necessary to take measures which will retain the rights of old creditors intact. Germany believes this goal will be attained if the revenues destined for the service of the old loans as well as for a new loan are submitted to foreign control."[45] In short, while the other powers sought definite arrangements between the Greek government and the various stockholders, Germany demanded direct intervention in governmental affairs. The British and French took a very cautious approach to the matter, since the establishment of an international commission would obviously encroach on the sovereignty of Greece. In spite of suggestions that Germany take a less extreme position, Berlin remained adamant. Afraid that cooperation in Balkan affairs might break down, Britain and France finally agreed to the establishment of such a commission, the provisions for which were now written into the Greek-Turkish Peace Treaty. The reaction of the Greek public was extremely adverse, but the government had no alternative and therefore accepted the foreign control of its revenues.[46]

The results were unexpected. Contrary to Greek fears of economic ruin at the hands of foreigners, the Greek situation improved by leaps and bounds. Greek credit revived, financial conditions improved considerably because of the commission's care in handling payments and new commitments, and Greece now entered into a period of prosperity such as it had not previously enjoyed. Peculiarly enough, now that Germany had won its point, German money played a smaller role in the Greek loans negotiated between 1897 and 1914, with the consequence that England and France obtained an ever greater financial

[45] Tsouderos, *Relèvement Économique de la Grèce,* p. 10; André M. Andreades, *Oeuvres Études sur Les Finances Publiques de la Grèce Moderne,* pp. 115, 117, 118; Politis, *Guerre Gréco-Turque,* p. 123; Levandis, *Greek Foreign Debt,* pp. 83, 94.

[46] Tsouderos, *Relèvement Économique de la Grèce,* p. 10; Politis, *Guerre Gréco-Turque,* pp. 122, 127, 130; Germany, *Die Grosse Politik der Europäischen Kabinette, 1871–1914,* vol. 12, pt. 2, no. 3250, von Bülow to Kaiser Wilhelm, 20 August 1897 (hereafter cited as *G.P.*); France, Ministère des Affaires Étrangères, *Documents Diplomatiques: Affaires d'Orient, Mai-Décembre 1897,* no. 26, Hanotaux to Geoffrey in London, 8 June 1897.

preponderance and an accompanying political influence with the Athens government.[47]

The political relationship existing between Greece and the Central Powers by the opening of the World War, however, was based on much more than simply economic ties. Although the Greek monarch, King George, came from the royal house of Denmark, he thoroughly identified himself with Greece's welfare. Until his assassination in 1913 his intention was to strengthen Greece by the acquisition of additional territories; and because the future of his country was clearly bound up with the Mediterranean, he inclined toward those major powers who had strong interests there—Britain, France, Italy, and Spain. The two states which he saw as natural enemies were Turkey and Bulgaria—Turkey because it refused to countenance Greek control of Macedonia, Crete, and the Ionian Islands, and Bulgaria because it wanted Macedonia for itself, and also constituted a Slavic threat to Greek well-being.[48]

In 1910 King George summoned Eleutherios Venizelos to the premiership. Venizelos was strongly in favor of maintaining close ties with France and England, and, like the king, he aimed at expansion of Greek territorial holdings. His advent to power further hardened Greco-Turkish hostility. There were two and a half million Greeks in Asia Minor and a particularly heavy population in Thrace and along the southern coast of Macedonia as far west as the port of Dedeagatch. Venizelos wanted those areas. The realization of his expansionist ambitions was impeded by the success of the Young Turk revolt in 1909, which had as its object the resuscitation of the Ottoman Empire. The Young Turk leaders announced a Turkification program in which was envisaged the destruction of Greek influence within Turkish territories. Therefore it was quite clear that Greek and Turkish policies stood diametrically opposed.[49]

Venizelos's desire to control Macedonia also produced ill feeling between Greece and Bulgaria. The intermixture of Greek and Bulgarian populations there made the drawing of borders most difficult, so that the division of Macedonia to the satisfaction of both states was

[47] Politis, *Guerre Grèco-Turque*, p. 140; Levandis, *Greek Foreign Debt*, p. 107; Andreades, *Finances de la Grèce*, pp. 125–26; Feis, *Europe, World's Banker*, pp. 287, 292; Tsouderos, *Relèvement Économique de la Grèce*, p. 54.

[48] Martin, *Greece of the Twentieth Century*, p. 42; Edouard Driault and Michel L'Heritier, *Histoire Diplomatique de la Grèce de 1821 à nos Jours*, 4:562–65.

[49] Crawford Price, *Venizelos and the War*, pp. 13, 20; Herbert Gibbons, *Venizelos*, p. 90; George Soteriadis, *An Ethnological Map Illustrating Hellenism in the Balkan Peninsula and Asia Minor*, pp. 1–16; Edouard Driault, *Le Roi Constantin*, pp. 54–56.

almost impossible to achieve. And yet in 1912 Greece and Bulgaria signed an alliance. What drew them together was the common enemy, Turkey. The alliance, while defensive in nature, had an additional military convention envisaging a joint attack on the Turks. This agreement, in conjunction with a previously arranged Serbian-Bulgarian accord, provided the diplomatic basis upon which the First Balkan War was to be launched against the Ottoman Empire.[50]

The military victory of the coalition proved to be a relatively easy matter, but the territorial settlements did not erase the hostilities between Greece and Turkey, on the one hand, or Greece and Bulgaria on the other. As a result of the Treaty of London of May 30, 1913, Greece now controlled the Aegean port of Salonika, incurring the wrath of the Bulgarians, who coveted it. Furthermore, during the war the Greek navy had occupied the Aegean Islands, which, because they were seen by the Turks as the first line of defense against attacks on Constantinople and Asia Minor, were considered to be of the most crucial importance to Turkish welfare. The disposition of these islands was referred to a Council of Ambassadors representing the great powers of Europe. Since the decision of the council was not immediately forthcoming, it remained impossible to establish amicable relations between the two adversaries.

While the disposition of the islands was still pending, the Second Balkan War was fought, in which Greece was allied with Serbia and Rumania against Bulgaria. The Treaty of Bukarest ended the conflict in August, 1913, but left Bulgaria seething with anger, particularly toward Serbia and Greece, which had divided Macedonia between them. The Greek border was now delineated by a line drawn east of the prized Macedonian port of Kavalla. The result of the peace settlement was that there were now two revisionist states, Turkey and Bulgaria, that saw in Greece a common enemy. Yet, there could be no healthy alliance between the two because they were themselves at loggerheads on the issue of which would control Thrace.[51]

In the midst of this difficult situation, Germany and Austria, concerned as they were with the development of a Balkan coalition to be intimately connected to the Triple Alliance, were forced to consider the relationship of Greece to that coalition. By August, 1913, the disagreement between Vienna and Berlin over the Greek issue was hot and heavy. It was clear that the clash of ambitions between Greece and

[50] Toynbee, *Greek Policy Since 1882*, pp. 15–16; E. C. Helmreich, *The Diplomacy of the Balkan Wars, 1912–1913*, pp. 76–77.
[51] Gibbons, *Venizelos*, pp. 126, 152; Helmreich, *Diplomacy of the Balkan Wars*, pp. 432, 339, 413–414; Harry Howard, *The Partition of Turkey*, pp. 64, 65.

Bulgaria made it necessary for the Central Powers to choose one or the other as a member of a Balkan alignment. Both could not be achieved. The Ballhausplatz took the position that Bulgaria was the better choice. The Bulgarian government had now been courting the Dreibund for some time, but Count Berchtold took his stand on additional factors. It appeared to him that a close tie with Bulgaria would be in no way disadvantageous to Germany's best interests. On the contrary, if a friendly connection between Bulgaria and Rumania could be established, it would be to the strong benefit of the Dreibund, since in the case of a war with Russia, the Rumanians could fulfill their military obligations without fear of being attacked from the rear by King Ferdinand. Berchtold did not intend to bar the door against Greece and to preclude its joining such a Bulgarian-Rumanian combination, but it was quite apparent to him that the gap between Greece and Bulgaria was large, that it could be closed only after much goodwill had been generated, and that at the moment the elimination of Greek-Bulgarian hostilities was hardly to be expected.[52]

Austrian thinking was also colored by the fact that Greek territorial ambitions cut across Austrian interests. When the First Balkan War broke out in October, 1912, a governmental conference in Vienna met to consider the question of Albania. It was decided that even at the expense of war Austria must prevent the eastern coast of the Adriatic from being controlled by another power. This meant that Austria must support the development of an independent Albania whose borders ought to be as extensive as possible. Vienna did, of course, accept the declaration of Albanian independence in November, 1912, but a problem developed in trying to settle the southern boundaries of the new state. The Greeks had long had their eyes on southern Albania, or what was called northern Epirus, and since they occupied part of this area during the First Balkan War, the Greeks found themselves at loggerheads with the Monarchy during the London Conference of Ambassadors when the question of border delimitation was broached.[53]

For Vienna the importance of northern Epirus was based on its strategic location. To control the area meant to control the entrance to the Adriatic Sea, and since the territory lay in a direct line with the heel of Italy, the Italians backed the Austrian government in opposing Greek extension there. In December, 1913, the Austrians and Italians

---

[52] Ö.-U. Aussenpolitik, vol. 7, no. 8157, Berchtold to Szögyény, 1 August 1913.
[53] Alfred F. Pribram, Austria-Hungary and Great Britain, 1908–1914, p. 164; Edith Stickney, Southern Albania or Northern Epirus in European International Affairs, 1912–1913, pp. 19, 20, 21, 24, 27–28.

DIPLOMATIC DISAPPOINTMENTS

proved successful when a commission set up by the Conference of Ambassadors decided that the area in question was to be evacuated by Greece and included in the Albanian state. As a compensation, the commission declared that Greece was to retain the Aegean Islands. Berchtold had won his point, but not without embittering Athens and straining relations between Vienna and Berlin. The Wilhelmstrasse was forced to support the Dual Monarchy. To Greek pleas for aid in the issue of southern Albania, Berlin replied that in a conflict between Greek, Italian, and Austrian interests, Germany would have to support its allies. Jagow wrote to the chargé d'affaires in Athens, Rudolf von Bassewitz, "An aspiring state such as Greece cannot get all its wishes satisfied at once. Rome was not built in a day."[54]

Nevertheless, Germany remained pro-Greek. Its desire to win Greece to the side of the Triple Alliance increased as 1913 wore on, and this was based on other factors than the distrust of Kaiser Wilhelm for the Bulgarian king and the latter's apparent perfidiousness. On March 18, 1913, King George of Greece was assassinated while in Salonika, and his son Constantine immediately assumed the throne. Constantine had completed his education at the universities of Leipzig and Heidelberg and he came away with a healthy respect for Germany. More than that, in 1889 he married Sofia, the sister of Kaiser Wilhelm, a marriage which the German Emperor not only sanctioned but attended. A warm relationship developed between the two men, and when Constantine proved himself a very capable military leader during the Balkan Wars, the Kaiser honored him with the baton of a German field marshal.[55]

The close tie between the two monarchs was reflected in a series of negotiations which went on between Berlin and Athens in the late spring of 1913. Minister Nicholas Theotoky, representing the Greek government in Germany, informed the Wilhelmstrasse at that time that Greece was prepared to join the Dreibund. Since Venizelos was known to be pro-Entente, von Jagow got in touch with the German minister in Athens, Albert Quadt, to check on the authorization of Theotoky to make such a direct statement. Quadt replied on June 23 that although Venizelos did not agree with such a direct connection with the Triple Alliance, the king did; Constantine was ready to override Venizelos's caution. In return for Greece's seeking a tie between itself, Rumania,

[54] Stickney, *Southern Albania*, pp. 1, 2, 27–28, 40; *G.P.*, vol. 36, pt. 1, no. 13923, von Jagow to von Bassewitz in Athens, 11 September 1913.
[55] Prince Nicholas of Greece, *My Fifty Years*, p. 243; Driault, *Roi Constantin*, pp. 46, 47, 79; Arthur Lee, *The Royal House of Greece*, pp. 34–36.

and the Dreibund, Constantine wanted German support for the continued possession of those territories which Greece now held.[56]

The Wilhelmstrasse's reaction was mixed. Both von Jagow and Bethmann-Hollweg were delighted with the idea of Greece turning toward their camp, but the Balkan crisis was still not settled and until it was, both felt that such a connection between Greece and the Central Powers could only directly involve Germany in the Balkan tangle. Constantine's demand for German support of Greek territorial holdings required a heavier commitment than Berlin wanted to make at this moment. The Kaiser agreed with his advisors and authorized what proved to be a cautious reply to the offer. Germany, it said, though joyful over the prospect of a close orientation with Greece, could not before the end of the Balkan crisis consider the question of a direct anschluss.[57]

Vienna agreed with this stand, and Berchtold, in conversations with von Tschirschky, expanded on the Austrian attitude. In truth, Berchtold was sympathetic to a connection with Greece, but his reluctance to go ahead was based on a long series of considerations. In the first place, since June, 1913, Greece had had an alliance with Serbia, the greatest Austrophobe country in the Balkan peninsula. Although the Greek representative to Vienna, Streit, had told him this alliance was directed only against Bulgaria, the Austrian foreign minister did not know the precise terms. On this basis, he could hardly take any strongly affirmative position with respect to Athens. Second, the Greeks wanted the town of Koritza in southern Albania, a concession which Austria was unwilling to grant. Third, Greek demands would engage the Monarchy in far-reaching questions: the defense of the Greek coasts against the Entente fleet, the covering of Greece's rear against a Bulgarian attack, and the support of Greek aspirations in Asia Minor. Moreover, Berchtold could not agree with Germany's eagerness to foster a Greek-Rumanian understanding. If one should be realized, Serbia and Bulgaria might join hands for purposes of self-defense against those two powers. While Austria was at loggerheads with Serbia it could not afford the risk of a Serb-Bulgarian combination, which would be a formidable one. Greece would hardly be in a position to serve Austrian interests, because it could not hold its neighbors in check. The only solution was to keep Serbia and Bulgaria

[56] *G.P.*, vol. 35, no. 13450, memorandum by von Jagow, 18 June 1913; no. 13452, von Jagow to Kaiser Wilhelm in Hamburg, 21 June; no. 13455, Bethmann-Hollweg to Wilhelm in Hamburg, 23 June.

[57] Ibid., vol. 35, no. 13456, von Jagow to Minister Albert Quadt in Athens, 25 June 1913.

apart and this required courting the Bulgarians. Thus, the idea of combining with Greece and using it as a substitute for Bulgaria was out of the question.[58]

Germany and Austria agreed to leave in abeyance the question of Greece joining the Triple Alliance, but it is clear that their strategies were really quite different. Germany wanted to wait until the Balkan atmosphere cleared and then, if conditions were right, to proceed with its pro-Greek policy. The Austrians also chose to wait, but, if conditions were right, to continue with a pro-Bulgarian policy, which they hoped could be worked out without irrevocably cutting the lines to Athens.[59]

The difference between Berlin and Vienna became clear when the two sharply disagreed on the disposition of Kavalla, just before the signature of the Treaty of Bukarest. The Wilhelmstrasse proved eager to fulfill Greece's ambition to control the Macedonian port. Greece, as one of the victors in the Second Balkan War, had strengthened itself considerably, so that von Jagow now saw it as a strategic factor in the Mediterranean "worthy of notice." "Our interests," he said, "would hereby be very essentially affected." If Greece did not get Kavalla there would be no possibility of its being drawn into the orbit of the Triple Alliance in the future. Berchtold's reaction was quite the opposite. The Bulgarians, he observed, wanted Kavalla for themselves, and because they had made overtures toward joining the Dreibund, Vienna could only recommend that Kavalla go to them and not to their Greek enemies. Sofia had pressed much earlier for Austrian support on the matter and the Monarchy could not now turn its back without repulsing Bulgaria and driving it into the arms of the Russians.[60]

The German rebuttal was that if Greek adherence to the Triple Alliance was desired, Greece must have Kavalla; Bulgaria could be placated by granting it concessions on the coast in the area of Dedeagatch. Berchtold agreed that eventually Bulgaria might be satisfied in this way but his bitterness over the matter was reflected in a private letter to Szögyény on August 8, two days before the Treaty of Bukarest was signed, when he remarked that the Kaiser had apparently made promises to Greece concerning Kavalla and "now Berlin demands

---

[58] Ibid., no. 13463, von Tschirschky to Foreign Office, 28 June 1913.

[59] Ibid., no. 13476, Berchtold to Szögyény in Berlin, 1 July 1913; Ö.-U. Aussenpolitik, vol. 7, no. 8157, Berchtold to Szögyény in Berlin, 1 August.

[60] G.P., vol. 35, no. 13700, von Jagow to Tschirschky in Vienna, 1 August 1913; no. 13702, von Tschirschky to von Jagow, 2 August; no. 13712, von Tschirschky to von Jagow, 4 August.

that we adapt our policy to this escapade." In the end Greece obtained the port but the Austrian attitude remained revisionist.[61]

Subsequently, in pursuit of a closer understanding with Greece, Germany sought to establish a workable agreement between Athens and Constantinople that would lead both governments to align themselves, side by side, with the Triple Alliance.[62] The policy failed, largely as a result of the Greco-Turkish dispute over control of the Aegean Islands. These islands, except for Tenedos, Imbros, and Castellorizo, were all awarded to Greece in February, 1914.[63] Both before and after this award the Turks refused to accept the Greek occupation of the Archipelago, and the fact that a Greek-Turkish treaty was signed in Athens in November, 1913, restoring normal diplomatic and commercial intercourse between the two, did not prevent the Turkish grand vizier's threatening war against Greece if the situation was not redressed. It was quite clear to the Austrians that the establishment of truly amicable relations between the disputants would be almost impossible. Hilmi Pasha, the Turkish ambassador to Vienna, flatly asserted at the end of August, 1913, that Turkey would never assent to an alliance with Athens because Greece was seen as the Ottoman Empire's most dangerous enemy. Prince Emil von Fürstenberg, legation secretary in Athens, had written to the Ballhausplatz at the same time, saying that a *modus vivendi* simply could not be worked out between the two. At the turn of 1914, Pallavicini in Constantinople wrote that with Enver Pasha, Talaat Bey, and Djemal Pasha now holding power in the Turkish government, the Turks would not shrink from a war with Greece. If the powers decided on the islands question in favor of the Greeks, Constantinople would quietly bide its time and then attack at the most propitious moment.[64]

By the spring of 1914 the struggle between Greece and Turkey had

[61] Ibid., no. 13701, von Jagow to Flotow in Rome, 2 August 1913; no. 13703, von Jagow to Tschirschky in Vienna, 2 August; no. 13713, Zimmermann to Tschirschky, 5 August; no. 13722, Zimmermann to von Treutler at Swinemünde, 6 August; no. 13725, Tschirschky to Bethmann-Hollweg, 5 August; footnote to no. 13751, Pourtales in St. Petersburg to Bethmann-Hollweg, 12 August.

[62] Ibid., vol. 36, pt. 1, no. 13842, von Jagow to Wangenheim in Constantinople, 8 September 1913; Harry Howard, *The Partition of Turkey, 1913–23*, p. 65.

[63] Karl Strupp, *Die Beziehungen Zwischen Griechenland und der Türkei von 1820–1930*, pp. 74–75. Tenedos and Imbros were strategically located with respect to the Dardanelles, while Castellorizo lay between Rhodes and the coast of Asia Minor.

[64] G.P., vol. 36, pt. 1, no. 13846, Wangenheim to Foreign Office, 10 September 1913; Ö.-U. *Aussenpolitik*, daily report of Berchtold, 22 August 1913; no. 8455, Legation Secretary Prince Emil von Fürstenberg in Athens to Berchtold, 23 August; no. 9165, Pallavicini to Berchtold, 7 January 1914; Helmreich, *Diplomacy of the Balkan Wars*, pp. 431–32.

not abated. That the Council of Ambassadors had assigned the islands to Greece meant nothing to Constantinople. Yet, Berlin remained convinced that a reconciliation could be accomplished, and in spite of supporting Athens on the islands question, Germany assumed the role of mediator between the combatants. The Wilhelmstrasse worked to establish a Greek-Turkish alliance but exercised caution in the process. It offered moral rather than specific, formal, diplomatic support. Wangenheim in May made the striking point that whether Germany wanted to or not, it would have to guarantee an eventual Greek-Turkish alliance with much more than simply moral protection. He declared, "We cannot fish in the troubled waters of eastern politics without getting our fingers wet."[65] The ambassador promised to continue working for the desired understanding, but he had little faith that it would develop. In his estimation, no experienced observer could believe a reconciliation possible between Hellenism and Ottomanism. Greece would never give up its Byzantine hopes, and the Turks, aware of this, hated the Greeks for it. He doubted very much that a peaceful settlement of the islands question could be found because the Turks had made the issue a question of national prestige.[66]

To be sure, there seemed to be every possibility of a new Greek-Turkish war occurring. In March, Enver Pasha said that Turkey would make good its claims to the islands in three or four months, meaning that Turkey would then be ready to make its move, having achieved naval supremacy over the opponent.[67] Enver's aggressive attitude was based on Turkey's having ordered two cruisers, then on the construction ways in England. Additional but unsuccessful attempts to purchase fighting ships were made in Germany, France, and Italy. To deter the Turks the three powers had refused the sale. As Germany pointed out, a war with Greece would hardly be in Turkey's interest since it would only bring down on Turkey's head the condemnation of the powers and would hasten the dissolution of the Ottoman Empire. There subsequently occurred a small naval race, for Greece, once aware of Turkey's maneuvers to strengthen its battle squadrons, countered by purchasing from the United States two warships, the *Idaho* and the *Mississippi*, in June, 1914.[68]

The thing which now brought the two enemies to the very brink of war was the persecution and atrocities perpetrated by each against the

[65] *G.P.*, vol. 36, pt. 2, no. 14582, von Jagow to Wangenheim, 2 May 1914; no. 14587, Wangenheim to von Jagow, 7 May.
[66] Ibid., no. 14587, Wangenheim to von Jagow. See also addendum.
[67] Ibid., no. 14555, Waldthausen to Bethmann-Hollweg, 3 March 1914.
[68] Ibid., footnote to no. 14555; Henry Morgenthau, *Ambassador Morgenthau's Story*, pp. 52–53, 55–56.

other's nationals. On May 20, the Turkish chargé d'affaires in Athens suggested to Venizelos that perhaps their countries could eliminate the friction existing between them by agreeing to an exchange of Turkish and Greek populations. By May 25 both governments had consented to an exchange involving the Greeks in Smyrna and in Thrace and the Ottomans in Macedonia. No sooner had the agreement been made than the Turks began mass persecution and deportation of Greek citizens. While Greece bitterly protested such measures, the Turks could similarly point to arrests, religious persecution, and atrocities of one type or another by Greeks against Turkish citizens on the island of Crete and in Macedonia.[69] Venizelos, responding to a very strong reaction by the Greek public, sent an ultimatum to the Turkish government on June 12. The note demanded the cessation of Turkish persecutions, compensation for damages, and future guarantees for the lives and property of Greeks living in Asia Minor. The Greek representative was instructed to break off diplomatic relations if the Turks did not reply favorably.[70]

The war, which now hung in the balance, was averted for two reasons: Turkey decided on a conciliatory attitude and offered Athens a positive answer, and the various powers responded coldly to Greece's sudden bellicosity. Rumania declared it would not support Greece in a war against the Ottomans and Serbia took the same attitude. France advised against hostilities, while the Kaiser cogently pointed out that if Greece opened hostilities, it would bear the odium of aggression among the major states. It was the apparent eagerness of the Turkish government to negotiate which now led Venizelos to agree to personal discussions with the grand vizier in Brussels. When, on July 28, Austria-Hungary declared war on Serbia, Venizelos was in Munich waiting to hear that the grand vizier had started for the meeting. Venizelos now asked that the Turk leader come there rather than to Belgium because of the tense European situation. Said Halim agreed to leave for Munich by way of Trieste on July 31, but the beginning of the World War precluded the scheduled conversations. So the negotiations between Greece and Turkey went no further, and the relations between the two remained undefined. The Kaiser's much dreamed of Rumanian-Greek-Turkish coalition was never to be.[71]

[69] Helmreich, *Diplomacy of the Balkan Wars*, p. 439; GFMA, ser. 1, reel 395, no. A 9909, Dragoumis to von Jagow, 19 May 1914; no. 152, Wangenheim to Bethmann-Hollweg, 28 May; A. F. Frangulis, *La Grèce et la Crise Mondiale*, pp. 111, 112.

[70] Frangulis, *La Grèce*, p. 112; G.P., vol. 36, pt. 2, no. 14609 and accompanying footnote, Quadt to Foreign Office, 14 June 1914; Wilhelm Stahl, ed., Schulthess' *Europäischer Geschichtskalender*, vol. 30, pt. 2, p. 865.

Actually, at the last moment, German policy had been reversed. When the Wilhelmstrasse heard of the intended Brussels negotiations, Wangenheim in Constantinople was instructed to discourage Said Halim from signing any alliance with Venizelos. The sudden German turnabout is explained by the events that occurred after the assassination of Archduke Franz Ferdinand. It was clear that Berlin would now have to support Austria against the Serbians. If it should come to war and the Bulgarians should join the Monarchy against the Serbs, Greece would come to the aid of the Serbian people. And if a Greco-Turkish alliance existed, the Turks would be forced to honor the *casus foederis*, would end by fighting Austria, and so would become the enemy of the Dreibund.[72] That Berlin now did what it could to block the realization of a Greek-Turkish accord also reflected German capitulation to Austrian pleas on July 5 for support of Vienna's pro-Bulgarian policy. Wangenheim now succeeded in extracting from the grand vizier a promise that he would sign nothing with Venizelos.[73]

Having once accepted the Austrian viewpoint, the Germans proceeded with all haste to smooth away the frictions between Turkey and Bulgaria and to align both powers on the side of the Triple Alliance. This *volte face*, interestingly enough, did not deter Kaiser Wilhelm, during the opening days of the war, from attempting to obtain the active participation of Greece on the side of the Central Powers. The German emperor acted in this respect with a certain logic, for he banked on his cordial relations with King Constantine, on the obvious pro-German tendencies of the Greek monarch, who had talked of his desire to sign a German alliance, and on the goodwill built by the Wilhelmstrasse in supporting the Greek claims to Salonika, Kavalla and the Aegean Islands. What the Kaiser failed to understand was that Constantine, though indeed pro-German, could not be verbally bludgeoned into submission.

When on July 23, Wilhelm heard indirectly from the German military mission in Constantinople that great amounts of war goods

[71] Stahl, *Europäischer Geschichtskalender*, vol. 30, pt. 2, p. 867; G.P., vol. 36, pt. 2, no. 14616, Waldthausen in Bukarest to Foreign Office, 17 June 1914; no. 14618, Quadt to Foreign Office, 17 June; no. 14631, Quadt to Foreign Office, 23 July (see here the marginal note by the Kaiser); Kautsky, *Deutschen Dokumente*, vol. 2, no. 405, Wangenheim to Foreign Office, 30 July.

[72] G.P., vol. 36, pt. 2, no. 14644, von Bassewitz to Foreign Office, 18 July 1914; no. 14645, Wangenheim to Foreign Office, 19 July; no. 14648, von Jagow to the Kaiser, 23 July (see here the marginal note of the Kaiser); Greece, "Diplomatic Documents, 1913–1917," *American Journal of International Law*, supplement to vol. 12, no. 11, G. Streit, minister of foreign affairs, to Venizelos, 11/24 July 1914.

[73] G.P., vol. 36, pt. 2, no. 14645, Wangenheim to Foreign Office, 19 July 1914.

were piling up in various Greek ports, that Greece was about to mobilize, and that it intended to attack Turkey at the Dardanelles, he instructed Minister Quadt to deliver to Constantine his strong appeal that Greece not proceed with such an attack. Turkey wished to join the Dreibund and Greece must not now fall upon "a worthwhile ally of the Triple Alliance."[74] On July 27, Constantine sent a long reply in which he stoutly denied that Greece was planning any kind of attack on Turkey. The war goods piling up in Greek ports were supplies ordered for the army the previous October. He did not want war and he looked forward to the results of the planned meeting between Venizelos and the grand vizier. He concluded with a rather impressive statement: "I beg Your Majesty to believe in my complete loyalty as a ruler, as a colleague, and as a man, and to believe that I have always told the plain, unvarnished truth and shall continue to do so. But the others must treat me just as honorably as I treat them, particularly Turkey."[75]

Kaiser Wilhelm now made a desperate bid for the entry of Greece on the side of the Triple Alliance. On July 30 Count Bassewitz was instructed to deliver orally to Constantine the offer that Germany would do everything it could to further good relations between Greece and Turkey. To quiet Greek fears of a possible Bulgarian-Turkish coalition, Wilhelm declared that if the conflict was localized between Austria and Serbia, the other two Balkan states would not be permitted to interfere. But if it should come to a general European war, then each of the Balkan states would have to make a choice between the Triple Alliance and the Entente. Concerning such a conflagration and the position of Greece, the Kaiser made his feelings quite plain: "I feel that it goes without saying that the very memory of your father, who fell at the hands of a murderer, will keep you and Greece from taking the part of the Serbian assassins against my person and the Triple Alliance. But even from the standpoint of pure usefulness to the interests of Greece it seems to me that the place for your country and your dynasty is at the side of the Triple Alliance."[76]

Further to convince the Greek monarch that Greece was not bound to support its alliance obligations with Serbia, he argued that "even Serbia, which cannot be saved from her fate except by Greek support,

[74] *G.P.*, vol. 36, pt. 2, no. 14647, von Jagow to the Kaiser, 23 July 1914, and marginal note of the Kaiser.
[75] Kautsky, *Deutschen Dokumente*, vol. 1, no. 243, the King of Greece to the Emperor, 27 July 1914.
[76] Ibid., vol. 2, no. 466, Imperial Chancellor to Kaiser Wilhelm, 30 July 1914; vol. 3, no. 504, von Jagow to von Bassewitz, chargé d'affaires in Athens, 31 July.

will understand that it is *force majeure* which determines the attitude of Greece." Playing upon Greece's heavy concern over possible Slavic domination of the Balkans, the Kaiser said, "No nation has regarded Greece's rise under your leadership with more envious eyes than has Russia. Never will there be a better opportunity than now for Greece, under the mighty shield of the Triple Alliance, to cast off the hegemony that Russia is endeavoring to impose upon the Balkans." As if all this were not enough to convince Constantine, he concluded with a threat: "Should you, against my confident expectations, align yourself on the side of the enemy, Greece would at once be exposed to the attacks of Italy, Bulgaria, and Turkey, and also, our personal relations would probably have to suffer forever as a result. I have spoken frankly, and beg you to communicate your decision to me without delay and with equal frankness."[77]

The arguments and the threat notwithstanding, Constantine stood his ground. His answer, forthcoming on August 2, was analytical, firm, and negative. The king stated that Greece would not come to Serbia's aid, but neither could Greece associate with Serbia's enemies and end by attacking that very country which, after all, was Greece's ally. The best interests, he asserted, were to be found not in participation in the war but in neutrality and in the preservation of the status quo in the Balkans as it was created by the Treaty of Bukarest. If Bulgaria came in against the Serbs and if Greece also joined, it would mean the disruption of that status quo, since the Bulgarians would take for themselves newly acquired Serbian territory in Macedonia. This would mean that the entire Greek northern border as far as Albania would be surrounded and, therefore, Greece would face an enormous Bulgarian threat. Such an addition of territory for Bulgaria would destroy the balance of power in the Balkans, where the domination of the Slavs "would then be assured." "These considerations," he concluded, "force us to neutrality and also in conjunction with Rumania to prevent Bulgaria from taking a hand."[78]

The Kaiser was furious. His reaction was to scribble "rubbish" in the margin of the telegram, and to issue more threats: "Tell Athens that I have made an alliance with Bulgaria and Turkey for the war against Russia and will treat Greece as an enemy in case she does not join us at once. . . . If Greece does not at once join us, then she will lose her position as a Balkan power and no longer enjoy our support in her

---

[77] Ibid., vol. 3, no. 504, von Jagow to von Bassewitz, 31 July 1914.
[78] Ibid., no. 702, the King of Greece to the German Kaiser through von Bassewitz, 2 August 1914.

desires. . . . It is not a question of the balance of power in the Balkans but of cooperation on the part of the Balkan states to free the Balkans from Russia forever."[79]

On August 4, Wilhelm talked with Theotoky, and told him that Turkey had signed with Germany and that Bulgaria and Rumania were also ranging themselves on the same side. The German ships in the Mediterranean would now join with the Turkish fleet. All the Balkan states were siding with the Central Powers, and Greece must do so too. Through Theotoky, the Kaiser appealed to Constantine as a comrade, as a German field marshal, as a brother-in-law. This was his last plea, he said. If Constantine did not join hands with him now there would be a complete break between the two states. The Greek minister panicked in the face of what seemed a solid Balkan wall of German allies. On the same day he wrote to his king, "I beseech you to weigh in the most careful manner the immense consequences for the present and the future which a refusal on our part to accede to the appeal of the Emperor could entail." And a week later Theotoky wrote to the Greek foreign minister, Streit, "As you see, we are isolated."[80]

Athens remained unruffled. On July 30 the Bulgarians had declared their neutrality, so that, at least for the moment, they were not going to actively join the Dreibund. The Turks and the Rumanians both had alliances with the Central Powers but both refused to acknowledge the *casus foederis* and simultaneously announced their neutrality on August 4. Greece was scarcely faced with a Balkan phalanx ready to fall upon its back. On August 7, Constantine replied to Wilhelm's desperate urgings by saying that while his sympathies were certainly with Germany, Greece could not now be of use to the Central Powers. The English and French battle squadrons would only destroy the Greek fleet and merchant marine, making impossible the concentration of the army. "Without being able to be useful," said Constantine, "we would be wiped off the map." In light of this he concluded that, "I am necessarily of the opinion that neutrality is imposed upon us." He nevertheless assured the Kaiser that "I shall not touch your friends, my neighbors, as long as they do not touch our local Balkan interests."[81]

The one country that concerned Athens more than any other was Bulgaria. On July 25 Theotoky had told Jagow that Venizelos felt very strongly about the Bulgarians. The premier intended to honor

[79] Ibid. (see Kaiser's marginal note).

[80] Greece, "Diplomatic Documents," nos. 19 and 20, Minister Nicholas Theotoky to the Greek king in Athens, 4 August 1914; no. 24, Theotoky to Streit, 11 August.

[81] Ibid., no. 21, Constantine to Wilhelm, 7 August 1914.

the military convention signed between Greece and Serbia in June, 1913, by which both had promised military aid if one was attacked by Bulgarian troops. Venizelos had declared that if Bulgaria intervened against Serbia, Greece would immediately take up its obligations.[82] When the Austrians declared war on Serbia, Venizelos was still in Munich, awaiting the grand vizier, but when he was queried by his own foreign minister as to what Greece ought now to do, particularly in light of Serbia's having requested a definition of Athens's position, his answer proved an interesting one. In a localized war between Austria and Serbia, Greece would see no obligation existing necessarily to participate. Only if Bulgaria mobilized would Greece act. If the localized conflict between Austria and Serbia became a general conflagration, Greece could not range itself with Serbia's enemies, for this would be contrary to Greek vital interests. And Venizelos underscored this position by asserting that, "I shall under no pretext whatever deviate from this policy."[83]

Greece did declare its neutrality on August 2, but in fact, Venizelos went back on his word; by the end of the month he had offered Greek services to the Entente, which at this time rejected them. It became quite obvious to diplomats at the Wilhelmstrasse that the best they could hope for was the continuation of Greek neutrality. The Greek position came as no surprise to the Ballhausplatz. As early as January, 1914, Berchtold, during a visit of Venizelos to Vienna, had learned where Greece would stand in case of a major war. Venizelos flatly stated that Greek interests made it necessary to remain aloof from binding obligations with the great powers. Venizelos was not interested, as he put it, in being pulled into "the vortex of *Weltpolitik*." Greece lay exposed because of its extensive sea coasts, and if the major states of Europe should ever go to war, Greece would remain neutral.[84]

While in the spring of 1914 Austria went along with German attempts to forestall a Greek-Turkish clash, Vienna had little faith that any lasting friendship could be established. Even as late as July 25, when it was well known that the grand vizier was to meet with Venizelos, Pallavicini was writing that the distances between Greece and Turkey were such that they could not be bridged. Nor did he consider the meeting anything but a Turkish attempt to gain time.[85]

---

[82] Ibid., no. 13, Theotoky to Streit, 25 July 1914.
[83] Ibid., no. 17, Venizelos in Munich to Streit, 2 August 1914.
[84] Ö.-U. *Aussenpolitik*, vol. 7, no. 9272, daily report of Berchtold, 30 January 1914.
[85] Ibid., vol. 8, nos. 10489, 10676, Pallavicini to Berchtold, 22 and 25 July 1914 respectively.

By July the Austrians were doing all they could to block the signing of a Greco-Turkish alliance, because, in conjunction with their policy aimed at obtaining Bulgarian adherence to the Dreibund, they now also sought Turkey as an ally. If the Greeks and Turks signed an arrangement, the desired Bulgarian-Turkish-Rumanian combination would become impossible to achieve. When Pallavicini extracted from the grand vizier the unqualified remark that he would in no way entertain signing an accord with Venizelos, the Austrians breathed more easily.[86] Nevertheless, Berchtold wanted no trouble with Athens, and after Austria's declaration of war on Serbia he sent careful instructions to the Austrian minister to Greece, Julius Szilassy. He was to explain to the government that Serbia had refused to accede to demands aimed at preserving Austrian interests, that Austria was not desirous of territorial expansion, and that the Monarchy hoped Greece would undertake nothing that might produce a more general war from what was merely a localized action. The Greek foreign minister was to be reminded of Athens's repeated assurances that the Greek-Serbian alliance was not directed against Austria-Hungary. Streit's answer was reassuring; he stated that in a localized war Greece would not aid its Serbian ally and would do so only if Bulgaria joined in against the Serbs.[87] For the moment, Berchtold was satisfied. The subsequent strongly neutral position espoused by Constantine after general war began led the Ballhausplatz to forge ahead with the desired Bulgarian-Turkish-Rumanian coalition.

In the war years ahead neither of the Central Powers was seriously to consider the possibility of Greece joining their camp. They had Greek neutrality; the subsequent machinations of Venizelos intended to involve Greece on the side of the Entente only increased the satisfaction felt by Germany and Austria in maintaining that neutral status.

So it was that with the start of the World War, Turkey, Bulgaria, Rumania, and Greece stood pat. All had declared neutrality. Nevertheless, neither Berlin nor Vienna despaired. With rapid, successful action in the field, these smaller powers might not be needed, or, if they were, at least three of them might still be won by astuteness at the bargaining tables. But the optimism of Germany and Austria notwithstanding, Greek support never became a realistic possibility and by August, 1914, the Central Powers had failed to achieve the desired Turkish-Bulgarian-Rumanian combination.

[86] Ibid., nos. 10489, 10598, Pallavicini to Berchtold, 22 and 24 July 1914 respectively; no. 10778, Berchtold to Szilassy, 27 July.

[87] Ibid., no. 10777, Berchtold to Szilassy, 27 July 1914; no. 10861, Szilassy to Berchtold, 28 July; no. 10935, Berchtold to Szilassy, 29 July.

Chapter 3

Military
Preparedness

An examination of military strength, plans, and preparations might at first glance seem an unnecessary digression from the main diplomatic theme. But it was on the basis of the preparedness of the Central Powers that the first crucial battles were decided. The outcome of those battles produced attitudes on the part of the two chiefs of staff which not only colored their individual views on mutual strategy, but also affected their stance on German and Austrian diplomatic policy.

Prospects on the Eve of the War

If the Central Powers faced an uncertain diplomatic scene, matters on the military side of the ledger were more reassuring, though both general staffs had their worries. From any long-range point of view there remained a good deal to be desired. Germany began the war with an extremely well-organized and efficient military machine whose striking power had long been recognized by other nations as nothing less than excellent. The Military Law of 1913 provided for heavy increases in recruitment and equipment, with well over a billion marks being set aside in the budget for military needs.[1] Germany could depend upon a war strength of almost 4,000,000 men, which, if reserve units were not included, meant 51 infantry divisions, 11 cavalry divisions, 1,012 field and heavy artillery batteries, and assorted specialized units. If reserves were brought into play, the General Staff could count on a very comfortable increase of 45 divisions in the all-important infantry arm. This, with other units, brought the total trained manpower to just short of 5,000,000. A reservoir of another 5,000,000 men, though untrained, could be tapped if needed.[2] In 1914 the army lacked combat experience, because Germans had not been called to arms against a major power since 1871. On the other hand, the standards of recruitment and training had been extremely high and German generals could count on a lightning-fast mobilization. In various campaigns of the World War the ability to handle shipment and massing of troops with almost flawless efficiency would more than once save the day.[3]

Austria-Hungary, too, boasted of no mean military organization. It could muster a wartime army of approximately 2,000,000 men with a field strength of 1,338,000. If all units and men not considered thoroughly trained were added, the total rose to well over 3,000,000. Immediately available as operative were 59 divisions of infantry and cavalry, and more than 500 artillery batteries. If all available manpower was considered—standing army, reserves, and untrained civilians—it meant that the Monarchy had a pool of 6,000,000. There was an officer corps, proud of its traditions, well educated, and well trained. Commanders were confident that the rank and file would perform well, for in spite of the rumblings and dissatisfactions of various groups within the Empire, the *esprit* and the discipline of the enlisted men were generally considered high.[4]

To the casual observer the Austro-Hungarian army would have seemed a smoothly-running machine, but the quality of its working parts left much to be desired. In the first place the Austrian General Staff had to deal with certain problems its German counterpart never faced, for example, the multinational character of the army. In an average group of a hundred soldiers only twenty-five were German. The remainder were likely to be: twenty-three Magyar, thirteen Czech, nine Serbo-Croatian, eight Polish, eight Ukrainian, seven Rumanian, four Slovak, two Slovene, and one Italian. Add to this a religious diversity involving Catholic, Protestant, Greek Orthodox, Jewish, Muslim, and other sects, and the task confronting the army leaders was hardly enviable.[5] Yet, out of this heterogeneity, the Austrian commissioned and noncommissioned officers were successful in fashioning an effective fighting force. Aiding them in this job was the peculiar mystique surrounding the Habsburg crown. National feeling or no, citizens felt duty-bound to serve their Emperor. When war was declared a unified and loyal response greeted the call to arms.[6] The unspoken question was whether the patchwork would stand the strain of a major war.

There were other problems. The army plan of recruitment was

---

[1] L. R. von Collenberg, *Die Deutsche Armee von 1871 bis 1914*, pp. 111, 122.

[2] Germany, Reichsarchiv, *Der Weltkrieg, 1914–1918: Kriegsrüstung und Kriegswirtschaft*, vol. 1, appendixes, table 19, pt. 2, p. 510; pp. 218, 221. The total figures meant calling all classes between seventeen and forty-five years of age.

[3] J. E. Edmonds, *A Short History of World War I*, p. 10.

[4] Franz Conrad von Hötzendorf, *Aus Meiner Dienstzeit, 1906–1918*, 4:225; Germany, Reichsarchiv, *Kriegsrüstung und Kriegswirtschaft*, 1:38–39; Austria, Bundesministerium für Heereswesen, *Österreich-Ungarns Letzter Krieg, 1914–1918*, 1:80.

[5] Edmonds, *World War I*, p. 10; Conrad, *Aus Meiner Dienstzeit*, 3:762.

[6] Austria, *Österreich-Ungarns Letzter Krieg*, 1:43; Bertrand Auerbach, *L'Autriche et la Hongrie pendant la Guerre*, pp. 1, 3.

based on the out-of-date Service Law of 1889 and it was only in 1912 that a new bill was enacted which aimed at a more efficient conscription and at refurbishing what were generally poorly equipped units. By 1914 improvements had been made but the desired and necessary excellence had not been achieved. Conditions in the infantry and cavalry were satisfactory but the equipment was old, and when it came to artillery the only truthful description was "inadequate." Not only were field howitzers outdated; there were still in service heavier artillery pieces which had been cast as early as 1880. A comparison with other states shows that Austria was outgunned even by Serbia by a ratio of fifty-four to thirty-eight per infantry division. The transportation system needed to handle this army was adequate, but the all-important mobilization of troop trains had not been planned to the exacting degree necessary.[7]

The source of many of these shortcomings was to be found in the constitutional structure of the Dual Monarchy, where the minister of war, unlike his German colleague, was forced to deal with two governments. He had to work with two ministers of defense, one Austrian, the other Hungarian, each of whom had authority over equipment and training. The credits for military needs had to be approved by both Austrian and Hungarian parliaments. It was only the insistence of Franz Joseph that kept the Hungarians from splitting the army into separate Austrian and Hungarian forces, an aim of Magyar politicians since 1902.[8]

In spite of these negative factors all was not black. In a full-scale war the Austrians could meet the needs of their own armed forces. The Monarchy could depend on leading munitions firms such as Skoda, Böhler, and Noot, and clothing requirements could be met through existing textile combines such as Weiss and Wetzler. Beyond this, a neat balance existed between the food-supplying eastern and the industrial western sections of the Empire.[9] The country had been prepared for all-out war by the passage of the War Service Act in 1913, which gave the government fullest powers in mobilizing the nation and its resources for war purposes. By this act the entire economy was placed at the disposal of the military in times of national emergency. A year before, officials, including the head of the General Staff, the

[7] Moritz von Auffenberg-Komarów, *Aus Österreich-Ungarns Teilnahme am Weltkriege*, pp. 35, 36, 40–44; Austria, *Österreich-Ungarns Letzter Krieg*, 1:31; Auerbach, *L'Autriche et la Hongrie*, p. 6.

[8] Auerbach, *L'Autriche et la Hongrie*, pp. 5, 8; Auffenberg-Komarów, *Aus Österreich-Ungarns Teilnahme*, p. 34.

[9] Auffenberg-Komarów, *Aus Österreich-Ungarns Teilnahme*, p. 46; F. P. Chambers, *The War behind the War, 1914–18*, p. 184.

minister of war, and certain civilian chiefs, had put together a memorandum calling for the establishment of what amounted to a dictatorial agency in the form of a War Surveillance Office. Such an office put the control of the political administration in the hands of the military, provided for the application of military laws to civilians, and even gave to the Supreme Command the control of import and export embargoes. Any and all disturbances that might occur on the domestic scene during war would fall under its authority.[10]

When war began this agency came into being. An imperial decree issued on July 31 turned over the political administration to the military, along with the entire railroad system and the telephone, telegraph, and postal services. In spite of its deficiencies, the Austrian army seemed ready for war.[11]

Germany, of course, did not face such problems. It was not forced to deal with heterogeneous nationality issues, with the problem of Magyar intransigence, or with a dual parliament. There was only one head of the army and that was the Kaiser, who wisely ceded full authority of command to his chief of staff. The entire nation responded when war came, with no opposition from political parties. The Reichstag voted the necessary finances, then dissolved and went home, convinced that the interests of the nation called for *Burgfrieden.* Control of the nation passed to the Kaiser, his chancellor, and the military chiefs.[12]

Thus, neither Vienna nor Berlin was alarmed when declarations of war were exchanged with their enemies. Both seemed ready for the conflict. The great flaw was their belief that such a war would be short and positive in its results. The two were unprepared for four years of combat. Germany had no huge stockpiles of materiel. No measures had been taken to organize the nation along the stringent economic lines needed for a massive war machine. Copper, tin, nickel, mercury, manganese, and chromium could not be supplied from within, and the petroleum, nitrates and graphite, jute, hides, hemp, resins, and rubber indispensable to a modern army had always been imported. In foodstuffs Germany could supply 75 to 80 percent of its own needs, but those foods which other countries provided were important: fodder,

---

[10] Joseph Redlich, *Austrian War Government,* pp. 56–63. Redlich points out that Germans and Magyars feared a challenge to their supremacy by various national events within the Empire. Hence one of the key functions of the War Surveillance Office was to eliminate any violent expression of this national feeling.

[11] Ibid., pp. 63, 80, 81.

[12] Erich von Falkenhayn, *The German General Staff and Its Decisions, 1914–16,* p. 4; Arthur Rosenberg, *The Birth of the German Republic,* pp. 73, 77.

dairy products, wheat, and legumes. The stocks on hand of all these items would soon prove insufficient.[13]

While prior to 1914 the Austrian monarchy had largely met its own food needs, it had depended on the cooperation of Hungary, which supplied a very heavy percentage of agricultural products. Once the war began, lack of this cooperation and the Russian invasion of Galicia and the Bukovina caused an increasing scarcity of food. In raw materials Austria had deposits of soft coal, anthracite, iron, tin, lead, and Chile saltpeter, but also relied on heavy imports from Germany for all of these. As in Germany, so in Austria no large stocks of necessary materials were on hand for a protracted conflict.[14]

To make matters more difficult there existed up to 1914 no really strong economic cooperation between the two allies. For years there had been much talk of producing a *Mitteleuropa*, a Middle European economic community, but it had not developed. Though a very close tie existed between German and Austro-Hungarian financial circles it was limited to banking corporations. Although Germany drew certain important products from the Dual Monarchy, most of its imports came from overseas nations. Austria itself had decreased its exports to Germany by 10 percent between 1892 and 1913. The Germans relied on sea routes for reaching the import-export markets of the Balkans and Turkey; therefore, nothing concrete had been done about building interconnecting waterways with Austria-Hungary. Prohibitive construction costs and the problems presented by natural features had left unrealized the projects for the Rhine-Main-Danube, Elbe-Moldau-Danube, and Danube-Oder waterways. In short, there had been no coordination between the two countries to establish a mutually beneficial economic system to meet wartime requisites.[15] Neither was prepared on the home front for anything but a brief campaign. It would take Walter Rathenau in Germany and Richard Riedl in Austria-Hungary to reform the economic fabric so as to withstand a long fight.[16]

One area in which heavy preparation had been made was in military strategy and troop disposition. Before the war there had been many

[13] Chambers, *War behind the War*, pp. 142, 144; Leo Grebler and Wilhelm Winkler, *The Cost of the War to Germany and Austria-Hungary*, pp. 8–9.
[14] Chambers, *War behind the War*, p. 184; Redlich, *Austrian War Government*, pp. 109–10; Geza Lukacs, *Die Handelspolitische Interessengemeinschaft Zwischen dem Deutschen Reiche und Österreich-Ungarn*, pp. 65, 67, 84, 85, 87.
[15] Henry Cord Meyer, *Mitteleuropa in German Thought and Action, 1815–1945*, pp. 68–71, 75–76, 78–79, 129–30.
[16] Chambers, *War behind the War*, pp. 145–48; Redlich, *Austrian War Government*, p. 129; Riedl was chief officer of the Ministry of Trade.

talks and letters between the German and Austrian chiefs of staff. These communications, aimed at cooperation, had begun in the time of the elder Moltke, and a close relationship between the two army heads had developed during the tenures of Alfred Waldersee on the German side and General Friedrich Beck on the Austrian.[17] Both Moltke and Waldersee recognized the problems which Austria would face in the east in a war against Russia, and in their planning they had devoted between one-third and one-half of their troops to an eastern campaign. Their thinking was based on the fact that since the French had increased their defenses and since the Russian mobilization would be hampered by a poor railway system, an offensive in the east would net rapid gains. During this action a holding and defensive operation against the French would be carried out.[18]

After 1891, however, the attitude of the German military, now led by Count Alfred von Schlieffen, changed. Schlieffen's feeling toward his Austrian colleagues was hardly warm. He did not consult them, refused to treat them as equals, and when he decided on a major shift in German strategy merely informed them that such would be the case, without considering the Austrian viewpoint on various problems.[19] As is now well known, Schlieffen looked to the west and to the destruction of what had already, by 1899, become a much stronger French army. The offensive he planned there meant relegating a mere one-ninth of the German army to the eastern front, and this fraction was to hold as best it could until the French had been defeated.[20]

The hard feeling aroused in Austrian military circles by Schlieffen's abrupt attitude was much eased under the younger Moltke. He took command in 1906, the same year that Franz Conrad von Hötzendorf succeeded Beck, and the two new chiefs developed a close friendship. In 1909 Conrad wrote to the German asking him what Germany's position would be with respect to a two-front war. Moltke's answer was from this time on to color Austrian military thought. Moltke stated, "I shall not hesitate to make an attack to support the simultaneous Austrian offensive. Your Excellency can truly rely on this promise which has been maturely considered. It is stipulated thereby that the movements of the alliance will be simultaneously carried through without hindrance."[21]

---

[17] Gerhard Seyfert, *Die Militärischen Beziehungen und Vereinbarungen Zwischen dem Deutschen und dem Österreichischen Generalstab vor und bei Beginn des Weltkrieges*, pp. 11, 12, 35.

[18] Ibid., pp. 43, 11, 32, 35.

[19] G. A. Craig, *The Politics of the Prussian Army, 1640–1945*, pp. 286–87.

[20] E. M. Earle, *Makers of Modern Strategy*, p. 189; Seyfert, *Militärischen Beziehungen*, p. 43.

What Conrad wanted was a simultaneous German and Austrian attack on Russia, carried out in a particular way. Before anything else could be done, Russian Poland had to be taken, and this meant cutting off a large strip of land 230 miles long and 200 miles wide which bulged between Galicia and East Prussia. This could only succeed if a large pincers was closed on the area, with German troops constituting the northern claw. For this move Conrad wanted twenty German divisions deployed in the east.[22] Moltke, however, had no intention of scrapping the Schlieffen plan, and Conrad himself understood that the major German strike would first come in the west. What happened in the course of the discussions and correspondence during the five years preceding the war was that each side talked in generalities. Neither understood with precision the exact moves and the exact timing planned by the other. Moltke believed the greatest Austrian strength would be massed against Russia, and since he saw Serbia as an inferior military power, he declared, "Secondary opponents should be treated secondarily."[23] On the other hand, Conrad planned his campaign in the east in accordance with Moltke's letter of 1909. Even though Moltke as late as the spring of 1914 had told him the west would require six weeks, Conrad assumed he would get greater assistance in a shorter time. As it turned out, the Germans allocated only seven first-line divisions for eastern operations, far below Conrad's expectations. And Conrad devoted much more strength to the Serbian theater than Germany had expected. The basic strategies of each ally may have been known by the other, but the all-important details remained undefined. This lack of clarity meant the frustration of the German and Austrian goal of quick military success.[24]

The Germans had their plans for a two-front war, and the Austrians had theirs. Before 1914 Conrad had developed a series of intricate steps to be taken if conflict arose with Serbia and Russia. He had worked out two plans: Plan B against Serbia and Plan R against Russia. To manage both he split his army into three segments. Echelon A, consisting of twenty-eight and a half infantry and ten cavalry divisions, was the

[21] Seyfert, *Militärischen Beziehungen*, p. 46; Austria, *Österreich-Ungarns Letzter Krieg*, 1:13.

[22] Seyfert, *Militärischen Beziehungen*, pp. 50, 53, 74; Austria, *Österreich-Ungarns Letzter Krieg*, 1:13; Winston S. Churchill, *The Unknown War: The Eastern Front*, p. 78.

[23] Seyfert, *Militärischen Beziehungen*, pp. 47, 48, 67, 72.

[24] Ibid., pp. 59, 61–62, 74; Germany, Reichsarchiv, *Der Weltkrieg, 1914–1918* (9 vol. ed.), 2:358. The seven divisions alloted by the Germans constituted the Eighth Army, which on paper contained fourteen divisions. The remaining seven, however, were composed of reserve troops, including third- and fourth-line quality.

strongest and would mass in Galicia against the Russians. A second group, consisting of eight infantry divisions and seven militia brigades, would march against Serbia. The remaining units, Echelon B, would join the Galician forces if Plan R came into effect. Otherwise, they too would swing toward Serbia.[25]

The great weakness in this plan was that if Russia did not immediately declare war in the event of an Austro-Serbian conflict, but came in after the reinforcing Echelon B had been committed to the Serbian front, the units in Galicia would have to bear the brunt of the Russian attack by themselves. Conrad had thought of this possibility, but he believed that in such a situation the shift of B Echelon could be effected rapidly enough to meet the Russian challenge. Events proved him wrong.[26]

It was well recognized by Germans and Austrians alike that without sufficient forces in the east they could not long hold out against the Czar's armies. The pressure brought to bear by ever-increasing Russian strength would buckle and then burst their lines asunder. Russia had a wartime strength of close to 5,000,000, of which 3,500,000 constituted the field army. In fighting units, this meant 114½ infantry divisions and 36 cavalry divisions—a most impressive striking force.[27]

The simple arithmetic may have been frightening to contemplate, but the effectiveness of the Russian forces as fighting units was something else again. The inefficiency of General Sukhomlinov, the minister of war, had resulted by 1914 in a Russian army ill-equipped to meet its opposition. Crucial deficiencies abounded. Artillery officers had not been properly trained for mass fire, infantrymen lacked knowledge of fortification, and technical units were not up to par. Ammunition stocks were insufficient, as were the numbers of rifles, machine guns, and artillery pieces available.[28]

In its strategy the Russian staff had planned not one major knockout blow against either Germany or Austria, but a two-pronged attack against East Prussia and Galicia. It was well known that because of a poor railway system Russia could not mass its troops quickly, but the rail network leading to these two fronts had been strengthened and

---

[25] Austria, Österreich-Ungarns Letzter Krieg, 1:4, 6, 7.

[26] Austria, Österreich-Ungarns Letzter Krieg, 1:8, 10; Seyfert, Militärischen Beziehungen, pp. 86–87.

[27] Austria, Österreich-Ungarns Letzter Krieg, 1:12. It was expected that Russia would have approximately thirty-five infantry divisions in the field by the twentieth day of mobilization and sixty divisions by the thirtieth. Nicholas N. Golovine, The Russian Army in the World War, pp. 107, 208.

[28] Golovine, Russian Army, pp. 12, 28–29, 126–31; A. A. Brussilov, A Soldier's Notebook, 1914–1918, pp. 16–17.

when the time came proved capable of meeting the initial needs. The real weakness lay in the trunk lines that connected the two theaters of operation, for these lines would prove incapable of handling a rapid and large shifting of troops from one theater to another along an extensive vertical front. This deficiency was highly significant in the coming campaigns.[29] Yet Russian mobilization proved to be more rapid than had been expected. Three weeks after the war began Russia had concentrated fifty-two divisions. Russian unpreparedness notwithstanding, the Central Powers had their hands full.[30]

The situation facing Moltke and Conrad in the east had been made worse by diplomatic events which by August led to the loss of over 400,000 Rumanian troops they had hoped to use. Under the guidance of King Carol, the Rumanian army had been rebuilt after 1908. By 1914 these forces were well organized, well trained, and essentially well equipped.[31] Both Conrad and Moltke had considered the part their Rumanian ally might play in the active campaign. Conversations had taken place in the autumn of 1909 with the Rumanian chief of staff, General Gregor Crajniceanu, and in 1910 Carol had promised military aid in case the Central Powers went to war with Russia. In the spring of 1910 plans were made for Rumania to deploy its forces so as to ease the Austrian right flank in Galicia, and two years later conversations on this issue became more specific. In November, 1912, Conrad visited Bukarest, gained a renewed promise from Carol of full Rumanian military support, and obtained in writing an arrangement with the new Rumanian chief of staff, Alexander Averescu, on actual troop dispositions and mobilization dates.[32]

The military relationship with Rumania had therefore become very concrete. By 1913, the picture had changed. The Balkan Wars and Rumania's diplomatic cooling toward Austria had by now led Carol to declare that he could no longer guarantee Rumanian military aid. Averescu was dropped as head of the army.[33]

By the turn of 1914 Conrad was worried over the whole question of Rumanian loyalty and he began to think of the necessity of planning for moves not with Rumania but against it. His memorandum in

[29] Nicholas N. Golovine, *The Russian Campaign of 1914*, pp. 56, 59, 67; idem, *Russian Army in the World War*, pp. 34–35.

[30] Golovine, *Russian Army in the World War*, pp. 183–84, 209.

[31] Austria, *Österreich-Ungarns Letzter Krieg*, 5:230; Conrad, *Aus Meiner Dienstzeit*, vol. 3, appendix 3; H. D. Napier, *The Experiences of a Military Attaché in the Balkans*, pp. 31, 64; *Statesmen's Yearbook*, pp. 1215–16, 1259.

[32] Austria, *Österreich-Ungarns Letzter Krieg*, 5:202; Conrad, *Aus Meiner Dienstzeit*, 2:19, 61–62, 351–56, 361–64.

[33] Conrad, *Aus Meiner Dienstzeit*, 2:494–96.

January showed him dealing realistically with the problem. He put little stock in a Rumanian return to the fold of the Triple Alliance, since he believed hostile elements within the country were powerful. He saw instead a coalition of France, Russia, Serbia, and Rumania as possible, and to offset this he wanted developed a combination of Bulgaria, Turkey, Albania, and possibly Greece. If Rumania could not be reattached to the Dreibund, he believed every attempt should be made to keep it neutral; if it came to war, Rumania must be pitted against Bulgaria. Unsure as to how events would shape themselves, he proceeded with preparations for a possible conflict in Transylvania with the former ally.[34]

The German military leaders were also well aware of Rumania's increasing coolness and by March, 1914, were quite concerned over the issue. It is interesting to note that at this time Moltke shared the views of the German diplomatic corps. He distrusted the Bulgarians and did not go along with Austria's shift of focus to Sofia. In a letter to Conrad he expressed his regret that Austria had decided to replace "a worthwhile ally" with "a doubtful and weak Bulgaria."[35]

The German general may have been misled to some extent by Carol's attitude, which continued to favor Germany and Austria. As late as August 7, 1914, Rumania asked Austria for its precise alignment of troops in Galicia in order to coordinate military support, but Conrad had no illusions. He told his military attaché in Bukarest that when Rumania had definitely committed itself, a Rumanian staff officer could then be sent to Vienna to be properly oriented.[36]

As things stood when hostilities began, the Central Powers could only hope their diplomats would somehow regain Rumanian affections. Until this happened, military support from this quarter was an impossibility.

Elsewhere the situation was no more comforting. There was the chance of utilizing over 400,000 Bulgarian troops, but again there was uncertainty. The diplomats had not succeeded in definitely winning Sofia. Even if a concrete tie had been established, the Bulgarian army, from the standpoint of strength and effectiveness, had to be considered in light of the mauling it had experienced in the Balkan Wars.[37] In short, the Bulgarians were not ready.

Turkey could not offer strong military support. The Turks counted their forces at over a million men, but the figure was unrealistic. In

[34] Ibid., pp. 536, 549; 3:755, 757–60.
[35] Ibid., 3:611–12.
[36] Ibid., 4:189.
[37] Ibid., vol. 3, appendix 3.

spite of the work done by Generals von der Goltz and Liman von Sanders in conjunction with the Turkish minister of war, Izzet Pasha, and his successor Enver Pasha, the army suffered from poor organization and poor equipment. The infantry was fairly well supplied but artillery was almost nonexistent and the cavalry very weak. Communications were poor, railroad facilities insufficient to meet the needs of war, distances great, and the terrain difficult. To make matters worse, a personality clash had grown up between Liman and Enver: the one a Prussian officer—well trained, precise and careful; the other young, rash, an "impatient revolutionary."[38]

Nevertheless, plans were made. In actuality, about 400,000 Turkish troops could be counted on, but only 150,000 could be assigned to combatting Russians in the Caucasus. The rest were split between a major force concentrated at the Straits and a lesser group designated for the Syria-Palestine area. The mobilization of Turkish forces began in August but was still not completed four months later, and even then the army lacked efficiency as a fighting unit.[39]

In spite of these various shortcomings, both the German and the Austrian staffs would have been glad to see immediate Bulgarian and Turkish participation. An increment of 800,000 men was no small sum. But their participation was not immediately obtained and while diplomats in Berlin and Vienna may have been optimistic, Conrad von Hötzendorf and Moltke could not live on hopes, could not win a war on the basis of *probable* allies. They faced a simple fact. They were entering the war alone. Even so, there was no lack of spirit and no lack of belief in final success. A letter from Moltke to his Austrian colleague best summed up the attitude: "The struggle will be a severe one for us. . . . We hope with God's help to carry it through. . . . It is an inward joy to me to be able to take part with you in this struggle. With God, my comrade!"[40]

[38] Maurice Larcher, *La Guerre Turque dans la Guerre Mondiale*, pp. 64–67, 69, 72, 75, 76; Otto Liman von Sanders, *Five Years in Turkey*, pp. 8–10.
[39] Larcher, *La Guerre Turque*, pp. 69, 73–74.
[40] Churchill, *Unknown War*, pp. 135–36.

Part II

Balkan Diplomacy of the Central Powers

Chapter 4

Turkey's
Declaration of War

The ink on the German-Turkish Alliance signed August 2, 1914, had barely dried when it became apparent that the Turks were not ready to honor their obligations. A cabinet sitting the day before had ordered a general mobilization, but actual participation was, for the moment, rejected, and rejected for various reasons. The alliance with Germany had been the work of only three men: Said Halim, Enver Pasha, and Talaat Bey. In the first days of August, Djemal Pasha, the minister of marine, and Djavid Bey, the finance minister, were told of its existence, but the rest of the government remained ignorant of the negotiations which had taken place with Berlin and Vienna. Most members of the Turkish government took a moderate and cautious view of the hostilities, and even the ministers mentioned above, with the exception of Enver Pasha, were wary of entering the war.[1]

An informal war cabinet was immediately set up, consisting of the grand vizier and the ministers of war, marine, interior, finance, and justice. Of these men, Said Halim, Enver, Djemal, and Talaat were inclined toward the Central Powers, but whatever their predilections, they were Turcophile first. By August 4 it had become clear that the war would not be limited but general, for on this day England declared against Germany and the day previous had seen the entry of France. The expected participation of Italy, Rumania, and Bulgaria on the side of Germany and Austria-Hungary did not materialize. The Turks realized their own mobilization would take time and until it was complete any action by Turkey meant a possible attack by Russia, England, and France against the Dardanelles, the Bosphorus, and along the extensive, unprotected land borders of the Empire. Then, too, an attack by Bulgaria through Turkish Thrace was seen as quite possible and until the position of Sofia was clearly defined, caution was a necessary keynote if Turkey hoped to avoid catastrophe. All of these conditions and considerations led to a Turkish declaration of neutrality on August 4.[2] Said Halim was quite in agreement with this neutral status, and stated that from a standpoint of diplomatic obligation

Turkey's decision was honorable. By interpreting the German-Turkish Alliance as being inapplicable to a situation of general war he could assert that the *casus foederis* simply did not exist.[3]

The problem of obtaining Turkish military action was more than a diplomatic one. In truth, the Central Powers were dealing with a group of Turkish statesmen who, while they were relatively young and had only recently taken over the government, were extremely ambitious and therefore calculating. Of the four men who really controlled the fate of Turkey at this time, three had risen to preeminence from lowly origins. Only Said Halim was a man of great wealth, coming from one of the richest princely houses in the Empire. In spite of his aristocratic background, he had supported the Young Turk movement, played a part in the revolution of 1908, and through his acquired political contacts emerged as grand vizier. His burning ambition to become khedive of Egypt, along with his definition of the best interests of Turkey, led him to favor Germany and Austria, but his nature was cautious and his approach generally conservative. A man of great polish and thoroughly Western in his attitudes, he much impressed the foreign diplomats with whom he constantly dealt. Theoretically, he was head of the government, but it was well known that the real control lay elsewhere—in the hands of Enver Pasha, Talaat Bey, and Djemal Pasha.[4]

Of these three, Enver was certainly the most colorful and the most determined to cut a wide swath in high circles. When the war began he was thirty-three. He had taken a mere five years to rise from the obscure rank of army lieutenant to the position of minister of war in 1913. Playing a large role in the formation of the Committee of Union and Progress, he participated in the 1908 revolution, was involved in the move on Constantinople in 1909, and was rewarded by being sent to Berlin as Turkish military attaché under the new government. He returned to Turkey with a Kaiser Wilhelm moustache and a profound belief in the superiority of German military techniques and practices. Handsome, rather dashing, and sure of himself, seeking to emulate

[1] Ahmed Emin, *Turkey in the World War*, pp. 63, 68, 72; Carl Mühlmann, *Deutschland und die Türkei, 1913–1914*, pp. 52–54.

[2] Emin, *Turkey in the World War*, p. 72; Mühlmann, *Deutschland und die Türkei*, pp. 55–57; Djemal Pasha, *Memories of a Turkish Statesman, 1913–1919*, p. 116.

[3] Mühlmann, *Deutschland und die Türkei*, p. 50; Izzet Pasha, *Denkwurdigkeiten*, p. 266.

[4] Henry Morgenthau, *Ambassador Morgenthau's Story*, p. 25; Alfred Nossig, *Die Neue Türkei und Ihre Führer*, pp. 59–60; GFMA, ser. 1, reel 393, report no. 194, Wangenheim to Bethmann-Hollweg, 20 June 1913; reel 394, report no. 88, von Kühlmann to Bethmann-Hollweg, 5 February 1917.

Napoleon, his great hero, Enver believed Turkey's destiny was inextricably linked to his own. Participation in the war was something he saw as the avenue to his own greatness as the future leader of the empire. His belief in the victory of the Germanic powers was unshakeable. Although he was impatient to declare Turkey a belligerent, his impetuosity was kept in check by a calculation that he could extract greater concessions from the Central Powers than were offered by the August alliance. Equally important was Enver's understanding that he needed the full support of Talaat Bey and Djemal Pasha, both of whom enjoyed great influence within the Young Turk Committee and both of whom initially hesitated to join in the war.[5]

In a special report to the German chancellor in January, 1914, Ambassador Wangenheim remarked that "The destiny of Turkey has through the appointment of Enver to the position of war minister, taken a very serious turn," but other observers thought that the most astute of the Young Turks, the man with the real political cunning, boldness, and *sang froid*, was the former telegrapher and present minister of interior, Talaat Bey.[6] A powerful, ox-like physique and glowing eyes made him an arresting figure; more significant was the way Talaat compensated for his spotty formal education with an iron will, a first-rate mind, and a talent for politics. As minister of interior he controlled the police and the administration of the provinces of the empire. This office gave him the keys to political patronage and thus to a political following. When the decision whether to enter the war had to be made in August, 1914, he was quite willing to temporize because, in spite of his pro-German proclivities, he wanted more evidence of possible victory through German success in the field.[7]

Finally there was Djemal Pasha, a small, heavy-set man who spoke

[5] "Enemy Portraits: Enver Pasha," *The New Europe*, 1, no. 5 (16 November 1916): 149–50; André Mandelstam, *Le Sort de l'Empire Ottoman*, pp. 101–92; Bernard Lewis, *The Emergence of Modern Turkey*, p. 221; Henri Seignobosc, *Turcs et Turquie*, pp. 39–40, 43–44, 48; Rafael de Nogales, *Four Years Beneath the Crescent*, pp. 24, 25, 28; Morgenthau, *Ambassador Morgenthau's Story*, pp. 30–32; GFMA, ser. 1, reel 393, report no. 7, Wangenheim to Bethmann-Hollweg, 9 January 1914.

[6] GFMA, ser. 1, reel 393, report no. 7, Wangenheim to Bethmann-Hollweg, 7 January 1914; no. 374, Minister Quadt in Athens to Bethmann-Hollweg, 28 December 1914; ser. 1, reel 394, von Kühlmann in Constantinople to Bethmann-Hollweg, 5 February 1917; Nossig, *Die Neue Türkei*, p. 30; Lewis, *Emergence of Modern Turkey*, p. 222.

[7] Nossig, *Die Neue Türkei*, pp. 30–32; Morgenthau, *Ambassador Morgenthau's Story*, pp. 21–24; Lewis, *Emergence of Modern Turkey*, p. 222; Take Ionescu, *Souvenirs*, p. 145; Seignobosc, *Turcs et Turquie*, pp. 45, 49–50; Mandelstam, *Le Sort de l'Empire Ottoman*, p. 101; GFMA, ser. 1, reel 394, no. 88, von Kühlmann to Bethmann-Hollweg, 5 February 1917.

fluent German and French, seemed outgoing and warm, had a smile for everyone, and was an opportunist of the first degree. A graduate of the War College and very active in the Young Turk movement, he soon emerged as an excellent organizer and highly competent administrator. Though he had no experience in naval matters, he had been given the cabinet post of minister of marine. Before the war Djemal had shown decided pro-French inclinations, but he proved willing to join the camp of the Central Powers if he could be convinced of their ultimate victory and of Turkey's welfare being served through such a connection. A wrong choice would, among other things, mean the frustration of his own personal ambitions, which encompassed a leading position in the future of Syria and Palestine.[8]

If Berlin and Vienna wanted Turkish military aid, they would have to satisfy this triumvirate.

The Naval Factor

Early on August 4, 1914, when it became clear that England would declare war on Germany, Jagow quickly sent instructions to Wangenheim to bring about a Turkish declaration of war against Russia, "today if possible." Turkish military strength might not be all that was desired, but the empire bordered on Egypt and the Caucasus so that participation by the Ottomans would tie up English and Russian forces which otherwise could be pitted directly against the Central Powers. Furthermore, since there was only one way into or out of the Black Sea, a belligerent Turkey meant Entente ships would run the gauntlet of Turkish guns at the Dardanelles.[9]

The German ambassador, considering the general temper at Constantinople, could not immediately carry out the instructions of the home office. Yet, within a few days, there occurred an event which decidedly tipped the scales in Turkey toward Germany and Austria and made the position of the Entente even weaker than it had been in the months preceding the outbreak of hostilities. On August 1 and 2 the English had commandeered the *Osman* and the *Rashadieh*, the two warships ordered and paid for by the Turkish government and nearing completion in English dockyards at that time. The seizure brought an immediate hostile reaction from the Turks, for it meant the loss of attempted parity with the Greek navy, a threat to Turkish interests in

[8] Seignobosc, *Turcs et Turquie*, pp. 53–55, 58; Lewis, *Emergence of Modern Turkey*, p. 221; Frederick Bliss, "Djemal Pasha: A Portrait," *The Nineteenth Century and After*, no. 514 (December 1919), pp. 1151–52.

[9] GFMA, ser. 1, reel 13, no. 313, Jagow to Wangenheim, 4 August 1914; Carl Mühlmann, *Oberste Heeresleitung und Balkan im Weltkrieg, 1914–1918*, pp. 21–22.

the Mediterranean. The rashness of the English was quickly turned to good advantage by the Germans. On August 1 the German cruisers *Goeben* and *Breslau* lay off Brindisi under the command of Admiral Wilhelm Souchon. Both Wangenheim and Liman von Sanders were in agreement that these ships should be immediately sent to Constantinople. It was more than merely a gesture to the Turkish ally. It was of vital importance that these ships strengthen the Turkish fleet and allow it to attack the Russian navy in the Black Sea. The addition of these cruisers would also protect Bulgaria and Rumania from any projected Russian landing and might conceivably make possible a Turkish thrust against Russian territory.[10]

On August 3 Berlin complied with the suggestions of its representatives, and Admiral Alfred von Tirpitz, minister of marine, ordered Souchon to break through to Constantinople. Eight days later the two ships dropped anchor at the Turkish capital, though the maneuver had not been without its difficulties. When the grand vizier heard that the German ships were ready to proceed up the Dardanelles, he "urgently requested" they wait, for he feared that the run of the *Goeben* and the *Breslau* might frighten the Bulgarians and lead them to attack Turkey on the grounds that the ships constituted an indirect threat. But if a Turco-Bulgarian alliance could be obtained, Said Halim would then announce the existence of the German-Turkish Alliance and the vessels might proceed as planned. In the meantime, he agreed to their cruising in "the vicinity" of the Dardanelles. Both Wangenheim and his Austrian colleague, Pallavicini, sought to exercise caution at this time and they suggested that Souchon wait for the precise call before proceeding to Stambul harbor.[11]

Suddenly, on August 6, the Turkish government decided to allow immediate passage. The fact was that they wanted the ships and decided they could justify the move by invoking their right as a neutral to call upon the fleets of friendly powers for aid. Thus, when on August 8 the German naval attaché asked Djemal Pasha for the loan of a coaling ship, the Turkish naval minister complied, and with the consent of Enver and Talaat sent it into the Aegean to meet the *Goeben* and the

---

[10] Djemal Pasha, *Memories of a Turkish Statesman*, p. 116; W. W. Gottlieb, *Studies in Secret Diplomacy during the First World War*, pp. 42–43; Moukhtar Pasha, *La Turquie, l'Allemagne et l'Europe*, pp. 269–70; "Posthumous Memoirs of Talaat Pasha," *New York Times Current History* 15, no. 2, (November 1921): 290; Maurice Larcher, *La Guerre Turque dans la Guerre Mondiale*, pp. 163, 166; GFMA, ser. 1, reel 13, no. 406, Liman von Sanders to von Moltke through Wangenheim, 2 August 1914; no. 407, Wangenheim to Bethmann-Hollweg, 2 August.

[11] GFMA, ser. 1, reel 13, no. 429, Wangenheim to Berlin, 4 August 1914; no. 437, Wangenheim to Berlin, 6 August.

Breslau. On the morning of August 11 Souchon asked for and received permission to run the Narrows.[12]

If the prewar naval agreements made by the members of the Triple Alliance had materialized, there would have been more than two ships standing off Constantinople. Germany, Austria, and Italy had agreed to assemble their naval forces at Messina to establish a combined Mediterranean fleet. The Italians, unfortunately for their allies, did not honor their commitments when war broke. Souchon arrived at Messina on August 5 and failed to find even the Austrians waiting. The Austrian naval commander declared his fleet was simply unprepared. The Germans therefore proceeded alone. Von Tirpitz had disapproved the whole idea, having originally wanted to attach the *Goeben* to his North Sea squadron or, failing this, to order it to attack and destroy the Suez Canal. But in talks with Bethmann-Hollweg, it became apparent that breaking through to Constantinople was of major political importance.[13]

The arrival of the German vessels did indeed have heavy repercussions. The existence of the German-Turkish Alliance was no longer a secret. On August 4 Kaiser Wilhelm had instructed Theotoky, the Greek minister in Berlin, to inform the Greek king that such an alliance did exist, and by August 8 the fact was known to the Entente powers. The appearance of the two ships gave diplomats a clear indication of which way the Turkish wind was blowing.[14]

For Wangenheim, the presence of the ships at Constantinople constituted a strong advantage, since they gave him an additional lever with which to press the Turks into the war. If it became necessary, the guns of the German cruisers could easily be trained on the Turkish capital to help persuade the Ottomans to take action. The Russians were now at a disadvantage, since the *Goeben* and the *Breslau* joined with the Turkish fleet could prevent a Russian attack on Constantinople. Moreover, the Germans had placed the Turkish government in a most difficult position. Supposedly the Ottomans were neutral but they had just provided a haven for a naval contingent of a declared belligerent. By international law Turkey had either to order the ships to leave within twenty-four hours, or strip them of armaments and intern them.

[12] GFMA, ser. 1, reel 13, no. 438, Wangenheim to Berlin, 6 August 1914; Djemal Pasha, *Memories of a Turkish Statesman*, p. 118. For a detailed examination of the run of the German ships see Barbara W. Tuchman, *The Guns of August*, pp. 137–59.

[13] Grand Admiral Alfred von Tirpitz, *My Memoirs*, 2:81–82; idem, *Politische Dokumente: Deutsche Ohnmachtspolitik im Weltkriege*, p. 60.

[14] Maurice Bompard, "L'Entrée en Guerre de la Turquie," *La Revue de Paris*, 14 (15 July 1921): 263–64.

Ordering the ships to leave meant they would have to meet the British squadron waiting to destroy them. Internment was something to which the Germans themselves would not agree. A remedy had to be found, for the British and French soon lodged a protest with the grand vizier, and the Turks recognized the possibility of the Entente's declaring the run of the *Goeben* and the *Breslau* to be a *casus belli*. Said Halim, Djavid Bey, and Djemal Pasha now solved the problem by suggesting that Wangenheim announce that Germany had sold the vessels to Turkey, their presence constituting only the final delivery. Wangenheim, with Berlin's approval, agreed to the fiction on condition that the English Admiral Limpus be replaced by Souchon as head of the naval mission in Turkey. The Turks accepted, and although Limpus did not leave for home until September, his post was filled on August 16 by Souchon, who now became commander-in-chief of the Turkish Imperial Navy.[15] Wangenheim had exploited the situation beautifully. By mid-August the Germans controlled not only the Turkish army but the navy as well, and it was the navy that was to prove crucial in forcing Turkey to take action at the start of November.

German-Austrian Concessions

The Turkish ministers were well aware of the implications of allowing the passage of the cruisers. It placed Turkey on the side of the Central Powers, participation or no; but before they went ahead, the Turks exacted their own price. Aside from securing the ships to strengthen their navy, they gained from Wangenheim certain assurances beyond those in the recently signed German-Turkish Alliance. Though the German ambassador had refused to put anything in writing, he verbally agreed that Germany would help Turkey in its quest to end the Capitulations and would support the Turks in obtaining regularizations of Caucasus borders and in securing a retrocession of the islands given to Greece as a result of the Balkan Wars. Initially these assurances seemed rather harmless since Wangenheim had attached the condition that they would only come into consideration if the Central Powers emerged from the war as absolute victors. On the strength of this proviso, Berchtold in Vienna had given Pallavicini

---

[15] Harry Howard, *The Partition of Turkey, 1913–23*, p. 96. Djemal Pasha, *Memories of a Turkish Statesman*, pp. 118–22. Limpus made the mistake of criticizing the state of the Turkish navy and going over Djemal's head. The latter administered the sternest of rebukes and Limpus resigned. Larcher, *La Guerre Turque*, p. 167.

authority to make the same verbal agreement.[16] It was quite obvious, however, that the Central Powers were doing all they could to maintain and strengthen their position with Turkey, the aim being to gain an active ally.

The Turks now proceeded to take good advantage of the bargaining power the war had given them. They wanted the immediate abolishment of the Capitulations, a series of economic and juridical privileges enjoyed by foreigners which were particularly onerous to the Turkish people. These privileges included freedom from the jurisdiction of Turkish courts, special protection of foreigners by their respective embassies, exemption from certain government taxes, and the enjoyment of a uniform customs tariff which could not be altered without the express permission of the foreign powers.[17] The subject of abolishment was first broached by Djemal Pasha on August 20 in a talk with Sir Louis Mallet, the English ambassador. Mallet proved cold toward the whole idea. The French and Russians were willing to make certain concessions on the matter but their price was something the Turks could not pay—the dismissal of the German military mission and the dismantling of the *Goeben* and the *Breslau*. The Turks, gauging the situation properly, now decided on a fait accompli. On September 9 Said Halim sent a note to foreign representatives setting October 1 as the date for abrogation of the Capitulations.

The powers formally protested, but they could not oppose the actions too strongly without damaging their diplomatic strategies. The Entente, eager for a continuation of Turkish neutrality, was forced, if grudgingly, to accept the move. The Germans and Austrians did not like the situation either, but a refusal to comply with the Ottoman decision would only have angered Turkish leaders and injured the main goal, Turkish wartime participation. To protest that their verbal assurances of aid in obliterating the Capitulations had been made with the postwar period in mind would certainly not have been to the immediate advantage of Berlin and Vienna. The Central Powers thus gave their approval with the hope of strengthening their position at Constantinople vis-à-vis the Entente. France, England, and Russia made the error of insisting that the question be further negotiated, thereby increasing Turkish rancor. Wangenheim and Pallavicini, on the other hand, offered the Porte assurances of the complete concurrence of their respective governments.[18]

---

[16] Staatsarchiv, PA, box 521, no. 407, Pallavicini to Berchtold, 6 August 1914; no. 285, Berchtold to Pallavicini, 7 August; Mühlmann, *Deutschland und die Türkei*, pp. 45–46.

[17] Emin, *Turkey in the World War*, p. 113; Edwin Pears, "Turkey and the War," *The Living Age*, no. 3674 (5 December 1914), pp. 584–85.

In this case Wangenheim and Pallavicini had to consider military matters as well as diplomacy. Initial successes of German and Austrian forces in the field during August had by the opening days of September been vitiated by the battle of the Marne and by reversals suffered by Conrad's forces at the hands of the Russian army. The Turkish neutralists therefore became even more cautious, an attitude revealed by Rifat Pasha, Turkish ambassador in Paris, who in September wired home: "The Russians have taken Lemberg. They dominate the road to Vienna. . . . Germany is isolated and doomed to defeat. Hostility to the Entente may endanger our very existence. The only sane policy for Turkey consists in obtaining advantages from the Entente by pursuing strict and sincere neutrality. . . . We should recall the fact that an extremist foreign policy has always been the cause of our misfortunes."[19]

Considering the unfavorable military situation, Bethmann-Hollweg wired Wangenheim that the active participation of Turkey was now urgent, and the solution of this matter, said the chancellor, "I lay in your energetic hands." A protest by the Central Powers against the abolishment of the Capitulations at this time would be out of the question.[20]

Germany and Austria gave way on more than the issue of Capitulations. One of the major considerations of the Ottoman government in delaying war action was financial. As early as 1913 the Turkish treasury was running a deficit of over ten million pounds and the Balkan Wars had heavily depleted available funds. The need for financial support came to the fore in September, 1914, and ended with the signing of a loan convention between Germany and Turkey in November, to which the Austrians gave their concurrence. Although the convention was not signed until after the Turks had entered the war, they had already procured a good sum by October. As the terms were negotiated, the Germans agreed to loan Turkey five million pounds at a rate of 6 percent interest with repayment to begin one year after the conclusion of peace. The first two million pounds were to be paid directly after the signature of the loan convention and the rest was to follow in installments of one-half million pounds each, the first to be delivered in December, 1914. The Turks, however, refused to take action in the field until the first two million had been received at

---

[18] Howard, *Partition of Turkey*, pp. 103–6; Gottlieb, *Secret Diplomacy*, p. 59; Jean A. Mazard, *Le Régime des Capitulations*, pp. 49–51, 116. See Mazard's Appendix I for the full statement issued by Said Halim on 9 September; Pears, "Turkey and the War," pp. 584–85.
[19] Emin, *Turkey in the World War*, p. 74.
[20] Mühlmann, *Oberste Heeresleitung*, p. 48.

Constantinople. By October 22 Berlin had complied and sent Wangen-heim the money. Behind the German willingness to grant such large sums stood the recognition that Turkey was in bad financial straits and would have to be supported as the only way to free the Turkish government from the mastery which had heretofore been exercised by Entente financiers. On September 2 the director of the Dresdner Bank summed up the situation when he pointed out that the Imperial Otto-man Bank, responsible for Turkish financial affairs, was almost entirely in the hands of its British and French directors. For Turkey, war with the very powers which controlled its money matters would be intoler-able. Aside from Turkey's real need for cash, it was clear that the German banks and the Wiener Bankverein must gain ascendancy. From the German point of view the loan was clearly a diplomatic, military, and economic necessity.[21]

The Germans and Austrians had dealt easily with the issues of Capitulations and money, but they proved incapable of dealing with one major problem which the Turks insisted must be solved before Turkey would take up arms—the lack of a formal Turkish understand-ing with Bulgaria. As it turned out, the Central Powers were able to involve the Turks without achieving this understanding, but the in-tense negotiations on the issue reflect their sense of urgency in winning the Ottomans.

The Balkan Wars had ended with the Bulgarians posing a threat to Constantinople because of their acquisitions in Thrace. The Turks would not move until this threat had been eliminated through the establishment of a Turkish-Bulgarian alliance. The grand vizier had told Wangenheim on August 4 that he wanted such an alliance "as quickly as possible," and that when such a proposal was made by Sofia he would immediately accept it.[22] Negotiations toward this end had already taken place in 1913 but had led nowhere; as the war opened they were at a standstill.

Both Central Powers now did everything they could to have these negotiations resumed and quickly brought to a successful conclusion. The Austrian and German ministers broached the subject with Rados-lavov in Sofia, and by August 6 the Bulgarian government had given Andrew Toscheff, its representative in Constantinople, authorization to

<hr>

[21] GFMA, St. Anthony's Collection, ser. 1, reel 46, no. 1306, Wangenheim to Berlin, 10 November 1914; no. 24825, copy of terms of the loan; no. 1039, Wangen-heim to Berlin, 15 October; nos. 1058 and 1076, Wangenheim to Berlin, 17 and 22 October; Emin, *Turkey in the World War*, pp. 93–94; Mühlmann, *Deutschland und die Türkei*, pp. 54–55.

[22] Talaat Pasha, "Posthumous Memoirs," pp. 289–90; GFMA, ser. 1, reel 13, no. 429, Wangenheim to Berlin, 4 August 1914.

conclude a treaty. The Central Powers nevertheless recognized that such an agreement would be difficult to obtain, for the Turks would demand a retrocession of western Thrace to which the Bulgarians would never consent. Berchtold now sent an instruction to Pallavicini, declaring it very important that he and his German colleague arrange the bases on which a Turkish-Bulgarian understanding could follow.[23] The Ballhausplatz saw much more involved in the issue than the entry of Turkey, for Berchtold stated: "It could be disastrous for us if the fears of the Bulgarian statesmen were confirmed that Turkey would be ready for a rapprochement only on the basis of Bulgaria's giving up western Thrace. This would rob us of the possibility of offering to Bulgaria an assurance of her present territorial possessions and hence could shatter in the last moment the goal of our diplomatic action—a combination of Turkey, Bulgaria, and Rumania."[24] He therefore wanted Pallavicini to still the grand vizier's fears concerning a Bulgarian threat to Constantinople. The ambassador was to point out that the major task for the Turks was to overpower Russia, a step which would not only secure Constantinople but increase Turkish strength in Asia Minor, the Caucasus, and Europe. Berchtold hoped the Turkish government would see it ought not to make demands on Bulgaria which would "compromise such a large goal."[25]

German diplomats were also doing all they could to bring the Turks and Bulgarians into accord. The Kaiser himself spoke with the Turkish ambassador in Berlin, urging that agreement be reached between Turkey, Bulgaria, and Rumania. To eliminate the issue of Turkish demands for a retrocession of western Thrace, Wangenheim suggested that Constantinople and Sofia recognize the inviolability of each other's present borders under a guarantee by Germany and Austria-Hungary, and that a military convention be signed which would allow for the passage of Bulgarian and Turkish troops through each other's territories.[26]

The solution was a good one but it was difficult to bring the parties together. The Turks wanted more than an agreement with Bulgaria. They wanted Bulgarian action in the field against Serbia before they themselves would make a move. Sofia would not commit itself to open participation on the side of the Central Powers at this time, since Greece had clearly stated it would come to the aid of Serbia in case of

[23] Staatsarchiv, PA, box 521, no. 394, Pallavicini to Berchtold, 4 August 1914; nos. 473, 482, Tarnowski to Berchtold, 5 and 6 August.
[24] Ibid., no. 281, Berchtold to Pallavicini, 6 August 1914.
[25] Ibid.
[26] Ibid., no. 408, Pallavicini to Berchtold, 6 August 1914; no. 392, Berchtold to Szögyény in Berlin, 10 August.

a Bulgarian attack. Toscheff demanded that the Turks agree to an immediate offensive against the Greeks. The truth is that the Bulgarians were reluctant to pursue negotiations because they highly mistrusted the Turkish government. The latter still insisted on regaining western Thrace, and though the Turks had signed an alliance with Germany, Radoslavov was not convinced of Constantinople's sincerity. Both Turkey and Bulgaria were anti-Russian but the Bulgarians saw the massing of Turkish troops around Adrianople as a sinister move; it was not out of the question that these troops would be used against the Bulgarians.[27]

Just as these discussions were going on, the Rumanian minister to Constantinople suggested a dreibund between Rumania, Greece, and Turkey which would provide for the neutrality of each. It was clear to Vienna that the Bulgarians would seek to join this neutral bloc. Such an *entente à quatre* would be precisely contrary to the needs of the Central Powers, that is, Balkan allies as active belligerents. The Germans seemed willing to entertain the Rumanian proposal, for it would at least define what had thus far been ambiguous, the position of Greece, something which had not failed to concern Berlin. Furthermore, Wangenheim felt that the Turkish-Bulgarian and Bulgarian-Rumanian disagreements were "not so settled that an open cooperation of the three armies could be thought of." The Ballhausplatz immediately scotched the whole maneuver. Berchtold took a strong position, declaring this was no time to worry about Greece; he believed the entire projected Balkan entente would only involve unnecessary delay through protracted negotiations, which in the end must fail. On August 10 he wrote to Szögyény, asking him to point out to Berlin that "We need Bulgarian active support in our struggle against Serbia, as we and Germany need Turkey as an ally." He wanted the negotiations between Sofia and Constantinople continued and brought to a conclusion without other considerations interfering. The cogency of his argument impressed the Wilhelmstrasse. On this same day Bethmann-Hollweg personally wired Wangenheim, instructing him that any Balkan pact of neutrality was "inadmissible," and that Turkey and Bulgaria must be induced to attack Russia and Serbia immediately.[28]

[27] Talaat Pasha, "Posthumous Memoirs," p. 290; Staatsarchiv, PA, box 521, no. 417, Pallavicini to Berchtold, 8 August 1914; no. 543, Tarnowski in Sofia to Berchtold, 11 August; GFMA, ser. 2, reel 12, no. 274, Quadt in Athens to Berlin, 11 August; report no. 97, Michahelles in Sofia to Berlin, 15 August. The report recapitulates the problem of Bulgarian participation. It points, among other things, to the fact that the troops massed at Adrianople were part of the Turkish general mobilization.

[28] GFMA, ser. 2, reel 12, nos. 457 and 463, Wangenheim to Berlin, 8 and 10 August 1914; Staatsarchiv, PA, box 521, no. 522, Tarnowski to Berchtold, 10

The German and Austrian representatives now redoubled their efforts. Michahelles, the German minister in Sofia, quieted the fears of Radoslavov over possible Turkish aggression by stating that the *Goeben* and the *Breslau* were ready to protect the Bulgarian coast and by offering a German guarantee of Bulgarian territorial inviolability. Pallavicini in Constantinople suggested to the grand vizier that an important personage such as Talaat Bey be sent to Bulgaria to conclude an arrangement. While Said Halim, still in favor of Turkey's maintaining neutrality, had proved open to the Rumanian suggestion for a Balkan entente, Pallavicini pointed out its unfeasibility since Greek and Turkish interests in the Aegean were incompatible. The grand vizier seemed won by the argument and on August 15 sent Talaat Bey and Halil Bey to negotiate with the Radoslavov government.[29]

Two days later Talaat developed the Turkish position in a conversation with Tarnowski. He said Turkey wanted an immediate attack by the Bulgarians on Serbia, in which case the Turks would turn against Russia. Turkey would not demand territorial concessions. It would be enough to see the Russian enemy defeated, a condition which would mean the securing of Turkey's future existence.[30]

Talaat did not find the Bulgarians badly disposed to signing the desired alliance. On August 19 an agreement was indeed reached but the alliance was merely *defensive* in nature and therefore of no value to the Central Powers. Berlin and Vienna needed an agreement between the two states which would mean immediate action by both. The real stumbling block to an *offensive* treaty of alliance rested on the insistence by Radoslavov that Rumania guarantee *in writing* that it would not attack the Bulgarians if the latter took action against Serbia. In an attempt to surmount Bulgarian fears of Rumania, Talaat suggested that a clause be placed in the Bulgarian-Turkish agreement whereby Germany and Austria-Hungary would guarantee that Rumania would not attack the Bulgarians if the latter took action against the Serbs. Further, in the case where Rumania did attack, the Central Powers would agree to take immediate military action against it.[31]

Berlin partially agreed to Talaat's suggestion. Michahelles in Sofia

---

August; no. 302, Berchtold to Pallavicini, 10 August; no. 392, Berchtold to Szögyény, 10 August; GFMA, ser. 2, reel 12, no. 457, Wangenheim to Berlin, 8 August; no. 350, Bethmann-Hollweg to Wangenheim, 10 August.

[29] Staatsarchiv, PA, box 521, no. 537, Tarnowski to Berchtold, 11 August 1914; nos. 432, 435, Pallavicini to Berchtold, 12 August; no. 458, Pallavicini to Berchtold, 16 August.

[30] Ibid., no. 592, Tarnowski to Berchtold, 17 August 1914.

[31] Ibid., no. 608, Tarnowski to Berchtold, 20 August 1914; no. 598, Tarnowski to Berchtold, 18 August. See chapter 5 below for details of the Turco-Bulgarian Alliance.

was instructed to tell Radoslavov that Bukarest had made repeated assurances to Germany that it would give the Bulgarians a free hand against Serbia and therefore Sofia had no basis for worry. The Germans were willing to give the desired guarantee in a secret explicative note. However, military commitments could not be made against Rumania, which was still, after all, an ally. The Austrians agreed completely.[32]

Talaat realized that this partial acceptance of his scheme would not be enough. The solution to the problem obviously lay in Bukarest, where he and Halil now proceeded personally to take up negotiations. His opinion that agreement between Bulgaria and Rumania would be difficult to achieve was quite correct. By September 1 it had become apparent that the Rumanians would make no formal statement in writing on the continuation of their neutrality. That the Turks had agreed to march against Greece if it supported the Serbs proved insufficient to impress Sofia.[33]

By September 15 the negotiations fostered by the Central Powers had broken down. Turkish and Bulgarian military officers had had conversations which it was hoped would lead to a military convention, but such a convention remained unsigned. The military agreement hinged on the satisfaction of diplomatic demands which had not been met. Rumania would not commit itself sufficiently to still Bulgarian fears; and without Bulgaria in the field, Constantinople refused openly to join the Central Powers against the Entente. Turkish caution would have to be ended by some other means.[34]

The failure to involve Turkey in the war worried the German and Austrian military. General Conrad von Hötzendorf, his Austrian forces in retreat before the Russian onslaught, had instructed his military attaché in Constantinople to get a Turkish diversion going at Odessa to relieve the eastern front. On September 17 the German High Command asserted it must have Turkish action and tersely concluded, "The general situation unconditionally demands this."[35] Certainly, the foreign offices were doing all they could to gain Turkish participation. However, neither Wangenheim nor Pallavicini was personally con-

[32] Staatsarchiv, PA, box 521, no. 307, Berchtold to Tarnowski, 20 August 1914. Berchtold reports the German position as it was made clear to him by von Tschirschky in Vienna.
[33] Staatsarchiv, PA, box 521, no. 608, Tarnowski to Berchtold, 20 August 1914; no. 700, Tarnowski to Berchtold, 2 September; no. 535, Pallavicini to Berchtold, 3 September.
[34] Ibid., no. 745, Tarnowski to Berchtold, 10 September 1914; no. 775, Baron von Mittag, first consul in Sofia, to Berchtold, 15 September.
[35] Joseph Pomiankowski, *Der Zusammenbruch des Ottomanischen Reiches*, pp. 81–82; Mühlmann, *Oberste Heeresleitung*, p. 48.

vinced that this was the proper time for Turkey to commit itself. Both ambassadors loyally followed their instructions but both were more clearly aware than Berlin or Vienna of conditions which made Turkish entry difficult or even undesirable. By September, Turkish mobilization was still incomplete and war supplies insufficient. Wangenheim estimated Turkey's lasting power in a war at roughly four to six weeks, given the present stockpiles. Concentration of troops at various strategic points had been going on since August but the distances were great, communication was poor, and more time was still needed to bring various units to full strength. Then, too, when war broke in August there were no precise plans for the direction a Turkish attack should take. These plans had to be developed in conjunction with Enver Pasha. Were the Turks to prepare an expedition against Odessa? Or were they to mount an attack against Egypt, or the Balkans, or the Caucasus? It is significant that as late as September 5 Pallavicini was still writing to Berchtold that Vienna and Berlin must come to an agreement on the goal of Turkish operations.[36]

That the necessary diplomatic ties between Turkey and Bulgaria had not been achieved failed to impress Wangenheim and Pallavicini as catastrophic. Both agreed with Talaat Bey that Turkey by its armed neutrality and its inclination toward the Central Powers played the important role of checking Bulgaria and Rumania. As long as Turkey constituted a military threat to the rear of each of these two states, neither would be prompted to join the Entente and attack the Germans and Austrians. With the unsure position of Bulgaria and Rumania, the neutrality of Turkey could hardly be seen as an adverse factor.[37]

All these considerations notwithstanding, the German and Austrian ambassadors continued throughout September to press the Turks to join in. It was at this time that the issue of sending the *Goeben* and the *Breslau* into the Black Sea became useful as a lever.

The idea of the Turkish fleet, led by the *Goeben* and the *Breslau*, entering the Black Sea for purposes of attacking the Russian navy had been current for almost two months. As early as August 4 the Austrian ambassador in Berlin, Szögyény, had wired Berchtold that the German

---

[36] Larcher, *La Guerre Turque*, pp. 74, 83; Pomiankowski, *Zusammenbruch*, p. 85. Pomiankowski, who served as Austrian military attaché in Constantinople, shows that by October the armies in the Caucasus and Palestine areas were not yet ready for operations. Larcher states that full concentration of Turkish troops was not completed until the end of the year. GFMA, ser. 1, reel 13, no. 779, Wangenheim to Berlin, 11 September 1914; Staatsarchiv, PA, box 521, report no. 55 P/B, Pallavicini to Berchtold, 9 September; no. 543, Pallavicini to Berchtold, 5 September.

[37] Staatsarchiv, PA, box 941, Krieg 21 A, report no. 57 P/A-B, Pallavicini to Berchtold, 22 September 1914.

government was seriously entertaining such a project. Officials soon understood that not only was the political scene unripe for such a move, but further, that such an attack, which would bring a Russian declaration of war against Turkey, could not be permitted because of the weak condition of fortifications at the Dardanelles. On August 24 Wangenheim wrote a summation of the situation to the German General Staff. German naval officers in Constantinople did not believe the Dardanelles could be held without the support of the guns of the *Goeben* and the *Breslau*. If these two ships ventured into the Black Sea, in their absence the Straits could easily be forced by the English flotilla which was standing by. Two days later Wangenheim wrote that if the *Goeben* and the *Breslau* were to guard the Dardanelles then "the possibility of a Black Sea action is out."[38]

Wangenheim's contention that the Dardanelles had to be made so strong they could not be taken, even in the absence of the German cruisers, was supported by the naval leaders. Admiral von Tirpitz and the chief of the German Admiralty staff, Admiral Hugo von Pohl, convinced Bethmann-Hollweg the ships would be free for "wider action" only after the Straits had been more thoroughly fortified, and while Bethmann saw that a Black Sea attack by the ships would pull Turkey into the war, he nevertheless took the advice of his naval commanders and decided to wait. By September 8 Admiral Guido Usedom, who had become commander of the Straits, speaking with Enver Pasha, still refused to guarantee the Dardanelles against an English-French attack. There was a great deficiency in mines and the largest part of the cannon needed repair. Usedom wanted more time. Aside from the guns, mines, and fortifications that would have to be installed, he wanted the Straits completely closed to all enemy ships.[39]

Since the condition of the Straits precluded the *Goeben*'s and the *Breslau*'s entering the Black Sea, it meant the impossibility of an attack on Odessa—a maneuver which had been under heavy consideration as a method of distracting the Russians. Liman von Sanders approved of the plan to attack Odessa, but unless mastery of the Black Sea was obtained, landings were impossible. Without such control, the German admirals gave any attempted amphibious expedition against the Russians no more than a 10 percent chance of success. But the idea of attacking Odessa was further pursued. Kaiser Wilhelm on September

<hr />

[38] Ibid., no. 374, Szögyény to Berchtold, 4 August 1914; GFMA, ser. 1, reel 13, no. 595, Wangenheim to the German General Staff, 24 August; no. 609, Wangenheim to Berlin, 26 August.

[39] GFMA, ser. 1, reel 13, no. 609, Wangenheim to Berlin, 26 August 1914; no. 26, Bethmann-Hollweg in Coblenz to the Foreign Office in Berlin, 28 August; no. 752, Wangenheim to Berlin, 8 September.

14 sent direct orders to Admiral Souchon, telling him how he was to proceed: "His Majesty, the Emperor, wishes an energetic advance into the Black Sea as soon as you feel strong enough and the defensive capacities of the Dardanelles have been secured against a forcing. The goal of the operation is the crippling of the Russian Black Sea fleet and hence the assertion of sea mastery in the Black Sea as a condition for the operations of the Turkish army which must be established via sea route."[40]

Admiral Souchon now brought things to a head. Apparently he had come to believe the Dardanelles could hold against an Entente attack. Impatient for action, he told the grand vizier he was not at Constantinople "to play the comedian," and he demanded that the fleet enter the Black Sea. If he did not get orders to do so, he would go without orders, and if not with the whole Turkish fleet, then at least with the two German ships. Enver Pasha, the one cabinet member who since the beginning of the war had been steadfastly in favor of Turkish action, issued secret orders at this time which permitted the desired foray. A Turkish cabinet crisis ensued on September 19 when the ministry caught wind of what was about to take place. The grand vizier was diametrically opposed to such a move, and demanded that Enver rescind the orders. Said Halim was quite convinced that if Souchon was allowed to go ahead, in spite of his contention that it was only for purposes of "naval practice," he meant to attack the Russian fleet and push the Turks into war. Enver Pasha refused to revoke the orders and the grand vizier threatened his immediate resignation. It was only through the mediation of Talaat Bey, who begged Enver not to call forth a major governmental crisis now, that Enver agreed to delay things, but not before he made it quite clear he would not rescind an order again. The rest of the ministry backed the grand vizier. Djavid Bey, for example, went so far as to suggest that the Turkish batteries at the Bosphorus fire on the *Goeben* and the *Breslau* if they ventured out.[41]

The affair brought a strong reaction from the Germans. Wangenheim told Said Halim that as long as the German ships sailed under the Turkish flag and as long as the interests of Germany and Turkey did not clash, the ships were "at the disposal of Turkey." However, these vessels were still German and therefore they would not take direct orders from the Turkish minister of marine. To illustrate German

[40] Ibid., no. 795, Wangenheim to Berlin, 13 September 1914; no. 43, Bethmann-Hollweg to Wangenheim, 14 September.

[41] Ibid., no. 834, Wangenheim to Berlin, 19 September 1914; no. 836, Wangenheim to Berlin, 19 September; Bompard, "L'Entrée en Guerre de la Turquie," *La Revue de Paris* 14 (15 July 1921): 276.

independence Wangenheim had suggested to Souchon that he send the *Breslau* and two torpedo boats to demonstrate in the Black Sea. On the other hand, the German ambassador promised that the admiral would take no action against the Russians without agreement first being reached through the Turkish High Command. While the *Breslau* did make a short run at this time, nothing resulted. On September 21 the Ottomans admitted that the German naval command had to hold true to German interests even if these collided with the Turkish. They therefore agreed they could not hinder the German ships from entering the Black Sea and attacking Russia if they chose, but they would not allow the Turkish fleet itself to participate and if hostilities occurred between the Germans and Russians, Turkey would refuse to identify itself with Germany.[42]

By September 24, Souchon, who had refused to take orders from the Turkish sultan or minister of marine on the ground that he was subject only to the command of his German superiors, had received an important directive from Berlin. It was the wish of the Kaiser that he sail out the whole Turkish fleet. Undersecretary Zimmermann, without waiting for the approval of Bethmann-Hollweg, instructed Constantinople that Souchon was to demonstrate with the Turkish fleet before the Rumanian and Bulgarian ports of Constanza, Burgas, and Varna. Aside from whether the fleet met and did battle with Russian ships, the maneuver was aimed at impressing Bulgaria and Rumania with Turkish strength, an impression which perhaps would help lead them to join the Central Powers. Pallavicini had suggested the maneuver earlier in the month and it had been considered as a possibility by various members of the Turkish government, Talaat Bey in particular. The idea had proved unacceptable to the grand vizier, who still feared Admiral Souchon would take the opportunity to attack the Russians, ending Turkish neutrality.[43]

Once Souchon had received the green light from Berlin, he was ready to move. The only thing holding him back was Berlin's insistence that he was to exercise caution and to plan his sortie in conjunction with political conditions as they were defined by Wangenheim. At the moment Wangenheim saw the situation as unfavorable and Souchon continued to wait. In spite of the impatience of German military and naval leaders for Turkish action, in spite of recognition by the

[42] GFMA, ser. 1, reel 13, no. 848, Wangenheim to Berlin, 20 September 1914; no. 847, Wangenheim to Berlin, 21 September.

[43] Ibid., no. 191, Jagow at Luxembourg to Constantinople, 24 September 1914; Staatsarchiv, PA, box 521, no. 553, Hohenlohe in Berlin to Berchtold, 24 September; no. 634, Pallavicini to Berchtold, 24 September; no. 578, Pallavicini to Berchtold, 12 September; no. 58/P A–E, Pallavicini to Berchtold, 28 September.

Wilhelmstrasse of the importance of immediate Turkish participation and the complete agreement of Austrian leaders that such participation was essential to a furtherance of the war, the necessary step was still being delayed at the end of September. A naval venture into the Black Sea had been postponed. It was obvious to German and Austrian circles that once such an operation did occur the Turks would be in the war.[44]

From the closing days of September to the end of October a series of developments made possible Souchon's naval attack. On September 26 a Turkish torpedo boat attempted to leave the Straits, running toward the Mediterranean. It was turned back by the English fleet, and Constantinople was told that henceforth Turkish warships leaving the Straits would be treated as hostile vessels. The English position was based on what was by now a well known fact—the whole Turkish fleet was under the control of German naval officers and therefore might open fire on the ships of the Entente. Turkey replied by officially closing the Straits, and in answer to the protests of the Entente's ambassadors, replied that the Straits would be opened as soon as the English and French naval contingents were pulled back from the vicinity of the Dardanelles. Sir Edward Grey, head of the English Foreign Office, refused. By September 29 the Straits had been further secured against any Entente action by the laying of two additional mine fields.[45]

While this event may have eased the minds of German admirals concerning an English-French naval breakthrough, making them more amenable to a naval engagement in the Black Sea, Wangenheim took a pessimistic view of the venture. In his opinion the benevolent neutrality of the Turks was of more value than a premature entry into the war. He pointed out that the closure of the Straits had completely cut communications between Russia and its allies via the Mediterranean, a crucial step which had been accomplished with Turkey remaining neutral. With a serious military check, the military and political worth of the Turkish ally would become negligible. Although Berlin believed

---

[44] GFMA, ser. 1, reel 13, no. 191, Jagow at Luxembourg to Constantinople, 24 September 1914; Staatsarchiv, PA, box 521, no. 634, Pallavicini to Berchtold, 24 September; no. 424, Berchtold to von Mittag in Sofia, 13 September; box 941, Krieg 21 A, no. 47, Baron Wladimir von Giesl at Austrian army headquarters to Berchtold, 2 September. On 13 September Berchtold had written to von Mittag saying, "For us the earliest attack of Turkey is desired." As early as 2 September, Conrad had told Baron Giesl, the Foreign Office representative at army headquarters, that he believed a landing at Odessa had great worth and that this landing could be effected only after mastery of the Black Sea had been obtained by the *Goeben* and the Turkish fleet.

[45] GFMA, ser. 1, reel 13, no. 906, Wangenheim to Berlin, 27 September 1914; no. 915, Wangenheim to Berlin, 28 September; no. 931, Wangenheim to Berlin, 29 September; Howard, *Partition of Turkey*, pp. 107–8.

the Turkish fleet would be victorious against the Russian, and Vienna was confident that such a victory would raise the prestige of the Central Powers in the Balkans, Wangenheim saw the possibility that Russian ships might remain in port and refuse to give battle. In that case the Turkish fleet would impress no one. In an actual contest between the two navies, he suggested, "A single lucky torpedo hit by the Russian fleet which would put the *Goeben* out of commission would also negate the whole Turkish fleet at the same time and make all military undertakings in the Black Sea impossible."[46]

Wangenheim's Austrian colleague certainly agreed with his caution, for Pallavicini felt that nothing would be more disadvantageous to their war effort than such an undertaking, which at the moment offered no guarantee of success. Neither Berlin nor Vienna was willing to accept the conservative viewpoint of these men. Zimmermann expressed astonishment at Wangenheim's attitude and Berchtold refused to believe in its validity. On October 7, Wangenheim's view was rejected by an instruction from the Wilhelmstrasse which simply directed him to "try by all means to get Turkey to attack." Again, the German ambassador may have disagreed with his superiors but he did as he was told, and Pallavicini followed his lead.[47]

At just this time a shift in the attitude of important Turkish statesmen made possible the desired Turkish participation within a month. Enver Pasha had, since August, lacked sufficient backing to make his interventionist view prevail. But by October 8 he had managed to convince Talaat and Halil that intervention was now in the best interests of Turkey, and by October 10 he had won Djemal Pasha, minister of marine, to the side of the action party. These three had of course been consistently pro-German, and their hesitation was not based on the question of whether to join the Central Powers, but on waiting until the time seemed most propitious. Their decision that conditions for action were now right rested on Enver's contention that mobilization had proceeded to the point where Turkey was secure. Sufficient troops were now massed around Constantinople and Adrianople to protect these cities against possible enemy attack. Three army corps could be dispatched to the south to guard against an English striking force from Egypt, and enough troops had been concentrated in Asia Minor to

---

[46] GFMA, ser. 1, reel 13, no. 985, Wangenheim to Berlin, 6 October 1914; Staatsarchiv, PA, box 941, Krieg 21 A, no. 481, Hohenlohe in Berlin to Berchtold, 1 September; box 521, no. 572, Berchtold to Pallavicini, 2 October; no. 679, Pallavicini to Berchtold, 7 October.

[47] Staatsarchiv, PA, box 521, no. 679, Pallavicini to Berchtold, 7 October 1914; report no. 59/P A–E, Pallavicini to Berchtold, 8 October; no. 587, Hohenlohe to Berchtold, 7 October.

protect Turkey against the Russians. Aside from considerations of mobilization, they were also much impressed with the advances being made by both Germany and Austria on the eastern front. If the Central Powers won and Turkey did not join them in the war, the Germans and Austrians would not help them to preserve Turkey.[48]

The one condition on which these officials insisted before Turkey could take up the cudgels was the guarantee of financial support. Unless this guarantee was forthcoming, the Turks would not only be unable to engage in active war, but partial demobilization would have to be ordered. Djavid Bey, finance minister, was already pressing for a reduction in men under arms, his position supported by the startling fact that the army was at this early date already on half pay. The Turkish war party did not demand immediate payment but asked Wangenheim to have on hand two million Turkish pounds in cash or in bars which could be handed over after Turkey became a belligerent. Financial negotiations between Germany and Turkey had been going on since September and they were not entirely concluded until November, but it is significant that by October 11 Wangenheim had already received the approval of Bethmann-Hollweg to make the necessary financial assurances.[49] On this same day Wangenheim met with Enver, Talaat, Djemal, and Halil, who agreed that Souchon was to be placed in complete command of the Turkish navy and would receive orders from Enver Pasha to attack the Russian fleet just as soon as Wangenheim had the money at his disposal. This agreement was kept secret from the grand vizier. Once the money had arrived, these four ministers would be able to present the grand vizier with the alternative of accepting their war plans or resigning his office. It was probable that he would go along but if he refused they were prepared to build a new ministry without him.[50]

[48] Ibid., box 941, Krieg 21 A, no. 380, Szögyény in Berlin to Berchtold, 5 August 1914; Szögyény at this early date discusses Enver's willingness for a general offensive. GFMA, ser. 1, reel 13, no. 1010, Wangenheim to Berlin, 9 October 1914; no. 1022, Wangenheim to Berlin, 11 October; Talaat Pasha, "Posthumous Memoirs," p. 293.

[49] GFMA, ser. 1, reel 13, no. 1022, Wangenheim to Berlin, 11 October 1914; no. 254, Jagow to the Foreign Office, 11 October (Jagow explains Bethmann's agreement); no. A 25385, unsigned report from Constantinople, 3 October, describes the poor financial condition of the Turkish government and Djavid's objections to mobilization; Staatsarchiv, PA, box 941, no. 515, Pallavicini to Berchtold, 29 August; he reports that Enver is ready to go to war.

[50] GFMA, ser. 1, reel 13, no. 1022, Wangenheim to Berlin, 11 October 1914; no. 985, Wangenheim to Berlin, 6 October. On 6 October, Wangenheim wrote that Enver would work out plans with Souchon on that day to make Souchon a Turkish admiral and commander-in-chief of the Turkish navy. This would give Souchon authority to control the actual sailing of the fleet. Staatsarchiv, PA,

By October 22 Wangenheim had received the two millions in gold. At the same time Enver sent through Wangenheim to General von Moltke his plans for the actual military campaigns his forces would undertake. The Turkish army in Armenia was to hold the Russians in the Transcaucasus area. Two corps would attack Egypt, but this campaign would necessitate another six weeks of preparation. If Bulgaria joined, Turkish forces would be used partially for a Serbian campaign and partially as insurance against Greek and Rumanian attacks. If Rumania also joined against the Entente, the main Turkish force would be used against Russia. Until the Balkan states decided to join the Central Powers, the major portion of the Turkish forces would remain in Thrace and in the area of the Sea of Marmora.[51]

The plans for Turkish action had been under consideration since August and had required much discussion and deliberation between the Germans and Turks; disputes and hard feelings had arisen. It was all well and good for Enver Pasha to boast at the end of August that he was ready to attack in the Caucasus or in Egypt or to land at Odessa, but Germans and Austrians in Constantinople were well aware of the problems posed by the relative weakness and unpreparedness of Turkish military forces. The failure of the Central Powers to win Bulgaria and Rumania eliminated the possibility of Turkish-Bulgarian-Rumanian military cooperation, and although Liman von Sanders had been instructed to work out a plan for a Balkan campaign involving the three armies, the idea was dropped once Wangenheim and Pallavicini became convinced that the insecure diplomatic scene made the project unfeasible.[52] The possibility of a campaign against Odessa was quickly overruled by German officials. Neither Souchon nor Usedom was willing to accept the responsibility for amphibious operations without mastery of the Black Sea. This left the Caucasus and Egypt as possible battlegrounds. The Caucasus posed a formidable problem. Its passes ranged to elevations of 7500 feet. Communications were extremely poor, with primitive roads and insufficient rail facilities. Then, too, since there existed a minimum of troops to carry out the campaign, its value to the Central Powers was questionable. Russia would hardly deflect large forces from the eastern front to parry such a weak Turkish thrust.[53]

---

box 521, no. 688, Pallavicini to Berchtold, 10 October 1914. Pallavicini explains that Enver, Djemal, and Talaat had the support of the Young Turk Committee, which meant they could form a new cabinet without difficulty, should the grand vizier resign.

[51] GFMA, ser. 1, reel 13, no. 1087, Wangenheim to Berlin, 22 October 1914.

[52] Staatsarchiv, PA, box 941, no. 515, Pallavicini to Berchtold, 29 August 1914; no. 409, Pallavicini to Berchtold, 6 August; no. 404, Szögyény in Berlin to Berchtold, 9 August; no. 394, Szögyény to Berchtold, 7 August.

In the case of Egypt, Liman von Sanders early disagreed with an attack there. In conference with Enver and his staff, he pointed to the lack of communications, the lack of troops, and to the small possibility of success. An attack on Suez would perhaps surprise the British but the latter's preponderance of forces would eventually mean a Turkish defeat. Liman apparently saw no value in any Turkish venture. By August 19 he was ready to throw up his hands and wrote to the Kaiser asking that the whole military mission be recalled. In his opinion, it could be of no service to the German war effort by remaining in Turkey. Liman clashed not only with Enver Pasha but with Wangenheim as well. Unfortunately, both Germans were nervous, high-strung, imperious types. It was not long before Wangenheim was complaining to Berlin that he found it extremely hard to obtain Liman's cooperation. The Kaiser sent a special telegram to the general, telling him to remain in Constantinople since his services were considered "most important and useful." In September, Liman was instructed to subordinate his views to the policies of the German ambassador.

Throughout September and October preparations for an Egyptian campaign were begun under the direction of Colonel Kress von Kressenstein, who set up his headquarters in Syria. The strong inclinations of German military and diplomatic leaders in Berlin and at general headquarters for an attack on Egypt were reflected in the instruction Bethmann-Hollweg sent to Liman von Sanders on September 17: "In the common interest, an undertaking against Egypt is of great importance. Therefore your Excellency should subordinate to this idea any doubts you may entertain as to the operations proposed by Turkey."[54] So Liman's objections were bypassed, and on October 24 Enver received from von Moltke approval of the plans he had submitted two days before. Von Jagow at German headquarters wrote the Foreign Office in Berlin, "The German High Command lays greatest worth now as before on the immediate fleet action in the Black Sea and the undertaking against Egypt."[55]

[53] Ibid., box 521, report no. 55/P-B, Pallavicini to Berchtold, 9 September; Pomiankowski, *Zusammenbruch*, pp. 94, 102; Otto Liman von Sanders, *Five Years in Turkey*, pp. 28–30.

[54] Liman, *Five Years in Turkey*, pp. 25–27; GFMA, St. Anthony's Collection, reel 77, no. 547, Liman von Sanders to the Kaiser, 19 August 1914; no. 546, Wangenheim to Berlin, 19 August; no. 17, Kaiser Wilhelm to Liman, 20 August; no. 1249/14, Jagow at headquarters to Zimmermann in Berlin, 27 September (Jagow refers here to the instructions sent to Liman which the latter quotes in his memoirs); Pomiankowski, *Zusammenbruch*, p. 101. For descriptions of Wangenheim and Liman von Sanders, see Morgenthau, *Ambassador Morgenthau's Story*, p. 90, and de Nogales, *Four Years beneath the Crescent*, p. 29.

[55] GFMA, ser. 1, reel 13, no. 305, Jagow at headquarters to the Foreign Office, 24 October 1914.

The Decision

The necessary money was available, the political backing existed, the military strategy was agreed upon. Enver now took the final plunge. On October 24 he sent instructions to Admiral Souchon ordering him to take the entire Turkish fleet into the Black Sea. Along with this instruction went sealed orders which were to be opened when the admiral received a telegram to do so. If the telegram read "Open sealed orders," it would mean Enver had convinced the cabinet to agree on action. If it read "Do not open orders," it would mean the cabinet had refused to go along. In this case Souchon was to create an incident with the Russians and bring about hostilities by his own initiative.[56] These instructions show that Enver doubted he could carry the cabinet in sufficient degree to obtain a majority consent for war. The fact that the German admiral was given authority to proceed without such consent reflects Enver's relying on a fait accompli to achieve what he might not be able to get through regular channels.

Even now the Germans in Constantinople were practicing caution. Halil Bey, minister of foreign affairs, was a man whose attitude also carried weight with the Young Turk Committee. He was inclined toward Enver's position but he and Talaat were reported to be wavering and Enver apparently decided to delay action until their position was more precisely defined. Halil's and Talaat's sudden misgivings were caused by Italy's declaration that if Turkey entered the war the Italians would "find it necessary to take precautions," since Turkey's involvement would cause ferment throughout the entire Mohammedan world, including Italian-controlled Libya. The idea of war with Italy along with the other Entente powers was definitely not appealing. Both men suggested Turkey wait until early 1915 before ending its neutrality. By then preparations in Persia, in the Caucasus, and in Egypt would be complete and the Ottoman Empire better prepared to meet its foes. Yet, by October 25 Wangenheim could report that Enver had succeeded in stiffening the backs of Talaat and Halil and had regained their support along with that of Djemal Pasha.[57]

With the four most powerful Turkish ministers now properly aligned, the stage seemed finally set. Souchon, acting on his orders of

[56] Staatsarchiv, PA, box 941, no. 720, Pallavicini to Berchtold, 22 October 1914; Enver had told Pallavicini what he planned to do; GFMA, ser. 1, reel 13, no. 1094, Wangenheim to Berlin, 24 October.

[57] Staatsarchiv, PA, box 941, no. 1115, Baron von Macchio in Rome to Berchtold, 23 October 1914; no. 720, Pallavicini to Berchtold, 22 October; report no. 62/P A-G, Pallavicini to Berchtold, 22 October; GFMA, ser. 1, reel 13, no. 1094, Wangenheim to Berlin, 24 October; no. 1107, Wangenheim to Berlin, 25 October; Staatsarchiv, PA, box 941, no. 734, Pallavicini to Berchtold, 26 October.

October 24, weighed anchor on the twenty-seventh and steamed into the Black Sea with the Turkish fleet. Contact was made with Russian contingents and hostilities between the two squadrons occurred on October 29–30. At the same time Souchon ordered the bombardment of the ports of Sebastopol, Odessa, Theodosia, and Novorossisk, an action successfully carried out.[58]

An immediate Turkish cabinet crisis followed, with the grand vizier and Djavid Bey hotly protesting Souchon's action. Said Halim demanded the admiral be ordered to break off all hostilities, declaring that some way had to be found to settle the issue peacefully with Russia and its allies, or he would refuse to take the responsibility for what would be open war and would tender his resignation. He now sent Djavid Bey to obtain the good offices of the French ambassador, Maurice Bompard. But the only peaceful settlement acceptable to the Entente was a disarming of the *Goeben* and the *Breslau*, the return of all German officers and crews to Germany, the end of secret relations with the Central Powers, and the acceptance by Turkey of a truly neutral position. The demands could not be met without ending all connection with Germany and Austria, and this not even Said Halim was willing to do. On October 30 the Russian, French, and English ambassadors in Constantinople, asking for their passports, broke off relations.[59]

Two days later the government crisis ended when Talaat Bey charged the grand vizier with having himself engineered the alliance with Germany and Austria-Hungary. Now he would have to accept the consequences of his own policy. At a special meeting at the home of Said Halim on November 1, Enver, Talaat, Djemal, and Halil prevailed upon him to remain in office as his patriotic duty. Although some members of the cabinet resigned, the decision of the grand vizier to remain in office ended the possibility of a split developing in Turkish political circles. A split might well have come about because Said Halim had a certain real following within the Young Turk Committee. His decision to go along meant that the war party now controlled a unified government. On November 11 Turkey published its official declaration of war, offering as an explanation that Russian ships had interfered with peaceful maneuvers of the Turkish fleet, and, having opened fire, menacingly moved in the direction of the Straits. The explanation was, of course, purest fabrication.[60]

[58] Staatsarchiv, PA, box 941, nos. 736 and 740, Pallavicini to Berchtold, 27 October 1914; GFMA, ser. 1, reel 13, no. 1146, Wangenheim to Berlin, 29 October; Staatsarchiv, PA, box 941, no. 762, Pallavicini to Berchtold, 31 October.

[59] Talaat Pasha, "Posthumous Memoirs," p. 293; GFMA, ser. 1, reel 13, no. 1205, Wangenheim to Berlin, 2 November 1914; Staatsarchiv, PA, box 941, nos. 757 and 768, Pallavicini to Berchtold, 31 October and 1 November.

Germany and Austria-Hungary now had the cooperation of the Ottoman Empire. It had by no means been easy to obtain. Three months of hard work had been necessary on the part of German and Austrian diplomatic personnel, working in conjunction with their own military and naval officers and with powerful and cautious Turkish politicians. The diplomatic position of the Central Powers had been strong in Constantinople when the war began in August, and had become stronger as a result of the positions taken on the issue of the Capitulations and financial support. Nevertheless, it was not strong enough to successfully put through a Turkish-Bulgarian alliance, which might conceivably have brought Turkey into the war much sooner.

When all factors have been weighed, it must be concluded that without the presence of the *Goeben* and the *Breslau* at Constantinople, Turkish participation in the war would not have been achieved in November. It was unquestionably the Germans, in conjunction with Enver Pasha, who ended Turkish neutrality by using these ships, along with the Turkish navy, to provoke a conflict with Russia. What had been needed was the proper moment, and that moment was decided by Enver Pasha, who in spite of his impatience to enter the war found it necessary to wait until his own political backing was assured. Political support had followed upon obtaining the necessary money to meet the expenses of belligerency, the military securing of the Dardanelles, and an army that seemed sufficiently mobilized to defend Turkey against its enemies. Crucial to the establishment of these necessary conditions for Turkish entry was the ceaseless pressure maintained by Wangenheim and Pallavicini and their exploitation of circumstances as they arose. Of the two allies, it was clearly Germany which figured as the dominant partner at Constantinople, but the Austrian ambassador was no mean diplomat and in astuteness he was every bit the equal of his German colleague. The cooperation existing between the two reflected the strong agreement of Berlin and Vienna on the urgency of Turkish support. If the two ambassadors faithfully followed the instructions of their home offices, they did not do so without personal reservations. They feared the harvest might be bitter. That the Turkish ally was to prove as much a liability as an asset vindicated their hesitancy.

[60] Staatsarchiv, PA, box 941, no. 775, Pallavicini to Berchtold, 2 November 1914; report no. 66/P A-D, Pallavicini to Berchtold, 11 November; Djemal Pasha, *Memories of a Turkish Statesman*, pp. 132–33; Djemal lists the following men who resigned their cabinet posts in protest: Effendi El Bustani, minister of agriculture and commerce; Mahmoud Pasha, minister of public works; Oskan Effendi, minister of posts; and Djavid Bey, minister of finance. These posts were filled by Achmed Bey, Halim Pasha, Shukri Bey, and Talaat Bey, respectively.

Chapter 5

The Turkish Ally

It must now have seemed to Berlin and Vienna that they could transfer attention to the less well defined positions of Bulgaria and Rumania. In truth, there was still much work ahead in Constantinople.

Holy War

One of the ways in which Turkey could aid the Central Powers was by declaring a Holy War—a war which would unite all Muslims against their Christian enemies. The Germans had considered using the religious weapon and certainly it was a fond idea of the Young Turks, who fostered the growth of a Pan-Islamic movement, closely bound to their program of Pan-Turanism. Enver had broached the topic when he offered his war program in late October, 1914. The reaction of Austria was negative. Berchtold was deeply concerned because a Holy War would immediately involve Italy's North African possessions and would lead in only one direction—the joining of Italy with the Entente. In addition, because there were Muslims in Bulgarian Thrace, a Jihad might produce dangerous estrangement between Turkey and Bulgaria. Berchtold wrote to Pallavicini in Constantinople and to Hohenlohe in Berlin, prior to the Black Sea bombardment, that Turkey must make sure the Holy War did not include opposition to the Central Powers, Italy, Bulgaria, or Rumania. Only England, France, and Russia must be singled out as the Christian enemies. Zimmermann in Berlin agreed with the Ballhausplatz and instructed Wangenheim to urge Turkey to work along these lines.[1]

There was really no need to impress Wangenheim with the point. He had chatted with his Austrian colleague concerning the matter on November 2 and both concluded the whole venture was not advisable. Once such a movement began it would be difficult to hold it within prescribed limits. What was anti-Russian, -English, and -French one day could easily become anti-German and -Austrian the next. If, for example, Turkish leaders sought to rouse feeling against the English in Egypt, this could more easily be done not through an anti-Christian movement, but by simply stressing the desirability of destroying

99

English political power there. In this way the Egyptian question could be handled without any overlapping into Libya, so that the danger of angering Italy would be averted.[2]

The avoidance of a Holy War proved impossible. On November 15 there were large demonstrations in Constantinople, following upon the sultan's declaration of a Holy War the previous day. He called upon Muslim manhood to fight the enemies of Islam—Russia, France, and England; all Muslims who did not take part in the struggle would be eternally punished. He concluded with the warning that any attack on the Germans or Austro-Hungarians would be the "very greatest of sins." The failure to exempt the Italians led Pallavicini to make strong representations to Enver and Talaat, for he had heard that the government in Rome was much disquieted over the proclamation. The success of his arguments on the inadvisability of rousing Italy was reflected a few days later in the Turkish press, which suddenly carried lead articles stressing that Italy was an ally of the Central Powers and so a Turkish friend.[3] The Austrian ambassador remained unimpressed; the Turks might have placated the Italians but they had made no mention of the Balkan states and had therefore given the Russians a lever with which to rally all Balkan peoples against the common Turkish enemy.[4] As things turned out, the Holy War proved ineffectual. It lacked organization, and the Turkish government, unable to provide the necessary arms to give the movement any real force, found itself relying on whatever it could muster in the way of a national army.[5]

A Second Turkish Alliance

While the Pan-Islamic issue was being discussed, another problem of much greater significance was brought to the fore at the insistence of the Turkish government. At the end of October, Halil Bey was sent to

[1] Joseph Pomiankowski, *Der Zusammenbruch des Ottomanischen Reiches,* pp. 96–97; Ahmed Emin, *Turkey in the World War,* p. 174; Staatsarchiv, PA, box 941, nos. 660 and 738, Berchtold to Pallavicini and Hohenlohe, 26 October 1914; no. 633, Hohenlohe to Berchtold, 27 October; no. 675, Berchtold to Pallavicini, 29 October. Pomiankowski points out that Enver viewed the religious war as a lever for realizing his Pan-Turanian ideas. These involved the incorporation of many areas, and significantly included Tripoli and Bengazi, thus running contrary to Italian interests in Africa.

[2] Staatsarchiv, PA, box 941, no. 773, Pallavicini to Berchtold, 2 November 1914.

[3] Ibid., no. 835, Pallavicini to Berchtold, 15 November 1914; report no. 68/P A-H, Pallavicini to Berchtold, 19 November.

[4] Ibid., report no. 68/P A-H, Pallavicini to Berchtold, 19 November 1914.

[5] Emin, *Turkey in the World War,* pp. 174–77. Emin points out that the Pan-Islamic movement did lead to stirring the Kurds and Arabs but was insufficient to endanger the existence of Entente colonies; Pomiankowski, *Zusammenbruch,* pp. 95–96.

Berlin and Vienna with a request that the existing alliance between the Central Powers and Turkey, signed August 2, be extended in scope and prolonged in time. The original alliance, which had been aimed against Russia for the duration of the Austro-Serbian conflict, was to end in 1918, and would be extended for an additional five years unless denounced by the parties concerned. The Turks now sought to have Germany and Austria guarantee their aid in the case of an eventual attack by England, France, or a coalition of Balkan states. The guarantee was to be extended not for five years but for ten.[6]

The same suggestions for a change in the terms were made to Wangenheim and to Pallavicini by Enver Pasha, Talaat Bey, and Djemal Pasha. They explained that while Turkey was now indeed a belligerent there was still an influential circle at home remaining strongly opposed to active participation and anti-German in outlook. This group was led by Djavid Bey, the finance minister, who was Francophile in his leanings. Djavid did not believe that the existing alliance with the Central Powers was to Turkey's advantage. Since it insured Turkey against Russia only for the duration, Djavid argued that it hardly went far enough. Nor was the extension for only five years sufficient to cover Turkey's needs. In the event of peace the Ottoman Empire would face no immediate danger from its enemies, who would be exhausted by the conflict. The danger would begin when those enemies had rebuilt their strength. In an attempt to undercut this political opposition, Enver, Talaat, and Djemal now sought to obtain an extension of the alliance terms, and in the process made the opposition appear more formidable than it was. In fact Djavid Bey and several others who agreed with his position resigned their cabinet posts in early November. Henceforth opposition to government policy was carried on more or less indirectly through Djavid and his supporters at the monthly meetings of the Young Turk Committee. While the Committee represented the one political group having sufficient organization and backing to unseat a government, that body was controlled by the triumvirate of Enver, Talaat, and Djemal. Talaat was himself the presiding officer at its sessions. The three men shrewdly exaggerated the importance of the opposition and so used it as a club in their diplomatic negotiations. It was not domestic politics that triggered their representations to the German and Austrian ambassadors. The changes they wanted would make the pact a very broad instrument which would strongly commit the Central Powers on Turkey's behalf. In the initial stages of negotiations the government carefully avoided

[6] Staatsarchiv, PA, box 521, nos. 760 and 778, Pallavicini to Berchtold, 31 October and 2 November 1914; GFMA, ser. 1, reel 13, no. 1205, Wangenheim to Berlin, 2 November.

requesting an entirely new agreement. The revisions, it said, could be incorporated by the mere addition of an annex to the original.[7]

The reaction of Wangenheim and Pallavicini proved positive. The German ambassador was ready to go along because he believed that the desired revisions would strengthen the position of the existing Turkish government. Pallavicini went further. He pointed to the fact that the end of the war would see Turkey attached to the power sphere of Germany and Austria. Thus it was to their own interest to protect the Ottoman Empire against any further attacks by traditional or potential enemies. For this reason he asked the Ballhausplatz for authorization to say that the Austrians and Germans were "prepared *in principle* to take account of Turkish wishes." He and Wangenheim could then hammer out the details after thorough consideration.[8]

The Austrian foreign minister, Berchtold, wrote to Pallavicini that he agreed with his long-range thinking on the issue and instructed him to give Austria's consent to the Porte when his German colleague received approval from Berlin. At the same time Vienna informed its ambassador to Germany, Gottfried Hohenlohe, that Austria was prepared to accept the extension desired by Turkey. Wangenheim had, of course, informed the Wilhelmstrasse of the overtures made to him. Undersecretary Zimmermann proved amenable and suggested at the home office that the desired extension simply be attached as an annex to the already existing treaty. Everything seemed to be going well.[9]

The German chancellor, however, had been thinking about the whole issue. He was no more eager to deal with the Turks now than he had been before the war. In a memorandum sent to Zimmermann's desk he declared his dislike for the proposal, saying that after the war it would be Germany's policy to free itself "from the nightmare of coalitions as much as possible." Germany had signed an alliance with the Turks in August only after very careful consideration, and he saw any addition as undesirable and dangerous. To commit Germany to support of the Turks against all states only meant fostering the development of a new coalition system. Bethmann recognized that it was in Germany's interest to protect Turkey, but he asserted that the victory

[7] GFMA, ser. 1, reel 13, no. 1205, Wangenheim to Berlin, 2 November 1914; Staatsarchiv, PA, box 521, no. 688, Pallavicini to Berchtold, 10 October; no. 778, Pallavicini to Berchtold, 2 November; Djemal Pasha, *Memories of a Turkish Statesman*, pp. 132–33; Alfred Nossig, *Die Neue Türkei und Ihre Führer*, p. 69; Henri Seignobosc, *Turcs et Turquie*, p. 63.

[8] Staatsarchiv, PA, box 521, nos. 778, 781, Pallavicini to Berchtold, 2 and 3 November 1914; GFMA, ser. 1, reel 13, no. 1205, Wangenheim to Berlin, 2 November.

[9] Staatsarchiv, PA, box 521, no. 776, Berchtold to Hohenlohe, 3 November 1914; no. 647, Hohenlohe to Berchtold, 4 November; no. 780, Berchtold to Hohenlohe, 4 November.

of the Central Powers would itself insure Constantinople against any threat from another nation, for example, England. If the Central Powers lost, they would be unable to defend Turkey against "all coalitions and eventualities." Nor did Bethmann feel that the Central Powers owed the Turks such a revised alliance simply because the Ottomans were now in the war. Active participation was only the fulfillment of Turkey's existing obligations. Besides, Turkey was now in the war, it could not back out, and therefore any revision was unnecessary and superfluous.[10]

Wangenheim strongly disagreed with the chancellor's position and on November 7 wired his own view of things. It was his desire to win the war by every means and, once it was over, to do away slowly with the hazards arising from alliances. There was, he said, no intelligent Turk who believed a diplomatic agreement with any European power to be absolute in terms of binding obligations. In any case the *casus foederis* was always open to interpretation. The extension desired by Constantinople was necessary if the war party there was to maintain its supremacy. The acceptance of these commitments by Germany and Austria was considered among the Turks to be a mere formality, while for the present Turkish cabinet such acceptance was a necessity in order to maintain a unified war effort.[11]

Zimmermann agreed with Wangenheim and was also in accord with Pallavicini, who believed the situation was not so safe as Bethmann felt it was; Zimmermann therefore pressed the chancellor to reverse his position. Several days later, on the urging of his own diplomats as well as those of Austria, Bethmann agreed to go along with the Turkish request. He was willing to extend the alliance to 1920, the year of expiration for the Dreibund; if a year prior to its expiration no objections were voiced, it should then be in effect until 1926. Beyond this date the Germans could offer nothing, for not even the Dual Alliance itself was regulated past that year.[12]

Bethmann's reversal was no real surprise. Germany had not liked the idea of a Turkish alliance but had signed one in August. It was willing, after some reluctance, to accept an extension now, in November. Behind this change of attitude stood the exigencies of war, something

[10] GFMA, ser. 1, reel 13, no. 97, Bethmann-Hollweg at headquarters to the Foreign Office, 15 November 1914; Staatsarchiv, PA, box 521, no. 655, Hohenlohe to Berchtold, 6 November.

[11] GFMA, ser. 1, reel 13, no. 1262, Wangenheim to Berlin, 7 November 1914.

[12] Staatsarchiv, PA, box 521, nos. 647, 655, Hohenlohe to Berchtold, 4 and 6 November 1914, respectively; no. 816, Pallavicini to Berchtold, 9 November; no. 668, Hohenlohe to Berchtold, 10 November; GFMA, ser. 1, reel 13, no. 100, Bethmann at headquarters to the Foreign Office, 10 November.

the Wilhelmstrasse never forgot. The Turks were now Germany's fighting allies, and for purposes of maintaining a united war effort Berlin went along despite qualms concerning the diplomatic future.

Informed of Germany's approval, the grand vizier was delighted. He particularly liked the fact that Germany was considering the time span in terms of the Dreibund because he had long wanted Turkey to be part of that grouping. If Austria and Italy were also to agree, it would mean the creation of a Vierbund. Said Halim now declared that he wanted Austrian concurrence, evidenced not merely by an exchange of notes on the forthcoming German-Turkish extension, but by a formal treaty instrument. At this point Austria began to consider the matter with much greater care.[13]

Pallavicini himself was in favor of such a Vierbund, for it was clear to him that with Germany now controlling the Ottoman army and navy, that country held the preponderant position in Turkey. If Austria wished to seek commercial and political advantages in Turkey after the war, it would be best to have Turkey join the Dreibund. Under such conditions Italy would also hold a privileged position at Constantinople. With both Italy and Austria pursuing their own interests in Turkey, Germany would find competition keener, and the prospects of German monopoly might therefore be reduced. It was on this basis that Berchtold decided to ask Berlin whether it was not advisable to inform Rome officially of the negotiations with Turkey. Behind this decision there also lay his fear that Said Halim might, through an indiscretion, inform the Italians of the talks. The fact that Italy was still a member of the Triple Alliance but had not been told by the Central Powers of their commitments to Turkey would certainly not make for progress in the Austro-Italian conversations taking place at this time on the question of the Italian Irredenta. The Germans agreed to inform Rome, but they demanded that the extension of the German-Turkish accord first be arranged in Constantinople. So far as a Vierbund was concerned, Berlin chose not to think in those terms at the moment. While Berchtold remained uneasy about keeping the Italians in the dark, he nevertheless wrote to Hohenlohe that "on this question the judgment of the German government must be considered as primary."[14]

[13] Staatsarchiv, PA, box 521, no. 799, Pallavicini to Berchtold, 6 November 1914; report no. 68 P/C, Pallavicini to Berchtold, 19 November.

[14] Ibid., report no. 68 P/C, Pallavicini to Berchtold, 19 November 1914; memo no. S 312, Berchtold to Hohenlohe, 20 November; no. 714, Hohenlohe to Berchtold, 25 November; no. 794, Berchtold to Hohenlohe, 7 November; no. 699, Hohenlohe to Berchtold, 21 November; no. 828, Berchtold to Hohenlohe, 23 November.

Berchtold's consideration of Italy's attitude toward Turkish negotiations reflects a sudden caution on his part. This caution changed to thorough and real opposition in the latter half of December. The Turks submitted a draft version of what they wanted, and what they wanted was a whole new treaty rather than simply a supplement to the old. The form of the new pact was to be the same as that signed in August—an alignment between Germany and Turkey to which Austria would give its consent. Of the six articles which formed the first draft, the Ballhausplatz reacted vehemently to two, Articles I and III. The latter stated that the accord would expire on the same date as the treaty of alliance existing between Germany and Austria-Hungary, namely, July 8, 1920. Berchtold protested that the date of the German-Austrian alliance was secret and ought not to be revealed. As to Article I, it stated that Germany would guarantee Turkey its territorial integrity and would defend it against an attack by a great power or by a coalition of Balkan states. It was this article which led to the strongest opposition from the Ballhausplatz throughout December and to much negotiation between Berlin and Vienna.[15]

The Germans themselves were hardly ready to throw all caution to the winds. They insisted on certain changes, most of which the Turks were willing to accept, and by the latter part of the month the new agreement was ready for signature. The German Foreign Office saw Article I as much too broad. The secretary of state, Jagow, insisted that Wangenheim have it changed so that German armed support would be given only in the case of an unprovoked attack. Moreover, a coalition of Balkan states could not include Rumania, because Rumania's old alliance with Germany and Austria was still valid, at least in a formal sense. Germany therefore suggested an explicative note wherein Rumania would be included as one of these Balkan states only if it gave up its neutrality to join the Entente powers in the present war. A third modification on which Berlin insisted had to do with England. English interests in Egypt and the Near East made an English-Turkish conflict highly probable; therefore Germany was willing to support the Turks only if Turkey was engaged in a conflict with England and another European state simultaneously.[16]

[15] Ibid., report no. 70 P/A-F, Pallavicini to Berchtold, 1 December 1914 (the report contains the original Turkish draft); nos. 936, 878, Berchtold to Hohenlohe and Pallavicini respectively, 14 December.

[16] Ibid., report no. 70 P/A-F, Pallavicini to Berchtold, 1 December 1914; no. 936, Berchtold to Hohenlohe, 14 December; no. 953, Pallavicini to Berchtold, 21 December; GFMA, ser. 1, reel 13, no. 1459, Jagow to Wangenheim, 15 December; no. 1508, Wangenheim to Berlin, 4 December (a second draft, containing the clause on England, is found here).

In the negotiations between Wangenheim and the Turkish government, the German ambassador found it necessary to eliminate the phrase "unprovoked attack." Halil Bey, with whom he considered the issue, said such a phrase provided too many loopholes through which the Central Powers could avoid giving their aid. To obviate Turkish hostility the Wilhelmstrasse was willing to drop the suggested wording. On the other hand, the Turks agreed to the explicative note on Rumania and accepted the inclusion of a clause calling for a military convention to be drawn up when peace was declared. This convention would define the precise conditions under which the *casus fœderis* could be said to exist in the event of an attack by Balkan states. By insisting on such a convention Berlin took the sting out of its commitment on Balkan affairs, for the commitment would not come until peace had been restored, and by that time Balkan conditions would be clarified. Germany would thus not be working in the diplomatic dark. Turkish acceptance of the demand for a clause on the convention meant that Berlin was now ready to promise aid to Turkey against a Balkan coalition, and Wangenheim was authorized to sign an alliance as early as December 21, assuming that Austria concurred.[17]

But Austria did not concur. On December 26 Berchtold wrote to Pallavicini in Constantinople, summarizing his position. The clause on the Balkan states was of much greater importance to Austria-Hungary than it was to Germany. The Monarchy bordered on three Balkan states and was therefore much more directly involved with Balkan issues. The Balkan Wars had shown what dangers lay in wait for powers which made alliances with or concerning these Balkan states. For these reasons Berchtold wanted the clause on a Balkan coalition completely dropped. Wangenheim was, of course, much disturbed by this attitude, for he was being heavily pressed by the Turks to conclude the alliance. He had been led to understand from the reports of the German ambassador in Vienna, von Tschirschky, that the Austrians were ready to go along. Clearly they were not at all ready to go along. Pallavicini now no longer agreed with his German colleague. He had grown as cautious as the Ballhausplatz and declared that Constantinople must either accept the phrase "unprovoked attack" or eliminate the clause on the Balkan coalition altogether. The Austrian attitude was based on the fear that, unless the phrase "unprovoked attack" was included, the Turks would have *carte blanche;* Pallavicini made his

[17] GFMA, ser. 1, reel 13, no. 1508, Wangenheim to Berlin, 4 December 1914; no. 1642, Wangenheim to Berlin, 17 December; Staatsarchiv, PA, box 521, no. 920, Pallavicini to Berchtold, 10 December; no. 953, Pallavicini to Berchtold, 21 December.

government's position quite clear when in conversation with Talaat Bey he said that Vienna believed the omission of the phrase would allow Turkey "every chicanery." In his deliberations with other members of the Turkish cabinet, Pallavicini consistently held to this position. When Halil Bey expressed surprise and reminded him that the beginning of talks on the new alliance had seen Austria quite favorable, the ambassador replied that it had then seemed only a question of guaranteeing Turkish territorial integrity through the addition of an annex to the original accord reached in August 1914. Now a defensive alliance of broadest scope was being considered. In talks with the grand vizier he stated that Austria could not assume the "wide obligations" which were obviously implied by the terms of Article I.[18]

The Germans understood the position taken by their Austrian ally but once having decided to go ahead on the alliance, they pushed for its rapid conclusion. Berlin sought to avoid arousing any harsh feeling or mistrust in Constantinople against the Central Powers at this time. More than this, Wangenheim much feared the antiwar feeling in certain Turkish circles. The conclusion of the alliance was therefore necessary if the position of the present Ottoman government was not to be made more difficult than it was—something which could easily impair the war effort. A long memorandum was drawn up by the German Foreign Office on January 2, 1915, and submitted to Berchtold in Vienna. It reviewed the situation, discussed the Austrian objections, and showed how the various difficulties could be resolved. In the first place, no *casus fœderis* against Rumania would be permitted so long as that country was bound to the Central Powers. This would be clearly pointed out by an exchange of notes on the issue of Rumania. Secondly, a military convention to be drawn up in the future would eliminate Austria's concern over a *casus fœderis* with respect to a Balkan coalition. The wording would be such that Austria would be obligated only if one of the Balkan states involved *bordered* on the Monarchy. The military convention thus would omit Bulgaria, and Austrian aid would be required only if the coalition involved Serbia or Montenegro, which had contiguous borders with the Monarchy. A preamble to the alliance would make certain that it was only a defensive one, and consequently the term "unprovoked attack" was superfluous.[19]

[18] Staatsarchiv, PA, box 521, no. 918, Berchtold to Pallavicini, 26 December 1914; no. 984, Pallavicini to Berchtold, 27 December; no. 987, Pallavicini to Berchtold, 28 December; report no. 79 P/A-B, Pallavicini to Berchtold, 31 December; GFMA, ser. 1, reel 13, no. 1223, von Tschirschky in Vienna to Berlin, 20 December.

[19] Staatsarchiv, PA, box 521, unnumbered memorandum, folio B, German Foreign Office to Berchtold through von Tschirschky, 4 January 1915.

Since Vienna could not deny the clear-cut logic of the memorandum, its opposition to the accord now ended. Nevertheless, Austria's caution continued to be much in evidence. Berchtold instructed Pallavicini to offer official Austrian concurrence to the alliance but at the same time emphasized in his instruction that the accompanying note on Rumania was an unconditional necessity. When Pallavicini told the grand vizier of Austria's official consent, he made sure that, in addition to accepting the necessity of the explicative note, the Turks understood that the military convention would exactly state the terms by which aid would be given to them. He also took great pains to make clear that the *casus fœderis* for an eventual attack by a Balkan coalition would become effective only if at least one of the attacking states was a direct neighbor of the Dual Monarchy. The Austrians were going to insist on taking the greatest care with respect to any overt military commitment. This fact was reflected in Pallavicini's reiteration to Wangenheim that the military convention would have to set very precisely the limitations and terms of aid to Turkey. What bothered Austria here was the fact that it was committing itself to an agreement whose terms would have to be worked out in the future, a situation which at best is always risky.[20]

A few days later, on January 9, the Kaiser sent Wangenheim final authorization to sign the alliance, and on January 11 the German ambassador and the grand vizier put their signatures to the document. It read:

> His Majesty the German Emperor, King of Prussia, and His Majesty the Ottoman Emperor, desirous of reaffirming the ties of amity which unite their Empires, and deciding to this effect to conclude a defensive alliance, have named their plenipotentiaries . . . who . . . have agreed to the following:
>
> I. The Two High Contracting Parties engage mutually to give aid, if need be with all their armed forces, in the event that one of them shall be the object of an attack on the part of either Russia, France, or England or a coalition composed of at least two Balkan states.
>
> II. Concerning England, the engagement assumed by Germany will come into effect only in the event that Turkey finds itself engaged in a simultaneous conflict with England and a second European state, where there is a concerted action by these two states or an armed action on the part of one European state against Turkey during which the latter finds itself at war with England.
>
> III. The present accord shall be in force from the date of signature and shall remain valid to July 8, 1920, in conformity with the stipulations

[20] Ibid., no. 10, Berchtold to Pallavicini, 5 January 1915; a copy of Berchtold's instructions was sent to Hohenlohe in Berlin as no. 19, on the same day; no. 19, Pallavicini to Berchtold, 6 January; no. 3/P, Pallavicini to Berchtold, 7 January.

of the treaty concluded by Germany and Austria-Hungary on December 5, 1912.

IV. Unless it is denounced by one of the High Contracting Parties one year prior to the date as stated above, the present accord will continue to be in force for a new period of six years, to July 8, 1926. In the event that Germany and Austria-Hungary fail to agree to extend the treaty existing between them beyond the date indicated, as mentioned above in Article III, Germany agrees to waive from that time on its right to denounce the present convention.

V. The Two High Contracting Parties intend to conclude, as soon as peace shall be reestablished, a special military convention, having as its object the regulation of the limits and conditions under which the co-operation of their land and sea forces will be effectuated.

VI. The present accord is to be ratified by His Majesty, the German Emperor, King of Prussia, and by His Majesty, the Ottoman Emperor, and the ratifications shall be exchanged within two months from the date of signature.

VII. The present accord is to remain secret and be public only following an agreement between the Two Contracting Parties.

The Germans submitted the explicative note concerning Rumania on the same day:

It is agreed that the *casus fœderis* will not be invoked by Turkey against Italy or Rumania while these states are the allies of Germany.

On January 12, the grand vizier accepted this note in writing.[21] If the Austrian ally had finally agreed to place no barriers in the way of a German-Turkish defensive alliance, it is significant that its reluctance to sign a similar document was not at an end. While the Turkish government pressed the Monarchy on the point, Vienna merely declared that its formal concurrence to the German-Turkish accord would soon follow. This concurrence did not come until March 21, and then it was given only through an exchange of formal notes. Further than this the Ballhausplatz would not go. The exchange might have been delayed still further, had it not been for Pallavicini's warning that the Turks might feel Austria had "left them in the lurch." Count Stephan Burian, who replaced Berchtold as Austrian foreign minister in January, proved as hesitant as his predecessor, if not more so. In his instructions to Pallavicini on March 11 he called attention to the need for the utmost secrecy on the whole matter. The Italians still did not

[21] GFMA, ser. 1, reel 13, no. 72, Berlin to Wangenheim, 9 January 1915; no. 102, Wangenheim to Berlin, 11 January. For the original text of the alliance, see copy attached to no. A.S. 383. Staatsarchiv, PA, box 521, report no. 6/P, Pallavicini to Berchtold, 16 January 1915. The report contains a copy of the alliance and explicative note.

know of the alliance with Turkey, and Austrian relations with Rome were ticklish enough at the time without increasing the problem through a leak. Even as late as July 29, 1915, the Turks were still trying to commit the Austrians as deeply as they could. Halil Bey suggested that the exchange of notes actually be ratified by the respective sovereigns. Pallavicini cut him off by pointing out that "sovereigns only ratify true treaties, not notes."[22]

The whole episode disclosed a Turkish diplomatic victory on the one hand while on the other it demonstrated basic differences in the way Germany and Austria were to look at diplomatic affairs during the war. Although in final form the alliance proved less comprehensive than the Turks had hoped it might, it gave them much broader commitments than they had ever had before. The accord associated them with the Dual Alliance itself, and that not merely for the duration of the war but also in peace-time. Turkish diplomatic isolation in the event of future conflict with the great powers of Europe or with Balkan states was now at an end.

As far as Germany was concerned, the principle of expediency dominated its policy. Bethmann-Hollweg did not like the idea of extending the initial alliance when this was first proposed by Halil Bey, but the uppermost consideration was to win the war. Rather than create enmity with a wartime ally, the Wilhelmstrasse accepted the idea of a second and broader accord. But in so doing the Germans were careful enough to modify the important clauses of the arrangement so as not to make Germany the cat's-paw of Constantinople.

While Germany was willing to take whatever steps were necessary to win the war, whether entirely desirable or not, Austria would not surrender its own future welfare to the war effort as a whole. This parochial attitude is understandable, considering the importance of the Balkan states to Austria's well-being. Any arrangement which concerned these Balkan states would produce an immediate Austrian wariness, merely because of their geographical proximity to the Empire, if for no other reason. Small wonder that the Ballhausplatz came to play the role of diplomatic "brilliant second" when it came to a far-reaching agreement with Turkey. Austria did not like the way the alliance was set up, and without provision for a military convention it is highly unlikely that the Monarchy would have gone along even to such a limited extent as it did.

[22] Ibid., no. 114, Pallavicini to Burian, 10 February 1915; no. 107, Burian to Pallavicini, 13 February; report no. 19/P, Pallavicini to Burian, 6 March; no. 1538, Burian to Pallavicini, 11 March; no. 265, Pallavicini to Burian, 21 March; report no 62/P, Pallavicini to Burian, 29 July.

Campaigns and Supply

While the negotiations for a broader alliance were taking place in November and December of 1914, Turkey began its military action. To the chagrin of the Central Powers, Turkey's acceptance of belligerent status produced a new set of worries which continued to plague diplomatic and military circles for the next year. As the months wore on a major concern for Germany and Austria became that of trying to keep the Ottoman war effort from collapsing.

By February it had been demonstrated that the Turkish armies were not capable of successful offensives against the Entente. The initial war plans of Enver had called for holding to the defensive against the Russians in the Transcaucasus area, but when the Turks declared war in November, the Russian forces there were already operational. Led by General Ivanovich Voronzov, these forces drew first blood when they struck to the southwest from Kars toward Erzerum and came in contact with the Turkish Third Army, then commanded by Hassan Izzet Pasha. It was now that Enver decided to take personal command on the Caucasian front. On December 6 he informed Liman von Sanders of his plan to sail immediately for Trebizond, taking with him an additional army corps to bolster the three already deployed. His intention was to advance on Sarikamish from Erzerum, with one corps approaching frontally while two others wheeled to the north and east through the mountain passes. Their aim was to envelop the Russian right flank, cut the line of communication between Sarikamish and Kars, and isolate and destroy the Russian army. The new corps arriving from Constantinople would advance up the Choruk valley, cross the mountains, and cut the railway line between Kars and Tiflis. Once this had been done, Enver envisaged the furtherance of his Pan-Turanist goal—an advance into Afghanistan and from there to India. Liman von Sanders, amazed at Enver's recklessness, vigorously opposed the whole idea. The height of the mountains would pose a formidable obstacle at any time, but it was now the middle of winter and the snow in the passes stood meter-high, the roads were poor, and supply would be extremely difficult. On this basis he refused to support the plan. Enver, with the backing of his German chief of staff, Friedrich Bronsart von Schellendorff, and Wangenheim, went ahead with his project.[23]

The result of the campaign was utter catastrophe for the Turkish units. Improperly equipped and undertrained, the Turks for over three

[23] Maurice Larcher, *La Guerre Turque dans la Guerre Mondiale*, pp. 83, 89; Winston S. Churchill, *The Unknown War: The Eastern Front*, pp. 269–70; Pomiankowski, *Zusammenbruch*, pp. 98, 102, 104; Otto Liman von Sanders, *Five Years in Turkey*, pp. 37–39.

weeks faced temperatures of 20 to 25 degrees below zero centigrade. Thousands froze in the mountains or died for lack of rations. Elements of the army still able to face the Russians were easily defeated and turned back. Of the original 90,000 men composing the Third Army, 12,000 survived. Enver Pasha kept the figures a secret.[24]

By January 4 the defeat in the Caucasus was apparent, but there was in preparation another offensive which, if successful, would have a profound effect on the war situation—the Turkish attack on Egypt with the Suez Canal as the primary target. Colonel Kress von Kressenstein had been sent to Syria in September to initiate the preparations. Liman von Sanders opposed this venture on the grounds that such an attack could at best succeed only temporarily. His objections overruled by Enver, Wangenheim, and Berlin, he could only watch with disapproval as Djemal Pasha left for Damascus to become the commander of the Egyptian expedition. Djemal had no illusions about the difficulties of his task, but he hoped that, with a bit of luck, the venture might succeed. The British troops outnumbered his 16,000 men by more than two to one, but the enemy had to guard a canal over 100 miles long. Counting on the element of surprise, he might be victorious if his troops attacked where they were not expected.[25]

While Enver's real enemy in the Caucasus campaign had been the winter, Djemal was plagued by the problems of the desert. The offensive could not be started until December or January, for only then was there sufficient rain to meet water needs. Also there existed a shortage of equipment necessary to transport artillery over desert wastes. As things developed the campaign was not undertaken until the very end of January. Then, after a week's march made entirely under the cover of darkness, the Turkish force stood ready to attack the canal. On the night of February 2–3 the fighting began, and by 4:00 P.M. of February 3, Djemal had given the order to retreat. The British forces were initially caught off balance but they recovered very quickly and seized the initiative. Djemal, realizing his troops would be needed for a possible defense of Syria and Palestine, refused the pleas of von Kressenstein for a fight to the last man.[26]

Thus, Austrian hopes for a Russian diversion in the Transcaucasus

---

[24] Pomiankowski, *Zusammenbruch*, p. 103; Churchill, *Unknown War*, pp. 270–71; Liman, *Five Years in Turkey*, p. 40.

[25] Liman, *Five Years in Turkey*, pp. 26, 43; Pomiankowski, *Zusammenbruch*, p. 10, Djemal Pasha, *Memories of a Turkish Statesman*, p. 155.

[26] Djemal Pasha, *Memories of a Turkish Statesman*, pp. 152–55; Pomiankowski, *Zusammenbruch*, p. 100; Larcher, *La Guerre Turque*, pp. 89–90; Liman, *Five Years in Turkey*, pp. 43–45; Djemal Pasha, *Memories of a Turkish Statesman*, p. 157.

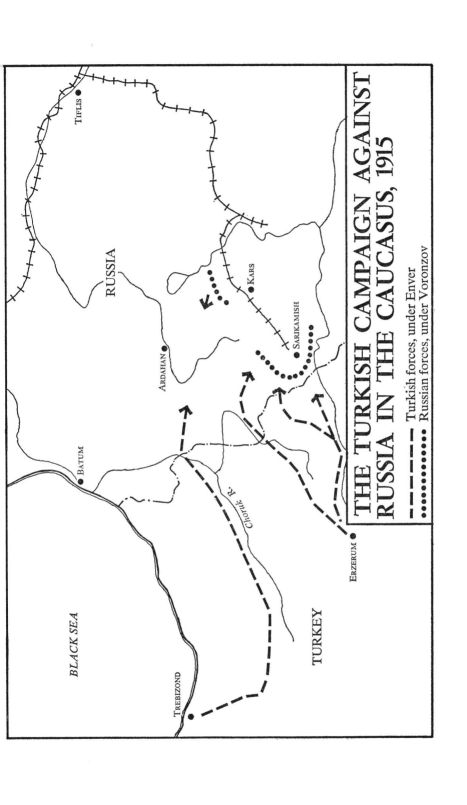

THE TURKISH CAMPAIGN AGAINST
RUSSIA IN THE CAUCASUS, 1915

Turkish forces, under Enver
Russian forces, under Voronzov

BLACK SEA

RUSSIA

TURKEY

TIFLIS

BATUM

ARDAHAN

KARS

SARIKAMISH

TREBIZOND

Choruk R.

ERZERUM

area had been shattered after a month's campaign, and German dreams of crippling the lifeline of Britain evaporated overnight. In 1915 no further attempts at offensive action were made by the Turks in either direction.

On March 18, six weeks after the Turkish attempt on Egypt, British naval units bombarded the forts at the Dardanelles and tried unsuccessfully to force the Straits. The Germans had been working feverishly for months to strengthen Turkish coastal defenses and adjacent waters against the possibility of just such an attack. Since August, 1914, artillery experts, engineers, and skilled German technicians had been sent to Turkey from the artillery school at Juterborg, the Kiel arsenal, and the western front. Between the entry to the Straits and the inner fortifications themselves, eight batteries of field howitzers had been mounted. Modern, rapid-fire cannon were placed at various locations along the coasts, interspersed with groups of dummy batteries intended to draw enemy fire. Nine rows of mines had been sown in the waters, with light guns mounted on the banks to destroy mine sweepers. Against the threat of U-boat attack an anti-submarine net had been dropped to a depth of over ninety feet. These defenses were formidable enough to defeat the British naval attempt, but German and Austrian leaders both in Constantinople and at home were deeply concerned. The problem they faced was simple enough to state but extremely difficult to solve: how to supply the Turkish ally with sufficient munitions as well as various other war materiel.[27]

On August 6, four days after the signing of the first German-Turkish Alliance, Enver Pasha made his first request to Wangenheim for munitions. Turkey needed a half million artillery shells, 200,000 rifles, and various additional supplies. As the weeks went on the list got longer—howitzers, trucks, electrical equipment, uniforms, and canned food. General Erich von Falkenhayn, then German war minister, agreed to pay the costs for meeting these needs out of German army funds. The most important items—the guns and ammunition—could be supplied by Krupp, but the real problem lay in transporting the weapons to Constantinople.[28]

The simplest route of transport was to Budapest and from there by rail through Serbia and Bulgaria to Constantinople. With Serbia still very much in the war, this route was impossible. An alternative lay in shipment from Budapest down the Danube to the Bulgarian river port

---

[27] Larcher, *La Guerre Turque*, p. 201; Pomiankowski, *Zusammenbruch*, pp. 112, 114; Churchill, *Unknown War*, pp. 305–6.

[28] Ulrich Trumpener, "German Military Aid to Turkey in 1914: An Historical Re-evaluation," *Journal of Modern History* 32, no. 2 (June 1960): 146–47.

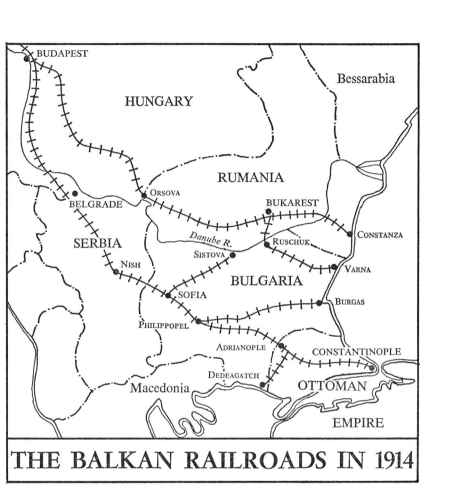

BUDAPEST

HUNGARY

Bessarabia

RUMANIA

Orsova

BELGRADE

BUKAREST

SERBIA

Danube R.

RUSCHUK

CONSTANZA

Nish

Sistova

VARNA

BULGARIA

SOFIA

BURGAS

Philippopel

Adrianople

CONSTANTINOPLE

Dedeagatch

Macedonia

OTTOMAN

EMPIRE

THE BALKAN RAILROADS IN 1914

of Sistova, where goods would continue by train, or to Ruschuk and from there by rail to the Bulgarian port of Varna on the Black Sea, and once again by water along the coast to the Turkish capital. The fact that Serbian guns were trained on the section of the Danube from Belgrade to Orsova made that route risky. The final route was by the railroad leading through Rumania to the Bulgarian border at Ruschuk and from there either to Varna, or up the Danube to Sistova, and thence to Turkey via Sofia, Philippopel, and Adrianople. It was the Rumanian route that was used during the first months of the war. Unfortunately, the Rumanians proved less and less amenable to allowing passage of munitions through their country. While neutral, the government was pro-Russian. It therefore reduced the number of freight cars which it permitted over the Bulgarian border to a mere trickle of some eight per day. On October 2 Bratianu, head of the Rumanian government, announced that no further shipments would be allowed at all. The use of bribery and the labelling of crates as "machine parts" had little effect. By November, when Turkey declared its belligerency, 200 cars loaded with war essentials lay motionless on German and Austrian sidings.[29]

The issue of supplying Turkey remained paramount for over a year, and indeed, became a burning question not only for the military leaders of the Central Powers but for the diplomats as well. Wangenheim had taken the measure of Turkish strength in September, when he wrote that considering the lack of any Rumanian assurance of through-passage for munitions, the Central Powers could count on Turkey's lasting four to six weeks in a shooting war. On November 13 he suggested that since Rumania had completely closed the shipment route to Turkey, the way would have to be cleared by occupying the northeast corner of Serbia, thus freeing the Danube. Zimmermann sent Falkenhayn a long *Denkschrift* on the matter in which he considered what might happen if the Ottomans succumbed to an enemy attack. He warned that if the Turks were forced to sue for peace the Central Powers might well see all the Balkan states joining the Entente. Therefore, the Turks would have to be supported to the fullest extent, and this meant that all other military considerations must be subordinated to an all-out offensive against Serbia. Falkenhayn could not at the moment proceed with this offensive, for he lacked the necessary troops. Both he and

[29] Carl Mühlmann, *Das Deutsch-Türkische Waffenbündnis im Weltkriege*, map 2 (see above, page 113); Carl Mühlmann, *Oberste Heeresleitung und Balkan im Weltkrieg*, pp. 72–73; Mühlmann also discusses the unsuccessful attempts in December 1914 and March 1915 to run the gauntlet of Serbian guns on the Danube; see his pp. 65, 99–100; see also Trumpener, "German Military Aid to Turkey," pp. 148–49.

General Conrad, much more concerned with the Russian armies in Poland, had first to stem the tide on the eastern front before they could look elsewhere. Besides, it did seem by the end of November that the Austrian forces already assigned to the Serbian theater might be enough. Under Oskar Potiorek the Austrians had taken Belgrade and the Serbian resistance appeared to be breaking. Then in the opening days of December came the strong counterattack of the Serbs and the retreat of the Austrian armies. By the beginning of the new year, the ray of hope for opening a road to Turkey had disappeared. The Serbs had driven their enemy back across the Danube.[30]

When in December, after surveying the military situation in the east, Falkenhayn decided that things were favorable enough to give attention to a special offensive against the Serbs, he talked with Conrad. The Austrian general refused to consider the move. He was convinced that the whole Balkan problem and that of supplying Turkey would be solved by the destruction of Russia. On this basis he refused to allot the necessary troops for a new Serbian campaign, and he consistently held to this position in January and February. Meanwhile, reports from Constantinople continued to speak of Turkey's grave condition as to military needs. Admiral Usedom, commanding the fortifications at the Dardanelles, estimated that the Straits could be held against one attack, but there was not enough ammunition to hold against two. Enver Pasha contacted Falkenhayn at the beginning of March and asserted that the opening of a route through Serbia was a question of life or death for Turkey. The German chief of staff answered that a Serbian campaign could not now be mounted. Aside from the poor weather and road conditions, it was questionable whether such a campaign, even if successful, could alleviate the Turkish lack of war supplies rapidly enough to be of profound significance.[31]

Falkenhayn had, throughout the early months of 1915, been heavily pressed by Bethmann-Hollweg, Jagow, and Zimmermann to attack the Serbs. On March 16 he lost his patience and sent off to Jagow a summation of the matter. It was not a question of a Serbian offensive depending on the goodwill of the German army. The problems on the eastern front far outweighed the attack desired by the Foreign Office. He pointed specifically to the miscarriage of the offensive against the Russians in the Carpathians. If anything was to be done against Serbia,

[30] GFMA, ser. 1, reel 13, no. 779, Wangenheim to Berlin, 11 September 1914; GFMA, St. Anthony Collection, reel 46, no. AS 2642, Wangenheim to Berlin, 13 November; Mühlmann, *Oberste Heeresleitung*, pp. 56–57, 58, 61; Churchill, *Unknown War*, pp. 268–69.
[31] Mühlmann, *Oberste Heeresleitung*, pp. 64, 80–81, 84–85.

it required Austrian cooperation—troops which, considering the serious Russian threat, Conrad von Hötzendorf would not allocate.[32]

Two days after Falkenhayn made this statement, the British navy attacked the Dardanelles. Although the attack was beaten off, the Turkish stock of artillery shells was reduced by one-third in the process. The question of munitions transport now took on even greater importance, especially after reports filtered through that the Entente was staging units in Egypt for an attempted land assault. Since their fleet had been unsuccessful, the British would use the army to capture the Straits. The Turks and Germans in Constantinople worked furiously to prepare for the new attack. Solely for purposes of protecting the narrows, Enver Pasha formed the Fifth Army—five divisions of infantry and a cavalry brigade—under the command of Liman von Sanders. The Germans had roughly a month's time to make preparations against the landing. When the enemy attack came on April 25 the Turkish forces of 60,000 men faced an Entente superiority of 30,000. Turkish stocks of artillery ammunition were woefully inadequate. Fortunately, however, there were plenty of cartridges to supply rifle and machine gun needs. This fact, along with the courage of the Turkish troops and the confusion of the enemy at crucial moments, allowed the Turks to successfully withstand the initial Entente offensive.[33]

Even though the Serbian campaign did not materialize at this time, attempts at supplying the beleaguered Turks did not slacken. At the end of March the Germans tried to send a steamer loaded with artillery shells and mines down the Danube. Just below Belgrade, Serbian guns blew it out of the water. Various other plans to get the necessary supplies to Constantinople were considered. Perhaps neutral ships could carry the ammunition to the port of Dedeagatch on the Aegean, whence it could be sent to Constantinople by rail; or perhaps a fast Austrian cruiser could steam to the Asia Minor coast with the important cargo. Patrols of the British and French fleet in the Mediterranean made such schemes impossible to realize. There was even the far-fetched suggestion that munitions be sent by manned balloons, which would be blown by favorable winds from southern Hungary to Bulgaria, whence the supplies could go on by rail. In the end the only methods by which Turkey was supplied in the spring months of 1915 were by German submarines and smuggling through Rumania. Neither was sufficient to meet Turkish needs.[34]

[32] Ibid., pp. 85–88.

[33] Pomiankowski, *Zusammenbruch*, pp. 124, 130–31; Liman, *Five Years in Turkey*, pp. 56, 57, 62, 75; Larcher, *La Guerre Turque*, p. 94.

[34] Mühlmann, *Oberste Heeresleitung*, p. 100.

By April both Falkenhayn and the German Foreign Office had succeeded in gaining consent from the Austrian High Command to mount a Serbian campaign. Conrad approved the date for the offensive —the second half of May. Underlying his approval, however, was his expectation at this time that Bulgaria would take part in the action. When it became clear that Sofia was not ready to act with the Central Powers, the Austrian general refused to carry through with the attack. His refusal was also based on two recent events: the German-Austrian breakthrough in Galicia in April and the negative turn taken by the Austro-Italian negotiations in late April and early May. The success in Galicia offered Conrad the great possibility of crippling the Russians once and for all; he therefore insisted that all available troops be concentrated in the east. Whatever units might be left over had to be reserved to ward off an Italian thrust, which seemed likely to occur in the near future. These Austrian considerations, and the fact that Falkenhayn could not muster sufficient German divisions to take on the Serbs alone, resulted in a further delay in freeing a Serbian passage to Constantinople.[35]

On May 20 Foreign Secretary Jagow summed up the situation in a wire to Wangenheim. His chief question was whether Turkey could continue the war if no passage for munitions through Serbia could now be obtained. Wangenheim's answer was not so discouraging as Jagow had feared. The Turks were determined to fight to the last man. They had enough ammunition to last a month; if the Russians were unable to effect a landing from the Black Sea, if no sizable reinforcements were landed by the British and French, and if enough arms could somehow be smuggled over the Rumanian borders, they might hold for two months. But beyond this the Turks could not stand.[36]

Turkish-Bulgarian Affairs

With only thirty to sixty days in which Germany and Austria could solve the Turkish problem, the work of the diplomats became once again a crucial factor. Negotiations with Bulgaria became inextricably bound to the plight of Turkish forces. Talks aimed at active Bulgarian support had been going on unprofitably since August, 1914. The Bulgarians bargained for gains in Macedonia, looked fearfully at Ru-

[35] GFMA, ser. 2, reel 13, no. 624, von Tschirschky in Vienna to Berlin, 1 April 1915; no. 51, Bethmann-Hollweg at general headquarters to the Foreign Office, 8 April; no. 195, Michahelles in Sofia to Berlin, 8 May; no. 504, Jagow to Falkenhayn, 18 May; no. 67, Falkenhayn to Bethmann, 20 May; no. 987, Jagow to Wangenheim, 20 May.

[36] Ibid., no. 987, Jagow to Wangenheim, 20 May 1915; no. 1189, Wangenheim to Jagow, 22 May.

mania—which might attack if Sofia sent troops against Serbia—and distrusted the Turks in Thrace. While the Russian moves on the eastern front had been parried, the Bulgarian government had yet to be convinced that the Central Powers would win. Nevertheless, the endeavors of the German and Austrian ministers in Sofia to obtain a Bulgarian commitment had not ceased by the spring of 1915. In May the urgency of a Serbian campaign to relieve the Turkish ally drove them to redouble their efforts.[37]

Concurrently with talks on the question of Bulgarian acquisitions in Macedonia, a strong attempt was made to obtain some kind of alliance between Bulgaria and Turkey. The Austrians played a major role in bringing the two powers together. Both Pallavicini and Burian saw that an accord between the two was more than just a means of getting the Bulgarians to aid in a Serbian offensive. Bulgarian-Turkish cooperation would affect the whole Balkan picture because it would negate the possibilities of a Rumanian or Greek attack against the Central Powers; neither Rumania nor Greece would move for fear of having to face a Bulgarian-Turkish combination. Burian saw, too, that if Turkey was to be of assistance against a belligerent Italy, it could only turn against the Italian possessions in Africa if its rear in Thrace was protected against a possible Bulgarian assault.[38]

The Bulgarian minister in Constantinople had merely to suggest to Pallavicini on May 21 that if Turkey granted the Maritza River as a border between Bulgaria and Turkish Thrace, giving the Bulgarians an unbroken railroad connection from Burgas to Dedeagatch, Sofia would then agree to an offensive-defensive alliance with Constantinople. The diplomats immediately went to work. Burian agreed that the Maritza line constituted a just basis for negotiation and he instructed Tarnowski in Sofia to sound Radoslavov on the issue. Pallavicini was told to work in close conjunction with his German colleague in Constantinople and to secure the alliance without delay. Berlin sent similar instructions to its representatives in both countries.[39]

Negotiations toward the desired Bulgarian-Turkish accord proved extremely difficult. Although Wangenheim had instructions from Berlin to work for such an agreement, he was not convinced this was the proper approach. His hesitancy stemmed from his belief that while

[37] Ibid., no. 67, Falkenhayn to Bethmann-Hollweg, 20 May 1915. Bulgarian relations with the Central Powers are considered in detail in chapters 6 and 7 below.

[38] Staatsarchiv, PA, box 873, no. 388, Pallavicini to Burian, 19 May 1915; no. 452, Burian to Hohenlohe in Berlin, 19 May. The latter recapitulates an instruction to Pallavicini which examined the implications of a Bulgarian-Turkish alliance.

[39] Ibid., no. 391, Pallavicini to Burian, 21 May 1915; no. 316, Burian to Pallavicini, 23 May; no. 234, Hohenlohe to Burian, 20 May. See map below, p. 125.

Bulgarian participation was necessary to defeat Serbia and clear the passage to Turkey, this participation would be gained only when Sofia was sure it need not worry about Rumania. In turn, the Rumanians could only be placated by Austrian territorial concessions in Hungarian-controlled Transylvania, and these concessions the Ballhausplatz could not make, simply because the Hungarians refused to consider them. Pallavicini not only was hampered by a German colleague who took a half-hearted attitude toward his scheme, but found it hard to deal with Turkish officialdom as well. The grand vizier believed, as did Wangenheim, that the key to Bulgarian action was Austrian concessions to Rumania. Pallavicini, after long talks, convinced Said Halim that these could not be made and gained his willingness to consider negotiating with Sofia on the basis of the Maritza line. While Talaat Bey and Enver Pasha objected to giving up the right bank of the river, since it would militarily expose Adrianople to Bulgarian attack, the Austrian ambassador finally succeeded in winning their approval to proceed with his desired project. The Turks, however, would not at this point consider any talk of concessions unless the Bulgarians took immediate military action.[40]

Radoslavov's policy was to play a cautious game, and he therefore offered only a benevolent neutrality in exchange for territorial concessions on the part of Turkey. He wanted not merely the Maritza River. He wanted the border in Thrace to be delineated by a line running between Enos and Midia. The grand vizier answered that if Bulgaria wanted Enos-Midia it would have to take it and his implication was clear.[41]

Not only did negotiations appear to be in danger of breaking down at this point, but there was also talk in Constantinople of open conflict between the two countries. Enver Pasha declared that he had been expecting the Bulgarians to attack since the start of the war, was prepared for them, and would be successful against them. Pallavicini, who was not impressed by such bravado, particularly in the light of Turkey's difficulties in the field, smoothed things over as best he could. He wrote to Burian that Sofia's request for concessions without offering anything in return was hardly workable, an observation with which Burian agreed. The Ballhausplatz instructed Tarnowski in Sofia to tell Radoslavov that "Austria-Hungary would never advise Turkey to take part in such a disadvantageous trade." Jagow, in Berlin, approved of Burian's attitude. Unable to push the Turks with regard to

---

[40] Staatsarchiv, PA, box 873, nos. 401 and 402, Pallavicini to Burian, 25 May 1915; report no. 39/P A-E, Pallavicini to Burian, 27 May.
[41] Ibid., no. 417, Pallavicini to Burian, 31 May 1915.

Enos-Midia, Radoslavov now went back to the idea of obtaining the Maritza River as a border, and negotiations were resumed.[42]

As June progressed the deadlock between the Bulgarians and Turks continued. Whereas Sofia insisted on the rectification of borders in Thrace, the Turks demanded that Bulgaria offer something in return. Radoslavov refused to go further than the promise of neutrality. Constantinople declared that this simply was not enough. By July 1, Pallavicini was discouraged and took a gloomy view of prospects for success. Constantinople continued to distrust Bulgaria, while the latter felt it was in a position to drive a hard bargain. To a considerable extent Sofia was able to do just this because the Entente had offered the Enos-Midia line in return for participation. The constant threat of Entente offers which might tempt the Bulgarians to declare against the Central Powers meant that the latter would have to pay a price to assure even benevolent neutrality on the part of Bulgaria, and this applied to Turkey as well. Even if Serbia should be defeated, any through passage of munitions to Turkey would be impossible without Bulgarian cooperation. As a matter of fact, Berlin was so concerned over the danger of the Dardanelles' falling that the Foreign Office declared Turkey ought to conclude with the Bulgarians at any price. Even the Enos-Midia line was not seen as too much to concede if it meant saving the Straits. Radoslavov knew that he was in a very strong position.[43]

On July 1, to help bring about a more positive Turkish attitude, Falkenhayn wrote to Enver Pasha that an understanding with Bulgaria was of pressing necessity, and he therefore suggested that Constantinople not delay in negotiating because of any worries it might have over the safety of Adrianople. On July 5 the Turks assented to Falkenhayn's remarks but the *sine qua non* for conceding the Maritza remained Bulgaria's immediate participation in the war. Radoslavov still refused to take the step.[44]

The whole issue was finally resolved by Germany and Austria. It was they who had been negotiating with the Bulgarians over Mace-

---

[42] Ibid., no. 417, Pallavicini to Burian, 31 May 1915; no. 252, Burian to Tarnowski in Sofia, 29 May; no. 332, Burian to Pallavicini, 31 May, explains the German position as reported by Hohenlohe to Vienna; no. 433, Pallavicini to Burian, 5 June; the last explains the grand vizier's being once again willing to talk of concessions, that is, the Maritza line.

[43] Ibid., report no. 44/P A-E, Pallavicini to Burian, 10 June 1915; report no. 47/P B, Pallavicini to Burian, 18 June; report no. 49/P B, Pallavicini to Burian, 24 June; no. 510, Pallavicini to Burian, 1 July; GFMA, ser. 2, reel 14, no. 1256, Jagow to Wangenheim, 1 July.

[44] Staatsarchiv, PA, box 873, no. 293, Hohenlohe to Burian, 1 July 1915; no. 524, Pallavicini to Burian, 5 July.

donia and who now agreed to sweeping concessions there. Impressed by the military successes of the Central Powers on the eastern front and by the war booty to be gained through establishing an open alliance with Berlin and Vienna, Sofia proceeded to take up negotiations for this alliance in July. On the twenty-third of the month Colonel Peter Gantscheff, the Bulgarian military representative, was ordered to German headquarters at Pless to consider a military agreement with Falkenhayn, while the German and Austrian ministers worked with Radoslavov to complete the terms of a diplomatic accord. One of the tidbits dangled before Bulgarian noses was the Maritza line in Thrace, which was promised if Bulgaria offered open military aid. At the same time Pallavicini, working in Constantinople, pointed out that since the fate of Turkey hung in the balance, sacrifices were necessary. The aim of his discussion was to soften the attitude of the grand vizier and make him more amenable to the increased demands the Bulgarians were about to submit. On July 25 it had been ascertained by Tarnowski that the Bulgarian diplomat Totschkoff was on his way to Constantinople. He would request that concessions be extended now to include both banks of the Maritza and the town of Kirkilisse.[45]

The new discussions proved fruitless. The Turks refused the new Bulgarian demands, and Totschkoff, had it not been for the pleas of Pallavicini, would have broken off talks and returned home. The most obstinate of the Turks proved to be Enver and Talaat, neither of whom would grant Bulgaria both banks of the Maritza. Most certainly they would not agree to give up Kirkilisse, which would have only increased Bulgarian control in what was seen as a rightful Turkish possession, rightful if for no other reason than because of the Muslim population living here. Both Germany and Austria supported the Turkish refusal to concede the town and declared the Bulgarian request too extreme. On August 11 Sofia answered by recalling Totschkoff from Constantinople.[46]

With the beginning of August, 1915, the diplomatic situation was poor and the military only a little better. The Turkish armies at the Dardanelles had managed to hold against the British and French at-

[45] Ibid., no. 806, Tarnowski in Sofia to Burian, 25 July 1915; no. 568, Pallavicini to Burian, 27 July. For a detailed discussion of Colonel Gantscheff's mission and the decision of Bulgaria to enter the war on the side of the Central Powers, see chapter 7 below.
[46] Staatsarchiv, PA, box 873, nos. 571 and 575, Pallavicini to Burian, 30 and 31 July 1915; no. 591, Pallavicini to Burian, 6 August; no. 419, Burian to Pallavicini, 3 August; no. 373, Burian to Tarnowski, 7 August; no. 887, Tarnowski to Burian, 11 August; no. 894, Tarnowski to Burian, 12 August.

tacks. Catastrophe had been averted by the recent construction of a munitions factory at Constantinople, by the discovery of a forgotten ammunition dump, by the failure of a Russian offensive to materialize against the Straits, and by the shrewd handling of the Turkish forces by Liman von Sanders and Enver. Although a period of stabilization set in after the initial assaults, the British began a new attack on August 6. The need for ammunition seemed more pressing than ever.[47]

The new attack on the Straits now led to a solution of the Turkish-Bulgarian impasse. On July 30 and 31 Falkenhayn had written to Enver explaining that the Serbian campaign hinged on agreement being reached with Gantscheff at Pless, and he therefore asked the Turks to accept Bulgarian demands in order to help him in his own attempts at successful negotiation. Constantinople held off as long as possible, though it again entered conversations with the Bulgarian representatives. Because Radoslavov now sought to conclude an alliance with the Central Powers, the Bulgarians dropped the demand for Kirkilisse. On August 17 Enver asked Falkenhayn whether Turkey could count on a German-Austrian action against the Serbs were Bulgaria to refuse its support or to go over to the side of the enemy. When Falkenhayn answered that in this case an operation against Serbia would no longer be considered, the Turkish government decided to give way. Five days later, on the twenty-second, an agreement was reached between Bulgaria and Turkey. Significantly, the actual signing was delayed until September 6, the day Bulgaria formally committed itself to the side of the Central Powers by signing an alliance and military convention with the Germans and Austrians.[48]

The terms of the Turkish-Bulgarian agreement provided for a new border in Thrace which gave Bulgaria not only the right bank of the Maritza but also the left bank to a depth of 2 kilometers. The border ran a distance of approximately 225 kilometers from where the Tundza River crossed the old border north of Adrianople to the mouth of the Maritza on the Aegean Sea. The railroad which ran from Dedeagatch northward to the Bulgarian Black Sea port of Burgas thus would be

[47] Liman, *Five Years in Turkey*, pp. 75, 83; Pomiankowski, *Zusammenbruch*, pp. 128, 132.

[48] GFMA, ser. 2, reel 14, nos. 240 and 244, Treutler at Pless to the Foreign Office in Berlin, 30 and 31 July 1915; Staatsarchiv, PA, box 873, no. 887, Tarnowski to Burian, 11 August; no. 591, Burian to Hohenlohe in Berlin, 17 August, explaining to Hohenlohe the new proposals of the Bulgarians; no. 628, Pallavicini to Burian, 18 August; memo no. 4225, Foreign Office, 22 August; this memo declares the agreement concluded; GFMA, ser. 2, reel 14, nos. 302 and 305, Treutler to the Foreign Office, 17 August; these telegrams inform the Foreign Office of the exchange between Enver and Falkenhayn; Staatsarchiv, PA, box 873, no. 1037, Tarnowski to Burian, 7 September.

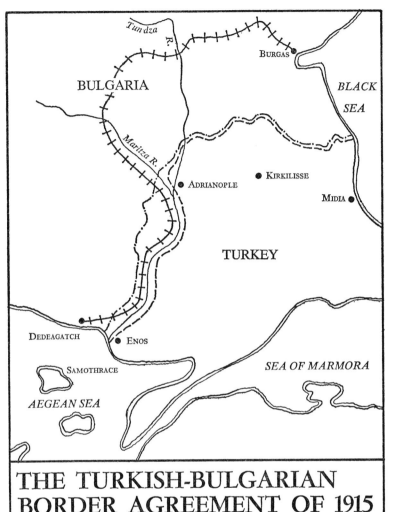

THE TURKISH-BULGARIAN
BORDER AGREEMENT OF 1915

_._._._._ Previous border

_____ New border

entirely under the control of the Bulgarians, though the Turks were to have the right to free use of the road for a period of five years and would obtain equal treatment with regard to shipment of goods on the Maritza itself. The borders were to be drawn by a delimitation commission consisting of one Austrian, one German, and one Swiss representative. It is interesting that this commission did not complete its work until November 20, since it faced the constant squabblings of Bulgarian and Turkish officials assigned to the project. Continual distrust and hostile feeling between the two groups made the work of the commission difficult to conclude and reflected the expedient nature of the agreement.[49]

Seen by itself, the agreement reached on border rectification was a minor one, but it played an important role in the broader context of solving the munitions problem for Turkey and of obtaining for the Germans and Austrians another ally. On the face of it, the accord was entirely one-sided, since it spoke only of concessions to Bulgaria. The price of immediate participation set by Turkey, however, was exacted by the Germans and Austrians in the alliance signed by Bulgaria with their representatives on September 6, and the Turks themselves formally agreed to nothing until they were sure that participation would definitely be forthcoming. They were in no way pleased over conceding additional areas in Thrace to the Bulgarians, but the Turkish leaders faced more than a munitions problem. Foodstocks and essential raw materials such as coal and petroleum were running low and there were reports of discontent amongst certain groups within Turkey, which led to the fear that reaction might pull down the government. There was no alternative but to satisfy the revised Bulgarian demands.[50]

The offensive against the Serbs started in October, and by the end of the month Germany could ship 100,000 rifles and carbines to Turkey by way of the Danube. At the start of November, forces under General von Mackensen took Nish, which opened the railway route to Constantinople, so that both Germany and Austria now shipped much-needed heavy artillery and munitions. By the turn of the year the stiffening resistance of the Turkish forces and the fast-degenerating condition of British and French units caused the latter to evacuate the Gallipoli Peninsula. The Dardanelles had been saved.[51]

The cost of the campaign in casualties had been heavy for both sides,

[49] Staatsarchiv, PA, box 873, no. 1037, Tarnowski to Burian, 7 September 1915; this telegram contains a detailed copy of the agreement as it was signed between Radoslavov and Fethi Bey in Sofia; report no. 84/P B, Pallavicini to Burian, 27 November.
[50] Ibid., no. 72/P B, Pallavicini to Burian, 3 September 1915.
[51] Larcher, *La Guerre Turque*, p. 104; Liman, *Five Years in Turkey*, pp. 106–7.

but it was Turkey which had suffered the greatest. Its losses totalled a quarter of a million men. It was no wonder that when Enver began to make plans for the coming year and suggested Turkey take on military obligations against the Entente in Europe, Falkenhayn rejected his proposals. Yet, in December, 1915, both men met at Orsova and agreed on future new military campaigns in the Caucasus, Persia, and Egypt. Since Turkey had almost suffered a collapse at the hands of the Entente, these new ventures would not easily succeed, if at all.[52]

In retrospect the first seventeen months of the war reflected the disadvantages of having Turkey as an ally. It had taken almost four months of diplomatic effort on the part of both Germany and Austria to convince Turkey its best interests would be served by openly joining the Central Powers against their enemies. When the Ottoman Empire became a belligerent in November, 1914, it was hoped the Turkish armies would constitute a sufficiently dangerous threat to divert Entente forces from the major theaters of operation in western and eastern Europe. Within a few months the poor showing of the Ottomans against the Russians in the Caucasus and the English at Suez demonstrated graphically how overoptimistic some German and Austrian leaders had been in their judgment of Turkish capabilities.

The problem of munitions existed from the start as a consideration. Early in 1915 it became an increasingly serious issue, and once the Dardanelles campaign began it became a major concern of high-ranking military and diplomatic leaders in Berlin, Vienna, and the Balkans. The question of supplying the Turks transcended that of merely supporting a weak ally. It became manifestly clear that the defeat of Turkey meant the defeat of German and Austrian ambitions concerning the whole Balkan alignment. Falkenhayn and Conrad von Hötzendorf were therefore unable to devote all their thinking to defeating the major enemy powers and were forced to develop a specific Serbian campaign to bolster the Turks. In the process of setting up the offensive, Bulgaria, because of the troops it could offer, became a key element in their considerations and forced German, Austrian, and Turkish diplomats to take measures and to grant concessions and guarantees to the Bulgarians which otherwise would have been unlikely.

The munitions question was the major issue with respect to Turkey throughout most of 1915, and the necessity of its solution helped bring Bulgaria into the fold of the Central Powers. Once Bulgaria agreed to enter the war, the campaign against Serbia could be mounted. The

[52] Pomiankowski, *Zusammenbruch*, pp. 144, 184–86; Erich von Falkenhayn, *The German General Staff and Its Decisions, 1914–16*, pp. 237–38.

success of the attack led to the collapse of the Serbs, to the solution of Turkish supply problems, and to the failure of England and France to establish any connection with their Russian ally through the Mediterranean. In spite of all this, the fact that Turkey began and continued as a weak comrade-in-arms justified the caution which in October and November, 1914, was suggested by Wangenheim and Pallavicini in Constantinople: a benevolently neutral Turkey would have been of greater worth in the struggle against the Entente than a Turkey marching off to war.

Chapter 6

Bulgaria Pursued

By the end of July, 1914, diplomatic circles in Berlin and Vienna were rather sure of one thing—that the negotiations which had been in progress for a formal accord with Bulgaria were about to reach a successful conclusion. Their confidence seemed justified when on August 2, the same day that Turkey aligned itself against the Entente, the Bulgarians submitted to the German and Austrian ministers in Sofia two basic principles which they sought to have incorporated in any alliance they might sign with the Central Powers. These principles involved the following demands: first, that the Triple Alliance guarantee Bulgarian territorial integrity against any attack from any side and obligate itself to aid Bulgaria in obtaining those areas to which it had a historic and ethnic right; and second, that after a successful Austro-Serbian war, Bulgaria was to obtain Serbian Macedonia. If Rumania and Greece chose to fight with the Dreibund, Bulgaria would guarantee their continued possession of the Dobrudja and Kavalla respectively, but if they should turn hostile, Bulgarian aspirations to these areas were to be satisfied.[1]

Both Germany and Austria readily accepted these two principles. On August 4 Berlin wired Michahelles, minister in Sofia, the authorization to sign a treaty. When Michahelles informed the home office that Tarnowski had not yet received instructions, the Germans hastily contacted von Tschirschky in Vienna to prod Berchtold, though the concern of the Wilhelmstrasse was quite unnecessary. To some extent Berchtold suffered from the poor opinion of his capacities as foreign minister that was current in high circles. His great interest in sports, his frequent attendance at turf and jockey clubs, and his unconcealed pride in his reputation as the best-dressed man in the Monarchy, marked him as a dilettante in the serious affairs of the diplomatic world. Nor was his image improved by his seeming to be shy, nervous, unsure of himself, and simply too nonchalant about affairs. Observers apparently forgot that he had, before his appointment as head of the Austrian Foreign Ministry, served with distinction as ambassador to Russia. In fact, he was a man of solid experience as a professional diplomat and his communications with Tarnowski in Sofia demonstrated precision and an exact awareness of the need for quick action. On August 3 he wired the minister that Vienna concurred with the Bulgarian demands and authorized him to conclude an alliance. Two days later he sent an even stronger instruction: "In consideration of the signing of the German-Turkish Treaty, which we accept, it is of the *greatest* importance that the signing of our agreement with Bulgaria take place *immediately*."[2]

By August 6 the Austrians and Germans had submitted a draft of the desired treaty to the Bulgarian government. Essentially, this draft contained the same stipulations as those which Tarnowski had carried in his briefcase since his return from the conference with Berchtold, July 10–16, though the wording had been somewhat changed and the stipulations made more concrete. Articles II and III contained the core of the alliance and would constitute the basis for the protracted negotiations soon to begin. The most crucial of the terms were the following:

Article II. Austria-Hungary guarantees the integrity of the actual territory of Bulgaria against attack from any state insofar as this attack is made without provocation on the part of Bulgaria.

If Austria-Hungary without any provocation on its part is attacked by a state bordering on Bulgaria the *casus foederis* will be presented for the latter as soon as it shall be demanded of it.

Article III. Austria-Hungary and Bulgaria agree in the wish that the amicable connection established between the Two High Contracting Parties and Rumania not be troubled by the circumstances envisaged in the preceding articles. In connection with this Bulgaria declares that it recognizes the frontier determined by the Treaty of Bukarest between Bulgaria and Rumania as definitive, a declaration which can only be altered by an aggression on the part of Rumania in the circumstances foreseen in the preceding article.

Austria-Hungary agrees to support Bulgaria by all its means for the eventual increase of territories of Bulgaria through annexation of provinces to which it possesses historic and ethnographic rights, and which are found or shall be found under the domination of Balkan states not allied to Austria-Hungary.

[1] GFMA, ser. 2, reel 12, no. 90, Michahelles to Berlin, 3 August 1914; Staatsarchiv, PA, box 513, no. 438, Tarnowski to Vienna, 2 August.

[2] GFMA, ser. 2, reel 12, no. 211, Berlin to Michahelles, 4 August 1914; no. 46, Michahelles to Berlin, 4 August; Staatsarchiv, PA, box 513, no. 219, Berchtold to Tarnowski, 5 August; Luigi Albertini, *Origins of the War of 1914*, 3:590; Victor Naumann, *Profile*, pp. 221–22, 227, 232; Solomon Wank, "The Appointment of Count Berchtold as Austro-Hungarian Foreign Minister," *Journal of Central European Affairs* 23 (July 1963): 147, 148; Hugo Hantsch, *Leopold Graf Berchtold*, 1:241–48; Staatsarchiv, PA, box 513, no. 218, Berchtold to Tarnowski, 5 August 1914 (italics in the original).

In this case the respective governments will come to an agreement on measures to be taken with respect to cooperation of their armies. Military questions, notably that of unity of operations, will be regulated by a military convention.[3]

While initially Tarnowski raised doubts that the Bulgarians would accept Article II, since it tied them immediately to any demands which Austria might make, he nevertheless submitted the draft as it stood.

Both Vienna and Berlin had been in closest contact with respect to the method of handling the alliance and had agreed that it would not be signed by the Dreibund but by the individual powers, as the Austro-Rumanian Alliance had been in 1883. Berchtold's concern with retaining Rumanian friendship was reflected in his informing Bethmann and Jagow that he would not allow a Bulgarian agreement to run contrary to that existing with Rumania.[4]

Initial Hesitations

To submit a draft was one thing but to have it accepted was quite another. Austria now desperately wanted the participation of Bulgarian forces. Because the Rumanians seemed ready to let Bulgaria intervene in Serbia with impunity, Tarnowski was ordered to press Radoslavov to mobilize troops immediately and to send a Bulgarian staff officer to cooperate with Conrad. Participation was extremely important since if Bulgaria sent its forces against the Serbs, Austria could transfer the largest portion of its armies from that theater to the Galician front, where troops were sorely needed. Sofia, however, was not ready to accept such an obligation.

The minister-president of Bulgaria had not been trained for the foreign service, but as a thoroughly seasoned politician he proved more than able to cope with the gambits of the German and Austrian ministers. Radoslavov had studied law at Heidelberg and was Germanophile in his inclinations, but he also understood the responsibilities of high office as these were defined by the best interests and welfare of his country. On the political scene since 1884, he had served as a cabinet member in various governments. His legal training and experience as chairman of the Bulgarian National Assembly gave him a firm comprehension of how best to maneuver verbally to achieve his own ends.

[3] GFMA, ser. 2, reel 12, no. 52, Michahelles to Berlin, 5 August 1914; Staatsarchiv, PA, box 513, no. 477, Tarnowski to Berchtold, 5 August; no. 3790, treaty draft.
[4] Staatsarchiv, PA, box 513, nos. 455, 462, Tarnowski to Berchtold, 4 August 1914; no. 213, Berchtold to Tarnowski, 3 August; no. 3790, Berchtold to Szögyény, 3 August.

While physically he has been described as looking like a maitre d'hotel, his mentality far surpassed such a station. Tarnowski and Michahelles found they were dealing with a clever statesman.[5]

Radoslavov fended off the German and Austrian importunities by offering a series of logical excuses—public opinion was not yet ready for such a war because the people were war-weary and exhausted; Bulgaria was not prepared militarily and lacked the money for such a conflict. Immediate mobilization, he said, was therefore not possible. Nor did he believe mobilization could be carried out until the actual signing of an alliance treaty took place and this had not yet occurred.[6]

His capacities notwithstanding, Radoslavov lacked the power of a Bratianu. He was always subject to the desires of King Ferdinand, who chose his ministers on the basis of their pliability. Although a constitutional monarch, Ferdinand maintained a tight rein on government foreign policy by manipulating Bulgarian political leadership. Radoslavov's excuses only reflected the fact that the king was in no hurry to sign an alliance which meant active participation in the war. Michahelles wrote to Vienna that "when the king has an important decision to make, he has the noticeable penchant for getting into his auto and leaving so that he cannot be reached." With a similar ploy, a well-timed illness, Ferdinand had avoided audiences on the draft of the treaty. When, on August 15, he finally gave the Central Powers a statement, he said only that he thought the guaranteed support of Bulgarian aspirations to historic and ethnological borders was not sufficiently exact. What he wanted was a precise delineation of the prizes Bulgaria could expect to gain.[7]

Yet much more than this was behind Ferdinand's reluctance. By the middle of August the military situation, as well as the diplomatic, prompted the king to take a cautious line. Both Michahelles and Tarnowski saw that one of the great deterrents to Sofia's acceptance of the alliance was the fact that Austria had accomplished nothing of real

---

[5] *Bulgarian Encyclopaedia*, p. 1305; Marcel Dunan, *L'Été Bulgare*, p. 53; *Wiener Zeitung*, 18 July 1913, supplement, p. 2.

[6] Staatsarchiv, PA, box 513, no. 215, Berchtold to Tarnowski, 4 August 1914. Czernin in Bukarest had wired that in the meeting of the Crown Council the Rumanians had agreed to allow Bulgarian intervention in Serbia. Carol hoped this would be a reflection of Rumanian friendship toward the Central Powers. No. 459, Tarnowski to Berchtold, 4 August; Tarnowski believed the Bulgarians could send 200,000 men against the Serbs. No. 472, Tarnowski to Berchtold, 5 August; no. 555, Tarnowski to Berchtold, 12 August.

[7] GFMA, ser. 2, reel 12, no. AS 1811, Michahelles to Berlin, 14 August 1914; Staatsarchiv, PA, box 513, no. 569, Tarnowski to Berchtold, 14 August; no. 571, Tarnowski to Berchtold, 15 August.

worth against the Serbs. Before taking action, Bulgaria would wait for positive results on the part of the Austrian armies.

From Bulgaria's standpoint its diplomatic situation was difficult indeed. The Russian minister had informed Ferdinand that if Bulgaria fomented trouble in Macedonia and had any hostile plans there, Russia, since it was at war, would see such action as unfriendly. This was little more than a veiled warning to Bulgaria not to take up arms unless it wanted war with Russia. In Tarnowski's words, Ferdinand was "quite impressed." Then, too, there was the question of Greece, which, although it had declared its neutrality, had nevertheless let it be known that because of its agreement with Serbia, it would mobilize if Bulgaria did so. Greece had not openly said it would declare war but there was nothing to lead Sofia to believe it would do otherwise.[8]

Even with the possibility of Russia and Greece becoming hostile, Bulgaria might still have been prompted to take the final step if negotiations with Turkey and Rumania had gone according to its wishes. The German and Austrian representatives in Sofia, Constantinople, and Bukarest did all that was possible to bring about a workable arrangement. The Turkish grand vizier had declared that without a Turkish-Bulgarian treaty Constantinople could make no move with respect to war, and therefore Wangenheim stressed the importance of a Turkish-Bulgarian accord. By August 6 Michahelles was able to report that Sofia had instructed its ambassador in Turkey to conclude an alliance and to seek out the aid of the German and Austrian representatives for this purpose. But neither Michahelles nor Tarnowski had any illusions about the ease with which Bulgaria could conclude agreements with Turkey and Rumania that would meet its requirements. On August 16 Tarnowski informed his government that "We cannot move Bulgaria without Turkey and Rumania being absolutely secure where Bulgaria must count on a war declaration by Russia and Greece. While the Bulgarians would like to complete understandings with Rumania and Turkey, they see these as difficult to obtain, and the German ambassador is of the same impression."[9]

Berlin and Vienna were hardly comforted by such reports, and the situation was made to seem worse because Wangenheim had reported

---

[8] Staatsarchiv, PA, box 513, no. 504, Tarnowski to Berchtold, 8 August 1914; GFMA, ser. 2, reel 12, no. 64, Michahelles to Berlin, 11 August; Staatsarchiv, PA, box 513, no. 471, Tarnowski to Berchtold, 5 August; GFMA, ser. 2, reel 12, nos. 274, 279, Minister Quadt in Athens to Berlin, 11 and 12 August.

[9] GFMA, ser. 2, reel 12, no. 416, Wangenheim to Berlin, 4 August 1914; no. 52, Michahelles to Berlin, 6 August; Staatsarchiv, PA, box 512, no. 582, Tarnowski to Berchtold, 16 August.

on August 15 that "it was as good as certain" that Turkey would take no action unless it was sure of Bulgaria and therefore sure of the safety of Constantinople. Nevertheless, five days later Michahelles and Tarnowski reported that a Bulgarian-Turkish Alliance had been signed on August 19. Arranged in seven articles, it called for an agreement on the part of each to respect the other's territories; to give mutual armed assistance if either was attacked by one or several Balkan states; to begin no move against one or several Balkan powers without previous agreement; and, in a case where one might undertake action with which the other could not concur, the latter was to maintain benevolent neutrality. Most significant was Article V, stating that Bulgaria would undertake no action in conjunction with Turkey unless Bulgaria was assured against Rumania, either by a Turkish-Bulgarian-Rumanian accord or by special arrangement between Bulgaria and Rumania concerning the issue of neutrality.[10]

The meaning of the terms is clear. If Turkey entered the war and was attacked by Rumania or Greece, it would have Bulgaria as an ally. For Bulgaria the agreement meant protection in the rear if it should decide to unite with Austria in an attack on Serbia. However, a Bulgarian decision to take action rested on the realization of Article V; and this was not to be the case. Concrete assurances of Rumanian benevolence could not be obtained. The Austrian ambassador in Sofia had pointed out to Berchtold that the treaty was defensive in nature, and that before it could become offensive Bulgaria must have a guarantee of Rumanian neutrality. The Bulgarians were so fearful of Bukarest that Talaat Bey had sounded Michahelles on the possibilities of appending a clause to the Bulgarian-Turkish accord whereby Germany and Austria would guarantee Bulgaria against Rumania if Bulgaria attacked Serbia. Berchtold refused, declaring such a guarantee in a bilateral Bulgarian-Turkish treaty to be impossible. In an instruction to Tar-

---

[10] GFMA, ser. 2, reel 12, no. 505, Wangenheim to Berlin, 15 August 1914; no. 84, Michahelles to Berlin, 20 August; Staatsarchiv, PA, box 512, no. 608, Tarnowski to Berchtold, 20 August; Albertini, *War of 1914*, 3:616–17. Albertini offers an exact copy of the Bulgarian-Turkish Alliance but he has made a mistake in the date. He declares it was signed on 6 August but this is on the basis of the Greek calendar. The fact that it was signed almost two weeks later is of some significance since if it had existed by 6 August it is possible Bulgaria might more easily have been prompted to take immediate action. For clarification of the date see GFMA, ser. 2, reel 12, memorandum no. 383. Albertini is also incorrect in declaring that the treaty's existence was not known until divulged by Halil Bey to Wangenheim on 17 December. Michahelles's and Tarnowski's telegrams of 20 August show that Talaat Bey, who signed the treaty with Radoslavov in Sofia, had divulged its existence to them, and they had, of course, immediately informed their respective governments.

nowski he wrote that Bulgaria had nothing to worry about because, "We have—as Herr Radoslavov knows—the most conclusive assurances from His Majesty King Carol as well as from the government that Rumania will give Bulgaria a free hand against Serbia and will not attack it. In our treaty draft we have, upon the desire of the Bulgarian government, given a framing to Article II which also satisfies the wished-for guarantee against Rumania."[11]

Bulgaria was not satisfied. Although he was much pleased by the agreement reached with Turkey, Radoslavov asserted that a formal accord would be necessary with Rumania. Once this was achieved Bulgaria would mobilize. Rumania, however, refused. Bratianu stated that any open treaty would, once signed, mean the hostility of Russia. To take sides with one of the power groups was not in Rumania's interest. Bratianu repeated that Bukarest would not hinder Bulgarian action with respect to Serbia, and King Carol went so far as to authorize Count Czernin to inform Ferdinand that he could count on Rumanian neutrality. When it came to offering assurances, the Rumanian minister in Sofia declared that his country would be benevolently neutral, but such an oral commitment was as far as Bukarest would go. By August 30 the diplomatic knot had not been successfully untied. No agreement had been reached between Bulgaria and Rumania, without which the Bulgarian-Turkish Alliance remained inoperative. The lack of a precisely defined diplomatic relationship with Rumania and Turkey meant Bulgaria would sign no treaty with Germany and Austria. Michahelles put it colorfully when he said that conditions required Bulgaria to have a Frederick the Great on the throne. Instead there was only Ferdinand, who was "fearful and completely unmilitary."[12] The minister underestimated his man, for the king's Machiavellian qualities made him a wily diplomatic opponent. It took little effort on his part to realize that he could afford to wait and bargain and that the initiative was now in his hands.

Michahelles's Austrian colleague had a better grasp of the Bulgarian problem. Adam Tarnowski had been posted to Sofia as minister in

[11] Staatsarchiv, PA, box 512, no. 608, Tarnowski to Berchtold, 20 August 1914; GFMA, ser. 2, reel 12, no. 83, Michahelles to Berlin, 18 August; see also frames 344–45 of the same reel for Berchtold's stand on the desired guarantee in the bilateral treaty; Staatsarchiv, PA, box 513, no. 343, Berchtold to Tarnowski, 19 August.

[12] Staatsarchiv, PA, box 512, no. 610, Tarnowski to Berchtold, 20 August 1914; no. 620, Tarnowski to Berchtold, 21 August; GFMA, ser. 2, reel 12, no. 86, Michahelles to Berlin, 21 August; no. 165, Waldthausen in Bukarest to Berlin, 21 August; no. 304, Tschirschky in Vienna to Berlin, 22 August; no. 205, Waldthausen to Berlin, 29 August; no. 213, Waldthausen to Berlin, 30 August; no. 97, Michahelles to Berlin, 23 August.

1911, after fifteen years spent learning his craft in various diplomatic assignments. Fluent in five languages, highly cultured, expert in Bulgarian politics, he nevertheless understood that he needed more than his own capacities to influence the Bulgarian government. He needed pragmatic conditions which did not exist. It was easy for Berchtold to suggest that he avoid giving Sofia the impression that Austrian policy relied on Bulgaria as a pivot. Success in this was quite another matter. And in a frank appraisal Tarnowski wrote:

> I cannot hide the truth, that because of the checks we have had militarily our position here is suffering. We are no longer regarded as protectors but we are seen as desirous of Bulgarian aid out of which will accrue to us a final victory.
>
> My advance is now much more difficult. I can now only coyly raise questions with respect to the Bulgarian action against Serbia. . . .
>
> The trust of the Bulgarian government in my counsel and word can scarcely have been deepened in these last days. I have given too many assurances which have not come about.[13]

The only solace that the Central Powers could take from the situation at this time was that Ferdinand was violently anti-Russian. In response to Russian threats to declare war on Turkey and march troops through Bulgaria, Sofia had clearly stated that while it would remain neutral such action would be repulsed.[14]

In spite of the negative turn of events, negotiations continued apace. On August 16 Radoslavov had requested changes in Article III of the alliance draft that would specifically offer Serbian Macedonia to Bulgaria, with guarantees of Macedonian border areas adjacent to Greece if the latter should declare war. Both Berlin and Vienna agreed concerning Serbian Macedonia but they were not willing to commit themselves on the Greek issue. By the end of August the Germans had grown impatient and demanded that a clause be inserted specifically tying Bulgaria to active military cooperation, without which the treaty was to be seen as void. Furthermore, Jagow instructed Michahelles to inform Sofia that if the treaty was not signed in six days, Berlin would break off negotiations. Fortunately this ultimatum was never delivered

[13] Staatsarchiv, PA, box 512, no. 294, Berchtold to Tarnowski, 17 August 1914. In this instruction Berchtold refused to change Article III to which Ferdinand had alluded on 15 August. "Enemy Portraits: Count Adam Tarnowski," *The New Europe* 2 (15 Feburary 1917): 151–54; Staatsarchiv, PA, Administrativ Registratur F 4, box 346, Tarnowski; Staatsarchiv, PA, box 512, no. 646, Tarnowski to Berchtold, 24 August 1914.

[14] Staatsarchiv, PA, box 512, no. 703, Tarnowski to Berchtold, 3 September 1914.

because Undersecretary Zimmermann, recognizing that such a tone would drive Bulgaria into the arms of the Entente, personally prevailed upon Jagow to soften German demands. The clause for active and immediate participation was also eliminated since almost all the diplomats concerned saw it as superfluous. Eventually, both the German and Austrian ministers declared orally to Radoslavov that their governments would consider the treaty ineffectual if Bulgaria did not take prompt action, although the Austrians considered even such a commentary ill-advised, for Berchtold believed any eagerness on the part of the Central Powers might be taken as a sign of weakness and might delay matters further.[15]

The month of September saw no change in the diplomatic situation; if anything, Bulgaria became even more hesitant. The failure of the Austrian offensive against Serbia and the defeat administered by the Russians in Galicia only increased Bulgaria's coyness. Although in October the war situation turned in favor of Austria on both the Serbian and Russian fronts, Sofia, while reacting favorably to the battle reports, nevertheless made no move. To some extent Bulgarian public opinion was a factor influencing the official position. Since traditionally Bulgaria had been pro-Russian and the people were not well disposed to the war, the government's neutral policy was popular. It was on the basis of such neutrality that Radoslavov maintained the confidence of the nation, pacified the Russophile elements, and was able to keep the parliamentary majority necessary to remain in power. Of the seven indigenous political parties, four stood in opposition to the government. Radoslavov headed the National Liberals but he depended for his continuation as minister-president on a coalition that contained a numerous element calling for moderation. It was not politically expedient for Radoslavov to throw in Bulgaria's lot with Germany and Austria and run the risk of turning himself out of office. He could decide to join these countries with impunity when the time was exactly right, but the moment had not yet arrived.[16]

[15] Ibid., no. 581, Tarnowski to Berchtold, 16 August 1914; no. 294, Berchtold to Tarnowski, 17 August; box 513, no. 472, Hamerle in Berlin to Berchtold, 28 August; no. 491, Hohenlohe in Berlin to Berchtold, 5 September; no. 501, Hohenlohe to Berchtold, 8 September; no. 736, Tarnowski to Berchtold, 9 September; no. 353, Berchtold to Tarnowski, 29 August.

[16] Ibid., box 513, no. 768, Baron Mittag, Austrian military attaché in Sofia, to Berchtold, 14 September 1914; box 512, no. 840, Mittag to Berchtold, 25 September; GFMA, ser. 2, reel 12, no. 994, Wangenheim to Berlin, 7 October; the Bulgarian Minister in Constantinople had discussed with Wangenheim the internal political scene in Bulgaria and pointed out that the pro-Russian element made things difficult for the government; no. 116, Michahelles to Berlin, 3 October; see also the attached memorandum of Lt. Tantilev, Bulgarian military attaché

By November the diplomatic picture had changed very little. The fact that Turkey now entered the war made no impression on the Bulgarian government, which steadfastly maintained its neutral position. Bulgarian-Rumanian negotiations were at a standstill; because Rumania and Greece had very friendly ties with each other, Sofia thought they might even have signed an accord. Bulgaria could not enter the war and find itself fighting Serbia, Rumania, Greece, and Russia. King Ferdinand labelled such a condition "catastrophical." To the persistent exertions of Tarnowski and Michahelles, Radoslavov, while friendly, reacted with merely vague assurances. He was pleased that Serbia seemed about to collapse. The moment when Bulgaria would intervene was coming closer and closer. Perhaps Bulgaria would intervene in a few weeks. But it could not do so at the moment, for there were still war preparations to be made; the army was not yet ready. Besides, he remarked, simply through its neutrality Bulgaria was aiding the cause of the Central Powers.[17]

Bulgaria Maneuvers

At this time Bulgaria held high cards, for it was also being persistently courted by the Entente powers. As early as August 24 Tarnowski reported that Sir Edward Grey had made an approach, suggesting that Bulgaria join a Balkan League along with Greece, Serbia, and Rumania. As payment it would be given Kavalla, the Serbian part of Macedonia, Monastir, and a part of the Dobrudja. When Berchtold heard of the offer, he told Tarnowski to mention in conversation with Radoslavov that none of Bulgaria's neighbors would willingly give up so much as a quarter of a meter of land. The Bulgarian leaders obviously agreed with the Austrian foreign minister, because their response to the Entente offer was quite negative.[18]

Fortunately for the Central Powers, the Entente had difficulty in

in Vienna; Staatsarchiv, PA, box 872, no. 1200, Tarnowski to Berchtold, 24 November; Dunan, *L'Été Bulgare*, pp. 71–78.

[17] Staatsarchiv, PA, box 872, no. 1030, Mittag in Sofia to Berchtold, 1 November 1914; GFMA, ser. 2, reel 12, Michahelles to Berlin, 30 October; no. 556, Bussche in Bukarest to Berlin, 7 November; Bratianu had denied that a formal accord existed with Greece but admitted relations were quite amicable. Staatsarchiv, PA, box 872, no. 1193, Tarnowski to Berchtold, 22 November. The remark of Ferdinand merely summed up what had been expressed to the German military attaché on October 10 when he spoke to Radoslavov. See GFMA, ser. 2, reel 12, no. A 27397, Richard von Mach to Berlin, 10 October; von Mach was the Sofia correspondent for the *Kölnische Zeitung*. Staatsarchiv, PA, box 872, nos. 1158, 1176, 1182, Tarnowski to Berchtold, 17, 19, 20 November.

[18] Staatsarchiv, PA, box 512, no. 644, Tarnowski to Berchtold, 24 August 1914; no. 334, Berchtold to Tarnowski, 26 August.

agreeing on precisely what to offer the Bulgarians, and Berchtold was right with respect to Serbia, Greece, and Rumania. All three proved loathe to give up territory to Bulgaria, which they distrusted. The Entente dropped serious negotiations for several months, but resumed talks with Sofia in November. On the seventh, the Russian minister met with Radoslavov for two hours and, in exchange for Bulgaria's agreement to proceed against Turkey, offered districts in Macedonia and the Enos-Midia line in Thrace. Radoslavov declined, saying that he had talked things over a few days before with his colleagues, and collectively they had decided to maintain neutrality. The English representative offered a similar proposition on November 18, and again Radoslavov refused. Six days later, on the twenty-fourth, the Entente powers finally submitted a joint note, vaguely worded, promising that in return for strictest neutrality with respect to Rumania, Greece, and Serbia, important territorial concessions would be granted to Bulgaria after the war. If Bulgaria attacked Austria or Turkey even greater concessions would accrue. The request for Bulgarian neutrality was based on the fact that Serbia was now in the greatest danger from a powerful and successful Austrian offensive. Radoslavov's reaction was to tell Michahelles that such vague concessions were worthless and that he would reject them.[19]

The Entente's failure to entice Bulgaria did not ease minds in Vienna and Berlin. Berchtold was much disturbed by the talks that Radoslavov was having with the enemy camp because he feared they might lead to an understanding between Bulgaria and Rumania providing for continued Bulgarian neutrality in the event of a Rumanian attack on Austria. By November 20 he already knew that, in addition to offering parts of Macedonia, the Entente was offering the Enos-Midia line in Thrace, and he therefore instructed Tarnowski to raise the ante. Austria promised not only Macedonia but the Pirot-Nish area as well. Tarnowski sounded Radoslavov in a tactful manner, mentioning that the Bulgarian's policy no longer seemed as clear and definite as it had been, for Sofia seemed more friendly to the Entente. He relayed Berchtold's information that Bratianu had gone so far as to state that if Bulgaria attacked Serbia and Greece came to the aid of the latter, Rumania would not attack Bulgaria's rear. Radoslavov, however, was anything but apologetic about his negotiations with the opposite camp.

[19] GFMA, ser. 2, reel 12, no. 236, Michahelles to Berlin, 7 November 1914; Staatsarchiv, PA, box 872, no. 1160, Tarnowski to Berchtold, 18 November; no. 1223, Tarnowski to Berchtold, 26 November; GFMA, ser. 2, reel 12, no. 266, Michahelles to Berlin, 25 November. For a more detailed delineation of Entente negotiations, see C. Jay Smith, Jr., *The Russian Struggle for Power, 1914–1917*, pp. 142–58.

In his opinion the political opposition at home necessitated continuing talks with the Entente. Besides, he could not help it, could he, if these powers made him proposals? His own sources of information told him Rumania would not stand by idly if Bulgaria attacked Serbia. From a purely military standpoint he felt Bulgaria could not take any action, since it had no munitions. When Tarnowski asked what Sofia would do if these munitions were supplied, the answer was a vague "the government would then have to decide."[20]

Germany also continued to press. In November, Count Tisza, the Hungarian prime minister, made a trip to German headquarters, where he spoke with Foreign Office officials, stressing that the best solution to the Balkan question was a rapid attack by Bulgaria on Serbia. Influenced by this, Jagow wanted renewed efforts made to gain Bulgarian participation. The Germans saw a Rumanian-Greek cooperative move against the Bulgarians as improbable, and felt that, even if it came, Rumania would be paralyzed because it would face a hostile Turkey. On receiving Jagow's views, Michahelles was somewhat perplexed as to how he might answer an impatient home office. He had had as much experience in dealing with the Bulgarians as his Austrian colleague, and if anything, was more forceful in pleading his case with Sofia. Clearly the Wilhelmstrasse did not appreciate the subtleties of Bulgarian thinking with respect to the posture of the Balkan states. Michahelles was himself rather cool and distrustful of Bulgarian motives, but obviously Sofia could not be swayed at the moment. He conferred with Tarnowski as to what he might say to Berlin. His fellow diplomat suggested that he merely declare they were both doing all they could, and that while to some extent Bulgarian public opinion favored a march on Macedonia, the decision rested with the government, which showed no signs of making that decision.[21]

The Austrians saw the situation with greater perspicacity than did the Wilhelmstrasse. On November 29 Tarnowski wrote a penetrating analysis of the scene. He pointed out that although the Bulgarians had not taken the position desired by the Central Powers, they were not insincere. Both the government and the king were decidedly favorable to Germany and Austria. That the Bulgarians had not joined them could be blamed on the uncertainty surrounding the outcome of the

[20] Staatsarchiv, PA, box 872, no. 667, Berchtold to Tarnowski, 20 November 1914; no. 697, Berchtold to Tarnowski, 27 November; no. 1245, Tarnowski to Berchtold, 29 November.

[21] GFMA, ser. 2, reel 12, no. 398, Jagow to the Foreign Office in Berlin, 22 November 1914; Arno Mehlan, "Das Deutsch-Bulgarische Weltkriegsbündnis," *Historische Vierteljahrschrift* 30 (1935): 772; *Meyer's Lexikon*, 8:402; Staatsarchiv, PA, box 872, no. 1198, Tarnowski to Berchtold, 23 November.

war and on their belief that the regulation of matters in the Balkans depended on more than simply the Germans, the Austrians, and themselves. In previous dispatches the Austrian minister had already mentioned that Radoslavov would have liked to obtain Macedonia by remaining neutral; Tarnowski now offered the opinion that if Bulgaria took action in Macedonia, it would do so only when the risks were the narrowest possible and when the taking could be done cheaply. This action would come when Austria had defeated Serbia and when Bulgaria's army was fully equipped and ready for war.

Tarnowski was not too concerned about Radoslavov's conversations with the Entente. He reported: "The policy of Radoslavov would in itself be dangerous for us, were the Entente in a position to offer Bulgaria favorable propositions. But they cannot and they cannot overbid us. Serbia will not make territorial concessions nor will Greece. . . . This guarantees us against the success of our enemies' intrigues. Only for a deal with Rumania can an eventual basis be found, which, however, as long as Bratianu will not cede the Dobrudja, is likewise non-existent. No pourparlers between Sofia and Bukarest have been opened." He concluded that as long as the military success of the Central Powers continued, Bulgaria would not turn against them.[22]

This was insufficient to soothe Berchtold's apprehensions about the possible effectiveness of Entente diplomacy, and he now instructed Tarnowski in detail. The enemy had offered Sofia concessions for mere neutrality; therefore, Austria and Germany could not afford to offer less. Tarnowski was to make clear to Sofia that if the Central Powers won, Bulgaria, even as a neutral, would emerge with more than it would if the Entente was victorious. In the latter case, Bulgaria would find itself faced with an enlarged Serbia and Rumania, while its own winnings would be slight. In choosing to join Germany and the Monarchy, Bulgaria would obtain "a frontier expansion which the Entente powers can never assign her."[23] Both Berlin and Vienna had already offered Radoslavov all of Serbian Macedonia and Pirot and Nish if Bulgaria joined in; they were willing to leave the way open for

[22] Staatsarchiv, PA, box 872, no. 1247, Tarnowski to Berchtold, 29 November 1914. For Radoslavov's desire to gain Macedonia peacefully, see no. 1233, Tarnowski to Berchtold, 26 November. Radoslavov had said he would like to acquire Macedonia in the same way that Greece had acquired Epirus. Stephan Burian, *Austria in Dissolution*, p. 133. Burian neatly summed up the quandary of the Entente when he stated that they could not offer territory to Bulgaria without meeting opposition from states they befriended. Serbia opposed cessions in Macedonia; Greece would not give up parts of Thrace; Turkish territory could not be offered without thwarting Russian ambitions.

[23] Staatsarchiv, PA, box 872, no. 708, Berchtold to Tarnowski, 30 November 1914. A copy of this instruction was also sent to Hohenlohe in Berlin.

satisfying Bulgarian aspirations to Kavalla and Salonika, though this would have to be worked out in conjunction with Turkey.

Contrary to his expectations in early August, Berchtold now recognized that a good deal of patience would be needed to win Bulgarian participation. He sought to maintain diplomatic forcefulness but not to threaten or push Sofia too hard, for, he wrote, "We must not place the Radoslavov ministry in a difficult position and we must not drive Bulgaria into the arms of the Entente, but through promising Turkish help and through presenting the advantages which Bulgaria could expect from an active participation on our side bring the Bulgarian government in our direction."[24] When all was said and done, Berchtold's promises of territory in exchange for Bulgarian neutrality were as vague as those of the Entente. Only for direct military cooperation was Austria, at this stage, willing to offer concrete concessions.

The Turks had also done all they could to assure Bulgaria and thus pull it into the war. Turkish officials were well aware that Bulgarian participation would considerably ease their own job. It would free those Turkish troops which had been assigned to guard the Adrianople area against a possible Bulgarian attack. It would lead to the fall of Serbia. At the least it would keep Rumania neutral if the latter proved unwilling to join in with the Central Powers. But attempts by Turkish diplomats to convince Bulgaria had led to no result by the opening days of December. Berchtold had ordered Pallavicini and Tarnowski to do all they could to obtain the signing of a Bulgarian-Turkish military convention, and the Austrian ministers had the support and cooperation of their German counterparts, who themselves had been instructed along these lines. By the beginning of December everything that could be done in this regard had been done, but Fethi Bey, the Turkish representative in Sofia, was still unable to report success.[25]

The Bulgarians not only refused Turkish overtures but also turned a cold shoulder to the additional territorial concessions now made to them. They argued that neutrality was not merely in Bulgaria's best interest, but was also advantageous to the cause of Germany and Austria-Hungary. In response to Tarnowski's urging that Bulgaria not wait to be given Macedonia as a present, but instead attack before Serbia was conquered, Tonchev, the finance minister, stated that the

[24] Ibid.
[25] GFMA, ser. 2, reel 12, no. 957, Tschirschky in Vienna to Berlin, 1 December 1914; Tschirschky offers here the Turkish thinking on the issue as given to him by the Turkish representative to Vienna, Halil Pasha; Staatsarchiv, PA, box 872, nos. 796 and 683, Berchtold to Pallavicini and Tarnowski, 24 November; no. 716, Hohenlohe in Berlin to Berchtold, 25 November; no. 883, Pallavicini to Berchtold, 26 November; no. 1284, Tarnowski to Berchtold, 5 December.

government believed Bulgaria's importance to the Central Powers would not end with the Serbian defeat. Indeed, Ghenadiev, boss of the powerful Stambulovist Party, declared that Bulgarian participation would not ease Austria's military task, since it would mean the inclusion of Greece and Rumania on the side of the Entente, involving Austria in a new Balkan war. Bulgaria's weak military condition would cause its defeat, Serbia would be saved by its new allies, and Turkey would be quite cut off. The war, declared Ghenadiev, was going to be a long one; Bulgarian strength should not be played out now but should be increased and used when it could be of greater worth—after the defeat of Serbia.[26] Tarnowski's reaction to all this was the impatient observation that Bulgarian aid would be of no value whatsoever when the war was over, when its forces would no longer be needed.[27]

Hard Bargaining Begins

Radoslavov's astuteness was soon manifest. If Sofia had accepted the original treaty draft of August, it would have meant accepting a military commitment. By December the Bulgarian policy of bargain and wait had been pushed a step further. Radoslavov now succeeded in obtaining from Berlin and Vienna a written declaration promising territorial concessions. In exchange, he offered nothing.

On December 7 the minister-president approached Tarnowski, declaring that he had been challenged by the opposition on the floor of the Sobranje to show what offers had been made by Germany and Austria-Hungary that could justify the refusal of those put forth by the Entente. He was willing to ignore the areas of Pirot and Nish, but he wanted to publish the offer of all of Serbian Macedonia. Tarnowski wrote to Berchtold that such a revelation should be made, but the desired note should be shown only to the Bulgarian party chiefs and not aired before the Sobranje itself. Berchtold immediately instructed Hohenlohe to bring the matter to Berlin's attention and then to send him quickly the reaction of the German Foreign Office. His own position was that no positive promises should be made to Sofia for mere neutrality but that the widest assurances should be given for that part of Serbian territory which was occupied by Bulgarian troops. To offer compensation for a merely neutral position was to offer a prize for Bulgarian inaction.[28]

[26] Staatsarchiv, PA, box 872, nos. 1176, 1312, Tarnowski to Berchtold, 19 November and 9 December 1914.
[27] Ibid., no. 1312, Tarnowski to Berchtold, 9 December 1914.
[28] Ibid., no. 1301, Tarnowski to Berchtold, 7 December 1914; no. 914, Berchtold to Hohenlohe, 9 December.

Jagow was completely in accord with Berchtold's view; however, he was willing to offer something for the Sobranje's satisfaction, though he wanted only an oral presentation by the German and Austrian ministers. He was not willing to go along with a published note unless Berchtold believed it absolutely essential. Written assurances should be presented after Bulgaria had agreed to a properly timed attack, and before things had been decided on the battlefield. Tarnowski and Michahelles cooperated carefully on this issue, informing Radoslavov that without active participation the desired pledge of territories could not be given.[29]

Radoslavov, remaining undaunted, put his request somewhat differently, declaring that what he really wanted was a written assurance for himself. He would keep the note secret and merely inform the Sobranje that he had received formal guarantees; when eventually he published a declaration, things would be stated in a quite general way.[30]

The idea of a secret note of guarantee was more acceptable to Berchtold, and he obtained Jagow's grudging consent for such a document. Jagow's hesitation was based on his doubt of Sofia's ability to maintain diplomatic discretion. Because Radoslavov had made known the promises of the Entente, there was no reason suddenly to assume that he would maintain silence now. Furthermore, the Wilhelmstrasse had received a discouraging dispatch from General von der Goltz, who had made a trip to Sofia and had talked with King Ferdinand. It did not look as though anything would come of the whole matter. Ferdinand spoke of current public opinion being against war, of the threat posed by Russia. He stated definitely that he would not now give up neutrality. Michahelles, reflecting Berlin's hesitation, told Radoslavov that no note was really needed. After all, the Bulgarians had for some time had in their hands an alliance draft which essentially offered more than the Entente would, by leaving Bulgaria free to take as much of Serbian Macedonia as it wanted. Nevertheless, Berlin gave way under the urging of the Ballhausplatz and of Hohenlohe. The latter remarked with resignation that written declarations rather than oral assurances seemed basic to the thinking patterns of Balkan statesmen.[31]

The Austrians were determined to try any possibility which might break up the log jam. Tarnowski felt Radoslavov could be trusted. On

[29] Ibid., box 872, no. 768, Hohenlohe to Berchtold, 10 December 1914; nos. 1325, 1328, Tarnowski to Berchtold, 11 and 12 December.
[30] Ibid., no. 1349, Tarnowski to Berchtold, 15 December 1914.
[31] Ibid., nos. 768 and 773, Hohenlohe to Berchtold, 15 and 17 December 1914; GFMA, ser. 2, reel 12, no. 3005, von der Goltz to Berlin, 15 December; no. 296, Michahelles to Berlin, 17 December.

December 19 Berchtold went ahead with the draft of a secret declaration. Jagow's cynical and serious insistence on tightening the wording so that Bulgaria could not try to take *all* of Serbia was reflected in the draft now sent by Vienna to Berlin for approval. It stated:

> Austria-Hungary [Germany] guarantees to Bulgaria that it will obtain after the war all the territories of the Kingdom of Serbia to which Bulgaria possesses historic and ethnographic rights and which it shall have occupied by its own troops.[32]

The reluctance of the Wilhelmstrasse to give its formal approval was demonstrated by Hohenlohe's being unable to wire German acceptance until some nine days after the draft had been received. Finally, on December 31, Berchtold authorized Tarnowski to present the declaration "as soon as you and your German colleague consider this necessary and useful." In conjunction with the text of the written note, Berchtold suggested that Tarnowski try to obtain as a precondition Radoslavov's agreement at least to place Bulgarian troops on the Serbian borders. Such a move would not endanger Bulgaria's neutrality, but it would serve to divert Serbian troops and ease the pressure on the Austrian forces. The suggestion had been made by Tarnowski in the middle of December, and Radoslavov had vaguely assured him that something like this would happen. In the end, the precondition failed. Radoslavov replied on January 4 that such displacement of troops was not possible for technical military reasons. On the same day Tarnowski submitted the note and two days later Michahelles presented an identical document. Before giving the declaration they had again made doubly sure that it would be held in absolute secrecy. Radoslavov strongly assured them of this, again remarking that he did not really want it for the Sobranje; he wanted it for himself. With such a note in his hands he could argue more convincingly with the king who had, of couse, not yet signed the treaty.[33]

The result of this maneuver was a Bulgarian diplomatic victory. The Bulgarians had signed no alliance treaty. They had not in the slightest way committed themselves to the Central Powers, yet they had managed to obtain the written pledge of Austria and Germany promising them the control of certain Serbian areas. Although control was based on occupation by Bulgarian troops, the time and manner of occupation

---

[32] Ibid., no. 954, Berchtold to Hohenlohe, 19 December 1914. This same draft was sent to Tarnowski on the same day as no. 766.

[33] Ibid., no. 792, Berchtold to Tarnowski, 31 December 1914; nos. 16, 22, Tarnowski to Berchtold, 4 and 6 January 1915.

were in no way defined. The fact that Bulgarian control would have the limitation of ethnographic and historical rights did not mean very much, since the phrase could be interpreted broadly.

In the early days of August, Berlin and Vienna had been confident that the Bulgarians would immediately enter the conflict against the Entente. Now, five months later, the confidence had evaporated. The Bulgarians were leading the Central Powers a merry chase. Both Germany and Austria had just presented the Bulgarian government with a written commitment and had obtained nothing in return. There was some solace, however, because the note did strengthen their hand in Sofia against pressure by the Entente representatives and friends of the Entente in the Bulgarian government. Then, too, the wording of the pledge offered territories only for participation in the war; Berchtold could therefore assert that his policy of offering nothing concrete in the way of territorial concessions for neutrality had remained intact. The Wilhelmstrasse could at least comfort itself with Radoslavov's promise that the offers would not be aired before the National Assembly. It was hoped that on the strength of the note Sofia might still decide to join. These were the considerations which had led the Germans to go along with Berchtold's persuasion that the formal note be proffered.

By the turn of 1915 neither Berlin nor Vienna could look forward to any immediate and significant change in Bulgaria's position. Certainly the heavy defeats inflicted upon Austrian forces in Serbia during December, forcing a retreat behind the Danube, had made a negative impression upon Bulgarian statesmen. Although the armies of the Central Powers had fared better on the eastern front, the results were in no way sufficient to lead Bulgaria to take a decisive step. In the opening days of January, Tarnowski talked with General Fitschev, chief of the Bulgarian army staff, who looked unfavorably upon Bulgarian participation. He had no faith in the Turkish forces, did not believe they would be successful in their Egyptian campaign against the British, and saw a combined Bulgaro-Turkish campaign against Russia as very risky. He felt that the war would be long and that Germany and Austria would emerge victorious, but not over a completely defeated enemy.[34] King Ferdinand had declared he was "sickened" by the reports from Serbia, and the reversals of the Austrian army were simply incomprehensible to him. These reports and the caution of his military leaders meant that he would certainly at this time refuse concrete commitments, notwithstanding his Russophobia.[35]

[34] Winston S. Churchill, *The Unknown War: The Eastern Front*, pp. 251–69; Staatsarchiv, PA, box 872, no. 8/P, Tarnowski to Berchtold, 9 January 1915.

Earlier in December, Jagow had tried further to influence the Bulgarian minister in Berlin by clearly stating that Germany as well as Austria expected Bulgaria would actively join them. He made it quite clear through Michahelles in Sofia that he believed the last moment for a Bulgarian attack had now come. But King Ferdinand and Radoslavov both remained unconvinced.[36]

While the Central Powers were doing all that was possible on the diplomatic level to commit Bulgaria, they also attempted to use finance as a lever in the same direction. The loan which had been ratified by the Sobranje on July 16, 1914, was scheduled to come into effect on September 30. That loan, it will be recalled, consisted of four separate contracts. According to the stipulations of the first contract, half the total sum of 500 million francs was to be paid on September 30. When the day arrived both Austria and Germany refused to grant the initial payment. The second contract, which was seen as a separate advance, had in actuality been put through on July 18 by the banking syndicate headed by the Diskonto Gesellschaft. This called for a loan totaling 120 million francs with Bulgarian treasury bonds as security, the deadline for repayment being set as August 1, 1915. The Central Powers did not see this sum as in any way part of the 500 million francs they were supposed to advance.[37]

As early as August 7, Tarnowski had wired that Bulgaria was asking for additional money necessary to meet its mobilization costs. Berchtold took the position that no financial support should be given to Bulgaria unless it signed a treaty of alliance with Vienna and Berlin. The Ballhausplatz sent its views to Szögyény in Berlin, who quickly wired that the Germans were in complete agreement. Undersecretary Zimmermann had declared that as soon as Bulgaria agreed to sign the alliance, the German government would influence the proper financial circles to grant the desired funds.[38]

[35] Staatsarchiv, PA, box 872, no. 1354, Tarnowski to Berchtold, 17 December 1914.
[36] Ibid., no. 756, Hohenlohe to Berchtold, 10 December 1914; no. 1324, Tarnowski to Berchtold, 11 December.
[37] Henri Prost, *La Liquidation Financière de la Guerre en Bulgarie*, pp. 38–39. Here and on succeeding pages Prost offers a basic sketch of the negotiations, carrying the story through 1918. For the precise terms of the loan granted in July 1914, which consisted of the four contracts dealt with in my chapter 1, see Arthur Raffalovich, *Le Marché Financier, 1913–14*, pp. 723–28, 734–37. For another informative treatment see Lübomir G. Leschtoff, *Die Staatsschulden und Reparationen Bulgariens, 1878–1927*, pp. 59–75. A consideration of the 120 million francs advanced in July is treated by Leschtoff, pp. 64–65, 68.
[38] Staatsarchiv, PA, box 513, no. 492, Tarnowski to Berchtold, 7 August 1914; no. 383, Berchtold to Szögyény, 9 August; no. 402, Szögyény to Berchtold, 9 August.

By August 10 instructions had been relayed to Sofia, and Radoslavov was informed accordingly. The two allies made it clear that they insisted on the signing of the alliance and, further, that money would be forthcoming only after the Bulgarian army had been mobilized. This position reflected the Wilhelmstrasse's view that without a Bulgarian declaration of war the Central Powers could not be sure that the money would not be used against them. Both Bethmann-Hollweg and Jagow were irritated at the neutral position taken by Bulgaria, and they felt that a money grant would not have even the "narrowest expectations" of pulling the Bulgarians into their camp. Vienna concurred.[39]

Initially, the Germans and Austrians staunchly maintained their position to withhold the large loan of 500 million, but in actuality the pressure of events forced them to open the purse strings. On October 17 General von der Goltz was in Sofia, and he reported to Berlin that the English were courting Bulgaria by offering a large loan at very good terms. A few weeks later he supplied the information that England was offering 200 million francs without interest and without any conditions except benevolent neutrality.[40]

The Bulgarian finance minister, Tonchev, had been in negotiation with Zimmermann, hoping to obtain money from the German and Austrian side, but he was astounded at the poor terms offered by the Berlin money market. First of all, the option on the great loan of July, 1914, had been postponed until August 1, 1915. Second, the most that the bankers would offer was 150 million at 9 or 10 percent interest. Fifty million would be given immediately but the major portion would follow only with Bulgarian mobilization.

Von der Goltz warned Berlin that Sofia had to take account of Bulgarian public opinion more than Germany seemed willing to recognize. He suggested that the whole issue be quickly settled, that the interest rate be lowered to 6 or 7 percent at most, that the 150 million be put through as a supplement to the originally projected loan but that the demand for mobilization be retained, and, finally, that the loan be handled not as a government matter but as a purely banking transaction, in order to reduce the complications.[41]

[39] Ibid., no. 254, Berchtold to Tarnowski, 10 August 1914; no. 491, Hohenlohe to Berchtold, 5 September. Radoslavov tried to obtain a smaller grant than the original 250 million; on 1 September he had mentioned to Tarnowski that he thought it would be an easy thing for Germany and Austria to loan his government 100 million francs. Tarnowski merely replied that any grant would come after mobilization, that is, military action. For this exchange, see Staatsarchiv, PA, box 513, no. 692, Tarnowski to Berchtold, 1 September 1914.

[40] GFMA, ser. 2, reel 12, no. 21, von der Goltz to Berlin, 17 October 1914.

As things turned out, von der Goltz's suggestion for a speedy conclusion of the loan was not accepted. Financial negotiations were protracted, for both Berlin and Vienna became aware in December that the Entente's attempts to win Bulgaria through vague territorial concessions had failed. The Central Powers had met the Entente challenge with a written note granting territorial gains to Bulgaria, but they delayed on the money issue and attempted to force promises of mobilization from the Bulgarians as a precondition for financial assistance. While the documents are not entirely clear, the evidence indicates that Sofia apparently threatened to cancel the original loan contracts, onerous at best, if a new advance was not forthcoming. Unwilling to risk the estrangement which would result from a financial break, and aware of the danger posed by Entente representations in Sofia, the Germans concluded a new loan with Tonchev in Berlin on January 31. Doctors Spitzmüller and Marcus, representing the Austrian-German banking syndicate, completed the arrangements on February 4. The Ballhausplatz went along with the decision because, as Berchtold had said six months before, "The Bulgarian divisions are still our cheapest troops."[42]

The new loan totalled 150 million francs at 6 percent interest, with the German and Austrian concerns each carrying half of the burden. Seventy-five million was granted immediately, the rest to be paid in the coming months. The Central Powers hoped and assumed that Bulgarian mobilization would be accomplished before the second installment was delivered. As we shall see, these hopes failed to materialize and Bulgaria ended by successfully obtaining the money it sought without meeting the precondition. By the start of 1915 Radoslavov had extracted a good sum without making any commitments at all. In the future he would extract more. His approach was to let things simmer and to profit from the increasing value Bulgaria came to have as a potential ally in the succeeding weeks and months.[43]

[41] GFMA, Foreign Office file no. 30512, von der Goltz to Berlin, 3 November 1914, and supplement, 4 November.

[42] Prost, *Liquidation Financière*, pp. 38–39; Viscount Grey, *Twenty-five Years*, 2:195–96; Staatsarchiv, PA, box 513, folio 6C, Foreign Office memo concerning Spitzmüller and Marcus; no. 390, Berchtold to Szögyény, 10 August 1914.

[43] Staatsarchiv, PA, box 513, folio 6C, Foreign Office memo; Leschtoff, *Staatsschulden und Reparationen Bulgariens*, pp. 66–67. With respect to the second installment and the demands for mobilization as a precondition, the documents in PA, box 513 show clearly the policy and that in the months of March, April, and May 1915 this policy failed. The document numbers are cited specifically in the further discussions of the money issue. See also *The Near East* 8, no. 197, (12 February 1915): 424. Reuters reported the loan of 2 February, calling it an installment of the 500 million. It had been released to the press as such but was in fact viewed by the governments concerned as a separate banking transaction.

Chapter 7

The Second Link

By the beginning of the new year it was obvious to both Germany and Austria that for the moment they could not obtain Bulgarian participation. Their diplomats had proved unsuccessful and their use of finance as a lever had failed. In addition, the Germans in particular had expended large sums for purposes of influencing public opinion. Through control of various Bulgarian newspapers and illustrated magazines they had attempted to propagandize the Bulgarian people to win popular support. In terms of obtaining Bulgarian military action these efforts met only with frustration.[1]

In spite of its disappointment over the turn of events, Berlin well understood that Sofia faced difficult problems. A report from Ambassador Bernhard von Bülow in Rome referred to a conversation he had with Ghenadiev, who was visiting that capital in late January, 1915. The Bulgarian envoy characterized the Russian situation as most delicate. The fact that many of his countrymen still saw Russia as their liberator from the Turkish yoke meant that war against the Czar would not be uniformly accepted. Tschirschky in Vienna had met with the new Bulgarian representative there, Andrew Toscheff, recently transferred from Constantinople. The Bulgarian minister had stated categorically that a campaign against Serbia was impossible because of the Greek-Serbian Alliance and the possibilities of conflict with Rumania.[2]

In the midst of the negotiations with the Bulgarians, Berchtold was forced to resign on January 13, 1915. His fall from office was not connected with the Bulgarian question but rather with that of satisfying Italian demands that the Monarchy cede the Trentino. Unable to win support within government circles for a policy which would have granted the concession, Berchtold, in the face of strong opposition, surrendered his portfolio to Count Stephan Burian. Burian, although previously the joint Austro-Hungarian finance minister, was no fledgling in the world of diplomacy, having served nine years with the Foreign Office at the ambassadorial level. In personality he was quite the reverse of Berchtold. Rather stiff and cold, with a penchant for examining things from the theoretical point of view, he was also accustomed to considering any problem from every angle before making his decision. Reluctant to take persons into his confidence, he acquired few friends at the Ballhausplatz, and Berlin found him difficult to work with in more instances than one. Yet, when it came to Bulgaria his attitudes prevailed for some while.[3]

These attitudes were based on two things: first, Burian's first-hand knowledge of Bulgarian psychology obtained between 1887 and 1895 when he himself had been minister to Sofia; and second, his daily contact with Berchtold over the last few months, which gave him a thorough orientation on all political details. On February 3, at a meeting of the Ministerial Council in Vienna he presented a summation of his views on Bulgaria's stand. It was patent, he said, that Bulgaria would continue its neutrality, which was understandable in light of the fact that it faced great dangers. If the Bulgarians agreed to join the Central Powers they faced a Greek and a Russian declaration of war, so that in spite of the assurances given to Sofia with regard to the pacific attitude of Rumania, they still feared an attack from this quarter. There were, he believed, perhaps more advantages than disadvantages in Bulgaria's insistence on neutrality. In the first place, neutrality kept a certain number of Rumanian troops occupied in watching the Bulgarian border. The Rumanians themselves would not enter the war on the side of the Entente for fear of an attack from Bulgaria, since such an attack would not constitute the *casus fœderis* for Greece. Secondly, intervention by Bulgaria at this time might actually interfere with Austria's preparations for a resumption of its Serbian campaign. Finally, Bulgarian neutrality would in no way set back Austria's war effort.[4]

Yet, Burian's calm and realistic appraisal of conditions did not mean he gave up all efforts to embroil Bulgaria. While he realized that "she would come in at what she judged the appropriate moment," he did not fail to mention in his first meeting with Toscheff that Bulgaria must keep its eyes open so as not to misjudge that moment.[5] Neverthe-

---

[1] Marcel Dunan, *L'Été Bulgare*, pp. 83–85.

[2] GFMA, ser. 2, reel 13, no. 42, Bülow to Berlin, 28 January 1915; reel 12, no. 48, Tschirschky to Berlin, 1 February 1915.

[3] Hugo Hantsch, *Leopold Graf Berchtold*, 2:717, 720, 723–24; Victor Naumann, *Profile*, pp. 232, 233; GFMA, St. Anthony's Collection, reel 24, memo no. 15, Tschirschky to Bethmann-Hollweg, 16 January 1915; memo no. 366, Ambassador Botho Wedel (successor to Tschirschky) in Vienna to Bethmann-Hollweg, 26 December 1916.

[4] Staatsarchiv, PA, box 312, Ministerial Protocol, 3 February 1915; Count Stephan Burian, *Austria in Dissolution*, pp. 17, 136; GFMA, St. Anthony's Collection, reel 24, Tschirschky to Jagow, 13 January 1915; Staatsarchiv, PA, box 312, Ministerial Protocol, 3 February 1915.

[5] Burian, *Austria in Dissolution*, p. 134; Staatsarchiv, PA, box 78, Instructions no. 52, Burian to Tarnowski, 6 February 1915.

less, in the forthcoming months he was forced to follow a much stronger policy, aimed at Bulgarian participation. It was at this time that Sofia began its next maneuver: to press unabashedly for territorial concessions while openly offering mere neutrality in return. When Toscheff mentioned to Burian that Radoslavov wanted an assurance of territory in Macedonia in return for Bulgaria's remaining neutral, the Austrian minister's reaction, while positive, was calculating. In a set of instructions to Tarnowski, he declared that such an assurance "would cost us nothing. In the case of victory that [promise] would be easy to fulfill. If there is no victory the situation would be devoid of application." He went on to state that such a general assurance would give the Bulgarian government a weapon against the "enticing promises, the golden mountains of the Entente," making Radoslavov's job easier with respect to the opposition at home. But Tarnowski was to make it clear that a regulation of conditions after the war "would take into account the *effective doings* of Bulgaria."[6]

When Tarnowski broached the whole subject with Radoslavov, the latter protested that he had not authorized Toscheff to mention the question of guarantees for neutrality. The Austrian was not taken in by the remark, and wrote to Vienna that Bulgaria sought to obtain all it could without taking any risks.[7] Events would show him to be quite right.

The German Initiative

Bulgaria's neutrality assumed greater proportions once the Entente began its attack on the Dardanelles. Bulgarian assistance was now needed to help eliminate the Serbs and so to open the route of supply to beleaguered Turkey. The German Foreign Office, with little hope of obtaining active Bulgarian support, was at this time forced to consider whether concrete compensations of territory should be offered simply to keep the Bulgarians neutral. On March 4, von Mach, a highly respected special correspondent in Sofia for the *Kölnische Zeitung*, wrote to Undersecretary Zimmermann informing him that Radoslavov was much worried over the possibility of British and French success at the Straits. If the campaign led to further Entente military action in the Balkan Peninsula, Bulgaria would be threatened. The political opposition in Sofia was now playing up this fear, making it increasingly hard for Radoslavov to maintain a friendly position to-

---

[6] Staatsarchiv, PA, box 872, unnumbered, Burian to Tarnowski, 10 February 1915; italics in the original.
[7] Ibid., no. 20/P, Tarnowski to Vienna, 22 February 1915.

ward the Central Powers. What he needed was an official and formal assurance that Germany and Austria were willing to offer more than the Entente could. Von Mach therefore advised a declaration offering Bulgaria "the territory of all the enemies of Germany and its allies to which Bulgaria had ethnographic and historic rights," with only neutrality being demanded in return.[8]

In the last days of February and the beginning of March, Toscheff in Vienna sounded both Burian and Tschirschky. He stated that the Entente powers had offered a part of Thrace up to the Enos-Midia line in exchange for Bulgarian neutrality and had put this in writing. Could not the Central Powers offer in writing a part of Serbia in exchange for Bulgarian neutrality, to serve as a counterweight to the maneuver of the enemy camp? Burian's answer was definite. He did not believe the Entente had given a written declaration. At best they might have made a verbal offer. Austria had already made clear how far it would go. In terms of additional written guarantees, Burian refused to offer anything at all nor was Tschirschky more amenable. The ambassador stated that Germany's agreement to give Bulgaria financial aid showed its support of the Bulgarian government. After the various assurances made to Bulgaria, its "see-saw policy" was surprising, particularly when it toyed with the idea of accepting offers of Turkish territories in spite of the close ties between the two countries. Tschirschky cut short any further debate by coldly saying that additional desires on the matter of compensations should be addressed to the German minister in Sofia and to Berlin.[9]

The Wilhelmstrasse itself did not take so adamant a line. The Germans would have liked Bulgaria to take action, but they agreed with Burian that its neutrality was "laudable and valuable." Significantly, they were now willing to offer "a more formal understanding" in exchange for neutrality, but that would depend on Austria's agreement to the move.[10] The Wilhelmstrasse had thus far worked in careful tandem with the Ballhausplatz, but in the course of the next six months the Germans took an increasingly stronger line with respect to obtaining a Bulgarian ally and on this matter ended by placing the Dual Monarchy in diplomatic leading strings.

During March the Germans once again began a diplomatic campaign to engage the Bulgarians, and, peculiarly enough, the question of

[8] Carl Mühlmann, *Oberste Heeresleitung und Balkan im Weltkrieg, 1914–1918*, pp. 52, 53; GFMA, ser. 2, reel 13, no. 8595, von Mach to Zimmermann, 4 March 1915.
[9] GFMA, ser. 2, reel 13, no. 45, Michahelles to Berlin, 8 March 1915; this constitutes Burian's position as presented to Toscheff in Vienna on 24 February; no. 567, Tschirschky to Berlin, 10 March.
[10] Ibid., no. 82, Zimmermann in Berlin to von Mach, 12 March 1915.

written guarantees for neutrality became bound up with obtaining Bulgarian participation in the war. The basis for the renewed diplomatic campaign was Falkenhayn's decision that a Serbian campaign was necessary to open the way to Turkey. He had to win Conrad von Hötzendorf's assent, but Conrad, who was preoccupied with the eastern theater, would not agree. The German Foreign Office did all it could to cooperate in this new attempt.

On March 21 Michahelles had reported that Radoslavov wanted the German military attaché to speak with his war minister on the military sections of a treaty. When Michahelles questioned King Ferdinand on Bulgarian action, the king answered that he first wanted to obtain the views of his military chiefs. A week later von Falkenhayn sent the German military attaché in Constantinople, Colonel von Leipzig, to Sofia: "Go immediately to Sofia for a few days, and, on the basis of your acquaintanceship with the king and leading men there, try to convince them it is to Bulgaria's own interest that it share with us and Austria an action against Serbia and not wait until we have arranged the matter."[11]

Falkenhayn's orders were more easily written than carried out, for to move the Bulgarian king assurances of a peaceful Rumania would have to be made. The part which Bulgaria might play in a Serbian campaign would have to be small so that the risk would not be too large. Murmurings were filtering through from Michahelles that Bulgaria wanted not only Macedonia but also the area of Serbia proper up to the Morava River. The General Staff thought the main goal was to get Bulgaria into the fight as soon as possible, but as Jagow patiently explained to Falkenhayn, a military convention would have to go hand in hand with political provisoes. Bulgaria would not settle for less.[12] By March 30 Falkenhayn had won over Conrad to the idea of a new Serbian campaign; but without Bulgarian participation Conrad still refused to move. In truth, Vienna, while it supported the German attempt to gain Bulgarian action, did so reluctantly. At this time Count Burian was much preoccupied with the whole Italian situation. The Germans hoped they could initiate a Serbian campaign by the end of April, and Burian agreed that such a campaign was highly desirable. It was not desirable, however, that Bulgaria take action against Serbia

[11] Ibid., no. 219, von Treutler at German headquarters to Berlin, 26 March 1915; no. 110, Michahelles to Berlin, 21 March; no. 223, von Treutler at German headquarters to Berlin, 28 March. Von Treutler served as Foreign Office representative attached to the German general staff.
[12] Ibid., no. 127, the military attaché in Sofia to Falkenhayn, countersigned by Michahelles, 26 March 1915; no. 131, Michahelles to Berlin, 27 March; no. 248, Jagow to Falkenhayn, 1 April.

unless Austria did so simultaneously. But Austria could not enter a new Serbian campaign with impunity unless an understanding with Italy had first been reached so that Austria's rear was protected. To obtain such an understanding within three weeks was something Burian much wanted to do though he saw it as very difficult to manage.[13]

Burian's thinking on the Italian situation allowed continuation of Bulgarian successes in effortlessly extorting money from the Central Powers. The second installment of the loan granted in January was due in two payments to be made on April 1 and 15. Michahelles had prompted Berlin to insist that Sofia meet the provisoes attached to completion of these payments—mobilization. The German minister saw seventy-five million francs dangled before the eyes of Radoslavov as an excellent means of persuading him to declare openly that Bulgaria would take military action. The financial bait should not be given up, "for it is basic to [the] Bulgarian character that the more one gives the more they want."[14]

Now, since Burian did not think mobilization of Bulgaria's army opportune until Italy had been rendered harmless, he asked that the loan be put through without the pressure envisaged by Berlin. Handling the matter in this way would certainly prove their good faith. Jagow consented and instructed Michahelles to inform the Bulgarians that the provisoes would be waived with respect to the first payment. He had come to the conclusion that holding up the money would probably not be enough to force Ferdinand to decide in their favor, whereas the ill humor produced by attempted coercion might lead to a complete breakdown of negotiations. So the payments were put through without any demands being made. In this matter, Germany and Austria were forced by other than Bulgarian considerations to give up their financial trump card.[15]

What had up to this point been a mere feeler by Bulgaria to obtain written guarantees in exchange for neutrality now became a full-blown

[13] Ibid., no. 232, Treutler to Berlin, 30 March 1915; no. 624, Tschirschky to Berlin, 1 April; no. 167/P Hohenlohe in Berlin to the German Foreign Office, 31 March.

[14] Ibid., no. 53, Michahelles to Berlin, 22 March 1915.

[15] Staatsarchiv, PA, box 513, no. 288, Tarnowski to Burian, 27 March 1915; no. 258, Burian to Hohenlohe in Berlin, 29 March; no. 131, Hohenlohe to Burian, 30 March; no. 301, Tarnowski to Burian, 31 March; no. 151, Hohenlohe to Burian, 8 April; no. 357, Tarnowski to Burian, 13 April; no. 210, Hohenlohe to Burian, 6 May. These documents show that each payment was granted in the hope that by the due date of the succeeding one, the Italian problem would be solved so that financial pressure could be brought to bear upon the Bulgarians for mobilization. The Italians were not successfully dealt with and so the political provisoes of the loan were simply discarded. GFMA, ser. 2, reel 13, no. 132, Michahelles to Berlin, 29 March; no. 256, Jagow to Michahelles, 30 March.

attempt. On April 8 Totschkoff, one of the chief leaders of a Bulgarian political faction called the Macedonian Committee, visited Berlin for unofficial talks with Jagow and Hohenlohe. For tactical reasons intended to deflate those Bulgarians who were favorable to the Entente, he suggested that the Central Powers grant written concessions for neutrality. If this was done there would be no reason to fear that Bulgaria would remain inactive; he pledged that, given the necessary guarantees, his party would overcome Ferdinand's reluctance. Jagow gave a careful answer, adding that his remarks were, of course, quite unofficial. The significant thing was that he agreed to a written guarantee for Bulgarian neutrality and was willing to grant certain Serbian areas. If, on the other hand, Bulgaria was willing to enter on their side, the Germans would go far beyond this and offer parts of old Serbia which "neither belonged to Bulgaria ethnographically nor historically, nor were occupied by Bulgarian troops." The particulars could be laid down in a military convention which Germany and Austria were now willing to conclude. The Central Powers recognized the value of Bulgarian benevolent neutrality, but a continuation of this status would obviously reduce the size of the concessions for which Bulgaria might hope.[16] Having made this statement, Jagow asked Hohenlohe to ascertain the views of Vienna, so that he might say that Germany's ally concurred.

While Burian was formulating his answer, von Leipzig was busy in Sofia. He came to the conclusion that Radoslavov and Ferdinand were not "in principle" against military cooperation, but he was also convinced they would participate only after the Germans and Austrians had begun operations and had actually crossed the Danube. On April 13 he met with Ferdinand for a long and frank conversation. It was apparent that the Bulgarian king feared a Russian attack, for the Russian minister, Alexander Savinsky, had threatened a declaration of war if Bulgaria attacked Serbia, and it was this threat which prevented the government from throwing in its lot with the Central Powers. Beyond this, Ferdinand had stated that the Entente had given him in return for neutrality a written promise of the following territories: the border line of Enos-Midia, the Greek districts of Seres, Drama, Kavalla, Bulgarian Macedonia, and the whole Dobrudja. Leipzig parried well by declaring that while the Entente might have made such offers, they could no more honor them than if they had promised Ferdinand the whole world. On the other hand, the Central Powers could support any guarantee they made, and what Bulgaria held by armed control at

[16] Staatsarchiv, PA, box 513, no. 28/P, Hohenlohe to Burian, 8 April 1915; GFMA, ser. 2, reel 13, no. AS 1524, Foreign Office report, Jagow, 8 April.

the end of the war would remain in its possession by fait accompli.[17]

Meanwhile, Burian had been thinking things over. The answer he sent by Hohenlohe on April 13 showed he was still reluctant to grant Bulgaria concessions. His approach remained consistent with the ideas he had expressed when he first took office, and he declared that Bulgaria "did not appear necessary for the attainment of our purposes." Nevertheless, he was willing to go along with offering the Bulgarians restricted concessions in return for neutrality, though he balked at the idea of granting them Serbian areas to which they had no claim, on the grounds that it involved "the further destinies of Austria-Hungary."[18]

Clearly, the Austrians wanted to take a much more cautious line than their ally. The documents show the course of developments in April and May, 1915. Germany was taking the initiative, and Austria, against its better judgment, was going along, applying a judicious brake wherever it could. Unquestionably Germany wanted desperately to pull in Bulgaria now that the Dardanelles campaign had placed the Turks in danger, and was willing to bid very high in order to do it.

By the beginning of May, Sofia had had a chance to assess the significance of the promises Totschkoff had received from Jagow in their conversation. Because Jagow seemed ready to raise the ante, and because the Entente was making bigger offers, the Bulgarians made a bold move. On May 9 Radoslavov dropped a bombshell into Michahelles' lap in the form of a declaration draft, which Germany was to sign. It read:

> The German government appreciates the neutrality observed up to the present by the Bulgarian government in the European crisis and declares that if this neutrality is maintained to the conclusion of peace, it guarantees to Bulgaria in compensation for its attitude of benevolence toward the allies the possession of Macedonia encircling the zones called 'contested' and 'uncontested,' such as were delimited by the Bulgarian-Serbian Treaty of Alliance of February 29–March 13, 1912, and conforming to the map annexed to this treaty.
>
> The above territories are guaranteed to Bulgaria independent of their being occupied or not occupied by Bulgarian troops at the time of the conclusion of peace. Moreover, Germany guarantees to Bulgaria a part of the territories actually possessed by Greece and Rumania by virtue of the Treaty of Bukarest of July 27, 1913, if one of these countries or both enter into war against the allies or solely against one of them. The extent of this piece of territory will be determined on the basis of the present declaration by a special accord between Germany and Bulgaria.[19]

[17] GFMA, ser. 2, reel 13, no. 156, Leipzig to Falkenhayn, 8 April 1915; no. 13948, Leipzig's report, 13 April.

[18] Staatsarchiv, PA, box 513, no. 307, Burian to Hohenlohe, 13 April 1915.

[19] Ibid., box 872, no. 464, Tarnowski to Burian, 11 May 1915; GFMA, ser. 2, reel 13, no. 63, Michahelles to Berlin, 9 May. See map, p. 159.

What was the purpose of this declaration? Radoslavov blandly declared that it was merely to meet the opposition of those Bulgarians who favored Russia. With such an agreement in his hands he could clearly show that the Central Powers offered as much as the Entente. The German minister's reaction was positive, for he wired the home office that in his opinion the Bulgarians were potentially the greatest power in the Balkans. To help them gain their territorial desires was to free them completely from dependence on Russia and to obtain a very close relationship between them and Germany and Austria-Hungary. Most crucial was his belief that such a declaration could be signed with impunity, since in his estimation Sofia was ready to join them in the war as soon as the Central Powers began operations against the Serbs.[20]

The German Foreign Office agreed with Michahelles; Jagow wired Tschirschky in Vienna, saying Berlin did not think the signing of the declaration would lead the Bulgarian government to lose any desire to participate in open war.

The Austrians did not at all respond as the Germans would have liked. Radoslavov had presented Tarnowski with a duplicate copy of the declaration two days after the Germans received theirs; when he sent it on to Vienna, Tarnowski remarked that he had received his copy later because the Bulgarians must have realized the impossibility of Austria's accepting their demands. On May 13 Burian sent his reactions to Germany. He stated most definitely that they must make a concrete distinction between what they would offer Bulgaria for its neutrality and what for its cooperation. Considering the fact that Germany's attempt to engage Bulgaria actively had thus far failed, it seemed to him to no purpose to grant "an all-engrossing premium for its neutrality." Concerning any promises by the Central Powers he declared, "I must absolutely refuse the undertaking of a *guarantee*." He believed it possible that the Central Powers would win their war without having to grant Bulgaria parts of Serbia. He was willing to concede areas in Rumania and on the Greek coast, but only if those powers made war on Germany and Austria, and if Bulgaria committed itself to active participation.[21]

The German Foreign Office had its hands full. On the one hand, it sought to meet the Bulgarian demands for concessions in the hope that Bulgaria would be led to join in, but on the other, it faced a balking ally. Terms had to be arranged agreeable to both Central Powers and at the same time acceptable to Sofia. Aside from this knotty problem, the

[20] GFMA, ser. 2, reel 13, no. 63, Michahelles to Berlin, 9 May 1915.
[21] Staatsarchiv, PA, box 872, no. 423, Burian to Hohenlohe, 13 May 1915; italics in the original.

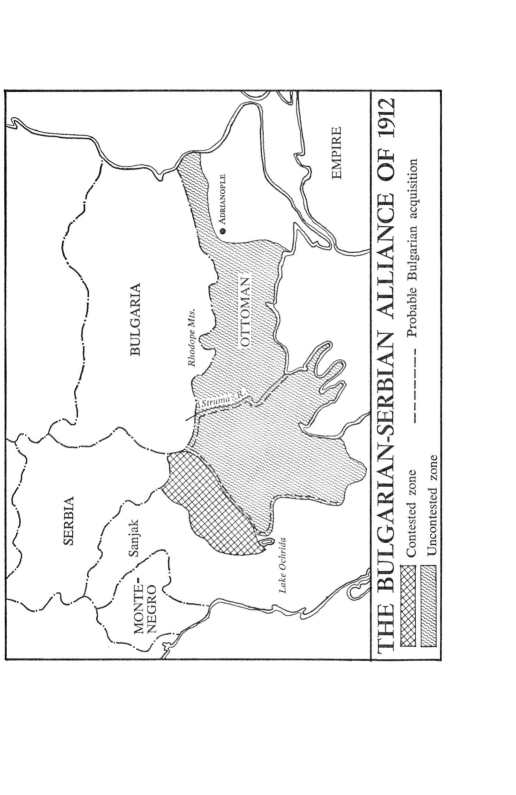

THE BULGARIAN-SERBIAN ALLIANCE OF 1912

Contested zone

Uncontested zone

—————— Probable Bulgarian acquisition

SERBIA

MONTE-
NEGRO

Sanjak

BULGARIA

Rhodope Mts.

Struma R.

OTTOMAN

Lake Ochrida

● ADRIANOPLE

EMPIRE

German High Command was pushing the Foreign Office to obtain a precise commitment from King Ferdinand. The situation concerning Italy had grown much worse, and by the middle of May it was quite clear the Italians would join the Entente. The question facing Falkenhayn was whether he and Conrad should hold their forces for an attack on Italy or go ahead with a campaign against Serbia. Bethmann-Hollweg had pointed out to him that the Serbian campaign was the more important, that they could probably still count on Bulgarian participation there, that such an action would deter Rumania, open a way to Turkey, and secure them in the Balkans. He suggested a merely defensive action against Italy. Falkenhayn, however, could not make his plans on the basis of probabilities. He wanted an answer from Bulgaria, he wanted it quickly, and it was up to the Foreign Office to get it for him. On May 18 he wired from headquarters that the answer must be obtained within forty-eight hours. He was willing to mount a Serbian campaign if Bulgaria definitely agreed to take part, and for such an agreement he was prepared to make every military concession. He therefore recommended that all political barriers be immediately cleared away. German troops could not enter Serbia alone, and without Sofia's promise to help, Conrad would not commit his forces. If Germany took on the campaign, Austria, facing the brunt of an Italian attack, could not allocate sufficient troops to Serbia, and the effect on a small German force in Serbia without Bulgarian aid could only be defeat.[22]

As German-Austrian negotiations on the declaration proceeded, Jagow did the best he could to smooth Burian's ruffled feathers over the steps Germany had taken. He began by agreeing with him. He admitted that a distinction should be made between concessions for neutrality and those for participation; that no guarantees should be given to Bulgaria for its territorial aspirations except for those areas which its troops held at the end of the war, or which were held by "our combined troops"; and that Bulgaria should obtain areas of Greece and Rumania only if those countries turned against the Central Powers. But, he said, they had to face the fact that a real difficulty had been presented by the Entente's offers for neutrality. He therefore suggested that the term "guarantees" be handled in such a way that Sofia understood they would do all they could at war's end to satisfy

[22] GFMA, ser. 2, reel 13, no. 60, Treutler to the Foreign Office, 18 May 1915; no. 394, Jagow to Michahelles, 19 May; no. 489, Bethmann-Hollweg to Falkenhayn, 17 May; unnumbered telegram from Falkenhayn to Bethmann, 17 May; no. 67, Falkenhayn to Bethmann, 20 May.

its ambitions, that satisfaction would depend on the military situation at that time and that "absolute guarantees" could only be given with respect to the areas which the Central Powers had actually occupied.[23]

Burian had protested that they might have the chance to make an advantageous peace before they had occupied the areas desired by the Bulgarians. It was, he remarked, "too much to ask that we give up this chance and pursue the war further only for the purpose of providing Bulgaria with enlargement of its territories without equivalents from Bulgaria." Yet, the Austrian minister was just as much aware as his German colleagues of the darkening Italian skies and of the immediate problems with which the allies were jointly faced. The war situation now forced him to change his policy. On May 18 Burian gave Tarnowski the green light, saying he agreed with Berlin "to support the wish of the Bulgarian government with respect to assurances of territorial extension for neutrality."[24] He authorized Tarnowski to cooperate with his German colleague and to draw up a declaration. The text, however, was only to mention the "uncontested zone." If Radoslavov was not satisfied they would then have to include the "contested zone" as well. Both Tarnowski and Michahelles would have to interpret properly the word "guarantee" in a secret note to be attached to the declaration, and the interpretation must clearly state that the guarantee of territories to Bulgaria would depend upon the areas which the Central Powers had occupied with their troops by the end of the war.[25]

The German and Austrian ministers worked quickly to produce a satisfactory text. Michahelles sounded Radoslavov on the omission of the "contested zone," and found him favorable. On May 21 the declaration along with an explicative note was submitted to the Bulgarian government. Except for omission of the contested zone, it offered precisely what Radoslavov had demanded in the draft submitted to Michahelles on May 9. It was only in the attached note that Germany and Austria managed to some extent to apply a checkrein:

> So as to give an authentic interpretation of the guarantee to which Germany [Austria] obligated itself in the Declaration, it is to be understood that the German [Austrian] government would do all possible at the conclusion of peace to procure for Bulgaria the territories in question. It will naturally depend on the military successes which Germany

[23] Staatsarchiv, PA, box 872, no. 223, Hohenlohe to Burian, 14 May 1915; GFMA, ser. 2, reel 13, no. 320, Jagow to Tschirschky, 14 May.

[24] GFMA, ser. 2, reel 13, no. 320, Jagow to Tschirschky, 14 May 1915; this instruction contains a summary of Burian's objections; Staatsarchiv, PA, box 872, no. 227, Burian to Tarnowski, 18 May.

[25] Staatsarchiv, PA, box 872, no. 227, Burian to Tarnowski, 18 May 1915.

[Austria] will have obtained at this moment as to whether Bulgarian aspirations will be realized in their entirety as indicated in the Declaration, and for this it would be very important that the territory Bulgaria wished to acquire be occupied at the time of the conclusion of peace by German [Austrian] troops or by its allies.[26]

Michahelles went further than his Austrian colleague. He submitted a second copy for the personal use of King Ferdinand, and along with this copy went a special memoir. In accordance with the policy of the German Foreign Office to seal the bargain as quickly as possible, Michahelles stated in the memoir that Germany was willing to offer, in addition, the contested zone, through the signing of a treaty of alliance, if Bulgaria decided on a military action. If Sofia wanted further guarantees, Germany was willing to discuss them and to arrive at a rapid agreement. In short, the memoir agreed to pay any price that Ferdinand and his government might possibly set for active cooperation. Vienna had not really agreed to such sweeping statements, but the Wilhelmstrasse had seized the reins.

While Burian had been influenced to make concessions by Conrad (who in early May had written that he now considered Bulgaria's military cooperation as "pressing and necessary"), he had done whatever he could to have the Germans take a more cautious line in the offers made. The question of the contested zone produced friction between the two allies. While both ministers in Sofia had been instructed to offer this area if necessary, Tarnowski made no mention of it when Radoslavov did not insist on having it included. Michahelles, through his memoir to the king, made it apparent that they would grant the zone in return for military cooperation only. But in the process of the negotiation, General von der Goltz, visiting Sofia, had told the influential politician Totschkoff that Germany was willing to include this territory in the declaration itself. Naturally, this information very quickly reached Radoslavov and King Ferdinand. Tarnowski complained to Vienna that von der Goltz had compromised Austria's position, and Burian wired Berlin that he regretted that the German representative "in ignorance of our general interests sought to reflect in his conversations a difference in the benevolent feelings of Germany and Austria." Jagow quickly promised Burian that von der Goltz would be more careful from now on. But the damage had been done. When Totschkoff was asked to put pressure on his government, as,

[26] GFMA, ser. 2, reel 13, no. 76, Michahelles to Berlin, 28 May 1915. The declaration and explicative note were submitted to Radoslavov not jointly by Germany and Austria but separately by each of the two ministers concerned.

from his earlier talks in Berlin, it was assumed he would do, he now refused. Totschkoff knew that Bulgaria could extract more Macedonian territory if it insisted.[27]

Sofia's reaction came quickly. Radoslavov was much pleased with the declaration. He could now, he said, go to the king with more than empty hands. Perhaps the king would be so satisfied he would even agree to sign an alliance. On May 22 Ferdinand gave his reply. Bulgaria would not enter the war. It was not the right time to decide on cooperation. He refused to sign an alliance and he refused to send an officer to Budapest to meet with Falkenhayn as had been previously suggested. The sending of military personnel would give the impression that Bulgaria had a secret alliance with the Central Powers, when in fact its position was benevolent neutrality. Therefore, in answer to Tarnowski's eager query, Radoslavov blandly answered, "Bulgaria must still wait."[28]

Bulgaria, the Diplomatic Victor

If the success of the Central Powers in Galicia had perhaps inclined the Bulgarians for a while to consider entering the war, the inclination quickly vanished as it became clear that Italy would join the Entente. A day after Ferdinand gave his response, Italy declared war on Austria-Hungary. This, along with the uncertain position of Rumania, led the Bulgarian king to an even more intractable stand. He was bolstered by Totschkoff and his Macedonian Committee which, in spite of all concessions, was dissatisfied with the declaration, and by the Stambulov Party, which sought further negotiation with the Entente.[29]

There was nothing to do but have Jagow inform Michahelles that the campaign against Serbia would now have to be postponed. The High Command hoped that in about two weeks the successful campaign against Russia in Galicia would be completed, and troops could

[27] GFMA, ser. 2, reel 13, no. 76, Michahelles to Berlin, 28 May 1915; Staatsarchiv, PA, box 872, no. 499, Tarnowski to Burian, 20 May; no. 9700, Conrad to Burian, 3 May; no. 503, Tarnowski to Burian, 22 May; no. 471, Burian to Hohenlohe, 23 May; no. 246, Hohenlohe to Burian, 24 May; no. 45/P, part B, Tarnowski to Burian, 24 May.
[28] Staatsarchiv, PA, box 872, no. 501, Tarnowski to Burian, 21 May 1915; no. 506, Tarnowski to Burian, 22 May; GFMA, ser. 2, reel 13, no. 76, Michahelles to Berlin, 28 May 1915.
[29] GFMA, ser. 2, reel 13, no. 245, Michahelles to Berlin, 29 May 1915; Staatsarchiv, PA, box 872, nos. 512, 513, 514, Tarnowski to Burian, 22 May; report no. 43/P, Tarnowski to Burian, 21 May. The Stambulov Party was led by Ghenadiev, who, after a trip to various capitals in Europe, had recommended a *rapprochement* with England and France.

be made available for Serbia. "In the meantime," said Jagow, "we must keep Bulgaria neutral under all conditions and maintain the possibility of Bulgaria's going along later." If the question of money arose, there were "inexhaustible funds available, should they be necessary."[30]

The Ballhausplatz reacted impatiently and negatively to the whole issue. On May 26 in his instructions to Tarnowski, Burian summed up the previous negotiations with Bulgaria, saying that since the opening of the war the attempts of the Central Powers had been practically without results and had led only to "delays, new terms, new demands, on which entry was made dependent." One thing did seem clear: that Bulgaria was determined to participate against Serbia only after Germany and Austria had actually begun operations. Even with respect to this the Central Powers had merely oral assurances. Therefore the foreign minister believed that their previous methods would have to be discarded. They simply had to know precisely what they could expect from this country. The Central Powers could not begin an operation for the success of which Bulgarian aid would be crucial, not knowing for sure "if and when this cooperation would actually come." Tarnowski was to discuss this matter quite frankly with Radoslavov, though in a most friendly fashion. To make sure the minister understood what was wanted, Burian repeated the immediate aim: "We must know precisely from which day on, where, and in what strength we can count on the Bulgarian offensive. Discuss with Herr Radoslavov ways and means for a political and military cooperation which could be realized practically and without further delay."[31]

These orders certainly disclose the fact that Burian, though formerly willing to hold Bulgaria neutral, had now swung over to the German point of view that aimed at full Bulgarian participation. The disparity between Vienna and Berlin would henceforth hinge on the price to be paid.

In answer to Tarnowski's urging, Radoslavov refused to give one bit of ground. He was friendly toward the Dual Monarchy. He could assert that most assuredly Bulgaria would not fight against the Central Powers; but at this time he was simply unable to discuss the question of open cooperation. Tarnowski frankly asked for reasons. Was it the war situation in general, or the Italian attack, or perhaps internal political problems? When would the moment for talking cooperation come? Radoslavov refused to give a precise answer. Perhaps he could say more shortly. For now Bulgaria would have to remain neutral.[32]

[30] GFMA, ser. 2, reel 13, no. 415, Jagow to Michahelles, 24 May 1915.
[31] Staatsarchiv, PA, box 513, no. 243, Burian to Tarnowski, 26 May 1915.
[32] Ibid., nos. 545, 546, Tarnowski to Burian, 28 May 1915.

One simple reason stood behind the refusal of the Central Powers to open a new offensive against the Serbs in the hope that Bulgaria would then follow. Both German and Austrian diplomats had been told by their respective military chiefs that Bulgaria would require approximately seventeen days to mobilize and another ten to deploy its forces. Since it was believed that the entire campaign could be handled in a month, the Bulgarian forces, from a military standpoint, would serve no purpose; and from a political standpoint the Central Powers would end by granting Bulgaria territorial concessions as a pure gift. Neither Berlin nor Vienna was willing to have Bulgaria collect wages without working for them.[33]

Sofia could afford to temporize. It had been negotiating with the Entente during the month of May, and on June 1 Radoslavov let go his next diplomatic fusilade. He informed Michahelles and Tarnowski that the Entente powers had made a new offer: both zones in Macedonia, Enos-Midia, Kavalla, diplomatic aid in obtaining the Dobrudja from Rumania, and financial support. The price—a Bulgarian attack on Turkey. Ferdinand and his minister-president were no more willing to accept this commitment than they had been willing to fight for Germany and Austria, and they said Bulgaria would not give up its neutrality. They were interested in seeing what reaction to the offer the Central Powers would have.[34]

In Berlin the reaction was near panic. To Jagow it seemed that the Bulgarians were ready to conclude with the Entente. There was no time to lose. Therefore they must immediately offer the Bulgarians both contested and uncontested zones in return for a benevolent neutrality, in writing, with no conditions. The explicative note was to be withdrawn and explained away as a misunderstanding.

The Ballhausplatz had a like case of the jitters, for Burian saw the Entente proposition as proof of how intensively the enemy was working to obtain Bulgaria as an ally. For him, the whole thing reflected a very critical moment. He therefore sent off the same instructions to Sofia as the Germans had. All of Tarnowski's influence was to be employed "to keep Radoslavov from being pushed from his former policy line."[35]

The respective ministers kept their heads and cooly analyzed the picture. They saw that the color of things had not changed in any

[33] Ibid., no. 243, Burian to Tarnowski, 26 May 1915; GFMA, memo. no. 2591, Jagow to Michahelles, 24 May.
[34] GFMA, ser. 2, reel 13, no. 259, Michahelles to Berlin, 1 June 1915; Staatsarchiv, PA, box 872, no. 572, Tarnowski to Burian, 1 June.
[35] GFMA, ser. 2, reel 13, no. 462, Jagow to Michahelles, 1 June 1915; Staatsarchiv, PA, box 872, no. 272, Burian to Tarnowski, 2 June.

way. They could, in fact, find not one danger to their interests. Their chiefs were obviously unimpressed by their evaluation, because both home offices sent instructions to submit a new declaration on the basis outlined by Jagow. On June 5 and 6 the declaration, without the explicative note, was delivered. To this Radoslavov stated that, except for the contested zone's being added, it was the same as the first; this was true enough, but in the meantime he had obtained everything he asked for.[36]

That Michahelles and Tarnowski were quite correct in believing the Entente had gained no ground is evidenced by the answer of Radoslavov to the Entente representatives on June 16. In response to the promises they had made, he offered a series of questions aimed at making their offer much more precise in its details. These details the Entente powers were not in a position to define.[37]

It seemed to the Central Powers they were getting nowhere. They had offered concession after concession and still the Bulgarians stolidly refused any commitment. But in reality the denouement of the drama had been reached. Six weeks after Radoslavov responded to the Entente proposition, King Ferdinand agreed to send a Bulgarian to German headquarters to draw up a military convention. Several things led Bulgaria to take this step, which constituted the prelude to a binding alliance. First of all, the Central Powers, true to Tarnowski's predictions, had been able to outbid their enemies for Bulgaria's services. By July 23 Michahelles could report that no answer had been given by Entente representatives to Radoslavov's note. Second, the war against Russia on the eastern front had gone very well. On June 19 Michahelles had told Sofia the victory over the Russians in Galicia was "as good as done"; the remark was underlined when Lemberg, the key city of Galicia, fell to the German forces under Mackensen. By July 13 a new attack was in progress aimed at shattering Russian resistance. For Sofia, these successes greatly reduced the Russian military menace.

[36] GFMA, ser. 2, reel 13, no. 269, Michahelles to Jagow, 2 June 1915; no. 282, Michahelles to Berlin, 4 June; Staatsarchiv, PA, box 872, no. 575, Tarnowski to Burian, 6 June; no. 493, Burian to Hohenlohe, 4 June. In Burian's wire to Hohenlohe he explained that Tschirschky had ardently pressed for his cooperation. Tschirschky wanted to assure Bulgarian neutrality by granting Bulgaria all its wishes.

[37] Staatsarchiv, PA, box 872, no. 648, Tarnowski to Burian, 17 June 1915; GFMA, ser. 2, reel 13, no. 177, Michahelles to Berlin, 15 June. Radoslavov had asked: Was the "uncontested zone" that of the Bulgarian-Serbian Treaty of 1912? What would be the "equitable compensation" the Entente mentioned as going to Serbia in return for the "contested zone?" How far would the hinterland of Kavalla reach and what would Greece obtain in Asia Minor as an indemnity? What basis would the Entente use for solving the Dobrudja question between Bulgaria and Rumania?

Along other military lines, Tarnowski had managed to excite the interest of the Bulgarians when, having received Burian's consent in late June, he intimated to Radoslavov that Austria had now decided on a Serbian campaign without regard to Bulgarian cooperation. When Radoslavov registered surprise, Tarnowski slyly remarked that the whole thing had been kept a military secret, but that if the minister-president had been willing to initiate talks through military representa-tives the Bulgarians would long ago have known the Monarchy's plans. Radoslavov's new attitude was reflected in his answer: previously that had been impossible but the situation was now different.

Third, as pointed out in an earlier chapter, serious negotiations between Bulgaria and Turkey had been resumed in May. By June, Sofia had become aware that it could not extract the area north of the Enos-Midia line from Constantinople without actual warfare with the Turks. Yet, by July, there was every chance of gaining Turkish assent to a border which followed the Maritza River. The Turks, working in conjunction with Berlin and Vienna, had set as a precondition Bulgar-ia's willingness to bind itself definitely to the Central Powers. Finally, the Bulgarians well knew that the option on the great loan agreed to in July, 1914, was scheduled to be picked up on August 1, and that on this same date the repayment of 120 million francs granted in July, 1914, was due. In short, the diplomatic, the military, and the financial scene in the summer of 1915 pointed to the obvious conclusion: it was now in Bulgaria's interest to conclude binding obligations with Germany and Austria-Hungary.[38]

On August 3, Colonel Gantscheff, a former military attaché in Berlin and a Bulgarian General Staff officer, arrived at Pless for conversations. Since Gantscheff's instructions gave him full powers to make a settle-ment, he immediately laid down Bulgaria's terms. Bulgaria demanded: 1) a new loan of 200 million francs; 2) a declaration that Germany and Austria would look upon Rumania and Greece as enemies if they attacked Bulgaria; 3) the immediate cession of Seres and Kavalla if Greece mobilized, and should Greece refuse the cession, German-Austrian military support for a Bulgarian declaration of war; 4) the sending of German troops to the Bulgarian ports of Varna and Burgas so that a Russian attack on these ports would meet German resistance; 5) a pledge by the Turks to ward off English and French naval attacks

[38] Staatsarchiv, PA, box 872, no. 797, Tarnowski to Burian, 21 July 1915; no. 843, Tarnowski to Burian, 31 July; no. 663, Tarnowski to Burian, 19 June; GFMA, ser. 2, reel 14, no. 387, Michahelles to Berlin, 23 July; Staatsarchiv, PA, box 872, no. 702, Tarnowski to Burian, 25 June; GFMA, ser. 2, reel 14, no. 388, Michahelles to Berlin, 23 July; Staatsarchiv, PA, box 872, no. 68/P, Tarnowski to Burian, 30 July. For the Bulgarian-Turkish negotiations, see above, chapter 5, pp. 119–28.

on the port of Dedeagatch; and 6) a recognition of Bulgaria's claim to all of Macedonia, and, in Serbia, the largest area possible as far as the Morava River and the Negotine Circle.[39]

The reactions of Berlin and Vienna were essentially positive. Jagow saw the demand for more money as certainly unpleasant, but acceptable because necessary. The other terms were unobjectionable, except for point 3, which he absolutely refused. Bulgaria would have to deliver a declaration of neutrality to Greece if the latter should take the same position. He was willing to accept Bulgaria's territorial demands in point 6 if Austria consented. Burian's reaction was likewise to accept all points except the third. In his opinion the Central Powers could not afford to "place the very worthwhile neutrality of Greece in question."[40]

On August 10 Gantscheff left Pless and hurried back to Sofia for conferences with his government. His opinion of the negotiations had been favorable. All seemed to be going well. The Germans had stressed that Bulgaria must speedily sign the convention since they wished to start the Serbian campaign by the end of the month. Michahelles had been instructed that if the Bulgarians wanted an alliance along with the military convention, he was to say Germany was ready to sign such an accord.[41]

It was now that negotiations became more detailed and nerve-racking, for rancor against Germany had been building in Vienna. Early in the previous month Burian had written to Tarnowski that Austria had no desire to force Bulgaria into a formal agreement. He observed, "A wish for an alliance or a need for an alliance does not exist on our side, but should the alliance be asked for on Bulgaria's side, we would then indeed have to go into it." His goal was Bulgarian military cooperation

---

[39] Staatsarchiv, PA, box 872, report no. 73 A-D/P, Hohenlohe to Burian, 4 August 1915; GFMA, ser. 2, reel 14, no. 259, von Treutler, Foreign Office representative at Pless, to Berlin, 3 August; no. 273, Treutler to Berlin, 7 August. Gantscheff dealt initially only with the Germans. The request by Vienna that an Austrian officer be included in the discussions was met by Falkenhayn's remark that he was in constant contact with Conrad and that the latter would be summoned to take part when the "situation became serious." This attitude was not in any way appreciated by Vienna and added to the general tensions between the two allies as the final negotiations proceeded.

[40] Staatsarchiv, PA, box 872, report no. 73 A-D/P, Hohenlohe to Burian, 4 August 1915; memorandum no. 4091, Burian to Hohenlohe, 6 August; GFMA, ser. 2, reel 14, no. 1947, Jagow to Tschirschky, 4 August. On point 3, Jagow elaborated by saying that a Greek-Bulgarian war must be avoided since such a struggle would be against German interests. It would cause the Bulgarians to swing their main strength against the Greeks, leaving Germany with the greatest work in a Serbian campaign.

[41] Staatsarchiv, PA, box 872, no. 362, Hohenlohe to Burian, 10 August 1915; no. 893, Tarnowski to Burian, 12 August.

and for this end he was agreeable to a signed military convention. A few days later the Austrian minister, in a resume of the problem, pointed to the difficult position into which he had been forced by Michahelles. The latter, on the basis of his instructions from Berlin, had openly raised the issue of alliance in such a way that the Bulgarians now had the impression that the conclusion of an alliance depended only on their own decision. Tarnowski had repeatedly pointed out to his German colleague that it was "basically inept to deepen such an impression," but to no avail. Jagow, having received Burian's views on the question through Hohenlohe, attempted to smooth things over by agreeing that the Austrian position was correct; however, he saw no way out. While they should perhaps not press heavily for such an alliance, he did not see how they could avoid one.[42]

Jagow's remarks in no way lessened the irritation of the Ballhausplatz. On August 2 Burian stated that while he was certainly aware of the general importance and significance of a Serbian campaign, from Austria's viewpoint its value now was highly questionable, since it would depend upon whether the Italian situation allowed such a blow before Austria had decisively defeated the Italian armies. Therefore Burian had hesitations on the whole Bulgarian issue at this time. He was not at all convinced that the approach was sound, and he was not made to feel any better when Tarnowski wired, "It is characteristic that between Radoslavov and [my] German colleague, the question of alliance always comes up." As the month of August went on, Germany increased its activities concerning a formal Bulgarian agreement, and on August 18 Burian wrote a strong message to Berlin saying, "The insistence with which Herr Michahelles works on the Bulgarians with relation to the alliance does not stand in accord with our mutual view." He reminded his ally that they had agreed Bulgaria was not to be offered an alliance but rather the reverse: "*It* was to be left to *ask* the Central Powers."[43]

August 16 had seen Radoslavov drop his first hint that an actual alliance would be demanded. When Gantscheff arrived back in Pless six days later, he had in his pocket a military convention, a draft of a formal alliance, and a secret annex, all of which the Bulgarians wanted signed concurrently. The Austrians took a very gloomy view of the

[42] Ibid., no. 333, Burian to Tarnowski, 3 July 1915; no. 741, Tarnowski to Burian, 5 July; no. 346, Hohenlohe to Burian, 31 July. Since the Turks had demanded that Bulgaria formally tie itself to the Central Powers as a condition for the completion of Bulgarian-Turkish agreements, Jagow felt the alliance would have to be accepted.
[43] Ibid., no. 570, Burian to Hohenlohe, 2 August 1915; no. 856, Tarnowski to Burian, 4 August; no. 592, Burian to Hohenlohe, 18 August; italics in the original.

maneuver, reiterating to Berlin that they did not need an alliance with Bulgaria, the Bulgarians needed them just as much, and, while the military agreement should be pushed to rapid conclusion, the alliance could be left for a later time. The Wilhelmstrasse readily admitted that mere military agreements were most desirable, but the question of opening the way to Constantinople was so important that Bulgarian participation in the war had become crucial. Sofia was thoroughly aware of the worth of Bulgarian cooperation, and Radoslavov saw the simultaneous signing of convention and alliance as a "foregone conclusion." The fact that Berlin did not want negotiations protracted any longer led to the staunch belief there that Bulgarian wishes would have to be granted.[44]

So it was that by August 22 the Germans had, by seizing the initiative, produced a double set of negotiations aimed at formal arrangements—one taking place in military, and one in diplomatic circles —with each dependent upon the other for success. Berlin had raised the ire of its ally, but Austria, while protesting, went along. The result was that fifteen days after Gantscheff returned to Pless with his three drafts, Bulgaria formally declared itself an ally of the Central Powers.

Gantscheff had presented his copy of the alliance and secret annex to the Germans on August 22. Radoslavov handed the Austrians their draft on the next day. While there were some differences, the copies were essentially the same. The alliance, consisting of fourteen articles, bound Germany and Austria to the following agreement: If Bulgaria remained *neutral* the Central Powers would grant it the contested and uncontested zones of Macedonia, according to the Bulgarian-Serbian Alliance of 1912, as far as the Serbian-Greek border. If Greece took part in the war against the Central Powers, Bulgaria would obtain Greek territory east of the Vardar Valley. If Rumania took part in the war against the Central Powers, Bulgaria would gain those lands ceded to Rumania by the Treaty of Bukarest.

If Bulgaria *took part* in the war it would then gain, in addition, the territory in Serbia which had been a portion of the Exarchate of Bulgaria before the Treaty of Berlin of 1878, and the area in old Serbia running from east of a line from Dancora Glara to Golema Cuca. If Greece and Rumania turned hostile, Bulgaria was to obtain the areas granted them by the Treaty of Bukarest and a rectification of the Bulgarian-Rumanian border as also drawn by the Treaty of Berlin. All these territories were to be granted whether or not Bulgarian troops occupied them by the war's end. A further stipulation, intentionally

[44] GFMA, ser. 2, reel 14, no. 324, Treutler to Berlin, 22 August 1915; no. 937, Tschirschky to Berlin, 24 August; no. 487, Jagow to Tschirschky, 24 August.

omitted from the Austrian draft, called for agreement to a Bulgarian-Albanian union if Albania proved favorable.

The secret annex consisted of an additional six articles: If Greece and Rumania joined the Central Powers, the latter would have to prearrange a revision of the Treaty of Bukarest to satisfy the territorial claims of Bulgaria. If Bulgaria undertook action against the Serbs, the neutrality of Rumania was to be assured by German and Austrian troops, sent to the Hungarian-Rumanian border to cover Bulgaria's exposure. The entire treaty was to come into effect five days after the Turks had evacuated the area they had agreed to retrocede to Bulgaria. (This clause referred to the Bulgarian-Turkish Alliance which was concurrently being drawn up.) Finally, the Central Powers would supply Bulgaria with all its war needs, guns, munitions, and so forth, and would grant 200 million francs in gold to meet Bulgarian war expenses, and any supplementary sums which might be required for this purpose. These monies were to be considered a war loan.[45]

The Bulgarians had finally put all their cards on the table. The price of their participation was the satisfaction of ambitions and aspirations dating as far back as the Treaty of Berlin in 1878. In offering his views on the draft, Jagow wrote to Michahelles on August 22, "Evidently Bulgaria believes the moment to have come when it can demand all from us." Burian's reaction was to find the stipulations totally unacceptable, for they were to him "unclear, contradictory, and [they] dealt almost exclusively with Bulgarian interests."[46]

Even Germany found the demands much too comprehensive, and by August 26 Jagow had reduced the alliance to five short articles: It was to run for five years, to guarantee Bulgaria against any attack made without provocation, to be ratified eight days after signature, and to remain secret. The secret annex declared the military convention an integral part of the alliance. No concessions were to be offered in the case of Bulgarian neutrality. For its participation in the war on the side of the Central Powers, however, Bulgaria was to obtain the contested and uncontested zones of Serbian Macedonia, and the Serbian area formerly belonging to the Exarchate. In the case where Rumania or Greece, or both, attacked Bulgaria without provocation, Bulgaria would be given freedom of action to reclaim the territories ceded to each of these countries by the Treaty of Bukarest. Berlin accepted the

---

[45] Staatsarchiv, PA, box 513, no. 77, Tarnowski to Burian, 23 August 1915; no. 78-B/P, Hohenlohe to Burian, 24 August.

[46] Ibid., folio 185, Jagow to Michahelles, 22 August 1915; no. 603, Burian to Hohenlohe, 25 August. As late as 25 August Burian was still asking that a military convention be signed immediately but without a simultaneous alliance. No. 396, Burian to Tarnowski, 28 August.

clause calling for a union of Bulgaria and Albania, but refused the Bulgarian demand for occupation of Turkish retroceded lands as a condition for the alliance to come into effect. Furthermore, Germany was willing to pay the 200 million francs, but the sum was to be granted in monthly installments of 50 million each, beginning when Bulgaria took action in the field. Additional sums would be forthcoming on the basis of "Bulgarian contributions" to the war effort.[47]

Berlin was so eager to get the convention and alliance signed that even before the Austrians were informed of the German modifications, Michahelles was instructed to submit them to Radoslavov. Michahelles carried out his orders on August 26, and Burian, hearing of it, immediately got off an indignant protest to the Wilhelmstrasse. He was amazed that such action had been taken, when Austria had to submit an analogous alliance draft. A previous mutual understanding was absolutely essential for purposes of offering precisely the same terms. Hohenlohe patiently tried to explain to Jagow that Austria's interests were much more bound up with the Balkans than were Germany's, and therefore Vienna had to work with greater caution. His remarks left no impression. The answer given him was that Falkenhayn was pressing for the conclusion of negotiations and that Michahelles had been told to go ahead because delay could not be allowed. The Bulgarians had 240,000 men ready to move and Falkenhayn wanted them.[48]

Informed of the German counterproposals, Burian was willing to accept these, but only as an outline for further negotiations. He demanded certain specific changes. The *casus fœderis* which would apply to Germany and Austria if Bulgaria was attacked must be made reciprocal, and the term "without provocation" must be inserted as a precaution against Bulgarian ambitions. The entire secret annex would have to be attached to the military convention; otherwise the clauses applying to Rumania and Greece would extend to the duration of the alliance rather than merely the war period. And the Bulgarian-Albanian union was unacceptable. Berlin was ready to accept Burian's remarks on the *casus fœderis* and agreed to eliminate the article on Bulgarian-Albanian unification, but absolutely refused to attach the

---

[47] Ibid., no. 608, Burian to Hohenlohe, 26 August 1915. He informed the ambassador that Tschirschky had delivered the German version to him. The German draft is found in folio 192.

[48] Ibid., no. 606, Burian to Hohenlohe, 26 August 1915; no. 379, Hohenlohe to Burian, 27 August; no. 385, Hohenlohe to Burian, 31 August. In no. 612, Burian had written to Hohenlohe on 29 August that "Just as on the Bulgarian side the draft of Gantscheff differs in a few points from that given us, our draft, even if it relies on the whole structure and chief contents of the German draft, would still show certain important differences"; Austria, Kriegsarchiv, Evidenzbureau "B" Akten, folio 5629, no. 620, Enclosure 3.

secret annex to the military convention for fear of disturbing the completion of this convention. To quiet Burian's fears on the Greek and Rumanian clauses, Jagow was ready to write in "for the duration of the present conflict," but he considered this Austrian worry without basis.[49]

Germany believed its ally's objections to be little more than formalities and continually stressed the urgency of concluding the whole matter as quickly as possible. Jagow informed Burian that Michahelles was ordered to treat with Sofia in simultaneous cooperation with Tarnowski, but that Vienna must complete its revisions in short order. Faced with this kind of pressure, the Ballhausplatz quickly formulated terms and on September 6 the alliance was signed in Sofia. In final form it took the shape of the German draft with enough changes having been made to obtain the necessary Austrian consent. It read:

Article 1. The High Contracting Parties promise mutual peace and friendship and to enter no alliance or agreement directed against the other.

They agree to follow a policy of friendship and to offer aid in their spheres of interest.

Article 2. Germany [Austria-Hungary] guarantees the defense of Bulgarian political independence and territorial integrity against all attack which could result without provocation on the side of the Bulgarian government.

Should Germany [Austria-Hungary] be attacked by a neighboring state of Bulgaria, Bulgaria is obligated to take action against this state as soon as this is demanded of it.

Article 3. This alliance remains in force until December 31, 1920; if it has not been modified six months before it expires it will remain in being for an additional year and will continue to be renewed yearly so long as notice is not given.

Article 4. This alliance shall remain secret until a new understanding is reached.

Article 5. This treaty will be ratified and the ratifications exchanged in Sofia eight days, at the latest, after signature.

SECRET ANNEX

1. Germany [Austria-Hungary] guarantees Bulgaria the acquisition and annexation of the following territories:

a. Present-day Serbian-Macedonia, including the so-called contested and uncontested zones, as delineated by the Serb-Bulgarian Alliance of February 29 (March 13) 1912 and by the map accompanying this treaty.

[49] Staatsarchiv, PA, box 513, no. 608, Burian to Hohenlohe, 26 August 1915; no. 379, Hohenlohe to Burian, 27 August.

b. Serbian territory east of the following line: the Morava River from where it joins the Danube to a point where the Bulgarian Morava and Serbian Morava join, following the watershed of both these rivers, running through the ridge of Tschernagora, the Katchanik Pass, the ridge of Schar-Planina, until reaching the frontier [delimited by the Treaty] of San Stefano Bulgaria. The border line is shown on the accompanying map and constitutes an inseparable part of the agreement.

2. In the case where Rumania, during the present conflict, attacks Bulgaria, its allies, or Turkey, without any provocation on the part of Bulgaria, Germany [Austria-Hungary] agrees that Bulgaria will annex the area ceded to Rumania by the Treaty of Bukarest, and [agrees] to a rectification of the Bulgarian-Rumanian border as delimited by the Treaty of Berlin.

3. In the case where Greece, in the course of the present war, attacks Bulgaria, its allies, or Turkey, without any provocation on the part of Bulgaria, Germany [Austria-Hungary] agrees to Bulgarian annexation of the area ceded to Greece by the Treaty of Bukarest.

4. Both of the concluding parties reserve the right of further agreements with respect to conclusion of peace.

5. Germany and Austria-Hungary mutually bind themselves to guarantee the Bulgarian government a war loan of 200 million francs, which shall be paid in four installments:

a. the first installment of 50 million francs on the day of mobilization.
b. the second 50 million a month later.
c. the third 50 million two months later.
d. the fourth 50 million three months after the day of mobilization.

The details of this loan shall be set by an agreement between the finance authorities.

If the war lasts longer than four months, Germany and Austria guarantee Bulgaria a new supplementary loan, if such proves necessary, and after previous agreement.

6. This agreement shall come into force together with the military convention.[50]

On the same day, the military convention was signed at Pless, calling for Bulgaria to take action against Serbia in thirty-five days, five days after the Austrians and Germans began the campaign. The latter two would contribute at least six divisions each and Bulgaria four. As soon as the way through Serbia had been cleared, Bulgaria was to allow transit of munitions for Turkey. The other stipulations which Gantscheff had submitted, concerning the defence of Varna, Burgas, and Dedeagatch, were accepted in their original form. Bulgaria agreed to

[50] Vasil Radoslavov, *Bulgarien und die Weltkrise*, pp. 188–90. Staatsarchiv, PA, box 513, no. 608, Burian to Hohenlohe, 26 August 1915; no. 379, Hohenlohe to Burian, 27 August. See map, p. 175.

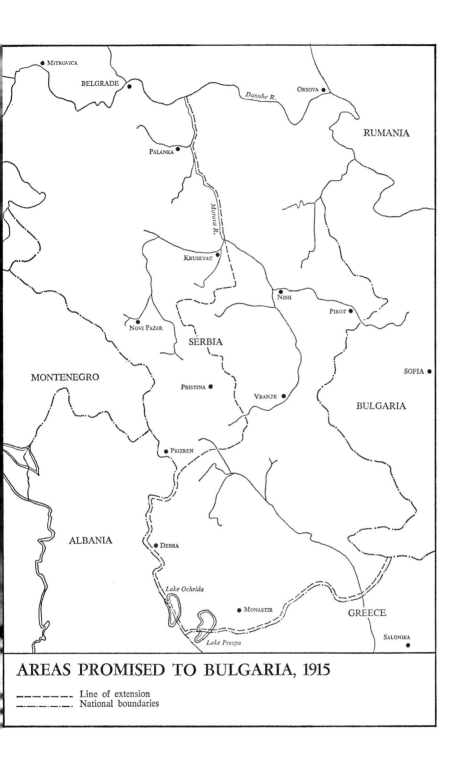

MITROVICA

BELGRADE

Danube R.

ORSOVA

RUMANIA

PALANKA

Morava R.

KRUSEVAC

NISH

PIROT

NOVI PAZAR

SERBIA

MONTENEGRO

SOFIA

PRISTINA

VRANJE

BULGARIA

PRIZREN

ALBANIA

DEBRA

Lake Ochrida

MONASTIR

GREECE

Lake Prespa

SALONIKA

AREAS PROMISED TO BULGARIA, 1915

———————— Line of extension
—·—·—·—·. National boundaries

maintain unconditional neutrality toward Greece and Rumania for the
duration of the campaign against Serbia, if these two states gave
assurances not to mobilize, to remain neutral, and not to attempt
occupation of Serbian territory. Finally, General von Mackensen was
to command the campaign, but an Austrian and a Bulgarian officer
were both to hold the positions of colleagues rather than mere attachés
on his staff.[51]

After thirteen months of hard negotiation Germany and Austria had
succeeded in obtaining Bulgaria as an ally. From early spring of 1915 it
had been the Germans who forced the issue. While Burian had initially
taken office with the belief that Bulgarian neutrality for the duration of
the war was acceptable, he had been forced by Berlin and by the events
of the war itself to slowly backwater. First he had agreed to concessions in exchange for neutrality. Then he had been won to the idea of a
Serbian campaign and to the establishment of an agreement with
Bulgaria in order to effectuate this campaign. Finally, he had been
forced to accept against his will the concurrent signing of an alliance.
He had done the best he could to make sure that Austrian interests
were not ignored, but in the end had been overridden by German
single-mindedness. German diplomats and generals knew only that the
war must be won. For this purpose they considered that extreme
concessions were quite justifiable, even if unpalatable. While their
tactics might cause Austrian rancor, everything else was secondary to
winning what was seen as a life-and-death struggle.

Austrian irritability became extreme in the final stages of the negotiations, and ill feeling remained after the signing of the alliance. On
September 5, Hohenlohe told Jagow that Austria felt it had been
treated most rudely and hoped such treatment would not be repeated.
As late as October 29, Tarnowski was still simmering over the way
Germany had steamrolled the negotiations. In a long report to Burian,
he declared that, "Germany . . . emphasized its wish for a lasting
alliance with Bulgaria so often, both officially and unofficially, that it
was impossible to remain within those boundaries which were the
intentions of your Excellency." He summarized the action of the
previous two years, and pointed out that Germany was really a new-
comer to the Balkans. It was Austria that had shown Germany the
worth of an alliance with Bulgaria, and without the experience of
Austrian diplomats, the Bulgarians could not have been secured as
allies. Tarnowski's position was not without justification.[52]

[51] GFMA, ser. 2, reel 15, no. AS 4506, Treutler to Berlin, 26 August 1915, copy
of the military convention. See also Radoslavov, *Bulgarien und die Weltkrise*,
pp. 190–93.

As far as the Bulgarians are concerned, their diplomacy demonstrates great skill. They had led the Central Powers step by step toward a fulfillment of their national ambitions, and the protraction of the war helped make their policy of hesitation highly successful. The increasing need of the Central Powers to mount a decisive campaign against Serbia and the fear in Berlin and Vienna that the Entente might successfully woo the Bulgarians were the two factors which gave Radoslavov his eventual diplomatic victory. If the Central Powers won, Bulgaria would emerge as the biggest power in the Balkans. At the time Bulgaria signed the alliance there was every reason to believe Germany and Austria would win; Russia reeled before their onslaught and the Italian military effort against them had not succeeded. Bulgaria had little to fear. The possibility of a Russian attack was slight because of Russia's weak condition. If the attack should come, however, guarantees against it had been offered by Article 2 of the alliance. The Greek king was known to favor a continuation of Greek neutrality. Since Bulgaria would join the war five days after the Central Powers attacked Serbia, it had the perfect opportunity to manufacture a border incident to justify its action on a basis of Serbian provocation. This would prevent the Greeks from honoring their alliance obligations to Serbia since the *casus fœderis* would not exist. Rumania was not likely to attack because of Russian reversals on the eastern front; and if it did, the alliance offered the same terms concerning Rumania as Greece. As things turned out, neither Rumania nor Greece budged an inch from its position of neutrality when Bulgaria declared war against the Serbs on October 14. Bulgaria made its commitment when it got what it wanted and when the moment seemed just right. Along with having obtained its territorial demands, Bulgaria had extracted large amounts of money from both Berlin and Vienna. By the time Bulgarian troops marched, Sofia had received or been promised a total of 470 million francs, and several additional millions had been poured into the pockets of Bulgarian politicians, ministers, and other high-ranking officials in order to smooth the way.[53]

[52] Staatsarchiv, PA, box 514, no. 81 A-F/P, Hohenlohe to Burian, 5 September 1915; no. 95 A-C/P, Tarnowski to Burian, 29 October; Burian, *Austria in Dissolution*, pp. 133-39; Burian's implication in his book that things went smoothly between Austria and Germany during these negotiations is obviously not borne out by the documents.

[53] Staatsarchiv, PA, box 514, no. 96 A-D/P, Tarnowski to Burian, 30 October 1915. German businessmen such as Roselius and Günther of the Deutsche Bank had distributed "gifts" with a generous hand, while the Diskonto Gesellschaft had granted King Ferdinand one million marks as a personal loan. In comparison to Germany, Austria had spent little. Tarnowski had used 250,000 francs; of this amount Radoslavov had received 100,000 for "pocket money."

When the alliance was signed on September 6, there was still over a month of preparation necessary for the Serbian campaign. Pressures were brought to bear upon Radoslavov by members of the opposition, made aware that Bulgaria was about to give up neutrality. The opposition demanded a calling of the Sobranje and threatened revolution. Neither Radoslavov nor the king was moved by these remonstrations, and they ordered general mobilization on September 21. In the opening days of October, the Entente delivered an ultimatum that Bulgaria declare it had not joined the Central Powers, and that German officers be dismissed from the Bulgarian army. Since the Bulgarian answer was not satisfactory, the English, French, Russian, Italian, and Serbian representatives asked for their passports on October 5 and 6. On October 13, Sofia declared that Serbian troops had for no reason attacked the Bulgarians at Belogradcik. Twenty-four hours later a declaration of war was sent to Belgrade.[54]

What followed was what might be expected. Under a three-pronged attack the Serbian forces were decimated, effective resistance was quickly broken, and by December the remnants of the Serbian army had been driven into the Albanian mountains. On January 18 King Ferdinand played host to the Kaiser at a victory banquet in Nish.[55] Two links had been forged in the Balkan chain which Germany and Austria were seeking to produce. Rumania, the third, would have completed the desired grouping, but it remained, and would continue to remain, outside the camp of the Central Powers.

[54] Ibid., no. 1092, Tarnowski to Burian, 18 September 1915; no. 1102, Tarnowski to Burian, 21 September; no. 1129, Tarnowski to Burian, 25 September; nos. 1203, 1205, Tarnowski to Burian, 5 and 6 October; no. 1260, Tarnowski to Burian, 13 October; Dunan, *L'Été Bulgare*, pp. 286–99; Dunan discusses in detail the confrontation on 15 September of the Bulgarian king by the opposition party leaders.
[55] Winston S. Churchill, *The Unknown War: The Eastern Front*, pp. 339–47.

Chapter 8

Rumania,
Uncertain Neutral

In the hectic first days of the war, when sides were chosen almost automatically on the basis of previous agreements, the Central Powers faced a Rumania which refused to honor its alliance obligations. In contrast to the situation in Turkey and Bulgaria, the obstacles to Rumanian intervention on the side of Germany and Austria were to prove insurmountable. If the inclinations of Turkish and Bulgarian officialdom were essentially hostile to the Entente—feelings which made easier the job of German and Austrian diplomats seeking to involve these two states in the war—the attitudes of most Rumanian statesmen were quite the reverse. Like King Ferdinand of Bulgaria, King Carol was pro-German but the political parallel ended there because the Rumanian sovereign did not enjoy a strong control of his own government. Ferdinand and Radoslavov were masters of the Sobranje, but Carol was much more dependent on his national assembly, led by Ion Bratianu, a man whose leanings toward the Entente powers were clearly evident. Bratianu's Liberal Party dominated the Rumanian parliament, enjoyed the confidence of the nation, and sought intervention on the side of France, England, and Russia. Its power was manifest in its occupation of eight of every ten seats in the Chamber of Deputies and seven of every ten in the Senate. Supporting the Liberals were one wing of the Conservative Party, led by Nicholas Filipescu, a strong nationalist, and the Conservative Democrats, whose chief was Take Ionescu. The only distinction existing between these groups was that the latter two parties sought to enter the war on the side of the Entente immediately, while the Liberals were more cautious.[1]

No powerful political faction sought active participation on the side of the Central Powers. Another wing of the Conservative Party, led by Alexander Marghiloman, favored Germany and Austria, but because of the temper of the nation, Marghiloman's faction could go no further than to advocate benevolent neutrality.[2] The strong antagonism of indigenous political elements constantly agitating the Rumanian public against Teutonism made the task of German and Austrian representatives that much more difficult.

The hostility toward Germany and Austria was based on the crucial issue of territorial aspirations. In negotiations with Sofia, Berlin and Vienna had been able to outbid the Entente powers for the simple reason that Bulgarian interests centered on Macedonia and Old Serbia, neither of which involved any great sacrifice for the Central Powers. Rumania's ambitions, however, could be satisfied only at the expense of the Austro-Hungarian Empire, since the Rumanians wanted Transylvania and the Bukovina, both of which were controlled by the Monarchy. The Entente proved perfectly willing to give away territory not its own, as long as relationships within its own family were not disturbed. But Germany and Austria found themselves at a definite disadvantage over the bargaining table in Bukarest.[3]

When war began Bratianu was certain of the approach he must take in order to best promote his nation's interests: neutrality and watchful waiting to see how the war would evolve and which side would emerge the stronger. Once this was revealed Rumania could act with the least risk for the most compensation. Such a posture seems the precise equivalent of that taken by the Bulgarians. The big distinction was that Bratianu expected the Entente would be the victor, hoped fervently it would, and within a short while made certain diplomatic promises to that coalition which reflected the strength of his convictions.[4]

His Francophilia notwithstanding, there were other considerations leading Bratianu to employ caution. In spite of the political power and influence that he exerted, he understood the position of the crown in Rumania and certainly realized that the king could not be ignored. Indeed, he had been appointed by Carol in 1913 to serve as minister-president because he was receptive to the king's wishes and did not offer strong opposition to the throne. Bratianu was a man capable of combining pleasantness and amiability with an iron-bound determination to get what he wanted. His strength lay in knowing when to make his bid. A man of great intelligence, he understood a good deal more than merely how to manipulate the political strings. He was aware in 1914 that although the Rumanian army was a good one, it lacked sufficient equipment and munitions for a full-scale modern war. To take the advice of the extremists who wanted immediate war against the Central Powers would mean risking immediate defeat. What made the weakness of the army even more striking was the geographical position of the country, which exposed it to attack from both Hungary

[1] Nicolas Basilesco, *La Roumanie dans la Guerre et dans la Paix*, 1:149–50.
[2] Ibid.
[3] Harry Howard, *The Partition of Turkey, 1913–23*, p. 166.
[4] Ibid.; Ottokar Czernin, *In Weltkrieg*, pp. 109, 127.

and Bulgaria. A simultaneous action from these two states would split Rumania in half, cutting off Wallachia from Moldavia and making effective resistance impossible. To make matters worse the Rumanian railroad system converged toward Russia rather than toward the Hungarian and Bulgarian borders. With 1500 kilometers of frontier to defend, with the capital city only 60 kilometers from Bulgaria, and with munitions orders worth over 200 million francs not yet filled by Germany and Austria, Bratianu would have to bide his time. All things considered, he could not now risk war.[5]

German-Austrian Disparity

Both Germany and Austria formally accepted Rumania's neutrality, but this did not keep them from persistent attempts to gain that nation as an active ally. Count Czernin, the Austrian minister to Bukarest, realistically appraised the situation three days before Rumania's declaration of neutrality on August 4, 1914. He wrote to Berchtold that if the Ballhausplatz wanted merely a neutral Rumania this was a rather safe bet because King Carol would not agree to an openly hostile position against the Central Powers. If Germany and Austria were successful in the field, Rumania would join them. If they lost, not even fear of an attack by Bulgaria would keep Bukarest from joining the Russians. As early as August 6, Czernin felt that no immediate cooperation could be achieved, but he nevertheless believed he must continue to strive for it. Berchtold accepted Czernin's report that the neutrality of Rumania was the most they could hope for at the moment, but he instructed the minister to continue attempts to win over the government.[6]

The Germans were rather more hopeful. Waldthausen, the German minister, believed it was quite possible that there could be sufficient change of opinion in Rumania to gain it as a partner. Should Russia attempt to go through Moldavia to reach the eastern front, the move would provoke Rumanian action against the Entente. On August 15, King Carol had declared that if Russia made such an attempt he would consider it a definite *casus belli*. Waldthausen's optimism unfortunately

---

[5] Marie, Queen of Rumania, *The Story of My Life*, pp. 534, 422–23; Mircea Djuvara, *La Guerre Roumaine, 1916–1918*, pp. 93–96; Nicholas Lupu, *Rumania and the War*, pp. 20–22. Von Hammerstein, the German military attaché in Bukarest, had declared that in a war with Rumania, Germany would occupy the country in ninety days. Constantin Minesco, *L'Action Diplomatique de la Roumanie pendant la Guerre*, p. 34.

[6] Staatsarchiv, PA, box 516, report no. Z 74/P, Czernin to Berchtold, 1 August 1914; no. 268, Berchtold to Czernin, 9 August.

had no real base. Even at a time when German forces were successful against the French and Russians and when the Austrians were holding in the Bukovina and Galicia, Carol frankly stated that public opinion could not be swung towards the Central Powers.[7]

Both Kaiser Wilhelm and Emperor Franz Joseph maintained a constant bombardment of letters to the Rumanian king, exploiting Carol's fear of Russian invasion. Although the left flank of the Austrian forces still held by the opening days of September, the right flank gave way, and on September 3 Lemberg fell to the Russians. Franz Joseph wrote to Carol that he understood the difficulties which the Rumanian king faced, but he pointed out that Rumanian armed support at this time "could essentially influence our success." What he asked was Rumanian occupation of Bessarabia, and he hoped Carol would bring his nation into battle as soon as possible. Kaiser Wilhelm followed through with a strong plea. If the right flank of the Austrian army should be shattered, he warned, "I need not describe the result of a Russian advance into Europe. The Balkans would then lie under Russian hegemony." Through military action Rumania could "break the Russian flood which threatened Europe. How joyous would be the outcome if the valiant Rumanians were to take part with us in victory."[8] The attempt to play on Rumanian fear of the Russian colossus failed. The fall of Lemberg in Galicia and the Battle of the Marne on the western front were not calculated to convince the Rumanians that the Central Powers would quickly win.

A rift now opened between Berlin and Vienna over the diplomatic strategy needed to gain Rumanian participation. Both Czernin and Waldthausen were aware by September 6 that Russia was offering Rumania the Bukovina and Transylvania in return for joining the Entente. A Conservative Party leader, Marghiloman, had told the Germans that if Austria offered to cede these areas to Rumania, Rumania would not only refuse to support the Russians but would attack them. Waldthausen wrote to the home office that in his opinion Bratianu was favorable to helping them and that the Rumanian public would be inclined to their side if these concessions were made. The minister therefore suggested that Berlin bring its influence to bear through Tschirschky in Vienna for Austrian consent to the necessary territorial grants. Bethmann-Hollweg, now at German headquarters in

[7] GFMA, ser. 1, reel 17, no. 137, Waldthausen to Berlin, 15 August 1914; no. 265, Waldthausen to Berlin, 7 September; letter from King Carol to the Kaiser, 7 September.
[8] Staatsarchiv, PA, box 516, folio 7 B, letter from Franz Joseph to Carol, 3 September 1914; report no. Z 78/P, Czernin to Vienna, copy of letter from Kaiser Wilhelm to Carol, transmitted 6 September.

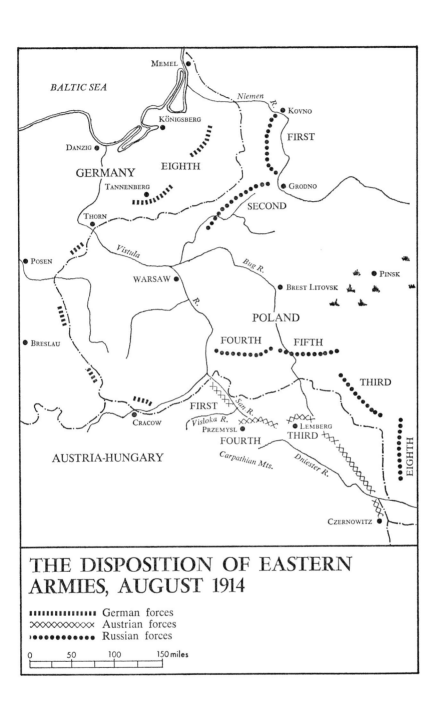

MEMEL

BALTIC SEA

Niemen R.

KOVNO

KÖNIGSBERG

FIRST

DANZIG

EIGHTH

GERMANY

TANNENBERG

GRODNO

THORN

SECOND

Vistula

POSEN

Bug R.

WARSAW

BREST LITOVSK

PINSK

R.

POLAND

BRESLAU

FOURTH

FIFTH

THIRD

FIRST

San R.

CRACOW

Visloka R.

PRZEMYSL

LEMBERG

FOURTH

THIRD

EIGHTH

AUSTRIA-HUNGARY

Carpathian Mts.

Dniester R.

CZERNOWITZ

THE DISPOSITION OF EASTERN ARMIES, AUGUST 1914

- ▬▬▬▬ German forces
- ✕✕✕✕✕✕ Austrian forces
- •••••••• Russian forces

0   50   100   150 miles

Luxemburg, instructed the Foreign Office: "We think that to move Rumania to take action it is urgently desirable that the Hungarian government guarantee concessions to the Rumanians and thus better public opinion with respect to the Danubian Monarchy." Tschirschky was to inform Vienna of the German government's view and urgently request that autonomy for Transylvanian Rumanians and the necessary border rectifications in the Bukovina be granted. If Rumania went over to the Russians, said the chancellor, the general situation as well as that in Galicia and the Balkans, would be "heavily compromised." A reasonable consideration of the military situation would lead Austria to see that heavy sacrifices were necessary, for things were serious. On the western front Germany faced an enemy superiority of 300,000 and in the east some twelve Russian corps. Germany could not send reinforcements to help its ally. Therefore Rumanian support was essential.[9]

Berchtold replied immediately and in very certain terms. Austria-Hungary had entered the war to "guarantee its integrity." If the Monarchy was now to be dismembered there was no sense in expending further blood and money and they might as well give their "hungry neighbors" the territories they demanded without a blow in defense. Furthermore, if Rumania was given the areas it wanted, Austria would be humiliated and Bukarest would demand even more.[10] Berchtold, fitting the Rumanian problem into the broader diplomatic context, asserted that if concessions were granted, it would also be the signal for Italy to make analogous territorial demands. For Austria to give up two provinces, or substantial parts of them, before any decisive battles had been fought, would demonstrate that Austria was unsure of its wartime capabilities. This would lead to doubts not only in Rumania, but also in Turkey and Bulgaria, would eliminate the possibility of Turkish-Bulgarian cooperation, and thus would only increase the striking power of the Russian forces against Germany and Austria-Hungary. The foreign minister concluded, "We do not underrate, certainly, the significance of Rumania's position, but we do not see under present conditions any clear way to swing Rumania from an ambiguous policy which involves no risk for Rumania and offers the possibilities of its reaping advantages by entering at a decisive turn."[11]

[9] Ibid., box 517, no. 496, Czernin to Berchtold, 2 September 1914; no. 524, Czernin to Berchtold, 6 September; Foreign Office report no. 4258, 7 September; GFMA, ser. 1, reel 17, no. 263, Waldthausen to Berlin, 7 September; nos. 36, 37, Bethmann-Hollweg in Luxemburg to Berlin, 7 September; entry no. AS 2012, Bethmann-Hollweg to Tschirschky, 9 September; see also Staatsarchiv, PA, box 500, no. 4315, Berchtold's report of Bethmann-Hollweg's arguments, 9 September.

[10] GFMA, ser. 1, reel 17, no. 365, Tschirschky to Berlin, 9 September 1914.

Behind Berchtold's strong reaction lay the attitude of Count Stephan Tisza, prime minister of Hungary. In the words of Czernin, Tisza was a man who "stood in awe of nothing and nobody" and who as a Magyar "knew no patriotism except that of Hungary." Aside from the leading political position he held within the Dual Monarchy, Tisza would under any circumstance have been a man to reckon with. He has been described as one possessed of an almost brutal will and with a psychological makeup as "cold as a sword blade." People both admired and hated him, though he hardly cared one way or the other. All his energies were directed toward one goal—the furtherance of Hungary —and most certainly this goal could only be compromised by giving up Magyar territory. The areas now in question lay under Hungarian control, and under Hungarian control they would remain. Tisza refused to concede one meter of ground, particularly in light of the fact that Rumania had offered no guarantee whatsoever that it would march against the Russians if the concessions were granted. Furthermore, he said, Rumanian desires with respect to the autonomy of Transylvania and the ceding of the Bukovina had been presented only in the form of diplomatic feelers; Tisza was unwilling even to consider what cessions might be made until the Rumanians submitted concrete conditions under which they would agree to cooperation. He was ready to make a binding statement concerning the Transylvanian Rumanians, but only after Rumania declared war on Russia, and not before.[12]

The German chancellor proved most impatient with the attitude of Berchtold and Tisza. His answer to Tschirschky declared that the Austrian position would be understandable if the Monarchy were strong enough to handle Russia militarily. Or, he asked sarcastically, were the signs of Austrian weakness, as reflected in its cries for military help, misleading? Bethmann instructed Tschirschky that Berchtold and Tisza would simply have to make concessions, even before Rumania declared war on the Russians. The sacrifices were worth the effort, since to obtain Rumania was also to gain Bulgaria and Turkey. To refuse Rumanian desires was to run the risk of seeing all three states in the camp of the opposition.[13]

[11] Staatsarchiv, PA, box 500, no. 4315, Foreign Office report by Berchtold, 9 September 1914.
[12] Czernin, *Im Weltkrieg*, pp. 184–86; Take Ionescu, *Souvenirs*, p. 142; Victor Naumann, *Profile*, pp. 207, 208, 219; GFMA, ser. 1, reel 17, no. 365, Tschirschky to Berlin, 9 September 1914; no. 387, Tschirschky to Berlin, 12 September.
[13] GFMA, ser. 1, reel 17, no. 5, Bethmann-Hollweg to Tschirschky, 10 September 1914; no. 42, Bethmann-Hollweg to Tschirschky, 13 September; Staatsarchiv, PA, box 517, no. 582, Hohenlohe in Berlin to Berchtold, 14 September.

Contrary to what Berlin believed, the Ballhausplatz was not being unnecessarily difficult. Count Czernin had analyzed the Rumanian scene much differently and much more correctly than his German colleague. Before his appointment as minister to Bukarest, Czernin had been absent from diplomatic service for ten years, but he had not lost his acumen. On September 11 he defined the situation as having grown worse. To count on the Rumanians was a "complete mistake," and in support of his view he stated that the Central Powers must face a country filled with hate against Austria-Hungary, a ministry which consciously worked against them, a king no longer in real control of his government, and an heir to the throne who not only was uncertain as to what he wanted but possessed a domineering wife, half English and half Russian. Generally courteous and tactful, Czernin told Berchtold that he considered Waldthausen a fool who was incapable of handling the job before him. For the German minister to say that Bratianu favored the Central Powers was absolutely erroneous. A few days later Czernin reported that Carol himself had told Waldthausen general public opinion was now so prejudicial toward the Germans and Austrians that an active Rumanian attack on their side was "out of the question." The basis for Carol's remark was the Austrian defeat on the eastern front, which had forced Conrad von Hötzendorf to order a general retreat behind the San River. Russian propaganda did not fail to take advantage of the situation and the impression in Rumania was highly disadvantageous to Austrian and German diplomacy.[14]

In spite of his pessimism Czernin believed that it was necessary to discover quickly what the precise demands of the Rumanians were and, if these proved acceptable, to deal with the matter at once. There was no time to waste, and the Ballhausplatz must state clearly what concessions it was willing to grant. He held out no hope of gaining active Rumanian participation, but concessions were necessary to keep Rumania even neutral.[15]

In Berlin it had become clear that Waldthausen was not satisfactory for the difficult job in Bukarest and on September 13 he was replaced by Hilmar von dem Bussche. Bussche was no Balkan specialist and at the age of forty-seven was still on the young side for occupying a minister's desk. But he had already seen almost twenty years of service

---

[14] Leo Santifaller, ed., *Österreichisches Biographisches Lexikon, 1815–1950*, p. 162; Marie, Queen of Rumania, *Story of My Life*, pp. 8–9; Staatsarchiv, PA, box 517, reports nos. Z 80 A-B/P, Z 82/P, Czernin to Berchtold, 10, 11 September 1914; nos. 577, 578, Czernin to Berchtold, 14 September.

[15] Staatsarchiv, PA, box 517, nos. 578, 579, Czernin to Berchtold, 14 and 15 September 1914.

at the Foreign Office and had held posts in German embassies on three continents. While at times he was rather abrupt, a fault for which Czernin eventually came to dislike him, Bussche at least had no illusions concerning the Rumanian problem. On his way to Rumania, von dem Bussche visited Tisza in Budapest. The fact that the Germans had been exerting all influence possible through Tschirschky was now reflected in Tisza's willingness to make certain concessions to the Transylvanian Rumanians in the way of reforms, a step which von dem Bussche believed would at least win a certain amount of precious time. Berchtold had told the Germans that Austria would also agree to border rectifications in the Bukovina and would cede the province of Suczawa, but this hardly impressed Berlin. By September 20 Bussche had seen both Carol and Bratianu and had talked with various leading Rumanian politicians as well. His impression was that such Austrian offerings would be insufficient to satisfy Rumanian ambitions. Bethmann was obviously in agreement since he wired Berchtold that small sacrifices were not enough when everything was at stake. Kaiser Wilhelm himself talked with Hohenlohe and urged that Austria "throw Rumania a crumb, by which action Rumania could be bought." The crumb to which he referred was not only the Bukovina but also Transylvania.[16]

The difficult situation of the Austrian army in the east led now to a series of soundings on the part of Bukarest, suggesting that Rumania occupy Transylvania to "protect" it against Russian incursions. The Germans were willing to accept the proposal and Wilhelm declared that if Rumania marched into the area Austria must then lodge only a light protest. No declaration of war must be forthcoming because Rumania had close ties with Italy. Both were held together by a mutual interest, that of obtaining territories from the Austro-Hungarian Empire. Since their territorial ambitions did not clash, they cooperated, and as events affected one, so they would affect the other. War with Rumania would mean war with Italy and the result for both Germanic empires would be disastrous.[17]

To these entreaties, Austria maintained a stern front. Vienna was

---

[16] GFMA, ser. 1, reel 17, no. 42, Bethmann-Hollweg to Tschirschky, 13 September 1914; no. 73, Fürstenberg to Berlin, 17 September; no. 53, Bethmann-Hollweg in Luxemburg to Berlin, 19 September; no. 338, Bussche to Berlin, 20 September; no. 51, Bethmann in Luxemburg to Berlin, 19 September; Staatsarchiv, PA, box 517, no. 534, Hohenlohe to Berchtold, 19 September; Marie, Queen of Rumania, *Story of My Life*, pp. 9–10.

[17] Staatsarchiv, PA, box 517, no. 586, Czernin to Berchtold, 16 September 1914; no. 534, Hohenlohe to Berchtold, 19 September; box 497, Denkschrift, January 1915.

willing to listen to Rumanian demands but thus far such demands had not been formulated. When Bukarest concretely laid down its proposals, Austria would in good time try to meet these halfway. As to the idea of Rumania's marching into Transylvania to "protect" it, Czernin thought it was time to state that such action would mean Rumania's "getting a bloody head," and certainly Berchtold and Tisza concurred. Count Forgach, section chief of the Austrian Foreign Ministry had called Undersecretary Zimmermann by phone. After mentioning the danger of such a step by Rumania, he had suggested Germany tell Rumania that it strongly disapproved of the contemplated action and would support Austria by sending troops to Transylvania and the Bukovina if necessary. Berchtold informed the ambassador in Berlin that aside from this issue any concrete proposals of concessions would at this time have no meaning. The Rumanians would not now cooperate with the Central Powers against the Russians, and indeed would see such proposals as reflecting a desperate situation for Austria. This, in turn, could only lead to strengthening the Rumanian conviction that it ought not to ally itself with Austria and Germany.[18]

The German government refused to agree with the Austrian interpretation. Kaiser Wilhelm in particular continually told Hohenlohe that Austria was being much too petty and would end by compromising the entire war effort. Bussche's telegrams had now begun to express a burning urgency. He believed conditions to be very critical and he asked that Tisza make at least some concessions to the Rumanians in Transylvania to allow him and his Austrian colleague the necessary time to maneuver. He hoped a decisive victory by the Germans in the west and by the Austrian forces in Galicia would have a quieting effect, so that Rumania could at least be kept neutral. The German minister suggested that Tisza agree to promise the following to the Hungarian Rumanians: the abandoning of the Apponyian School Law, which would de-Magyarize the schools in Rumanian districts of Transylvania; allowing the use of the Rumanian language; and voting arrangements to be permitted by district. Berlin followed through and Tschirschky made a trip to Budapest expressly to insist that Tisza do something. The Hungarian prime minister finally agreed to go along and said he would publish the concessions in an open letter to the Rumanian Metropolitan in Hermannstadt. The Metropolitan could then answer in a warm and public letter which would agree to the offers. In this way the Bukarest government and Rumanian public

[18] Ibid., box 517, no. 534, Hohenlohe to Berchtold, 19 September 1914; unnumbered memo, Czernin to Berchtold, 19 September; no. 597, Berchtold to Hohenlohe, 18 September; no. 563, Berchtold to Hohenlohe, 19 September.

opinion would become more favorable to Austria and to the Central Powers.[19]

The question of when the letter should be published was not easily settled. Tisza wrote to Berchtold on September 22, saying, "We must not give up this trump uselessly." The fact was that Russia was very busy at this time making offers to the Rumanian government and these offers were known to Czernin and Bussche alike. Czernin wrote a letter to Berchtold on this same day in which he urged that the concessions not be made at the same time as the Russian offers. If they were published now, they would only be met with scorn, for it would be unmistakable that the Monarchy had acted merely to offset the Russian move. If, said Czernin, concessions were going to be made, they must be large enough to be meaningful; otherwise they would have played their best diplomatic card without effect. If Emperor Franz Joseph publicly declared that concessions in the widest sense would be forthcoming after the war, if Austrian and German diplomats remained calm and let the Russian manuevers blow over, and if the Central Powers were successful against the Russians in the field, he hoped Rumania could be kept from joining the enemy. By September 24 King Carol had become quite ill and Czernin drew a dark picture. The king was their one advantage. As long as he lived Rumania would take no action on the side of the Entente. If he died the Central Powers would have to count on an open attack by Rumania, since his successor would be Ferdinand and one could expect anything from him. The Rumanian ministry was for proceeding against Austria-Hungary; only Bratianu and the minister of interior, Vasil Mortzun, were still for neutrality. To offer concessions in Transylvania at this moment would "ring like a bad joke." The effect, he said, would be like "quenching a burning house with a garden hose."[20]

While Czernin and Bussche agreed that concessions should be forthcoming and that these should not be lost in legislative detail, they disagreed on the timing. Bussche wanted things immediately and unconditionally resolved. Czernin held strongly to the view that the step could be effectively taken only after a strong military victory. Both saw the necessity for an emergency step if Rumania could not be held back from marching into Transylvania and the Bukovina. Czernin asked for permission, in such a case, to give the Rumanians the right to

[19] Ibid., no. Z 81/P, Hohenlohe to Berchtold, 23 September 1914; daily report of the Austrian Foreign Office, no. 4457, 21 September; GFMA, ser. 1, reel 17, unnumbered telegram, Tschirschky in Budapest to Berlin, 22 September.

[20] Staatsarchiv, PA, box 517, unnumbered letter, Tisza to Berchtold, 22 September 1914; unnumbered letter, Czernin to Berchtold, 22 September; unnumbered letter, Czernin to Berchtold, 24 September.

occupy the areas in question, with Carol understanding that after the war they would be evacuated, Rumania obtaining Bessarabia and Suczawa as a substitute.[21]

The Ballhausplatz answered this latest suggestion with an absolute refusal. Berchtold accepted Tisza's argument that to permit such a move would reflect Austro-Hungarian weakness, that Rumania, once in Transylvania, would attempt to expand into other Rumanian-populated sections of Hungary and that such "a military promenade" would have a discouraging effect inside and outside the Monarchy. He therefore instructed Czernin that he and his German colleague were to make sure Bukarest understood that such a move would mean the beginning of hostilities. The Ballhausplatz believed this strong position would inspire greater caution in the Rumanians and "bring them to their senses." So that Germany would understand precisely the position of Austria-Hungary, Berchtold, in a conference with Tschirschky, categorically stated that a Rumanian march into Transylvania and the Bukovina would mean an immediate declaration of war.[22]

For several weeks Czernin and Bussche had been aware that a Crown Council would once again be called. Considering the temper of the majority of ministers and the opposition parties, both expected the meeting to result in a Rumanian decision to join the Entente. To their surprise, on October 2 the government and opposition issued a joint communiqué declaring that the policy of neutrality would be continued. The German and Austrian ministers breathed more easily. Czernin wired: "For the moment the Central Powers are safe." A noticeable calm had settled over Bukarest during the week preceding the council, and Czernin attributed it to the good reports coming in from the Serbian front and to the new Austrian offensive in Galicia. Should things go badly in the military campaigns, he believed the mood would once again shift.[23]

But the Rumanian attitude had not changed because of things on the battlefields. In actuality, between September 26 and October 2, Russia had entered into serious negotiations with Bukarest which resulted in

[21] Ibid., unnumbered letter, Czernin to Berchtold, 24 September 1914; no. 656, Czernin to Berchtold, 25 September; GFMA, ser. 2, reel 17, no. 365, Bussche to Berlin, 25 September.

[22] Staatsarchiv, PA, box 517, nos. 548, 549, 550, Berchtold to Czernin, 25 and 26 September 1914; a series of unnumbered letters by Tisza to Berchtold and Czernin expressing the above views was written 13-29 September, also in PA, box 517; GFMA, ser. 1, reel 17, no. 217, Jagow at German headquarters to the Foreign Office, 29 September; Jagow summarized the Austrian position.

[23] Staatsarchiv, PA, box 517, memo, Czernin to Berchtold, 3 and 9 October 1914; GFMA, ser. 1, reel 17, no. 93, Bussche to Berlin, 2 October; Staatsarchiv, PA, box 517, memo, Czernin to Berchtold, 30 September.

the signature of a Russo-Rumanian agreement. The Rumanians gained Russian consent to an annexation of Transylvania and part of the Bukovina, the line to be drawn according to ethnic majority, and this in return for mere benevolent neutrality. Thus, no reason existed why Rumania should take open action against the Central Powers. Bratianu believed the Entente would win and he therefore had only to wait patiently to satisfy Rumanian territorial aspirations. War was unnecessary, and to make sure that this was avoided he refused the Russian demand that Rumania close the lines of communication between the Central Powers and Bulgaria and Turkey, which ran through his country; certainly if he had acceded to this demand, Germany and Austria would have been antagonized.[24]

In addition to reaching agreement with Russia, Bratianu signed an accord with Italy. Their ambitions for territorial gain, along with a mutual concern for a beneficial solution of the Straits question, led both powers to maintain a close contact as events unfolded. The accord, signed on September 23, stated that neither would end its neutrality without a previous notice of eight days to the other, and that they would take the same action to "safeguard their respective interests."[25]

Thus, by the opening days of October the Central Powers had failed to involve the Rumanians in the war against the Entente. Germany had been convinced that it was only necessary for Austria to grant certain territories to obtain this participation. Berlin had unfortunately not perceived the real color of things. Austria's refusal to make territorial grants to Bukarest was based on more than just Tisza's refusal to go along with a cession of Transylvania and the Bukovina. Rather, it resulted from a combination of Tisza's Hungarian nationalism and the realization that territorial sacrifices at this time would not obtain the desired result. Tisza had finally consented to publish legislative concessions intended to conciliate Hungarian Rumanians in the hope that this would have a positive effect on Bukarest. The Ballhausplatz had offered minor territorial cessions—border rectifications in the Bukovina—in exchange for Rumanian participation but refused to make such rectifi-

---

[24] C. Jay Smith, Jr., *The Russian Struggle for Power, 1914-1917*, pp. 27, 29; Howard, *Partition of Turkey*, pp. 167–68.
[25] Count Stephan Burian, *Austria in Dissolution*, pp. 64–65; Howard, *Partition of Turkey*, p. 141; Leonard A. Magnus, *Rumania's Cause and Ideals*, pp. 72–73. Magnus goes so far as to declare that the Rumanian Crown Council definitely decided on neutrality on 4 August when the Italian minister, Baron Fasciotti, informed Carol of Italy's decision to remain neutral. A copy of the Italo-Rumanian accord of 23 September 1914 is to be found in Staatsarchiv, PA, box 518, no. 3509, Berchtold to Hohenlohe, 18 June 1915.

cations merely for Rumanian neutrality, as suggested by von dem Bussche. Berchtold pointed to the remarks of the Italians when the Austrians had made offers in the Bukovina for Rumanian *action*. Italian diplomats had spoken of the desperate situation in which the Monarchy must obviously find itself to make such promises. Said Berchtold, "What impressions the purchase of mere *neutrality* must awaken can be easily foreseen." Not only would Vienna then stand open to further Rumanian blackmail, but the assurance of territories for mere neutrality would reduce to an absolute minimum the chances of Rumanian active cooperation against Russia. The Austrian foreign minister had agreed to Jagow's urging that Rumania be promised Bessarabia in the case of victory over the Entente, but both Bussche and Czernin were quite certain such an offer would have little result.[26]

The most striking fact was that by the end of September, relations between Rumania and its former allies had deteriorated to a degree where German and Austrian diplomats were working not to gain Rumanian active cooperation but simply to retain Rumanian neutrality. It is clear that this neutrality was maintained because the Rumanian government felt its own interests could best be served by such a position, rather than because the Central Powers succeeded in their diplomatic action. Vienna had threatened war if Rumania attempted occupation of Transylvania and the Bukovina, and Bukarest was not yet in a position to take such a gamble.

Unsuccessful Maneuvers

October and November saw no reduction in the differences of opinion existing between Germany and Austria as to how the Rumanians should be handled. The calm which had settled on Bukarest after its reassertion of neutrality on October 2, and an improvement of the military situation on the eastern front against the Russians, led von dem Bussche repeatedly to ask Berlin for stronger representations in Vienna. He believed that Tisza must now publish his concessions to the Hungarian Rumanians without further delay. Bussche constantly asserted that Tisza's point of view was narrow-minded and injurious to their cause in Rumania, and his superiors heartily agreed. Hohenlohe did what he could to convince the Germans that Tisza was attempting to

[26] GFMA, ser. 1, reel 17, no. 67, Bussche to Berlin, 27 September 1914; no. 232, Bussche to Berlin, 6 October; no. 199, Jagow to the Foreign Office, 5 September; no. 380, Bussche to Berlin, 30 September; Staatsarchiv, PA, box 517, no. 4581, daily report of the Austrian Foreign Office, 30 September. This report gives Berchtold's position on the granting of concessions in the Bukovina which was passed on by Bussche to Berlin in the above cited no. 232.

meet the situation half-way. The Hungarian prime minister refused to publish the concessions at this time because he did not believe their publication would have any positive result unless it was seen to stem from his own friendly attitude toward the Rumanians rather than from the war situation. Czernin had written that Bukarest believed a settlement of the "Transylvanian question" to be worthwhile, to which Tisza replied that in his opinion there was no "Transylvanian question." There was only a question of concessions to Hungarian Rumanians, and for this he had plans.[27]

Czernin himself now felt that the time was ripe for the publication but he differed strongly from his German colleague in approach. Von dem Bussche wanted immediate publication and was not very much interested in the details. Czernin understood that the real issue was one of content. If, after the concessions were made, the Hungarian Rumanians proved dissatisfied, the move would have no effect on Bukarest whatsoever and would, if anything, only increase hostility against Austria-Hungary.[28]

Behind Tisza's hesitation to publish the concessions in October stood certain recent events. There had been a Russian advance into the Carpathians, and King Carol had died on October 10. The Austrians judged the Rumanians properly. At the moment they would not foresake neutrality, and, concessions or no, they would certainly not now participate against the Russians.

Apparently the Germans actually believed Rumanian participation on their side could be gained by granting concessions, for Bussche had reported the remark of the Rumanian general, Dimitri Iliescu, that a swing of Rumanian public opinion depended on Tisza's decision. Bethmann-Hollweg instructed Tschirschky to urge a "prompt solution" and to request an audience with Franz Joseph on the matter. That Berlin placed too much weight on the possible effects of publication was brought out by Berchtold when he wrote to Hohenlohe in Berlin; he stated that Ferdinand, the new king, had clearly said, "any constellation is possible but not an action against Russia."[29] Nevertheless, Berlin continued its strong appeals in Vienna. On November 3 Bethmann wired Tschirschky that reports showed the Austrian army

---

[27] Staatsarchiv, PA, box 517, no. Z 87-B/P, Hohenlohe to Berchtold, 6 October 1914; no. 738, Czernin to Berchtold, 10 October; unnumbered letter, Tisza to Czernin, 17 October.

[28] Ibid., no. 725, Czernin to Berchtold, 9 October 1914; no. 803, Czernin to Berchtold, 27 October.

[29] Ibid., unnumbered letter, Tisza to Berchtold, 1 November 1914; no. 648, Hohenlohe to Berchtold, 4 November; GFMA, ser. 1, reel 18, no. 83, Bethmann-Hollweg at general headquarters to the Foreign Office, 26 October; Staatsarchiv, PA, box, 517, no. 784, Berchtold to Hohenlohe, 5 November.

to be very weak and that Germany was in no position to offer the necessary aid. Rumanian help must therefore be obtained: "Vienna and Pest must finally realize that political sacrifices cannot be too high to save the situation." He referred to the unfavorable current in Rumanian public opinion, and he laid the guilt at the feet of the Hungarian government, which could not decide on sufficient concessions.[30]

Continual German insistence finally led Tisza to make the move. The concessions were published on November 8 as an open letter addressed to the Metropolitan, Archbishop Metianu, and appeared in the Vienna *Fremden Blatt.* Tisza did not expect the publication to have any great result, but he agreed to it because of German pleas on the one hand, and, on the other, because of Turkey's recent entry into the war on the side of the Central Powers, which had produced a sobering effect in Rumania. Tisza's expectations proved to be correct. While the letter spoke of revisions in school laws, of the use of the Rumanian language by state officers, and of revisions in voting procedures, these issues were dealt with in very general terms. The Rumanians in Hungary reacted positively but the reaction in Rumania itself was poor. King Ferdinand declared that the concessions were too small and though he himself was favorable to the Central Powers, he could do nothing since his people were against them. Rumanian newspapers proved hostile, alleging that the concessions were an attempt to win Rumania at the last moment. The attitude was best summed up by the Rumanian newspaper *Facla:* "Today it is too late for a reform of the Volkschule laws, for a reform of voting rights. Today we want Transylvania and we shall have it!"[31]

The idea of issuing concessions as first developed by von dem Bussche had led to nothing but hard feeling between Germany and Austria. Just before their publication Bussche had apparently told various Rumanians that the forthcoming concessions were due to the efforts of the German government and that while Tisza had refused to guarantee the autonomy of Transylvania, Germany would manage to put this through, too. The latter remark evoked an immediate response from Tisza, who wrote to the Ballhausplatz that, "It would be in the interests of the situation if Herr von dem Bussche would contradict

[30] GFMA, ser. I, reel 18, no. 95, Bethmann-Hollweg to the Foreign Office, 3 November 1914.
[31] Staatsarchiv, PA, box 517, newspaper clipping, 8 November 1914; no. 808, Berchtold to Hamerle in Berlin, 12 November; GFMA, ser. I, reel 18, no. AS 2532, Bussche to Berlin, 7 November, a recounting of Dr. Roselius's talk with Ferdinand on 6 November; Staatsarchiv, PA, box 517, no. 5268, report from Austrian Foreign Office Newspaper Archives to Hohenlohe, 18 November; Count Stephan Tisza, *Briefe, 1914–1918,* 1:101, 102, 105.

this in suitable ways." Berchtold lost no time in asking Germany to inform its minister that he was meddling in affairs which were a "purely internal business of the Hungarian government." In reply, Undersecretary Zimmermann simply said Berlin had the fullest confidence in Bussche's tact and caution, and he attributed the supposed statements to Rumanian agitators.[32] Zimmermann's remarks convinced no one; two weeks later Tisza was at German headquarters to tell the Kaiser, the chancellor, Jagow, and Zimmermann that he would not stand for Germany's meddling in Hungarian affairs. In a telegram to Czernin in which he summed up the results of the meeting, Tisza wrote, "I hope the idea of further concessions to Rumania, which the Undersecretary rather emphasized, and the others more weakly presented, has been dashed from their heads. In any case I have categorically declared that on this issue there can be no talk."[33]

The whole question of Transylvania reflected a basic disparity in the viewpoints of Germany and Austria. German leaders believed the war had to be won and at any cost. The Austrians wanted victory but sought to emerge from the conflict possessing no less than when they entered it. In the months to come this difference was to make perfect cooperation on Rumanian policy impossible to achieve.

While Berlin and Vienna sought somehow to deal with the issue of concessions to Rumania, they tried simultaneously to cement relations between Rumania and Bulgaria. The distrust between the two Balkan states was seen as a definite barrier to the establishment of the desired Turkish-Bulgarian-Rumanian bloc. The effect of the distrust was contrapuntal, for without sufficient guarantees of friendship from Rumania, Bulgaria would not give up its neutrality to fight against the Entente. And certainly without Bulgarian assurances of a continued respect for Rumanian territorial integrity, the Rumanians would in no way be led to fight against Russia, for their rear would stand open to a possible Bulgarian attack.

In the initial months after the outbreak of war, the Central Powers attempted to obtain a formal understanding between Rumania and Bulgaria, but the attempt proved unsuccessful. It has already been shown that in August, 1914, Rumania was willing to offer oral assurances of its neutrality if Bulgaria should attack Serbia, but it refused to put these assurances in writing. The Bulgarians would have very much liked a formal agreement, but Bratianu rejected an accord that would be aimed essentially against Russia. Victory was not in sight for either

[32] Staatsarchiv, PA, box 517, no. 789, Berchtold to Hohenlohe, 6 November 1914; no. 661, Hohenlohe to Berchtold, 7 November.
[33] Ibid., box 500, unnumbered telegram, Tisza to Czernin, 26 November 1914.

the Central Powers or the Entente, and the Rumanians would not make any definite decision until the war's outcome was more certain. On August 22 Berchtold expressed to Czernin his irritation over Bratianu's refusal to sign what would have been a written treaty of neutrality, a measure which in his view aimed only at soothing relations between the two countries.[34]

The Rumanian king supported Bratianu's refusal because he feared that publication of such a treaty would evoke an attack from Russia, for the treaty would oblige Rumania to stand by while Bulgaria defeated the Serbs, who had Russian support. Bratianu had systematically nourished in Carol the fear that if Russia attacked Rumania, the people would rise in revolt against the crown. Nevertheless, the king sent a telegram to Ferdinand of Bulgaria on August 29, assuring him of his friendship. At the same time George Derussi, the Rumanian minister in Sofia, received instructions to inform the Bulgarian government that Rumania would maintain neutrality if the Bulgars decided to undertake action in the war. In exchange for these oral assurances Rumania dared to suggest a written declaration from the Bulgarians to the effect that "The Bulgarian government would strictly respect and consider as absolutely definitive all the clauses of the Treaty of Bukarest and of its annexes concerning the state of things between the two countries." What Rumania sought to eliminate by this declaration was the possibility of Bulgarian attempts to regain part of the Dobrudja. The Bulgarian reaction was to declare that "if Roumania wants it in writing, she must give something in writing." In answer to Tarnowski's remark that an assurance of benevolent neutrality by Rumania ought to be enough, Radoslavov replied that his government "would think things over." The only thing forthcoming was a formal note from King Ferdinand thanking King Carol for his assurances of Rumanian neutrality.[35]

The possibility of a written agreement between the two Balkan states thus came to nothing. Bethmann-Hollweg saw the position of the Central Powers as having worsened in the Balkans, since the desired Balkan bloc that might have broken Russian influence permanently could not now be brought about. But Berchtold turned the diplomatic failure to good advantage. The Ballhausplatz was well aware of the increasing agitation in Rumania against the Monarchy and equally

[34] Ibid., box 517, no. 426, Czernin to Berchtold, 21 August 1914; no. 344, Berchtold to Czernin, 22 August.

[35] Ibid., no. 441, Czernin to Berchtold, 24 August 1914; no. 469, Czernin to Berchtold, 29 August; no. 470, Czernin to Berchtold, 29 August; nos. 677, 682, Tarnowski to Berchtold, 29 and 30 August; no. 691, Tarnowski to Berchtold, 1 September.

aware that Rumania strongly feared Bulgaria. If the Central Powers could not effect an understanding between the two states and clear the way for gaining both as allies, then they could at least play on the Rumanian fear of a Bulgarian attack, to forestall any flight to the camp of the Entente. He instructed the legation in Sofia to influence Radoslavov to produce a statement that Bulgaria would declare war on Rumania if Rumania joined Russia. A few days later Radoslavov mentioned to the German minister that he had told the Rumanian representative, Derussi, that in the case of a Rumanian attack on the Dual Monarchy, Bulgaria would march its troops into the Dobrudja. Simon Radeff, the Bulgarian minister in Bukarest, was instructed to make the same remark to the Rumanian government. Radeff apparently did not act on his instructions, and the result was perplexity in the minds of Rumanian statesmen as to Bulgaria's exact position; but the confusion helped to produce a cautious policy and prolong Rumanian neutrality. The specter of a Bulgarian threat slackened the desire of various Rumanians advocating war throughout the next three months.[36]

[36] GFMA, ser. 1, reel 17, no. 46, Bethmann-Hollweg at general headquarters to the Foreign Office, 17 September 1914; Staatsarchiv, PA, box 517, no. 447, Berchtold to von Mittag, first consul in Sofia, 18 September; box 497, Denkschrift issued by the Foreign Office, January 1915; box 517, no. 527, Berchtold to Czernin, 22 September; no. 680, Czernin to Berchtold, 29 September; Bratianu had told Czernin that Radeff had declared Bulgaria only wanted to be friends with Rumania and would allow it to attack the Monarchy; no. 876, Tarnowski to Berchtold, 1 October; GFMA, ser. 1, reel 17, no. 167, Michahelles to Berlin, 28 September; no. 176, Michahelles to Berlin, 2 October; Staatsarchiv, PA, box 517, no. 941, Czernin to Berchtold, 21 November; no. 826, Berchtold to Czernin, 22 November; GFMA, ser. 1, reel 18, no. 656, Bussche to Berlin, 23 November; no. AS 36462, report from *Frankfurter Zeitung*, summarizing the Rumanian situation, 21 December.

Chapter 9

Rumania, Point
and Counterpoint

By December, 1914, both Germany and Austria were convinced that they could count on Rumanian neutrality at least until February, because of Rumania's military situation. In late November, Günther Bronsart von Schellendorff, the German military attaché in Bukarest, had written a long report to the War Ministry in Berlin discussing current opinion in Rumanian military circles. Army men were not in favor of war at this time, for there was no eagerness to take on a difficult winter campaign with forces still not entirely prepared. If there was to be participation at all, they wanted it in the spring. Then, too, there were the dispatches of Bussche and Czernin discussing the new Rumanian king. Since his accession to the throne in October, Ferdinand had consistently declared that he was favorable to the Central Powers, that he would insist on neutrality, and that Bratianu agreed with him to undertake no action against Austria. While there had been continued agitation for war by pro-Entente politicians such as Filipescu, Ferdinand, remaining undisturbed, observed that "Dogs that bark much do not bite."[1]

Rumanian Coolness Continued

It is not difficult to explain the basis for the king's adherence to neutrality. He was uninterested in joining the Entente because all of his inclinations were toward Germany. Born into the house of Hohenzollern-Sigmaringen, he had been sent to Rumania at the age of twenty to obtain the necessary grooming for the Rumanian crown under the direction of Carol, his uncle. Like Carol he had an overwhelming faith in the invincibility of the German army. This pro-Germanism was nevertheless offset by several other factors. First of all, the king had a shy, quiet, and retiring personality, which made it difficult for him to cope with the strong will of Bratianu. Second, his wife was pro-Entente, since she was the niece of the king of England and cousin of the Russian Czar. And third, Ferdinand possessed a great sense of his duty as the new Rumanian crowned head. In his address to the Rumanian

National Assembly when he assumed his duties on October 12, 1914, Ferdinand promised, "I will be a good Rumanian," and he meant it. He proved capable of laying aside his own prejudices to serve the future welfare of his adopted country. In the end his own timidity, the strength of Bratianu's will, the influence of the queen, Rumanian public opinion, the territorial offers of the Entente, and the general military situation forced him to turn his back on his German heritage. His position was a thoroughly unenviable one, for he remained torn between his natural pro-German attitudes and his sense of obligation to the Rumanian people. For almost two years, he was to choose neutrality as the best way out of a most difficult situation in which he was faced with a personal dilemma on the one hand, and on the other with constant entreaties from the representatives of both groups of belligerents.[2]

If Berlin and Vienna could not expect a great deal from the king, neither could they hope for much support from the Rumanian people. On December 9 Berchtold wrote a summation to Hohenlohe in which he depicted a dark Rumanian scene. On the basis of various sources of information the Ballhausplatz now judged that Rumania might well enter the conflict during the spring of 1915. By February the army would be ready for war. The question of which camp Bukarest would choose rested on what might happen on the battlefields, for Rumania would join the stronger side. Certainly there was much hatred against Austria-Hungary and against Germany, too, since the influence of Gallic culture predominated. The one thing which could swing Rumania toward the Central Powers was a reawakening of respect for their military strength. If Germany and Austria proved successful against Russia, there was a chance of obtaining Rumania as an ally. Until the outcome on the eastern and Serbian fronts had been decided, Berchtold believed the policy must be to seem self-assured and friendly in diplomatic circles while working secretly to prepare Rumanian public opinion.[3]

[1] GFMA, ser. 1, reel 18, no. 155, Bronsart to the War Ministry in Berlin, 20 November 1914; no. AS 2792, letter from Bussche to Zimmermann, 27 November; no. 738, Bussche to Berlin, 7 December; Staatsarchiv, PA, box 517, no. 815, Czernin to Berchtold, 29 October; Czernin reported his first conversations with the new king and found him more favorable than he had expected; Count Stephan Burian, *Austria in Dissolution*, p. 66; Leonard A. Magnus, *Rumania's Cause and Ideals*, p. 82.
[2] Marie, Queen of Rumania, *The Story of My Life*, pp. 4–7, 23; C. Diamondy, "Ma Mission en Russie, Octobre 1914–Mai 1915," *Revue des Deux Mondes* 60 (November–December 1930):422–23.
[3] GFMA, ser. 1, reel 18, no. AS 34517, secret letter to Hohenlohe in Berlin (unsigned, but clearly that of Berchtold), 9 December 1914; secret letter of Czernin to Berchtold, 2 December, attached.

By this time von dem Bussche was quite in agreement with this interpretation. The German minister also stressed the importance of the outcome of the fighting, stating: "If we are victorious they will remain neutral, *perhaps* even go with us."[4]

Both foreign offices were well aware of much hostile feeling in Bukarest. The reports which filtered in during December and January evaluated the position taken by various political parties and the attitudes of the public. Representatives of the Liberal Party in the Rumanian Senate were said to be 70 percent in favor of war on the side of the Entente, and in the Chamber of Deputies half of the Liberals took the same view. Ionescu's Conservative-Democratic Party was decisively against Germany and Austria, and of the Conservative group led by Marghiloman two-thirds were in favor of participation with the Entente. Newspapers supporting the Central Powers were boycotted, reports of German or Austrian victories were seen as false. In the cafes, the private clubs, and on street corners people talked of war with Austria-Hungary by the first of March. Bronsart, however, believed—and he proved to be correct—that *if* the Russians were decisively defeated by the middle of February and if the Italians made no move, the Rumanian government would stand pat, whichever party was in control.[5]

Certainly, as 1915 opened, the Central Powers counted on the fortunes of war to bring their diplomacy success. The necessity of a victory in the field led Conrad von Hötzendorf to press the Germans for a great offensive in the east, and by January 9 Kaiser Wilhelm had overridden Falkenhayn's objections. On January 19, Conrad wrote Tisza a letter which illustrates the importance that military considerations had come to have with respect to diplomacy. Conrad thought that if the action soon to begin against the Russian forces in the Carpathians could be successfully completed by the middle of February, an Italian declaration of war against Austria-Hungary could be averted. And Rumania, since it followed the lead of Italy, would also hold its hand.[6]

In early 1915, the real concern of the Central Powers centered on the Italian situation. As Rome decided, so would Bukarest, and in the

---

[4] GFMA, ser. 1, reel 18, no. 316, Bussche to Berlin, 18 December 1914; italics in the original.

[5] GFMA, ser. 1, reel 18, no. AS 36462, *Frankfurter Zeitung*, to the Foreign Office, 21 December 1914; no. 20, Bronsart von Schellendorff to Foreign Office in Berlin, 15 January 1915.

[6] Winston S. Churchill, *The Unknown War: The Eastern Front*, pp. 273–78; Count Stephan Tisza, *Briefe, 1914–1918*, 1:159. The Italian Consulta was scheduled to meet on 18 February 1915.

month of January the outlook with respect to Italy seemed poor. It was at this time that Burian replaced Berchtold, and shortly after his appointment, the new foreign minister travelled to German headquarters for high-echelon conversations with Bethmann-Hollweg, Jagow, and the Kaiser. Both the chancellor and Jagow tried hard to convince Burian of the necessity of granting the Trentino to Italy to assure its neutrality. Burian refused, for he did not believe an Italian attack imminent and, sparring for time, insisted that the best policy was to maintain a courageous and bold front.

Only the Kaiser spoke of Rumania, because the German officials were convinced that Rumania's position was entirely dependent on the Italian decision. Wilhelm assured Burian that his minister in Bukarest had spoken in plain language to officials there, making certain that they understood Germany would support Austria militarily if Rumania attacked it.[7] Wilhelm's remarks demonstrate that Rumania's intention of gaining Transylvania had not been deflected. On January 15 von dem Bussche had made quite clear to the Rumanian government that under no condition would Germany stand by quietly in case of an attempted Rumanian occupation. His representations indicate Berlin's recognition that at the moment a strong united front was necessary to reduce the Rumanian desire for war.[8]

During this month Czernin was very busy taking the pulse of the Rumanian patient. In the course of seven days he had three private audiences with the king in an attempt to ascertain his precise point of view. Ferdinand refused any commitment, but what he did say led Czernin to conclude that the patient might be growing worse. If, said Ferdinand, the Austrians were now to suffer defeat, Rumania would immediately intervene, for it could not emerge from a division of the Monarchy with empty hands. He reaffirmed his personal pro-German point of view, said he had told the political opposition that to go against the Central Powers meant breaking with his whole German past, but concluded by remarking that he could not ignore the wishes of his subjects for a "Greater Rumania" without risking revolution. Nevertheless, there was still hope that Rumania might remain neutral if the armies of Franz Joseph proved successful. Czernin reported to the Ballhausplatz, "There is no doubt that we are nearing a decisive stage and there is no time to lose."[9]

[7] Staatsarchiv, PA, box 503, Denkschrift no. 686, discussion of Burian's trip to Berlin and German headquarters, 27 January 1915.

[8] GFMA, ser. 1, reel 18, no. 60, Bussche to Berlin, 15 January 1915.

[9] Staatsarchiv, PA, box 519, nos. 51, 65, 77, Czernin to Burian, 13, 16, 19 January 1915.

Though Czernin was worried, he carried out the bold-front policy advocated by Burian. On January 15, he talked for over two hours with the queen, who was known to be very influential with her husband. When she asked Czernin for his "objective" point of view, he maintained that if Rumania attacked the Central Powers it would "disappear from the map of Europe." By choosing the side of the Entente it could only lose, for it would become the vassal of Russia. Therefore it was obvious that the best position for Rumania was neutrality. In an interview with Prince Stirbey, confidant of the king, Czernin countered the statement that Rumania would join Austria-Hungary after a decisive defeat of Russia by curtly saying that, in that case, Rumania would no longer be needed.[10]

That this cold approach seemed to Czernin a good gambit was borne out by a coincidence occurring in the last days of January, when Bratianu became aware of Austrian troop concentrations in the Bukovina. Just then Czernin was in Vienna for conversations on the outcome of Burian's visit to German headquarters. Bratianu, his fears increased by Czernin's absence, jumped to the conclusion that the forces were being massed for an attack on Rumania. He was quieted only after the Austrian minister hurried back and gave assurances that the troops were being deployed against Russia, as in fact they were. On February 1 Czernin reported that this "storm in a glass of water" had subsided, but the panic it produced allowed him to take the measure of his opponents. Rumania was afraid of war with the Central Powers, at least for the time being, and while the diplomatic strategy of assurance and coldbloodedness might not gain Rumanian active cooperation, it would at least keep Bukarest peaceful.[11]

Austria's Inelasticity on Concessions

The uncertainty of the Rumanians as to the outcome of the war was reflected in a letter of Ferdinand to Kaiser Wilhelm on January 25, 1915, ostensibly written as a birthday greeting. The king declared that he sought to avoid having his country commit itself to a bad adventure, that is, war against the Central Powers, but his position was difficult considering thirty years of agitation within Rumania to regain Transylvania. If Rumania came out of the war with no profits it would be

[10] Ibid. nos. 58, 59, Czernin to Burian, 15 January 1915, no. 90, Czernin to Burian, 21 January.

[11] Ibid., unnumbered memo, Tschirschky in Vienna to Burian, 27 January 1915; no. 86, Burian to von Szent-Ivany, 27 January (von Szent-Ivany substituted for Czernin while the latter was in Vienna); no. 144, Czernin to Burian, 1 February; unnumbered report, Czernin to Burian, 2 February.

seen by his people as a moral defeat. Although Bratianu had already been promised Transylvania and the Bukovina by Russia in return for the maintenance of neutrality, Ferdinand now suggested to Wilhelm that the Central Powers at least guarantee Rumania the Bukovina as compensation for its remaining peaceful. Bukarest was obviously weighing war events most carefully. If the Entente should lose the war, Ferdinand and his government wanted still to emerge with some kind of territorial addition.[12]

Kaiser Wilhelm's answer was well put. He made no mention of ceding territories in exchange for neutrality. Instead he played upon the long-standing Rumanian fear of Russia, pointing to Rumania's role as a "bulwark on the lower Danube against the Slavic threat." While the Kaiser admitted that Ferdinand's position was difficult, he suggested that for the good of Rumania the king should maintain its present neutrality. Because the Russian offensive had been stopped and the military situation of the Central Powers had improved, he returned to the possibility of active Rumanian support: "It appears to me that the moment for a change is not yet past, but rather [is] favorable."[13]

The hint at active participation was not without basis. Carp, one of the few prominent Rumanians who consistently retained his pro-German and interventionist leanings, had approached Czernin earlier in January with a plan. He believed that if Austria offered Bessarabia and a part of the Bukovina in return for Rumanian cooperation, promising these concessions in a written treaty, Ferdinand would march against Russia. If Carp was given the firm support of both Berlin and Vienna, he would try to put the plan into effect.[14]

Von dem Bussche, informed of Carp's proposal, at once requested that Berlin exert "the most urgent and sharpest influence" on the Austrians to have them accept. The question was raised by Jagow when Burian visited German headquarters, but the latter refused any commitment until he could study the problem. Czernin, having anticipated the reaction of the Ballhausplatz, talked with Carp on February 2; though he declared that Austria would consider ceding Bessarabia, he stated flatly that it would not offer so much as one Bukovinian village. Two days later the expected arrived in the form of an instruction from Burian that not only must Czernin avoid discussions of actual territorial cession, but he must not even consider cession on a hypothetical level. That would give the impression of Austrian weakness

[12] GFMA, ser. 1, reel 18, no. AS 391, Ferdinand of Rumania to Wilhelm, 26 January 1915.

[13] Ibid., no. AS 395, letter from Wilhelm to Ferdinand, 31 January 1915; see also Staatsarchiv, PA, box 519, no. 54, Hohenlohe to Burian, 31 January.

[14] Staatsarchiv, PA, box 519, no. 106, Czernin to Burian, 23 January 1915.

and its decided need for Rumanian support. On February 8 Burian informed Czernin of the underlying reasons for his refusal of the plan. He pointed out that Ferdinand had said he was at the moment unable to pursue a line of active intervention. It was not certain that the king would accept Carp's project. Austria would be in the position of having pledged itself to a written promise without obtaining any specific assurances in return. The whole success of the plan hinged on Carp's being chosen to head the government, but such a choice was exceedingly unlikely, notwithstanding the burning political ambitions of the man. Finally, there was no reason to believe that a promise of such territories would in any way reduce the hostility of Rumanian public opinion.[15]

The Germans had all along disagreed with Vienna's position, and they did not change their opinion now. In conversations with Burian, who found the whole Carp proposal problematical, von Tschirschky expressed the belief that the gesture was worthwhile for it would help bring Carp to power. Burian's reply was that Carp simply would not be summoned to head the government; if Ferdinand made such an attempt, he might run the risk of a coup d'état, a risk which he would definitely avoid. Tschirschky, unimpressed by this reasoning, told the Wilhelmstrasse he believed Burian's policy to be based on Tisza's view that the project was not feasible. Bussche, on learning that Vienna was willing to offer the same old concession of Bessarabia, remarked briefly that he found Austria's position "shortsighted."[16]

Nevertheless, the Wilhelmstrasse saw that the Austrian ally had to be supported. When Alexander Beldiman, the Rumanian minister in Berlin, decided in February to go to Bukarest in an attempt to convince his own government that it should honor its old alliances with the Central Powers, he asked for a private letter from the German government to make his case stronger. While the Wilhelmstrasse provided the letter, it did not go beyond promising Bessarabia in return for cooperation, the most the Ballhausplatz was willing to grant.[17]

A German offensive in the northeast began on February 7 and two weeks later the Russian Tenth Army lay decimated at the hands of the German eastern forces. Czernin's earlier remarks that Rumanian war

---

[15] GFMA, ser. 1, reel 18, no. 129, Bussche to Berlin, 25 January 1915; no. 88, Jagow to the Foreign Office, 26 January; Staatsarchiv, PA, box 519, no. 146, Czernin to Burian, 2 February; no. 114, Burian to Czernin, 4 February; no. 129, Burian to Czernin, 8 February.

[16] GFMA, ser. 1, reel 19, no. 52, Tschirschky to Berlin, 1 February 1915; no. 185, Bussche to Berlin, 3 February.

[17] Ibid., unnumbered letter, von Jagow to Beldiman, 17 February 1915; see also Staatsarchiv, PA, box 518, folio 68, duplicate.

spirit reacted to the military situation like a pressure gauge proved to be accurate. During these days Rumanian attitudes toward the Central Powers improved. But von dem Bussche was no more certain of these attitudes than Czernin, for he declared that the improvement would have to be even greater and that a military setback would immediately produce an opposite trend. When he bluntly asked the king if Rumania would now attack with them, Ferdinand answered that the proper moment had still not arrived. Bukarest remained determined to wait for something decisive. The Rumanian attitude was prompted not by the success of the German Wehrmacht in the north, but by the Austrian failure to destroy Russia's hold on the Carpathians. By March 2 von dem Bussche was again reporting a worsening of opinion toward Germany and Austria. The German minister had heard that Rumania would still remain neutral, though there was one event, said Bussche's sources, which would lead Rumania to take the field against its former allies: the end of Italian neutrality.[18]

The Italian situation had continued to deteriorate, so that the anxieties of German diplomats and military men increased during February. On the twentieth Burian, accompanied by Conrad von Hötzendorf, again visited German headquarters for discussions with Bethmann-Hollweg. The chancellor saw the eleventh hour approaching and tried hard to obtain Austrian consent not to an immediate cession of the Trentino but to an eventual promise of the area. Stressing the danger now at hand, Falkenhayn offered the opinion that the entry of Italy and the consequent entry of Rumania on the side of the Entente would mean victory for the enemy.

Burian said he was well aware of the Italian problem, but a postwar cession of the Trentino would be impossible; and to make such a promise now would only raise new difficulties in negotiations. Conrad agreed with Falkenhayn's analysis of the military situation, but he concurred with Burian's refusal to consider giving up the Trentino. It would in his view, not be enough to satisfy Italian ambitions.[19]

The Germans were not made to feel any easier when, in the opening days of March, Bussche reported that Bratianu, while still wishing to maintain neutrality, had said that if Italy went against the Central Powers, Bukarest would be unable to hold back the tide of public opinion and would be forced to go along.[20] Czernin heard the king

[18] Churchill, *Unknown War*, pp. 293–99; Staatsarchiv, PA, box 519, unnumbered report, Czernin to Burian, 2 February 1915; no. 225, Czernin to Burian, 16 February; GFMA, ser. 1, reel 19, nos. 345 and 352, Bussche to Berlin, 2 and 4 March.
[19] Staatsarchiv, PA, box 503, Denkschrift no. 1164, 21 February 1915.
[20] GFMA, ser. 1, reel 19, no. 357; Bussche to Berlin, 5 March 1915.

make the same remark. A deep impression had been made on both Ferdinand and Bratianu by the Italian representative, who circulated the news that a crisis was approaching in Austro-Italian relations. Czernin and Bussche, in concert, made light of this statement. On the contrary, von Bussche asserted, an understanding had been reached between Austria and Italy. Czernin blandly stated that the Ballhausplatz counted with certainty on a continuance of Italian neutrality. When, in the middle of the month, the Austrian minister again spoke with the queen, he played his hand even more boldly. According to the picture he drew, Italy would remain neutral, and the Entente would lose the war. If Rumania wanted "a drubbing" it need only attack Austria, a move calculated to destroy Rumania and the dynasty with it. If Rumania wanted to remain neutral, this was acceptable to the Central Powers, but the country would emerge from the war with empty hands. If it joined them, Bessarabia would be given as a reward. In his report to the home office Czernin explained that such a strong tactic was necessary because if the Rumanians once believed Austria no longer had confidence in itself, the game was lost.[21]

Bukarest knew that things were not going well between Rome and Vienna and it was not swayed by the strategy of the German and Austrian representatives. In February, 1915, Italy had signed an additional accord with Rumania which not only maintained the agreement made in the previous September, but provided additional stipulations which brought about a defensive alliance between the two. The accord stated that if Austria-Hungary should be guilty of an unprovoked aggression against either party, both would act together against the Monarchy. In the face of this, Ferdinand could hardly have been impressed by Bussche's insistence that an understanding had been reached with the Italians, because when the king had asked for details Bussche could only reply weakly that these were not known to him.[22]

The lack of confidence in the Central Powers was also reflected in the steadfast refusal of Bratianu and the king to allow through passage of munitions to besieged Turkey. Throughout March, Bussche attempted to open the way for shipments of war goods. He argued that the fall of the Dardanelles and the control of Constantinople by a victorious Russia would not be in the economic interests of Rumania, but would mean a Russian stranglehold on Rumanian exports. Bratianu replied that Rumanian public opinion would not allow shipment, and

[21] Staatsarchiv, PA, box 519, no. 318, Czernin to Burian, 4 March 1915; no. 341, Czernin to Burian, 8 March; no. 364, Czernin to Burian, 11 March; unnumbered memo, Czernin to Burian, 18 March.

[22] Ibid., box 518, no. 3509, Burian to Hohenlohe, 18 June 1915; no. 364, Czernin to Burian, 11 March.

that he was thus forced to refuse. What he did not mention was the apparent assurance given him by the English and French representatives that the Straits would be internationalized after the war, which, of course, would dispose of the Russian threat. Given the allied naval attack on the Straits in March, the fragile relationship between Austria and Italy, and the continued lack of any decisive action against Russia, Rumania remained unimpressed by the importunities of German and Austrian diplomats.[23]

By the beginning of April, Berlin and Vienna had no greater hope of changing Rumanian attitudes. Jagow wired the German ambassador in Rome that "all means have been used in Bukarest including the 'golden keys'—sums fantastic in nature—and all has failed." The question for Germans and Austrians alike was how long the neutrality would last. German rancor against Tisza had not lessened throughout the winter in spite of the many conferences and discussions. Bethmann was sure nothing could be done with Tisza, for he said, "I have already personally convinced myself of the absolute inflexibility of this Hungarian bull."[24] He believed that by the time Tisza might come to make the necessary concessions it would be too late.

Even as Bethmann wrote these words he must have been aware that they oversimplified the issue, because the German Foreign Office kept a very close watch on the Rumanian domestic scene. The men with the greatest political power and influence remained pro-Entente: the Conservative, Filipescu, was pro-French; the Conservative-Democrat, Ionescu, was pro-British; the Liberal, Costinescu, pro-Russian. Bratianu, while he continued to take a cautious approach and never unequivocally committed himself, yet believed the Entente would win. The king, though a Hohenzollern, was not going to endanger his crown through a stiff-backed, pro-German policy. In addition, the Rumanian public had been bombarded by anti-Austrian and anti-German propaganda through the newspapers. Those with the biggest circulation had

---

[23] Austria, Ministerium des Aussern, *Österreichisch-Ungarns Rotbuch, Diplomatische Aktenstücke betreffend die Beziehungen Österreich-Ungarns zu Rumänien, Juli 22, 1914, bis August 27, 1916* (hereafter cited as Austria, *Rotbuch*), no. 27, Czernin to Burian, 18 March 1915; GFMA, ser. 1, reel 19, no. 398 Bussche to Berlin, 10 March; no. 455, Bussche to Berlin, 18 March; no. 458, Bussche to Berlin, 19 March; no. 113, Dr. Spiess in Bukarest to von Bussche, transmitted to Berlin 20 March. Spiess was a German newspaper correspondent who had talked with Costinescu, minister of economic affairs in the Bratianu government. It was Costinescu who told him of the Entente promises to internationalize the Straits. No. 417, Jagow to Bülow in Rome, 25 March; Jagow summarized the situation in regard to Rumania and mentioned the Entente promise to internationalize the Dardanelles.

[24] GFMA, ser. 1, reel 19, no. 417, Jagow to Bülow, 26 March 1915; no. 1467, Bethmann-Hollweg to General Director of Hamburg-Amerika Line, Albert Ballin, 5 April.

been bought by Russian money and most of the others had turned favorable to the Entente.[25]

In spite of all this, the Germans still, rather superficially, designated Tisza as the key to the Rumanian problem. They were convinced that Rumanian interests were essentially anti-Russian, and only Tisza's intransigence stood in the way of a settlement. The issue would be raised again. Although the diplomatic scene during April was static, fortunately this was not the case on the battlefields. By April 25 the offensive of the Austrian forces had caught fire, and in conjunction with the German South Army, forced a Russian retreat from the Carpathians. On May 2 a new united offensive began in Galicia which would eventually crush the entire Russian line. Against this military backdrop, the events of May and June and the decision of Rumania to maintain neutrality in spite of the Italian declaration of war against Austria-Hungary become comprehensible.

In early May, negotiations between the Central Powers and Italy were stalemated. Bratianu declared that if Italy made war, he would be in a very difficult position in maintaining Rumanian neutrality. By May 11 Czernin could speak of victories in Galicia, but Bratianu, though impressed, proceeded to exploit the basic German and Austrian fear that Rumania would join the Entente. There was no surety that Rumania would remain quiet if Italy should be lost. German diplomats began again to suggest that Austria make concessions in the Bukovina and Transylvania. Jagow telegraphed Tschirschky in Vienna to advise Burian to make another attempt, and later the German chancellor sent Tschirschky a long instruction on the same lines. Bethmann quite agreed with the opinion of Bülow in Rome, who had remarked that Austria should not make the same mistake with the Rumanians that it had made with the Italians and waste precious time by protracting negotiations. If the offers to Bukarest came too late, the country might be driven into the camp of the enemy. Even if Rumania made no move after the Italians declared war, it might nevertheless make such binding commitments to the Entente that breaking the connection would be impossible. By the middle of May, Berlin was fully aware that Bratianu, in spite of reiterations of neutrality, was in serious negotiation with the Russians. Though it was also known that the Russians were not reacting favorably to Bukarest's increased demands for Rumanian Bessarabia, part of the Bukovina, Transylvania, and the Banat, the Germans were clearly worried.[26]

[25] Ibid., no. AS 1368, unsigned report, 20 March 1915; no. AS 8485, unsigned Denkschrift, 8 March.

Now Czernin himself came to the conclusion that the time might be ripe to make an offer. The favorable results in the Galician campaign might conceivably be used to lever the Rumanians into active coopera- tion. Extensive concessions in combination with additional military successes would be necessary. Austria could offer terms in exchange for immediate participation, or let the Rumanians make the approach, setting forth their demands for continued neutrality. Czernin favored the first gambit, since the Dardanelles campaign and the imminent Italian attack might cause Rumania to decide against a rapproche- ment.[27]

Czernin had been visited by Mortzun, the minister of the interior, who unofficially told him that if concessions were now made he and Bratianu would raise such a storm that the feeling against the Central Powers would change within weeks, perhaps even days. Rumania could not continue its "dance on eggs" much longer and would have to choose sides. Czernin believed Mortzun's visit was not really "unoffi- cial" but inspired by Bratianu. At the same time the Entente was working feverishly to gain Rumania. Vienna had to make a decision; Czernin warned that what might succeed today might fail if they waited longer.[28]

But the reaction of the Ballhausplatz was negative. In answer to direct representations made by Tschirschky in Vienna, Burian stated that concessions made in Transylvania and the Bukovina would have no effect beside the greater offers of the Entente, which the Monarchy could not meet. Bratianu, he said, might indeed be involved in discus- sions with the Entente, but the stumbling block was the Banat, which Russia was unwilling to grant. He believed the Rumanians would wait and decide on the basis of military events. Czernin had been ordered to put out feelers and to maintain closest contact with Bratianu. To Czernin the foreign minister wrote instructions that under no condi- tion would Vienna offer anything at all for Rumanian neutrality, and he was to give the impression that neutrality was simply to be ex- pected. To make offers for its continuation could only be seen as signifying Austrian fear and would not lead to the desired results. Bukarest knew it could expect to receive Bessarabia after Russia was

[26] Ibid., no. 736, Bussche to Berlin, 13 May 1915; no. 219, Jagow to Bethmann-Hollweg, 4 May; no. 747, Bussche to Berlin, 15 May; no. 1522, Bethmann-Holl- weg to Tschirschky, 17 May; no. 754, Bussche to Berlin, 16 May; no. 759, Bussche to Berlin, 17 May; no. 776, Bussche to Berlin, 19 May.

[27] Staatsarchiv, PA, box 519, no. 620, Czernin to Burian, 21 May 1915.

[28] Ibid., no. 621, Czernin to Burian, 21 May 1915; nos. 626, 627, Czernin to Burian, 22 May.

defeated; if this was not enough then the Rumanian government must make its wishes known.[29]

Burian and Conrad once again conferred with the German ally at Pless, two days after the Italians had declared war on Austria-Hungary. Rumania was now the prime policy consideration. The Germans realized that offers of territory without counter-guarantees of participation could lead to Rumania's continually raising the ante, and to what Bethmann called a "footrace with the Entente Powers." The Austrian foreign minister developed the issue further. Offers should be made to the Rumanians only with very great care. Bukarest must be impressed again and again with the idea that it could obtain only momentary advantages from joining the Russians. Burian was not against discussing further territorial rewards but he wanted the first overtures to come from the Rumanian government. This approach, along with the fear Rumania would experience if the Central Powers could bring about a Bulgarian-Turkish defensive-offensive alliance, might be enough to gain Rumania.

Jagow agreed that the Austrian position was logical, but he pointed out that logic had not worked with the Italians and might not work now. There was no time to wait for Rumanian overtures. They had to strengthen the position of the favorable element in Rumania at once, and therefore it was the Central Powers who had to make promises. No rewards should be given for neutrality; the condition should be cooperation. And while they could not meet the Entente proposals, concrete offers should nevertheless be tendered, with Rumania clearly understanding it could take them or leave them. Burian thought if this tack was taken the Rumanians would not take their offers but leave them—in short, declare war. Von Jagow's willingness to use strong tactics had already come to light when he had written to Bussche that the successful outcome of the Galician campaign might lead to an ultimatum to Bukarest in order to obtain through passage of munitions to Turkey. The protests he received from both Bussche and Czernin had forced him to drop the idea. The one advance made at the conference at Pless was Burian's final agreement to offer a part of the Bukovina along with Bessarabia as an exchange for Rumanian participation.[30]

[29] GFMA, ser. 1, reel 19, no. 761, Tschirschky to Berlin, 19 May 1915; Staatsarchiv, PA, box 519, no. 485, Burian to Czernin, 23 May.

[30] Staatsarchiv, PA, box 519, no. 3252, report and resume of Burian's conference at Pless, 25 May 1915; no. 637, Czernin to Burian, 24 May; GFMA, ser. 1, reel 19, no. 676, Jagow to Bussche, 23 May; no. 792, Bussche to Berlin, 24 May; no. AS 2586, Jagow at Pless to the Foreign Office, 25 May.

Bukarest Unimpressed

The Germans could now feel they had softened Austria's implacable stand, but their diplomats could not take all the credit. Falkenhayn had repeatedly urged that the Rumanians be won over, and Conrad von Hötzendorf had himself written to Burian, saying nothing must be left untried to assure that Rumania did not attack Austria. However, the decisive factor in Burian's acceptance of the principle of concessions in the Bukovina was Tisza's change of mind. The Hungarian prime minister, by April much concerned over the developments in Rome, had written to the Ballhausplatz: "I am not a nervous man but I must feel the full weight of the moment." In May, Italy's preparations for an attack on Austria-Hungary made him recognize that the policy towards Rumania must be changed if the Rumanians were to be kept from joining the Entente. On May 23, the day Italy declared war, Tisza wrote to Burian that the Rumanian danger was very great, for the Russians might decide to fulfill Rumanian territorial aspirations. The counterweight to this was to be found, he said, not only in establishing a Bulgarian-Turkish alliance, but also in negotiating concessions in the Bukovina in return for Rumanian cooperation. He made it quite patent that no part of Transylvania could be amputated. The Bukovina itself was enough; and he pointed out that a grant of territory there was no bagatelle, for it contained, after all, 273,000 Rumanians.[31]

The instructions which Czernin received were not simple to carry out. Burian left him with the difficult job of obtaining Rumanian support but without making promises that could not be fulfilled. Rumania could expect a piece of the Bukovina if it acted, but Czernin was not to shoot the bolt carelessly. If Austria offered the Bukovina before Rumania committed itself, Bratianu would merely take this as his cue to ask for more and the maneuver would be worthless.[32]

On May 28 Czernin sent a discouraging wire, saying that negotiations on the active entry of Rumania had reached a dead end. Bratianu had flatly stated that Rumanian entry on their side was at the moment impossible; at this time, only neutrality could be expected. Bukarest was waiting to see how the Italians did on the battlefield. Bratianu hinted that Austria ought to concede the Bukovina for neutrality, since

[31] GFMA, ser. 1, reel 19, no. 676, Jagow to Bussche, 23 May 1915; Staatsarchiv, PA, box 517, no. 540, Count Thurn, Foreign Office representative at Austrian military headquarters, Teschen, 23 May; box 519, unnumbered letter, Tisza to Burian, 23 and 24 May; Tisza, *Briefe*, 1:186, 216, 222–25.

[32] Staatsarchiv, PA, box 519, nos. 500 and 512, Burian to Czernin, 24 and 26 May 1915.

this would help strengthen his position. If this was granted, perhaps later Rumania could join the Central Powers. Czernin retorted that his country would not cede so much as a quadrameter of land for neutrality. If Rumania sought to enter the war and help them, he would present the terms that Vienna was willing to grant. The Central Powers did not need Rumania and were not in Bukarest as suppliants, but rather sought to assure joint advantage.[33]

Burian applauded his minister. He evaluated as worthless Bratianu's suggestion of concessions for neutrality which might then be followed later by Rumanian participation. There were prizes to be given but only if Rumania joined while its forces could still be of value against the Russians. Burian believed Russia would be completely defeated in Galicia within two weeks. But because Bratianu had broached the question of the Bukovina, Burian felt that negotiations were not, as Czernin thought, at a dead end. Therefore, Czernin was to continue offering concessions in the Bukovina but only for Rumanian cooperation.[34]

Berlin was impatient to seal the bargain somehow and now not only diverged from Vienna's policy of no territorial prizes for neutrality but attempted the unheard of—influencing an ally's diplomatic representative to ignore the instructions of his own foreign minister. Von Jagow went so far as to tell Bussche that the Austrian minister should seize the initiative. Czernin must not allow himself "to be intimidated through Viennese hesitations," permitting catastrophe to strike again, as it had in the Italian negotiations. Jagow contended that if Czernin exceeded his instructions, Burian would accept the fait accompli. If the Germans could not immediately obtain Rumanian participation, they were ready to offer all of the Bukovina to the River Pruth in exchange for benevolent neutrality. Their thinking was based on the absolute necessity of getting munitions through to the Turks. If Rumania once agreed to such a through transit, its neutral position would be heavily compromised and it would unavoidably be driven into their camp by the resultant alienation of Russia. Berlin was convinced that if the promise of the Bukovina was not given soon, it would be too late. The decision must be made quickly and no price was too great if the tie between Bukarest and St. Petersburg could be cut.[35]

[33] Ibid., no. 658, Czernin to Burian, 27 May 1915.
[34] Ibid., no. 529, Burian to Czernin, 29 May 1915.
[35] GFMA, ser. 1, reel 20, no. 718, Jagow to Bussche, 29 May 1915; no. 88 Falkenhayn by Treutler at Pless to Berlin, 30 May; Staatsarchiv, PA, box 519, unnumbered report, discussion between Count Hoyos in Berlin and the secretary of Bethmann-Hollweg, 30 May.

Czernin and the Ballhausplatz maintained a mutual *sang froid*. Burian chose to temporize; if the Rumanians decided to take action on the side of the Central Powers he would not be small about concessions. To Czernin he wired that it was time to ask Bratianu for a clear answer to the question of Rumania's conditions for immediate cooperation. In short, what was Bratianu's price?[36] Czernin put the matter to him bluntly, but Bratianu refused any commitment, declaring that along with the Bukovina part of Hungary would have to be granted. At any rate, Rumania's decision could not be made rapidly and Burian would have to wait.[37]

By the end of the first week in June nothing had been achieved. King Ferdinand supported Bratianu, maintaining that the government could not make the decision now because of the Italian attack. Had this not come, the victories of the Central Powers against Russia might have allowed for participation. The king and Bratianu were convinced they might face revolution if they joined Germany and Austria. Neutrality would be endangered by a through passage of munitions. Bratianu furthermore refused to make Rumania's wishes known. He wanted an offer to come from the Central Powers before discussing cooperation. It was evident to Czernin that Rumanian aid at the moment was simply not possible. If they wanted the Rumanians they would have to pay more, and this meant concessions in Transylvania.[38]

In Vienna, the new feelers by Bratianu for an actual grant of territory in Transylvania met with an immediate and flat refusal. Count Tisza on hearing the Rumanian allusions dubbed the maneuver an "undiscussable absurdity."[39]

Germany, aware that Vienna would remain adamant on not ceding any Transylvanian land, now returned to the idea of granting additional rights to Hungarian Rumanians. The whole Rumanian problem was back where it had begun in the late summer of 1914. There were now two additional worries: Rumania might succumb to the eager courting of the Entente, and the Dardanelles might be lost for lack of supplies in Turkey unless Rumanian benevolent neutrality could be obtained. Berlin, therefore, made desperate attempts to soften the Austrian position. Matthias Erzberger, a member of the German Reichstag, was sent to Hungary for conferences with Tisza in the

---

[36] Staatsarchiv, PA, box 519, no. 539, Burian to Czernin, 31 May 1915; GFMA, ser. 1, reel 20, no. 796, Tschirschky to Berlin, 30 May.

[37] Staatsarchiv, PA, box 518, no. 684, Czernin to Burian, 1 June 1915.

[38] Ibid., no. 691, Czernin to Burian, 3 June 1915; report no. 55/P A-B, Czernin to Burian, 9 June; no. 741, Czernin to Burian, 11 June.

[39] Ibid., no. 594, Burian to Czernin, 10 June, 1915; Tisza, *Briefe*, 1:247–48.

opening days of June. He asked that linguistic, administrative, and political privileges be granted to the Hungarian Rumanians, but this time they were to be offered in a very specific form. Tisza replied that the plan would have no influence on Bukarest's decision either in the direction of open cooperation or of benevolent neutrality, and for Germany to raise such an issue with the Rumanian government "would have catastrophic consequences." Erzberger disagreed, saying that such concessions *would* be significant, that Germany was not attempting to meddle in Hungarian affairs, that it was all a question of saving Turkey and with it the position of the Central Powers vis-à-vis the Balkan states in general.[40]

Bethmann-Hollweg decided on confidential talks with the Hungarian prime minister and invited him to Berlin. In a conversation on June 17, Bethmann essentially recapitulated the remarks of Erzberger, but went somewhat further. In return for Rumania's permitting through transit of munitions, Germany was prepared to guarantee it heavy financial support. Austria must offer three southern districts of the Bukovina. If Bukarest should agree and then make the additional demand of concessions to the Hungarian Rumanians, the German government wanted Vienna's authorization to say that it knew Hungary intended to "effect various measures." Tisza agreed and went home, seemingly much impressed with the crucial condition of Turkey, and seemingly willing to gain the support of Burian and Franz Joseph for the German scheme. But in fact he believed the Turkish predicament had been exaggerated, for at the start of the Dardanelles campaign it had been said that the Turks could not hold out more than six weeks and they had now lasted almost five months. He was sure they could hold on much longer and he therefore felt that the Central Powers could afford to handle Rumania with composure.[41]

It was quickly apparent that the Austrians were dragging their feet. The German chancellor now became extremely irritated. First of all, Burian refused to make the desired offers unless Rumania would give

[40] Tisza, *Briefe*, 1:229–35.
[41] Ibid., pp. 251, 254, 256–57; GFMA, ser. 1, reel 20, no. AS 3204, report of the conversation by Bethmann-Hollweg, 17 June 1915. The specific proposals for Hungarian Rumanians suggested by Bethmann were: a reform of voting rights, which would mean a Rumanian voting majority in 35–40 voting districts; a consideration of Rumanians in the filling of official posts; an increase in Rumanian schools of various types (college preparatory, agricultural, and trade schools); Rumanian to be the language of instruction; an increase in endowments for Rumanian churches; the use of Rumanians in administration; and correction of the borders of the Bishopric of Hajde Dorogh. While Tisza repeatedly declared to Bethmann that these would be thoroughly ineffectual as a means of obtaining the desired result, he nevertheless agreed to accept them.

open cooperation. To grant Bessarabia, the Bukovina, and privileges for Hungarian Rumanians simply in exchange for the transport of war goods to Turkey was in his estimation very risky. There was no guarantee that the transit could actually be carried off successfully, and, even if it was, what then could Austria offer Rumania for active participation if it had already given away everything possible? He suggested that both powers offer territorial compensation but only for military cooperation within a promised period of time. As the first act of good faith Rumania must allow passage of munitions to Turkey. Furthermore, Burian resented the idea of Germany exclusively making a demarche in Bukarest. The issue of extended rights to Rumanians in Transylvania was the affair of the Monarchy, and he wrote to Hohenlohe in Berlin that he wished "to present *our* offer exclusively through *our* representative, who would proceed simultaneously with his German colleague." Aside from this he told Tschirschky that he wanted to think further about the extended privileges suggested by Bethmann. Tisza had not been sent to Berlin as an official negotiator but only to talk out the question. When Tschirschky pointed out that certainly Berlin had the right to see the Tisza-Bethmann meeting as more than a mere "loose conversation," Burian impatiently remarked that the guaranteeing of concessions to Rumanians in Transylvania was not really the issue. The issue was giving up territories belonging to the Monarchy and for mere Rumanian neutrality this was quite impossible.[42]

On June 25, Bethmann, accompanied by von Jagow, went to Vienna in an attempt to unravel the whole matter through personal talks. Their concern and their discussion hinged on Turkey's successful defense, necessary to keep the Balkan states from throwing over neutrality and joining the enemy. Burian stood his ground so that there was nothing left for the Germans but to accept his proposed strategy. He now instructed Czernin to make the offers of Bessarabia and the Bukovina, along with German financial assistance, in exchange for Rumanian participation within thirty days. No mention was to be made of extended rights to Hungarian Rumanians unless Bratianu first broached the issue. If Bukarest refused the desired cooperation, Burian was willing to have Czernin ask what the Rumanian price would be for through transit.[43]

---

[42] Staatsarchiv, PA, box 518, no. 3533, Burian to Hohenlohe, 21 June 1915; no. 278, Hohenlohe to Burian, 20 June; GFMA, ser. 1, reel 20, no. 198, Bethmann-Hollweg, consul in Budapest, 20 June; no. 98, Fürstenberg to Berlin, 20 June; no. 854, Tschirschky to Berlin, 20 June.

[43] Staatsarchiv, PA, box 518, no. 3610, recapitulation of conversations between Burian, Bethmann-Hollweg, and Jagow, 25 June 1915; no. 639, Burian to Czernin, 25 June. GFMA, ser. 1, reel 21, no. 863, Tschirschky to Berlin, 25 June.

Czernin now hurried off to see Bratianu but got nowhere. The minister-president proved noncommittal. As to the thirty-day limitation, he said they would have to wait and see what the month would bring. If there was then no doubt as to conclusive victory over Russia, cooperation might be possible. Through transit of munitions would signify the same thing, in his view, as active participation, which in the face of Rumanian public opinion he was not in a position to approve. When, two days later, Czernin bluntly asked Bratianu how much he wanted as a price for through passage of supplies, he received a blunt answer: "*You* propose a price to me. . . . You have said you would never consent to make us territorial concessions in Hungary."[44] Czernin could make no comment.

In the month of July the condition of Turkish munitions was still alarming and the fall of the Dardanelles still quite possible. Thinking at the Wilhelmstrasse was almost completely taken up with the problem of supplying the Turkish ally. Both Berlin and Vienna again considered the idea of issuing an ultimatum to Rumania for benevolent neutrality, and in the course of the month the idea was again rejected. While Bussche and Czernin agreed that an ultimatum might work, they saw that the condition for its success would lie in the capacity of the Central Powers to buttress their demands with force. Bethmann-Hollweg was willing to support Falkenhayn, who saw an ultimatum as the solution to the Turkish munitions problem, but the chancellor refused to take the step unless the General Staff could offer the necessary troops to back it. Falkenhayn could make no such promise at the moment since the Russian campaign necessitated all available troops. In Vienna, Burian proved unwilling to go along with the scheme, but because he wanted to make a strong impression on the Rumanians, he asked Conrad if 150,000 troops could be spared to be massed in the Bukovina. Conrad thought not and supported his German colleague in the belief that such an allotment would be possible only after the Russians had been conclusively defeated.[45] Unable to attain the necessary assurances from their military chiefs, the diplomats once again set aside the strategy of ultimatum.

In spite of Bratianu's rebuff of Czernin's representations at the end of June, Berlin continued to seek Rumanian consent for arms shipment. In

[44] Staatsarchiv, PA, box 518, no. 813, Czernin to Burian, 26 June 1915; no. 820, Czernin to Burian, 28 June (italics in the original).

[45] Ibid., no. 841, Czernin to Burian, 3 July 1915; GFMA, ser. 1, reel 21, no. 214; Falkenhayn, through Treutler at Pless, to Berlin, 16 July; no. 871, Bethmann-Hollweg to Falkenhayn, 19 July; no. AS 3852, Bethmann-Hollweg to Falkenhayn, 23 July; Staatsarchiv, PA, box 518, no. 236, Burian to Conrad, 10 July; no. 12750, Conrad to Burian, 11 July.

the first week of July, Kaiser Wilhelm again wrote to Ferdinand. With no pretense at subtlety he defined the situation at the Dardanelles as very serious, speaking of the possibility of Turkish defeat at Gallipoli unless munitions were gotten through. The surrender of Gallipoli, he said, meant the surrender of the Dardanelles and Constantinople, and the establishment of Russian control. The result could only be detrimental to Rumanian interests since Russia would proceed to establish its hegemony over the Balkans. It was Wilhelm's opinion that even on the basis of international law, through passage of munitions would not be inconsistent with neutrality. After all, the United States was shipping war materiel to the Entente. Bussche, too, did the best he could to press Bukarest. In conversations with Bratianu he warned that if Rumania refused to allow passage of arms and if the Dardanelles fell, the offers which the Central Powers were willing to make would not go up, but down. Rumanian hesitation could only result in a loss for Rumania itself.[46]

The Rumanians continued to refuse. In spite of successes in the field by the Central Powers, public opinion had not become more favorable toward them. Russian retreat was not enough. Bukarest wanted a decisive defeat of the Czar's armies before it would consider commitments to Germany and Austria. Only under that condition might public attitudes and those of political circles allow such a commitment. There was, said Bratianu, one other possibility for effecting this change, and this lay in heavy territorial concessions. Obviously, however, the Austrians would not agree. On July 31, King Ferdinand answered Wilhelm's letter politely but firmly. With the attitudes prevailing in the nation, allowing through passage of munitions to Turkey would harm rather than aid the cause of the Central Powers. Therefore his government would have to wait until a more favorable time.[47]

Ferdinand was following the policy of Bratianu, who had convinced him of the wisdom of caution, but in truth the king was now more favorable toward action against the Entente. In a long conversation with Bussche at the beginning of August he agreed it was not in Rumania's interests to have Russia controlling the Straits. In mid-July, Ferdinand had talked most seriously with Bratianu on the whole matter of munitions, declaring that he did not want to see the Dardanelles fall. Bratianu saw the munitions question as a maneuver by Germany and

[46] GFMA, ser. 1, reel 21, no. AS 3499, undated but clearly sent in the first days of the month; no. 22, Bussche to Berlin, 21 July.

[47] Staatsarchiv, PA, box 518, no. 833, Czernin to Burian, 2 July 1915; GFMA, ser. 1, reel 21, no. 22, Bussche to Berlin, 21 July; no. 63, Ferdinand's answer to Wilhelm by Bussche, 31 July. Austria, *Rotbuch*, no. 38, Czernin to Burian, 16 July.

Austria which, if successful, would compromise Rumania's neutrality and draw the nation into war before it was ready to take part. Bratianu's interpretation prevailed.[48]

The Austrians had no greater success than the Germans in attempting to reverse Bukarest's stand. On July 20 Burian instructed Czernin to remind Bratianu of the fact that Austria had offered territorial concessions for Rumanian military cooperation, provided such cooperation came within a month. The month had now almost expired and Austria awaited an answer. Bratianu replied that military cooperation was totally out of the question as long as the Rumanian people believed, as they still did, that the Entente would win. He asked that Burian prolong the time limit, for certainly Rumanian aid would remain of great worth for some time to come. Czernin's warning that Rumania now faced a time of decision made no impression.[49]

The Ballhausplatz refused the extension, and in a letter to Tisza, Burian told why. In spite of his own displeasure with the idea and only because of German insistence, he had offered Rumania the Bukovina. The offer had not produced the desired effect, and in the process of making the concession Austria had actually agreed to give up its inviolability. To Czernin went the order that a second time-period for the offered lands would not be given. New concessions would perhaps be made but they would be on the basis of changed conditions. The conditions Burian alluded to were the continued success of the German and Austrian armies against Russia.[50]

There was still another possibility for obtaining Rumanian cooperation. On July 27 Marghiloman, one of the prominent Conservative Party leaders, conversed with Czernin for over two hours. The Rumanian leader sought to bring pressure upon the king to reconstruct the cabinet by replacing Bratianu with Majorescu, who was favorable to Germany and Austria. Once in power, this cabinet, in which Marghiloman would himself hold a prominent position, would immediately grant the through passage of arms and pledge itself to attack Russia within a given period. Before he went to the king, however, he wanted *in writing* the concessions that Austria was willing to offer with respect to the Bukovina and the Hungarian Rumanians. Czernin was ready to propose a draft and Bussche also went along, feeling that Marghiloman needed something other than empty hands if he was to

---

[48] GFMA, ser. 1, reel 22, no. 271, Bussche to Berlin, 2 August 1915; Staatsarchiv, PA, box 518, unnumbered report, Czernin to Burian, 14 July.

[49] Staatsarchiv, PA, box 518, no. 695, Burian to Czernin, 20 July 1915; no. 883, Czernin to Burian, 22 July.

[50] Ibid., unnumbered letter, Burian to Tisza, 30 July 1915; no. 718, Burian to Czernin, 2 August.

deal effectively with Ferdinand. The Wilhelmstrasse was ready to try, and Jagow requested Tschirschky to sound the Austrian foreign minister. Burian would not agree. There was no guarantee that a new Rumanian cabinet would actually do what Marghiloman believed it would. Nor was Burian willing to make formal and written promises in the name of the Monarchy to a private individual, at the moment a mere ministerial candidate. Burian did not close the door entirely, since he was much interested in continuing discussions with men of Marghiloman's stripe, who might possibly influence Bratianu to lead the country in the proper direction. But in reality the scheme died aborning.[51]

A year after the war began, therefore, no progress had been made with the Rumanian problem. The attempt to gain active cooperation by offering Bessarabia and the Bukovina had failed. An ultimatum was not feasible. Vienna had rejected the idea of collusion with Rumanian politicians for purposes of overthrowing the Bratianu government. The route through Rumania, so desperately needed to aid Turkey at the Dardanelles, remained closed. The problem of Turkey's continued belligerency, which had assumed such great proportions, particularly in the minds of the Germans, led to the only solution possible for holding the Straits: the Turks would be supported by mounting a Serbian campaign, in this manner clearing the necessary passage through Bulgaria. It was now that negotiations between the Central Powers and Bulgaria, intended to develop such an offensive, entered what were to be the final stages.[52]

Fortunately for the Central Powers, their offensive against the Russians continued its strong forward momentum in August and early September. It was this fact which held back the Rumanians from joining the Entente. Aside from Bukarest's being impressed by the military successes of Germany and Austria in the east, there was really no reason why Rumania should at this time trouble to enter the war. The situation for the Czarist armies was so poor by August that St. Petersburg now satisfied the demands for territorial concessions which Bratianu had sought from the Entente since May. The price Bratianu paid for Russian oral assurances was only the vague promise of entering the war against the Central Powers "at a favorable moment."[53]

---

[51] Ibid., no. 904, Czernin to Burian, 27 July 1915; no. 710, Burian to Czernin, 29 July; GFMA, ser. 1, reel 22, no. 1127, Bussche to Berlin, 6 August; no. 1957, Jagow to Tschirschky, 7 August; no. 918, Tschirschky to Berlin, 9 August.

[52] GFMA, ser. 1, reel 21, no. 921, Jagow to Treutler at Pless, 27 July 1915; no. 1450, Zimmermann to Halil Bey in Constantinople, 1 August.

[53] C. Jay Smith, Jr., *The Russian Struggle for Power, 1914–1917*, pp. 291–94, 299, 303–4, 305–9. Bratianu had demanded and was promised the entire Banat, the Pruth River as a frontier in the Bukovina, Ruthenia (Sub-Carpathian Ukraine)

Their territorial ambitions satisfied at no immediate cost, the Rumanians could afford to remain aloof and to avoid involvement. They knew an offensive against Serbia was in the offing because Bethmann-Hollweg had told them so. Through Beldiman, he had informed Bukarest that since Rumania refused through transit of war materials, the Central Powers would open a route through Serbia in conjunction with Bulgaria. Bethmann had dropped this information because both Berlin and Vienna were concerned over what the Rumanian reaction would be when the attack actually did occur. When Bussche and Czernin personally sounded the Rumanian king, they received the comforting statement that in the case of an attack against Serbia, any idea of Rumania coming to its support would be "entirely erroneous." By September 3 Bratianu had reiterated his policy of neutrality, and told Bussche his government would take no hostile action if Serbia was invaded. He also vehemently denied that Rumania now had an obligation to join the Entente or that he had made any agreement with the Entente at all. The first of these assertions was correct; the second was not, and the Wilhelmstrasse knew it. On September 6 a German secret agent in Bukarest wrote directly to Bethmann-Hollweg, pinpointing what had happened: oral understandings with the Entente for action against the Central Powers, but only when the time was right.[54]

The very vagueness of the Rumanian obligation was enough to keep Germany and Austria nervous and the nervousness turned to alarm when, as a result of Bulgarian mobilization on September 21, Bratianu began to talk of ordering a partial mobilization as a means of self-defense. Czernin remained calm, for he understood his opponent thoroughly. The Austrian minister said Bukarest knew very well indeed that neither Austria nor Bulgaria nor Germany was planning to attack the country, and he concluded with what was almost a threat: Rumanian mobilization would have "the most serious results." In the face of hostile Rumanian demonstrations before the German and Austrian legations and demands by Filipescu and Ionescu for immediate mobilization, Bratianu refused to issue the necessary orders. He was no more ready to fight now than he had been in the previous months.[55]

with a western frontier from the junction of the Theiss and Danube Rivers to Szegidin.

[54] GFMA, ser. 1, reel 22, no. AS 4221, Beldiman to Bukarest, 12 August 1915; nos. 112 and 115, Bussche to Berlin, 20 August; no. AS 4556, Bussche to Berlin, 25 August; no. 143, Bussche to Berlin, 3 September; no. A 26977, report no. 35, Herr "33" to Bethmann-Hollweg, 6 September.

[55] Staatsarchiv, PA, box 519, no. 47, Czernin to Burian, 23 September 1915; no. 51, Czernin to Burian, 24 September; report no. 87 A-C/P, Czernin to Burian, 27 September; GFMA, ser. 1, reel 22, no. 349, Bussche to Berlin, 30 September; no. 873, Bronsart to Berlin, 1 October.

In spite of Czernin's bluster, neither Vienna nor Berlin was ready to throw caution to the winds. To eliminate any concern Rumania might now have, it was decided to deliver formal assurances to Bukarest that the Central Powers had no idea of hostilities against Rumania. Bulgaria declared its friendly intentions by way of a telegram from the king on October 11, the day Bulgarian troops crossed the Serbian border. Two days later similar statements were made by Germany and Austria.[56] Bukarest seemed calm.

Now that the Serbian campaign was under way the people who really worried about Rumania were the German and Austrian military leaders. Rumors reached Conrad at Teschen, his headquarters, that there was danger Rumania would allow Russia to transport troops over its soil in order to aid the Serbs. If Rumania permitted this, Russia could attack the Bukovina and Transylvania across the Rumanian borders. Conrad's forces, preoccupied with Serbia, would be unable to meet the threat. The diplomats now put out feelers to define the situation. When approached on the matter both King Ferdinand and Bratianu immediately stated that the Russians had made no threat or demands concerning such transit. Actually, the Russians had begun negotiations along these lines on October 23, but Rumania would not hear of an idea which clearly meant involvement, and informed the Entente it would meet a Russian march-through with force. This attitude had been directly transmitted to St. Petersburg by November 13.[57]

The Germans in particular remained convinced that there was reason to worry. They sent Prince Otto Metternich as a special representative to talk with Bratianu and the king and queen. Metternich was to attempt somehow to bind the Rumanians closer to the Central Powers and, failing this, at least to secure a more certain Rumanian neutrality. The mission proved totally unsuccessful.[58]

[56] Staatsarchiv, PA, box 519, no. 1058, Czernin to Burian, 1 October 1915; no. 810, Burian to Czernin, 3 October; no. 437, Count Larisch (substituting for Hohenlohe) in Berlin to Burian, 4 October; no. 446, Hohenlohe in Berlin to Burian, 9 October; no. 820, Burian to Czernin, 10 October; nos. 72, 80, 84, Czernin to Burian, 11, 13, and 14 October.

[57] Staatsarchiv, PA, box 519, no. 80, Czernin to Burian, 13 October 1914; no. 6181 and enclosure, Conrad at Teschen to Burian, 14 October; unnumbered report, Czernin to Burian, 15 November; no. 1163, Czernin to Burian, 12 November; GFMA, ser. 1, reel 22, no. 1346, Bussche to Berlin, 13 October; reel 23, no. 1374, Bussche to Berlin, 18 October; no. 1393, Bussche to Berlin, 23 October; no. 1418, Bussche to Berlin, 27 October; no. 1468, Bussche to Berlin, 4 November; no. 1506, Bussche to Berlin, 13 November; Smith, *Russian Struggle for Power*, p. 340.

[58] GFMA, ser. 1, reel 23, no. 929, Metternich to Jagow, 10 November 1915; Staatsarchiv, PA, box 519, unnumbered resume of Metternich's report, 10 November; unnumbered report, Czernin to Burian, 15 November.

Bussche did what he could in this direction too. On November 20 he talked with King Ferdinand. After stressing the fact that Rumania might become a battleground, he suggested that a German-Rumanian defensive plan be drawn up by the respective military staffs against any possible Russian threat to Rumanian soil. The idea for this had originated with Falkenhayn, who was genuinely worried over the possibilities of Russian troops striking at the Central Powers through Rumania. Ferdinand, who immediately saw the diplomatic implications of the proposal, refused and simply replied that there was nothing to fear from Russia. When Bussche tried another tack and asked whether Rumania would remain neutral under *all* conditions, the king offered the wary answer that it would "unconditionally *for the time being* remain neutral."[59]

The Austrian diplomats were much less concerned over the Rumanian situation at this time, simply because they took a more accurate measure of things. Czernin knew Bukarest would make no commitments now, whether military or guarantees of neutrality for the war's duration. He therefore took a poor view of Bussche's latest attempts and sent off to Vienna very astute analyses of the Rumanian picture in the early winter of 1915. He pointed out that the victories on the Russian front and the entry of Bulgaria made a declaration of war by Rumania against the Central Powers quite impossible at the moment. Only some "rash step" by Germany or Austria would drive the Rumanians into the enemy camp. Nor need the Central Powers fear a Russian march through Rumanian territory. If anything, the Russians and their allies now had but one watchword concerning Rumania—to keep it neutral—for Russia was militarily in a most unenviable position. The dangerous moment, the time to worry about Rumanian participation on the side of the Entente, would come in the spring when Russia would attempt a new offensive. If the Central Powers wanted to actually win Rumania, the time to act was now, when they held the trump cards in the form of military success. But military victories were by themselves not enough. Czernin therefore suggested that the Ballhausplatz make renewed and greater offers of territorial concessions within the Austro-Hungarian Monarchy. These might lead Ferdinand to construct a more conservative ministry through which Rumania might be won.[60]

---

[59] GFMA, ser. 1, reel 23, no. 581, Falkenhayn to Berlin, 14 November 1915; no. 1536, Bussche to Berlin, 18 November; no. 1540, Bussche to Berlin, 20 November; Staatsarchiv, PA, box 519, no. 1188, Czernin to Burian, 19 November; no. 1193, Czernin to Burian, 20 November, italics in the original.

[60] Staatsarchiv, PA, box 519, unnumbered report, Czernin to Burian, 25 November 1915; report no. 111 A-E/P, Czernin to Burian, 7 December.

A week later the Ballhausplatz answered. Burian was in no way moved to give up his former policy on concessions. He agreed to offer Bessarabia as before, but he refused to discuss the idea of granting areas within the Monarchy. Nor did he want Czernin mixing in Rumanian domestic politics. If any conservative ministry came to power, it must come naturally out of the internal situation itself, or the ministry would be branded as a German-Austrian mouthpiece, providing the liberals with a real basis for agitation against the Central Powers. Burian insisted that Czernin continue to give the impression they neither feared nor needed Rumania.[61] The Austrian minister must have reacted with utter frustration to this unbending attitude and seeming incapacity to look ahead. However, there was nothing he could do but comply with his instructions.

The fact that no Russian attack through Rumania materialized brought a more tranquil attitude in Berlin. The successes against the Serbs produced a certain optimism but there was a great difference between the attitudes of German diplomats and German military leaders on how Rumania ought now to be handled. Falkenhayn, feeling the full flush of victory, wanted a much stronger approach in Bukarest and talked of economic sanctions if Rumania proved uncooperative. Jagow had a much better sense of proportion. They had won greater influence in Rumania of late, but, he declared, this was no time for threats or coercion. Force could be used only "when Rumania had no other choice than to accede unconditionally to our demands."[62]

It was the diplomats' caution which prevailed, for there was more at stake than things military. The Central Powers could not afford to alienate Bukarest by any rash act for the simple reason that they needed foodstuffs, primarily grain, and the Entente blockade made Rumania now the potential big source of supply. By winter of 1915, neither Germany nor Austria could meet its grain requirements. If the Central Powers had a need to buy, the Rumanians had a need to sell. Not only had the normal channels for export, the Dardanelles and the Danube, been closed as a result of the war. The Rumanian government had also followed a policy of prohibiting exports in order to conserve foodstuffs for an emergency. Tremendous surpluses caused dissatisfaction among Rumanian farmers and led to continual pressure for the elimination of the prohibitions. Both Germany and Austria understood the predicament which faced Bukarest on this issue. The only method

[61] Ibid., no. 987, Burian to Czernin, 15 December 1915.

[62] GFMA, ser. 1, reel 23, no. 1625, Bussche to Berlin, 7 December 1915; no. 516, Bussche to Bethmann-Hollweg, 30 December; no. 10115, Falkenhayn to Jagow, 15 December; no. AS 6124/15, Jagow to Falkenhayn, 20 December.

of exporting left open was by railroads which led to the Austro-Hungarian border. Berlin and Vienna saw the possibility of fulfilling their own grain requirements and achieving their diplomatic goals at the same time by forcing Rumania to its knees on a critical economic matter.[63]

The issue was taken up again and again by German and Austrian diplomats, especially from July, 1915, on. It was von dem Bussche who first saw the possibilities of tying the Rumanian harvest to political affairs. In July every attempt was being made to obtain Rumanian approval of munitions transport to Turkey. At this time Rumania had five million tons of grain on its hands from the harvests of 1914 and 1915. Therefore Bussche suggested an exchange of grain purchase for through transit of war materials to the Turks. Surplus or no surplus, however, Bukarest refused to be blackmailed and the idea was dropped. In the following month Berlin and Vienna explored the political benefits which would accrue through a purchase of the entire Rumanian grain stock available, for certainly this sort of economic interest would politically tie Rumania to the Central Powers. Burian had initially thought this tactic worth considering but he applied a brake after analyzing the internal political scene. The big stumbling block to concluding any large economic deal was the finance minister, Emil Costinescu, whose opposition was certain. There was not a more anti-German and anti-Austrian official in Bratianu's government. It was decided to let the project wait until it became clear whether a conservative ministry containing more friendly politicians would actually replace Bratianu's cabinet.[64]

In September, an import syndicate was formed which unified German, Austrian, and Hungarian grain-buying agencies into one unit. The purpose of this consortium was to apply systematic leverage and to monopolize the purchase of Rumanian cereals. Two things happened

[63] George D. Cioriceanu, *La Roumanie Économique et ses Rapports avec L'Étranger de 1860 à 1915,* p. 402. Gustav Gratz and Richard Schüller, *Der Wirtschaftliche Zusammenbruch Österreich-Ungarns,* pp. 42–46. Gratz and Schüller point to the fact that in 1915 Austria-Hungary was running a deficit of 20.6 million quintals of grain. GFMA, ser. 1, reel 23, no. AS 6167, Jagow to Falkenhayn, 20 December 1915. Jagow discusses Germany's grain shortage, particularly in oats. George Ionescu-Sisesti, *L'Agriculture de la Roumanie pendant la Guerre,* pp. 19, 21–24, 26–28.

[64] Staatsarchiv, PA, box 518, no. 699, Burian to Czernin, 22 July 1915; GFMA, ser. 1, reel 22, no. A 22810, copy of a report by Henry Newman, newspaper correspondent, on the grain issue, submitted to the German Foreign Office through Erzberger, 31 July; Staatsarchiv, PA, box 519, no. 4008, Burian to Hohenlohe in Berlin, 2 August; report no. 78 A-D/P, Czernin to Burian, 21 August. GFMA, ser. 1, reel 22, no. AS 27339, Erzberger to the Foreign Office, 18 September; this report gives a breakdown of the political leanings in the Rumanian government.

to block its effectiveness. First, the Rumanian government took the precaution of establishing an official Central Commission with which the consortium found negotiations difficult because of the commission's caution. Secondly, the British offered to purchase a large amount of the 1915 harvest on condition that the remainder would not be exported. Though the Rumanians did not accept the British proposal, England did buy sizable quantities of grain which it was content to have kept in Rumanian warehouses simply to foil the attempts being made by the Central Powers to obtain a monopoly. Nevertheless, the consortium patiently continued deliberations and, by offering high prices and a payment in gold, achieved a large contract, which was signed on December 22. The agreement called for the purchase of over 500,000 tons of cereals and legumes, 50,000 carloads.[65]

Another contract was to follow in March, 1916. Before Rumania made its decision to join the Entente, the Central Powers would obtain from it over 23,000,000 quintals of grain, that is, well over 2,000,000 tons. This was of considerable value, but the fact remained that the attempt to bind Rumania irrevocably to Germany and Austria through an all-engrossing economic commitment had failed by December, 1915. This failure buttressed the conviction current for some time that the Rumanians would not allow themselves to be coerced, no matter how this might be attempted. Thus it is not difficult to imagine Jagow's impatience when Falkenhayn naively suggested in December that economic force be applied.[66]

[65] Ionescu-Sisesti, *Agriculture de la Roumanie*, pp. 28–34, 38; Hans Loewenfeld-Russ, *Die Regelung der Volksernährung im Krieg*, pp. 386–87. Before unification the separate German, Austrian, and Hungarian grain purchasing agencies were known as the Zentraleinkaufsgesellschaft, Kriegs-Getreide-Verkehrs Anstalt, and Kriegs-Produktion Aktiengesellschaft, respectively.
[66] GFMA, ser. 1, reel 23, no. 10115, Falkenhayn to Jagow, 15 December 1915; nos. 6124 and 6167, Jagow to Falkenhayn, 20 December.

Chapter 10

The Rumanian
Link Unforged

As the new year of 1916 opened the Central Powers were enjoying
their best military position since the start of the war. This was particularly the case on the eastern front where they had forced the Russian
armies into a major retreat. The threat to the Dardanelles and to
Turkey had been stopped and Bulgaria felt the full flush of victory,
having aided in the prostration of Serbia. Yet, diplomatically speaking,
Berlin and Vienna had been frustrated in obtaining the Balkan coalition
as it had been conceived in August, 1914, for the third link, Rumania,
remained unforged.

In January, 1916, von dem Bussche was called home for high-level
conversations, during which he spoke with Falkenhayn. The general,
in a confident mood because of recent military events, now called for
an end to the pussyfooting policy being pursued with Bukarest. In his
view what was needed was an ultimatum demanding Rumanian participation. If Rumania refused to comply, it should be pointed out that the
country would quickly be brought to its knees with the aid of Bulgarian and Turkish military cooperation. Falkenhayn's idea was not accepted by the Wilhelmstrasse, but the orders given to Bussche were
very strong, to say the least. He was to tell King Ferdinand that the
Bratianu ministry was no longer acceptable and its continuance could
only mean an open break between Germany and Rumania. Berlin's
impatience had increased when it was learned that Bratianu had sent
troop units to the Hungarian frontier and that England had successfully purchased 80,000 carloads of Rumanian wheat on January 7.
Viewing these acts as hostile, the German Foreign Office told Bussche,
"We must clearly see whether we have [in Rumania] an enemy or a
friend." Shortly after returning to his post, Bussche had an audience
with the king during which he was anything but tactful. He accused
Bratianu of insincerity, called him a liar, and demanded that the king
reconstruct the cabinet so that it would contain ministers favorable to
the Central Powers. In the light of Bratianu's actions, all of which he
described as more or less unfriendly to Germany and Austria, Bussche

226

pointed out that relations between Berlin and Bukarest were reaching the "danger point." In the end, if things continued as they were, it would mean war.[1]

Ferdinand was not intimidated. He replied that he had thought of a cabinet change which would exclude Bratianu and replace him with the Conservative, Majorescu, who was pro-German. But it was plain that the Conservative Party was badly split into factions and that Majorescu could not carry a majority. Even if the king disregarded this, the desired result would not be achieved; the new cabinet would be seen as an instrument of the crown's and the reaction of the Rumanian public would place Ferdinand in an untenable situation.[2]

Burian, upon receiving word from Czernin of the harsh German tone, was quite upset. He wrote the Austrian minister that von dem Bussche's attitude was hardly proper, especially since threats were of no use unless one intended to carry them out. He could scarcely assume that Germany would choose such an extreme measure as war merely because the Rumanians refused to change their government. He could understand and, indeed, suggested, that appeals be made to the king in the form of "urgent protestations" against Bratianu's subterfuges, but threats were to be employed only when they could be distinctly advantageous. Czernin could not have agreed more. "I may err," he said, "but I believe that athletic poses in diplomatic wars can only have a purpose if the opposite side does not recognize them as such. I asked my German colleague what would happen if Bratianu, in spite of this demarche, remained in office and I received no answer."[3]

Increased Uncertainty

Czernin was now convinced, in light of the favorable military position enjoyed by the Central Powers, that Rumanian cooperation in the field was no longer needed nor, in terms of the future, desirable. What was required was *benevolent* neutrality, though it was clear that as long as the Bratianu ministry remained in power there would be no shift in that direction, either. While disapproving of Bussche's rather brawny approach, he concurred with his German colleague on the need for energetic representations to the king aimed at putting the

[1] Staatsarchiv, PA, box 520, no. 95, Czernin to Burian, 25 January 1916; report no. Z 6/P, Czernin to Burian, 28 January; GFMA, ser. 1, reel 24, no. A 2133, Jagow to the Prince of Hohenzollern, 24 January; no. 126, Bussche to Berlin, 26 January.

[2] GFMA, ser. 1, reel 24, no. 126, Bussche to Berlin, 26 January 1916; Staatsarchiv, PA, box 520, no. 95, Czernin to Burian, 25 January.

[3] Staatsarchiv, PA, box 520, report no. Z 6/P, Czernin to Burian, 28 January 1916.

Conservatives in the saddle. If the king could be induced to appoint Majorescu as minister-president, Czernin wired Burian, then "we would have attained all . . . that your Excellency wishes. Not cooperation—for Majorescu would also work against this—but the most benevolent, widest, most certain neutrality possible. Majorescu would personally guarantee all we wished." Czernin was totally opposed to an ultimatum requiring Rumanian participation because he feared it would have a boomerang effect and throw Rumania into Russian arms.[4]

In a controlled but frank manner, the Austrian minister now attempted to push Ferdinand into making a cabinet change. The king refused, as he had in his conversations with Bussche, but he did take some pains to explain that he was well aware of Bratianu's chicanery and that in the future the minister-president's attitude would change. The change was hardly profound, since Bratianu merely tacked before the storm by offering repeated assurances, once again, of continued neutrality. The main goal of Berlin and Vienna, that of obtaining a drastic change in the make-up of the Rumanian government, fell short of success. As Bussche put it in a telegram to Jagow on February 14, "Talk has achieved nothing."[5]

Bussche's evaluation was not entirely correct, because Ferdinand had been sufficiently affected and impressed to write directly to Bethmann-Hollweg, assuring him that as crowned head he wished to maintain Rumania's neutral stance. He took some pains to point to his particular dilemma in the hope that Germany would understand his difficult position. He emphasized that while he was a monarch he could not buck the current of both chambers in the Rumanian Parliament and public opinion in general. In light of that mood he had to think of his own fate and the fate of his dynasty as well. The telegram reflected what both Central Powers had known for some time—that although Ferdinand essentially favored them and was annoyed at his own prime minister, he lacked the necessary strength, energy, and daring to prod his country in their direction.[6]

There was only one thing which Germany and Austria could count on at this time and it was expressed by the German military attaché in Bukarest in four words: "The Rumanians are afraid." They were afraid because of the condition of the military map and the apparent weak-

[4] Ibid., report no. Z 6/P A-L, Czernin to Burian, 28 January 1916.
[5] Ibid., no. 118, Czernin to Burian, 31 January 1916; GFMA, ser. 1, reel 24, no. AS 571, Bussche to Jagow, 14 February.
[6] Staatsarchiv, PA, box 520, report no. Z 15/P A-E, Czernin to Burian, 3 March 1916; GFMA, ser. 1, reel 24, no. A 5283, Erzberger to Berlin, 26 February. Erzberger had made a special trip to see the king 18-20 February, and reported his impressions.

ness of the Entente. Should they now decide to join that Entente, Rumanian troops would face Turks and Bulgarians to the south, and Hungarians and Germans to the north and west. The English and French forces which had landed at Salonika were too weak to come to their aid effectively, while the Russians would probably be defeated in Bessarabia in any attempt to help. Such a situation meant that no Rumanian politician would risk a war against the Central Powers.[7]

That the Rumanian government appreciated the delicacy of its own position was soon borne out. German intelligence reported that Bratianu not only continued to increase troop dispositions along the Hungarian border but also strengthened the number of units facing Bulgaria. In early March, Falkenhayn pointed to these activities and to the disturbing fact that the number of Rumanian soldiers left to guard against a Russian incursion from the north was almost non-existent. Any lasting neutrality seemed unlikely, so he asked Jagow to discover whether Bukarest intended to send troops to the Russian border. The secretary wasted no time in requesting Bussche to interrogate the king on just how he could square neutrality with such pointed and one-sided military shipments. The Bulgarians, even more exercised than Berlin, stated that if the Rumanians continued to strengthen their armies on the Bulgarian border, war between the two states would be possible "from one moment to the next."[8]

Apparently Jagow believed that war with Rumania was now probable. This was not the view of the Ballhausplatz nor even of Bussche, though the German minister spoke very seriously with Ferdinand about the issue and told him the Rumanian shipment of troops could not be taken lightly. It was very possible, he explained, that because of the current excitement in Bulgaria "the guns could go off by themselves." Ferdinand eased the situation when he replied that he would order Bratianu to send on furlough one-third of the men massed against Bulgaria. Tensions were further reduced when, on March 21, the Rumanian grain commission signed a contract with the German, Austrian, and Hungarian Central Purchasing Company, guaranteeing to the Central Powers shipment of 140,000 carloads of assorted cereals.[9]

Burian proved much less concerned about troop concentrations than

[7] GFMA, ser. 1, reel 24, no. 320, Bronsart von Schellendorff, military attaché in Bukarest, to the German War Ministry, 28 January 1916.

[8] GFMA, ser. 1, reel 24, no. 128, Falkenhayn at Pless to von Jagow through Treutler, 3 March 1916; Staatsarchiv, PA, box 520, no. 83, Hohenlohe in Berlin to Burian, 4 March.

[9] GFMA, ser. 1, reel 24, no. 351, Bussche to Berlin, 9 March 1916; no. 333, Bronsart through Bussche to Berlin, 6 March; unsigned supplemental report to no. AS 1213, 2 April.

the Wilhelmstrasse. As it turned out, his evaluation of the Rumanian actions was accurate. He prognosticated that the Rumanian army would not make any move now. The danger would come in the spring when Russia would begin an offensive that many believed might be the decisive turning point of the war. The Rumanian assemblage of troops on the Hungarian and Bulgarian borders was aimed, he thought, only at a demonstration to draw off Bulgarian units and make them unavailable against the other Entente fronts, particularly in the Balkans. In spite of these opinions the Austrian foreign minister did not let the issue pass but told Czernin to raise the question of the lack of Rumanian soldiers on the Russian frontiers and, in a vigorous way, "to demand" that Rumania defend its neutrality against any Russian invasion. When Czernin saw the king, Ferdinand's reaction was to maintain staunchly that neither he nor Bratianu would allow a Russian march-through and that Russia had already been notified its forces would be fired upon if they ignored Rumanian neutrality. Again and again Ferdinand repeated, "Your concern is unfounded." Speaking with Emanuel Porumbaru, who officially though not in fact was the Rumanian foreign minister, Czernin told him precisely that a Russian march-through was something for which the Central Powers would hold Bukarest strictly accountable. All reactions considered, Czernin came away from the excitement convinced that a Russian armed passage through Rumania would not be permitted "at the moment."[10]

Berlin had reacted very strongly to Rumanian troop dispersements and Vienna had been at least disturbed, but both allies now used their knowledge of Rumanian uncertainties to excellent advantage. While Austro-Hungarian units were sent to bolster positions along the Rumanian border, the Bulgarians, who were itching for a conflict, moved an additional division into position against what they hoped would soon be their open enemy. Radoslavov sent a sharp note to Bratianu protesting recent border incidents. Bratianu now became very excited and agitated. It was well known that he cooperated with the Entente as closely as he could, that Russia was helping Rumania to prepare for war by shipping it horses, coal and other supplies, but the minister-president was hardly ready for a break with the Central Powers. He asked Germany and Austria to intercede with Sofia and force the Bulgarian government to end its menacing stand. Czernin was delighted with Bratianu's nervousness, for, as he wrote the Ballhausplatz, it was just such fear of a Bulgarian strike that would keep Rumania neutral. He was himself somewhat concerned about Bulgarian bellicos-

[10] Staatsarchiv, PA, box 520, no. 71, Burian to Hohenlohe, 6 March 1916; no. 151, Burian to Czernin, 7 March; no. 252, Czernin to Burian, 10 March.

ity, particularly if Radoslavov intended to attempt to reconquer the Dobrudja, a move which Czernin believed would be the most unfortunate one possible. But if Sofia sought only to arouse panic in the Rumanians, he was all for it, because Rumania would be constrained to send troops to the Russian border and so demonstrate its wish for continued neutrality. In such an event, the policy of keeping Rumania a nonbelligerent would have succeeded. What Czernin called the "ministerial fear thermometer" was on the rise, and heat from Bulgaria could be used to keep it high. In an interview with Bratianu he suavely advised him that he had nothing to worry about so long as Rumania established a correct neutral posture, and this would depend on the policy of the Rumanian government.[11]

Von dem Bussche did not react in the same way. When the Rumanian government requested him to ask that Berlin use its influence to reduce Bulgaria's obvious animosity, he readily complied, causing Czernin to bemoan the fact that his German colleague had failed to properly exploit the diplomatic possibilities. What really nettled him was Bussche's lack of consistency in his approach to their common adversary. In a special report to the home office in March, Czernin showed his impatience and fervent dislike when he reported that after Christmas Bussche had returned to Bukarest with instructions to use sharp or even threatening words, but since then his severity had "melted like butter in the sun." Although Bussche might return to his post "all pumped up again," his firmness always proved to be transitory. "Contact with this gentleman," Czernin concluded, "and the unfortunate unconditional necessity of friendly feeling are the much less enjoyable sides of my activities."[12]

Burian, however, was much more in accord with Bussche's immediate reaction, because he himself was much disturbed by the possibilities of Bulgarian military attacks against the Rumanians. He let Czernin know that as soon as definite signs of warlike action appeared, Vienna would do all it could to urge officially that Sofia remain quiet. He pointed out that unfortunately Bulgaria could not be counted upon to do precisely what would best serve German and Austrian interests, though at present he had no reason to believe Sofia was planning any rash step. In the end Radoslavov did just what his allies wanted him to

[11] GFMA, ser. 1, reel 24, no. A 5283, report by Erzberger on his trip to Bukarest, 18–20 February 1916; no. 358, von Bussche to Berlin, 11 March; no. 935, Bronsart in Bukarest to Berlin, 19 March; Staatsarchiv, PA, box 520, no. 262, Czernin to Burian, 13 March; no. 267, Czernin to Burian, 14 March; no. 276, Czernin to Burian, 17 March; report no. 19/P, Czernin to Burian, 20 March; no. 252, Czernin to Burian, 10 March.
[12] Staatsarchiv, PA, box 520, no. 262, Czernin to Burian, 13 March 1916.

do—controlled the hotheads, mostly military men, who wanted immediate war with the Rumanians, while he continued to maintain sufficient pressure through additional troop dispositions to keep Bratianu
worried and still neutral.[13]

Impact of the Brussilov Offensive

The catalytic agent that finally proved responsible for the long-
feared Rumanian decision to join the Entente was the Russian offensive
led by General Alexei Brussilov. The attack, originally planned only as
a diversionary movement on the southeastern front, started on June 4
and raged on until the following September. In the course of this
offensive, which was stopped only after some fifteen German divisions
had been sent from the west, the Russians reoccupied areas ranging in
depth from 25 to 125 kilometers. The first impact of Brussilov's forces
proved too much for the Austrian armies against whom the campaign
was launched, and the resulting negative impression in Bukarest of the
Central Powers' endurance had much to do with Bratianu's decision to
forsake neutrality.[14]

From the start of the Brussilov advance, it took another ninety days
for Bratianu to make his final commitment to the Entente and to
convince the king that the move was a wise one. On the assumption
that the Brussilov attack would not succeed, both Germany and Austria decided to deal further with Bratianu's conservative opposition,
which they hoped might bring sufficient pressure to bear upon the king
to change the government.

Indeed, it was Marghiloman, still pro-German-Austrian, and still one
of the Conservative leaders, who seized the initiative. He was ready to
go to the king, whom he believed he could influence to join the Central
Powers, but he had to have definite offers of concessions in his hand.
Toward the middle of June he bluntly asked Czernin the following:
Could the Austrian minister guarantee that Hungarian Rumanians who
had fled to Rumania would be given amnesty? Could the Hungarian
Rumanians still count on concessions from Tisza? Would Austria-
Hungary be willing to better Danubian transit conditions, for example,
improve the passage at the Iron Gates? Could Rumania count on
obtaining territories in the Bukovina? To the first three questions,
Czernin answered yes. To the question on concessions in the Bukovina

---

[13] Ibid., no. 176, Burian to Czernin, 18 March 1916; no. 253, Tarnowski to
Burian, 21 March; no. 303, Czernin to Burian, 24 March; no. 179, Pallavicini to
Burian, 27 March; GFMA, ser. 1, reel 24, no. 442, Bussche to Berlin, 26 March.

[14] For a fuller discussion of the Brussilov campaign see chapter 13 below.

he replied he would have to confer with Burian. On June 24 the Conservative leader was told that Vienna had decided concessions in the Bukovina were impossible. Even now the Austrians remained implacable when it came to surrendering territories. Berlin was not surprised at the Austrian response, for when Marghiloman made his first indirect sounding to Tschirschky through a friend in Vienna, von Jagow's reaction was that the Rumanians would have to satisfy themselves with concessions in Bessarabia. There was no reason for him to think that the Ballhausplatz would now change what had been its consistent attitude since August, 1914. Even Bussche refused to broach the subject with Czernin, who had become extremely touchy when it came to territorial bribes.[15] Once again the Austro-German attempt at political maneuver had failed.

Once Brussilov began his forward movement, Czernin had no doubts as to the seriousness of the situation. As he so aptly put it, "Diplomatic work can postpone and retard dangerous Rumanian steps. In the last analysis it cannot prevent them. The facts provided by cannon are much stronger than diplomatic strategems. To the cannon belongs the last word and they will decide." In his opinion, continued successes by the Russian armies would sorely strain Bratianu's neutrality, but while the minister-president expected Russian victory he would still continue to wait for something decisive. Burian instructed Czernin to show no preoccupation with recent Austrian military reversals, though he secretly admitted that until they could stop the Russian advance in the Bukovina, there could be no way of counteracting Rumanian public opinion, which had been heavily affected by the successes of Brussilov and by the agitations of what was now an excited, vocal, and revivified nationalist element.[16]

Czernin and Bussche remained calm in this crucial moment. Both agreed that while Bratianu was clearly expecting their defeat he would not yet move, and both pointed with almost uncanny accuracy to the time when Bratianu would throw in his lot with the enemy—the second half of August. Their calculations were based on the fact that Rumania could not get its munitions orders filled by the Entente for another six to eight weeks, that the military successes needed to push Bratianu over the brink could not be achieved overnight, and that the government would not order general mobilization until after the sum-

---

[15] GFMA, ser. 1, reel 25, no. AS 1860, Tschirschky to Bethmann-Hollweg, 1 June 1916; no. 224, Jagow to Tschirschky, 4 June; no. 261, Bussche to Berlin, 14 June; no. 283, Bussche to Berlin, 24 June.

[16] Staatsarchiv, PA, box 520, report no. 35/P, Czernin to Burian, 19 June 1916; no. 331, Burian to Czernin, 21 June.

mer harvests had been completed. If the German and Austrian forces could bring the Russian surge to a real halt, the situation would change, though as Bussche pointed out at the end of June, "In spite of all our assurances, this has heretofore not been the case."[17]

On July 1 Bratianu dropped his guard. In a conversation with the Austrian minister, in which the latter expressed his wonderment over the change in Rumania's attitude, a change that was bringing the country closer to war with the Central Powers, Bratianu declared that things were different now. "The war," he said, "is coming to an end," and as proof he pointed to the exhaustion of Germany and Austria and the strength of the Entente, particularly that of the Russians. There was no doubt that Bratianu was making political and military preparations for combat. Czernin concluded that if the Central Powers could not stop the Russians "we must count on war with Rumania."[18]

By July, neither Berlin nor Vienna had given up all hope of restraining Rumania from entering the war, but the hope was very slight. The question now was not whether Rumania would decide to participate but when that decision would be made. Czernin observed that almost the whole Rumanian army was now in agreement on taking action, that approximately a third of the Rumanian Liberal Party supported Filipescu's desire for war, and that Bratianu had assured various nationalists there was no doubt of Rumania's entering the fight. Neither minister knew that on July 4 Bratianu had gone so far as to inform the Russians that his country was ready to intervene as soon as a formal treaty had been signed. However, it was very clear by the middle of the month that the Rumanian minister was engaged in most intimate negotiations with the Entente representatives. When Bratianu was challenged on this he replied blandly that while he wanted to remain neutral he had to enter into talks with the Entente, since if the Russians came over the Carpathians the Rumanian position would be difficult.[19]

There was little expectation of reversing the Rumanian trend because although the Brussilov offensive had by now lost its momentum, the Russians had not been forced into a major retreat. In an attempt to delay Rumania further from making any irrevocable decision, von dem Bussche warned Ferdinand that Rumania was not Italy and that, unlike the Italian instance, if Rumania declared war on Austria-Hungary, German troops would take immediate action. The remark seemed to

[17] Ibid., report no. 38/P, Czernin to Burian, 28 June 1916; GFMA, ser. 1, reel 25, no. 837, Bussche to Berlin, 30 June.
[18] Staatsarchiv, PA, box 520, no. 39/P A-B, Czernin to Burian, 1 July 1916.
[19] Ibid., no. 533, Czernin to Burian, 8 July 1916; GFMA, ser. 1, reel 25, no. 316, Bussche to Bethmann-Hollweg, 9 July; no. 11, Bussche to Berlin, 12 July.

have no profound effect on the king but it did produce a significant reaction in Vienna. Burian telegraphed to Hohenlohe in Berlin, saying that Germany had made the same sort of declaration to the Italian government a year ago and yet when Italy declared war against the Monarchy, Germany had made no move to support its ally. While German inaction in this case could be rationalized on the basis of the alliance with Italy not being identical with both Central Powers, this was not the case with the Rumanian alliance, which in each instance was quite the same. Burian instructed Hohenlohe to get a definite commitment from the German government that it would for a certainty immediately declare war on Rumania if Bukarest declared war against the Monarchy. When Hohenlohe broached the matter with Jagow, the German foreign secretary offered the strongest assurances that if it came to a conflict with Rumania, Germany would take immediate steps. Jagow was somewhat irritated by Hohenlohe's distrust and rather petulantly added that if oral assurances were not enough to ease Burian's fears, a formal declaration could be given to the Monarchy, though this would, of course, first have to be authorized by the Kaiser. The Austrians remained unconvinced and Hohenlohe took the question directly to Bethmann-Hollweg. Not until July 25 did Burian relax on the matter. The German chancellor was sufficiently worried over Austrian mistrust specifically to authorize Tschirschky in Vienna to assure Burian that Germany would immediately declarate war if Rumania went against Austria. This was further bolstered by German press releases announcing that German and Bulgarian troops would be distributed along Rumanian borders. Bussche was told to inform both Bratianu and King Ferdinand that a Rumanian mobilization would be seen as a direct provocation against which Germany would take counter measures.[20]

While Berlin and Vienna were busy getting commitments for unanimity between themselves, their diplomats were trying to gauge Bratianu and the extent to which he had or had not already committed Rumania to the Entente powers. Bussche sounded Ferdinand on July 21, stating that he had definite reports proving that Bratianu was negotiating with the Entente for a formal accord and that the minister had already gone very far on the matter. While the king agreed that his

[20] GFMA, ser. 1, reel 25, no. 303, Bussche to Berlin, 2 July 1916; Staatsarchiv, PA, box 520, no. 524, Czernin to Burian, 2 July; no. 3346, Burian to Hohenlohe, 11 July; report no. 81 A-E/P, Hohenlohe to Burian, 14 July; no. 203, Hohenlohe to Burian, 17 July; GFMA, ser. 1, reel 25, no. 23, Jagow to Bussche, 19 July; no. 34, Bethmann-Hollweg to Tschirschky, 22 July; Staatsarchiv, PA, box 520, no. 184, Burian to Hohenlohe, 23 July; no. 590, Czernin to Burian, 24 July; no. 14, Czernin to Burian, 25 July.

government was being fervently urged by the Entente to conclude an arrangement, he insisted that nothing had actually been signed. On July 23 Ferdinand reiterated this. Bussche came away from his interviews with the impression that the king did not want to go to war and that Bratianu would only obtain his approval for such a step with difficulty. The German minister wrote the Wilhelmstrasse that he would continue to influence the king "with all means" since when it came to talking with the prime minister "in light of his cunning it is difficult to know what he intends."[21]

The strategy of influencing the king to check his own prime minister had previously worked to a very limited degree, but it was the only one left and the Central Powers knew it. Bratianu was now taking a much bolder stand and was no longer affected by Bussche's strong protests. When the latter confronted him with reports that a Rumanian mobilization was imminent, Bratianu retorted that these were false, that Germany could do as it wished but in any event he, Bratianu, was "master in his own house." When Czernin suggested that renewed troop movements were reflecting a very serious situation, he was fobbed off with the implausible statement that these were only "little garrison exercises."[22]

Czernin as much as Bussche attempted further direct negotiations with Ferdinand, since the Ballhausplatz believed that these might still succeed. On July 18 Burian had written his minister a very secret and private letter in which he said that there was no way of judging whether Bratianu's tactics were aimed at a further drawing out of things or at reaching an immediate agreement with the enemy. It seemed to Burian quite purposeless to reproach Bratianu from a moral standpoint but he believed it would be different with the monarch. Since Ferdinand had little self-assurance in political matters, some worthwhile effect might be gained by making him aware of the moral repercussions involved in Rumania's breaking its word. The alliance between Rumania and Austria and Germany was still in effect, and according to the first article of that agreement the signatory powers would enter into no alliance which would be directed against one of them. Czernin was in despair when on the twentieth he wrote his chief: "What can be done in this country is done, as far as my strength permits, to paralyze Herr Bratianu. I do not know of any other means." But he dutifully plowed on and a week later Ferdinand told

[21] GFMA, ser. 1, reel 25, no. 22, Bussche to Berlin, 21 July 1916; no. 29, Bussche to Berlin, 23 July; no. 342, Bussche to Berlin, 19 July.
[22] Ibid., no. 843, Bussche to Berlin, 26 July 1916; Staatsarchiv, PA, box 520, no. 574, Czernin to Burian, 20 July.

him he did not believe Bratianu had widely committed himself, and if this had happened then such a commitment would not bind the crown. From a constitutional point of view, Czernin knew this was accurate enough, but not even a strong monarch such as King Carol had been able to resist the wishes of those holding the political majority.[23]

What worried the Austrian minister was the possibility that Bratianu might present the king with a fait accompli. Not only did the prime minister hold the high political cards in Rumania, but if he obtained a written promise for extensive territorial concessions from the Entente, Ferdinand would not and could not stand against him. His concern on the matter was well founded because both Central Powers had learned with surprising precision what territorial concessions the enemy were now offering Bukarest. Burian listed them for Hohenlohe on July 28 as Transylvania, the Banat to the Theiss River, the Bukovina to the Pruth, and Czernowitz. In addition to territory, Bratianu was holding out for a series of military stipulations, though as far as Czernin could tell he had not yet obtained all he wanted. Until Bratianu achieved his major military demands he would not confront the king.[24]

In truth no fait accompli would be necessary at all, since Ferdinand, while he might not like Bratianu's tactics, was by this time in tow. Czernin himself defined the king as a mere tool in his minister's hands. This being the case, Czernin and Vienna agreed that the Central Powers must continue to treat Bratianu in a friendly manner, leave the door open for a rapprochement, and thus avoid driving the prime minister into an irrevocable arrangement with the Entente. So it was that at the end of the month Czernin saw his adversary for a long conversation. In answer to the frank charges that Bratianu was preparing for war, seriously and intimately negotiating with the enemy, and planning for an imminent mobilization, the Rumanian minister countered with a series of remarks which Czernin in his report to the Ballhausplatz labelled as out-and-out lies. If, said Bratianu, he gave the Entente hope that Rumania would enter now on its side, he did this only for internal reasons. Public opinion was very excited and his approach was a gambit aimed at cooling off the hotheads. His policy

---

[23] Staatsarchiv, PA, box 520, no. 3477, Burian to Czernin, 18 July 1916; nos. 574 and 591, Czernin to Burian, 20 and 27 July.

[24] Ibid., no. 591, Czernin to Burian, 27 July 1916; unnumbered private letter, Burian to Hohenlohe, 28 July; GFMA, ser. 1, reel 25, no. 263, unsigned memo containing Burian's information on the secret Rumanian-Russian negotiations, 29 July. That Burian was essentially correct in his listing of Entente territorial concessions is demonstrated by the clauses of the final treaty submitted to Bukarest by the Russians. See C. Jay Smith, Jr., *The Russian Struggle for Power, 1914–1917*, pp. 413–14.

was that of delaying the Rumanian commitment as long as possible so as to give the Central Powers the chance to redress the military situation against the Russians and by so doing to "cool Rumanian war lust." He was not now thinking of war largely because he did not wish to worsen the position of the Monarchy and Germany. Bratianu ended the interview by waxing sentimental on his and Czernin's long and friendly relationship. In his analysis of the talks, Czernin wrote to Burian that as far as he was concerned they only reflected Bratianu's convictions that "our collapse is imminent. He wishes now to fall upon us." The two things which gave Bratianu pause in making such a decision were Germany's declaration that it would stand squarely behind the Monarchy, and the recent Bulgarian troop movements to the Rumanian border. Because of these events Bratianu would still hold off. Any estimation of the future decisions of Bukarest, the minister suggested, rested on the question: "Is Rumania still afraid or no longer afraid? Upon this hangs the whole political problem, and the king will no longer help us if Bratianu is not afraid anymore." Borrowing Cato's response to the Carthaginian threat, Czernin ended his remarks with what seemed to him the only effective solution to the whole frustrating business: "Sed ego autem censeo Bratianum esse delendum."[25]

Rumania Chooses

The month of August opened with no reduction of tension in sight. Both German and Austrian military intelligence reported a stepping up of Rumanian war preparations. By August 3 Rumanian reserve units were being called to the colors. While actual mobilization had not been called for, men aged twenty to forty-six had been ordered to report to the police stations for pre-mustering procedures. Troop dispositions involving five army corps were under way and the greatest activity was in the west where units facing Transylvania and the Bulgarian border were put on near or full war standing. Materials for army use were being requisitioned throughout the country, schools turned into hospitals, defensive gun emplacements set up in major cities. By August 11 there were thirty carloads of ammunition arriving each day from Russia and facilities had been expanded in Jassy to receive the larger Russian freight cars.[26]

[25] Staatsarchiv, PA, box 520, report no. 48/P, Czernin to Burian, 29 July 1916; see also no. 15, Czernin to Burian, 26 July.

[26] Ibid., no. 1050, resume of military reports, June–August 1916, Intelligence Bureau of Austrian General Staff, 8 August; GFMA, ser. 1, reel 25, no. 2499, Col. von Hammerstein-Gesmold, German military attaché in Bukarest to the War

When Czernin confronted Bratianu with his knowledge of these military preparations, the latter continually denied that Rumania had any aggressive intentions. What seemed to be troop movements to the borders were only those men returning to their units who had been sent on furlough to help with the harvests. There was nothing to worry about. There was not the slightest reason, he said, to assume that Rumania would now give up its neutrality. On August 8 the two statesmen had it out in a bitter exchange. Czernin began by saying that if Bratianu wanted war he "could and would have it" and he was not to think that Czernin was so obtuse as to be blind to Rumanian preparations. But if war came, Rumania would find the borders very well defended. Bratianu insisted that all the preparations were purely for internal reasons and because Rumania was worried about a Bulgarian attack. He believed it was very possible that Vienna and Sofia wanted to do away with Rumania. Czernin retorted that the whole idea was laughable and if proof of this was desired, all the Rumanians had to do was to demobilize their troops and declare a definitive neutral status. In this case Austro-Hungarian and Bulgarian units would be pulled back from the Rumanian border areas. Bratianu countered by charging that the Central Powers had hundreds of spies watching Rumania's moves while he himself had no way of controlling Austrian or Bulgarian troop movements. Insofar as demobilization of Rumanian units was concerned, this was totally impossible. Czernin would just have to trust him and believe that he was doing everything he could to maintain a neutral position.[27]

Even now, just one week from signing a formal arrangement with the Entente, Bratianu put out feelers for territorial concessions from the Monarchy. Burian had offered him a part of the Bukovina in early 1915. If Austria repeated the offer it would do much to help him maintain Rumania's neutral status. Of course, in the final analysis that status would depend on Russia's being defeated. To the feeler concerning the Bukovina, Czernin replied that he was worried about Bratianu's mental state. And on this note the conversation ended.[28]

Bratianu maintained the same bold front with Bussche, to whom he offered strong assurances of continued neutrality. How, asked Bussche, could this be squared with the Rumanian troop assemblages and dispo-

Ministry in Berlin, 3 August; unnumbered report, resume of von Hammerstein's 4 August communiqué, 5 August; no. 165, von Hammerstein to von Luckwald, legation secretary at army headquarters, 11 August.
[27] Staatsarchiv, PA, box 520, no. 19, Czernin to Burian, 1 August 1916; no. 22, Czernin to Burian, 2 August; unnumbered telegram, Czernin to Burian, 8 August.
[28] Ibid., unnumbered telegram, Czernin to Burian, 8 August 1916.

sitions? What about the Rumanian Third and Fourth Corps being moved toward Transylvania east of Ploesti? The answer was simple— these were merely troops returning to their original units from furlough. Bussche's comment to the Wilhelmstrasse was that Bratianu "openly lied."[29]

The only area where Bratianu admitted that Rumanian troop concentrations had been increased was on the Bulgarian border. It was from the Bulgarian quarter, he asserted, that Rumania feared an attack. Bussche's assurances that Rumania had nothing to fear from the Bulgarians as long as the Austrians were not attacked made no impression. Bratianu would not be calmed and said that, as in the case of the Balkan Wars, the Bulgarian military could go against the wishes of the Bulgarian government. When Bussche declared that he knew exactly what he was saying when he told him that "Rumania has nothing to fear if it remains quiet," Bratianu remarked that he did not wish to undertake anything against the Central Powers. He knew that Berlin distrusted him but people there were being quite unjust and Bussche would discover that he, Bratianu, was right.[30]

Bratianu maintained his deception until the delivery of the Rumanian declaration of war on August 27. On August 18, a day after he signed an alliance with the Entente, to which was attached a military convention binding Rumania to begin its participation on August 28, he told Bussche that Vienna was mistaken in counting on a Rumanian attack. The two Austrian corps sent to the Rumanian border could be used better elsewhere. And when Bussche stated that Rumanian preparations had now gone well beyond the defensive, Bratianu vehemently denied this. On August 26, one day before the Rumanian declaration of war was delivered at the Ballhausplatz, Bratianu told Czernin unblinkingly that he "wished to, could, and would remain neutral."[31]

Aside from having their representatives do everything to influence Bratianu in a positive way, the Germans and Austrians explored the desirability of using various other methods to dissuade the Rumanians from taking the leap. The difficulty in reaching a decision as to the most effective approach lay in the terrible uncertainty of the situation. Neither Bussche nor Czernin was sure whether the Rumanians had

[29] GFMA, ser. 1, reel 25, no. 871, Bussche to Berlin, 5 August 1916.
[30] Ibid., reel 26, no. 881, Bussche to Berlin, 12 August 1916.
[31] Staatsarchiv, PA, box 520, no. 637, Czernin to Burian, 18 August 1916; no. 40, Czernin to Burian, 26 August; for the final negotiations of Rumania with the Entente see Smith, *Russian Struggle for Power*, pp. 412–17, and Alfred J. Rieber, "Russian Diplomacy and Rumania," in *Russian Diplomacy and Eastern Europe, 1914–1917*, ed. Alexander Dallin, pp. 269–75.

formally committed themselves to the side of their enemies. No one could tell for certain whether the king was fully aware of the degree to which Bratianu consorted with the Entente.[32] The possibilities of an ultimatum were considered and then dropped, as was the suggestion of a threatened Bulgarian invasion of Rumania. Czernin believed either of these two blunt approaches would be "the worst thing which we can do at the moment," and his view was that of Bussche, Burian, and Jagow as well. Neither Falkenhayn nor Conrad was eager to commit troops against Rumania, so that both chiefs proved to be as cautious as the diplomatic leaders. Conrad suggested a collective demarche on the part of Germany, Austria, Bulgaria, and Turkey, declaring that while all were far from having any desire to attack Rumania, each would see any Rumanian action against one as an action against all. This suggestion was rejected by Burian as being rather purposeless, and by Jagow, who reminded Vienna that Germany had already made strong representations along this line to the Bukarest government.[33]

On August 7 Burian wrote to Hohenlohe that it was entirely possible Russia might march through Rumania with strong forces. If this occurred and if the Central Powers took it passively, the Rumanian government would probably limit itself to a "Platonic protest." Armed opposition to such a Russian move would occur only if Rumania was informed that a Russian invasion would be matched by one mounted by the Central Powers, a counter-move which would turn Rumania into a battleground. Burian was ready to have Czernin say this to Bratianu, but he wanted Germany to cooperate and instruct Bussche to do the same. And Burian was ready to make a similar request in Sofia and Constantinople. Von Jagow agreed with the suggestion but while Bussche would be instructed to make an analogous remark, he believed that no general, official demarche ought to be made since Bratianu could easily take it as a threat and this was most certainly undesirable now. Burian was quick to inform his colleague that he had no official or formal demarche in mind, but only wanted the respective ministers to inform Bratianu, in an oral and friendly way, of the Central Powers'

---

[32] Staatsarchiv, PA, box 520, no. 32, Czernin to Burian, 9 August 1916; no. 235, Hohenlohe to Burian, 10 August; no. 624, Czernin to Burian, 12 August; report no. 52 E/P, Czernin to Burian, 16 August; no. 638, Czernin to Burian, 19 August; GFMA, ser. 1, reel 25, no. 853, Bussche to Berlin, 27 July; no. 859, Bussche to Berlin, 28 July; no. 872, Bussche to Berlin, 8 August.

[33] GFMA, ser. 1, reel 26, no. 204, Jagow to Falkenhayn, 10 August 1916; no. 316, Jagow to Michahelles, 10 August; no. 318, Falkenhayn to Jagow, 10 August; no. 52, Bussche to Berlin, 10 August; Staatsarchiv, PA, box 520, no. 615, Czernin to Burian, 10 August; no. 58, Conrad to Burian, 7 August; no. 3907, Burian to Conrad, 10 August; no. 233, Hohenlohe to Burian, 8 August.

intentions. The gambit was tried but only received Bratianu's assurance that he would do all he could to avoid a fight on Rumanian soil.[34] Conrad von Hötzendorf's nerves proved unable to take the mounting strain. On August 12 he wrote to the Ballhausplatz that the Rumanians were certain to attack the Monarchy. It was only a question of days before the offensive would come and since to simply wait for that move was unwise, he suggested that the Monarchy along with its allies fall upon Rumania without bothering about formalities, to assure themselves of a victory through surprise. Vienna answered that only after they were quite certain the Rumanians had joined the Entente could the question of opening a surprise attack on Rumania be aired and this, clearly, would be dependent on existing military strength. Berlin was toying with the idea of open hostilities, too, but in a somewhat calmer way. Writing to Falkenhayn, von Jagow asked whether it would be more desirable to hold off the eventual conflict as best they could and to let the break come from the Rumanian side, or to go ahead with a preventive conflict. Falkenhayn replied that delaying the fight rather than forcing the situation was the lesser of two evils.[35]

The result was that both German and Austrian policy ended by being hamstrung through caution. Even the project of having the Kaiser send a personal letter to King Ferdinand to ascertain more thoroughly where the crown stood was watered down and finally sent off as an essentially innocuous birthday greeting on August 23.[36]

Attempts to affect Rumania's decision by working through leading Rumanian political figures also came to nothing. King Ferdinand successfully held at bay men such as Majorescu and Carp by telling them he would take no action without consulting the Conservative opposition. The crowned head played his role beautifully. When on August 23 Bussche told him it was well known that Bratianu had proceeded very far with the Entente, Ferdinand only asserted that he did not know how far his prime minister had gone. Besides, as king he was not bound; then too he was about to call a Crown Council which was also not bound and would do what it thought right. Once the news was out

---

[34] Staatsarchiv, PA, box 520, no. 197, Burian to Hohenlohe, 7 August 1916; no. 233, Hohenlohe to Burian, 8 August; no. 200, Burian to Hohenlohe, 9 August; GFMA, ser. 1, reel 25, no. 875, Bussche to Berlin, 9 August.

[35] Staatsarchiv, PA, box 520, no. 69, Conrad to Burian, 12 August 1916; no. 365, Burian to Conrad through Friedrich von Wiesner at headquarters, 13 August; GFMA, ser. 1, reel 26, no. 955, von Jagow to Falkenhayn through Kurt von Grünau, chancellor's representative, 20 August; no. 564, Falkenhayn to Jagow through Grünau, 20 August.

[36] Staatsarchiv, PA, box 520, no. 235, Hohenlohe to Burian, 10 August 1916; GFMA, ser. 1, reel 26, no. 569, Bethmann-Hollweg to Jagow, 21 August; no. 66, Bussche to Berlin, 21 August; no. 578, Grünau to Berlin, 23 August.

Theobald von Bethmann-Hollweg and Gottlieb von Jagow in Rome, 1910

Leopold von Berchtold

Stephan von Burian

Stephan Tisza

Franz Conrad von Hötzendorf

Erich von Falkenhayn

Paul von Hindenburg

August von Mackensen

Enver Pasha

Talaat Bey

Djemal Pasha

Hans von Wangenheim

Johann von Pallavicini

King Ferdinand of Bulgaria

Vasil Radoslavov

Adam Tarnowski

Gustav Michahelles

King Ferdinand of Rumania   Ion Bratianu

Hilmar von der Bussche

Ottokar von Czernin

Heinrich von Tschirschky

Gottfried von Hohenlohe, as a younger man

that a Crown Council was to be held, Czernin talked with Majorescu in the hope of spurring Rumanian Conservative leaders to undermine the plan for the council's meeting. Majorescu agreed that such a meeting would be a dangerous matter because of the make-up of the body. Those who would be invited to attend the session fell into three groups: all of the present ministers of the government, Filipescu and Take Ionescu, and Carp, Majorescu, Marghiloman, and Rosetti. The last group favored the Central Powers and while they would fight for neutrality, they could not keep the other two factions from deciding on war. When Bussche pointed this out to the king, Ferdinand answered that if the majority voted for participation he would be unable to ignore that vote. To Czernin he said that while he himself did not want war and really desired to continue neutrality, the crown could not stand alone on the issue. He therefore was unable to assure the Austrian minister of Rumania's impartial position in the future.[37]

The council met on August 27, but before it gathered, Bratianu had sworn "high and holy" in a conversation with Czernin on August 26 that he had no intention of declaring war on the Monarchy, and after the council was over Czernin would have all the proof he needed to demonstrate that Bratianu had been telling him the truth. The prime minister insisted that Rumania would take up arms only if attacked. His shocking duplicity was demonstrated the next day, when Foreign Minister Porumbaru sent the following declaration of war to the Dual Monarchy:

> On the order of his government, the undersigned Minister of Rumania has the honor to remit to his Excellency the Minister of Foreign Affairs, the appended notification.
>
> *Edgar Mavrocordato M.P.*
>
> The alliance concluded between Germany, Austria-Hungary and Italy had only, according to the declarations of these same governments, a character which was essentially conservative and defensive. Its principal object was to guarantee the allied countries against all attack from outside and to consolidate the state of things created by the anterior treaties. It was in the desire to have its policy in accord with these pacific tendencies that Rumania joined this alliance.
>
> In view of the work having to do with its own domestic reconstruction and faithful to its firm resolution to maintain an element of order and equilibrium in the region of the Lower Danube, Rumania did not cease in contributing to the maintenance of peace in the Balkans. The last Balkan War, in destroying the status quo, imposed a new line of

[37] GFMA, ser. 1, reel 26, no. 390, Bussche to Berlin, 14 August 1916; no. 896, Bussche to Berlin, 23 August; Staatsarchiv, PA, box 520, no. 38, Czernin to Burian, 23 August; no. 39, Czernin to Burian, 26 August.

conduct upon it. Its intervention hastened peace and the reestablishment of equilibrium; it was content for itself with a rectification of the frontier which gave it a greater safety against aggression and which at the same time repaired the injustice committed to its detriment at the Congress of Berlin. But, in the pursuit of this goal it was deceived, ascertaining that it did not meet with the attitude which it had the right to expect from the Ministry in Vienna.

When war was declared, Rumania, as did Italy, declined to associate itself with the Austro-Hungarian declaration of war of which it had not been previously informed by the Vienna cabinet. In the Spring of 1915, Italy declared war on Austria-Hungary; the Triple Alliance no longer existed. The reasons which had determined the connection of Rumania to this political system disappeared at the same time. In place of a grouping of states seeking by common effort to work to assure peace and the conservation of the de facto and legal situation created by the treaties, Rumania found itself in the presence of powers making war precisely with the goal of transforming from top to bottom the old arrangements which had served as the basis of their Treaty of Alliance. These profound changes were evident proof for Rumania that the goal which it pursued in joining the Triple Alliance could no longer be attained and that it would have to direct its view and its efforts toward new paths; moreover that the moves undertaken by Austria-Hungary took a menacing character with respect to the essential interests of Rumania as well as to its most legitimate national aspirations.

In the presence of so radical a modification of the situation created between the Austro-Hungarian monarchy and Rumania, the latter fell back upon its liberty of action.

The neutrality which the Royal Government imposed upon itself following the declaration of war, was done contrary to its desires and interests, having been adopted following the assurances given at the start by the Imperial and Royal government that the Monarchy, in declaring war against Serbia, did not do so in a spirit of conquest and that it did not pursue territorial acquisitions in any way. These assurances have not been realised.

Today we find ourselves faced with a factual situation involving great territorial transformations and political changes of a nature that constitutes a grave menace to the security and future of Rumania.

The work of peace which Rumania, faithful to the spirit of the Triple Alliance, had attempted to accomplish, was made sterile by the same ones who had called for its support and defense.

In adhering in 1883 to the Central Powers group, Rumania, far from forgetting the blood ties which connected the populations of the Kingdom of Rumania to the Rumanian subjects of the Austro-Hungarian Monarchy, viewed in the amicable relations and the alliance which was established between the three great powers, a precious pledge for its domestic tranquility as well as for the amelioration of the fate of the Rumanians of Austria-Hungary. In effect, Germany and Italy, which had reconstituted their states on the basis of the principle of nationality, were unable to acknowledge the legitimacy of such a principle, upon which their own existence was based. As for Austria-Hungary, in the amicable relations which were established between itself and the Kingdom of Rumania, it found assurances for its domestic tranquility as much as for our common borders; for Austria-Hungary was not without understanding at what point the discontent of the Rumanian population would be apparent to us, threatening at each instant the good relations between the two states.

The hope that this point of view was justified through our adhesion to the Triple Alliance was shattered. During a period of more than thirty years the Rumanians within the Monarchy not only never saw a reform introduced of a nature to give even a semblance of satisfaction, but they were, on the contrary, treated as an inferior race and condemned to submit to the oppression of a foreign element which only constituted a minority in the midst of the diverse nationalities of which the Austro-Hungarian state is composed. All of the injustices thus suffered by our brothers established a continuous state of animosity between our country and the Monarchy which the government of the kingdom could only appease at the price of great difficulties and numerous sacrifices.

When actual war was declared, it was hoped that the Austro-Hungarian government, even at the last hour, would end by convincing itself of the urgent necessity of ending this injustice which endangered not only our relations of amity but even the normal relations which must exist between neighboring states.

Two years of war during which Rumania has maintained neutrality have proved that Austria-Hungary is hostile to all internal reform which would better the life of the peoples which it governs. It has also been demonstrated that it [Austria-Hungary] is prompted to sacrifice those whom it is without power to defend against external attack.

The War, in which almost all of Europe has taken part, has placed in discussion the gravest problems touching on national development and even on the existence of states; Rumania, moved by the desire to contribute to the hastening of the end of the conflict and under the necessity of safeguarding its racial interests, sees itself forced to place itself at the side of those who would be able to assure the realization of its national unity.

For these reasons, it considers itself from this moment on in a state of war with Austria-Hungary.

[signed] *E. Porumbaru*

Bukarest 16/27 August 1916
9 P.M.[38]

On August 27, just after the adjourning of the Crown Council meeting, Carp had talked with Czernin and Bussche, and though he had been sworn to secrecy concerning the deliberations, he advised them both to "immediately pack your bags." The king had stood firmly behind Bratianu during the session. The Ballhausplatz was therefore in no way surprised at the war declaration which came that evening at

---

[38] Staatsarchiv, PA, box 520, entry no. 226; see also Austria, *Rotbuch*, no. 110.

nine. Burian instructed Hohenlohe to say in Berlin that Austria expected Germany would directly follow with its own declaration of war against Rumania; he then wired Tarnowski in Sofia and Pallavicini in Constantinople that the Monarchy saw immediate action against Rumania by Bulgaria and Turkey as "self-understood."[39]

The German government, true to its promises, acted at once. Von Jagow telegraphed to Bussche on the twenty-seventh: "We intend to declare war on Rumania. For this the concurrence of the Bundesrat will be rapidly obtained. As soon as this formality is met, your Excellency will demand your passports and say to the government that, since Rumania has declared war on our ally, we likewise consider ourselves in a state of war with Rumania." On the twenty-eighth, M. N. Burghele, substituting for minister Beldiman as Rumanian representative in Berlin, was handed the official German notification. Burghele, tears in his eyes, responded: "War with Germany! Such is the harvest of the work of my ancestors."[40] His disappointment was nothing compared to that in Berlin and Vienna, for the long game in Bukarest had finally been played out. Austria and Germany had lost.

The Rumanian problem had never really come close to an affirmative solution since the start of hostilities in 1914. King Carol had remained loyal to the Central Powers, trying in vain to make his government honor long-standing treaty obligations. But Bratianu had always been partial to the Entente camp and as the war went on these inclinations became even more deeply rooted. His refusal to embroil Rumania at an early stage in the conflict was never based on any uncertainty as to where his sympathies lay but only on the question of when Rumania could participate in the war with impunity. King Ferdinand was indeed a Hohenzollern and did not always agree with Bratianu's opinions nor with his actions. However, Ferdinand respected his minister's shrewdness when Rumania's best interests were at stake, and therefore ended by not opposing his policy. And that policy was a simple one to state: the greatest number of territorial concessions with a minimum risk for the Rumanian people. The Entente offered the most for the least. When the military situation was right, as it was at the time of the successful Brussilov offensive, Bratianu accepted that offer.

[39] GFMA, ser. 1, reel 26, no. A 25493, Bussche to Bethmann-Hollweg, 30 August 1916; no. A 25494, Bussche to Bethmann-Hollweg, 2 September; Staatsarchiv, PA, box 520, nos. 220, 335, 305, Burian to Hohenlohe, Tarnowski, and Pallavicini respectively, 27 August.

[40] GFMA, ser. 1, reel 26, nos. 53 and 351, von Jagow to Bussche through Constantinople and Sofia, 27 August 1916; no. A 23120, memorandum by Jagow, 28 August.

Germany had always believed that even large concessions to Rumania were a necessary sacrifice to the war effort, but the territories Rumania coveted most could only be offered at the expense of the Austrians, who would have been forced to give up considerable portions of the Monarchy itself. The difference in point of view made victory on the diplomatic front impossible, notwithstanding liaisons with Rumanian opposition leaders, economic schemes, and attempts to influence the crown.

Keeping Rumania neutral throughout 1915 had been accomplished by military successes of striking proportions against the Russians. Brussilov's attack in the spring of 1916 demonstrated just how tenuous that neutrality was. Though the Russians were halted, the damage to the Austrian and German military image had been done, and this in conjunction with the decisions of the Entente to guarantee Bratianu what he wanted, proved to be the deciding factor. Faced with the military and diplomatic strength of the enemy, Austrian and German strategy fell apart. The Central Powers ended by rejecting a forceful policy which they feared would irrevocably alienate the Rumanian government. The alternative of moderation and a more subtle diplomatic approach proved ineffective against Bratianu, who handled his political opposition and the king most adroitly. Czernin and von dem Bussche ended with no high cards to play. The result was the Rumanian declaration of war.

Part III

The High Commands— Unity and Disunity

Chapter 11

Initial Operations

It remains to treat of the relationship between the German and Austrian high commands. That relationship involved a series of problems concerned with strategy and specific combat situations and needs, but it went beyond the requisites of the battlefields, bringing the military chiefs into close contact with their respective foreign offices. On the one hand, the diplomatic corps were used to help settle military disputes or to help implement the strategems of the general staffs. On the other, military leaders at times attempted to influence diplomacy in order to meet their own obligations more easily or were pressed into service to aid in attaining foreign policy goals. While each of the two groups tended to guard what it saw as its own specialized domain, the complexities of the war and the high stakes involved necessarily blurred the limits of their authority.

Friction Begins

The very first weeks of the war saw the beginning of animosities between the two general staffs, animosities that were frequently smoothed over but never eliminated. Germany's declaration of war against Russia, delivered on August 1, 1914, immediately produced a difficult military situation, a conflict on two fronts, east and west. When Kaiser Wilhelm wrote to the Austrian Emperor on July 31, saying that Germany would itself mobilize against the Russians, he advised Austria to relegate the Serbian campaign to a secondary position and direct the major part of its forces against the Czarist armies. In the following days von Moltke, the German chief of staff, sent a series of telegrams to Conrad, his Austrian counterpart, in which he urged not a merely defensive action against the Russians but a full attack. Conrad loyally rose to meet the challenge, for the small German army that could be marshalled to protect East Prussia would hardly be enough to stem the oncoming enemy tide.[1]

While the Austrian chief of staff had indeed agreed to mount an attack on the Russians, he had done so with reservations as to the outcome. As early as August 1, Conrad had already put into execution his Plan B, which called for a major offensive action against Serbia while leaving only some thirty-eight and a half divisions to defend the eastern borders of the Monarchy. To bolster the Serbian offensive, an additional army, the Second, had been entrained and was on its way to the Serbian borders by the time war broke on the Russian front. This army would be desperately needed for the action in the east, but it would not now be available until its troops reached the depots in the southwest and were retrained and reshipped. On August 6, Conrad informed his commander of the Serbian theater, Potiorek, of the planned new disposition but it was impossible to begin the actual transport until August 18. This situation proved to be of major importance in the outcome of the battle against the Russians, since Conrad could pit only three armies against the four of Grand Duke Nicholas, the Russian commander.[2]

When the full-scale Austrian offensive in the east began on August 23, it had not been carefully planned in its details, had not been coordinated with German forces, and, in the words of one observer, was "undertaken in the blue, in space." The failure of the attack was due to more than haste. Conrad had decided on a thrust which would carry two of his armies north and east, deep into Russian Poland in the area between the Vistula and Bug rivers. The rest of his forces were to strike the Russians east of Lemberg. The success of the venture rested on two crucial assumptions, both of which proved wrong. First, there was the belief that the Russians would be unable to mobilize rapidly enough to meet the thrust. But by the time the engagement took place the Austrian commanders faced four fully massed armies, outweighing theirs by approximately 200 battalions. Although initially Conrad's forces succeeded in advancing, the enemy's superiority in numbers slowed this advance and forced the Austrians on the defensive. They now found their flanks threatened, experienced a constantly increasing Russian pressure, and by September 1 had given up the key city of Lemberg. Ten days later, realizing he faced disaster, Conrad gave the order for a general retreat of his exhausted troops. Nor was the retreat a minor withdrawal, since there was no place where an effective defense could be set up before the Austrians reached the Visloka River, 160 kilometers behind the originally established line. By September 26 the Austrians had lost all of eastern Galicia and stood

[1] Franz Conrad von Hötzendorf, *Aus Meiner Dienstzeit, 1906–1918*, 4:156–57, 166, 195; Winston Churchill, *The Unknown War: The Eastern Front*, pp. 135–37.
[2] Churchill, *Unknown War*, p. 122; Freiherr Hugo von Freytag-Loringhoven, *Menschen und Dinge*, p. 203; Conrad, *Aus Meiner Dienstzeit*, 4:165, 383. See map, p. 183.

with their backs against the passes of the Carpathians. If the Russians broke through those passes, the Hungarian Plain would lie before them. The military situation for Austria-Hungary was critical.[3]

Less than two-thirds of the 900,000 men who initially met the Russians were still available. The Austrian casualties had totalled the frightful sum of 250,000 dead and wounded, and an additional 100,000 were now prisoners. Conrad laid the blame for his crushing defeat on his ally, and a decided rift now opened between German and Austrian headquarters. In taking the offensive he had made a second miscalculation: the assumption that, although the major part of the German armies could not be shipped to the east for six weeks, he would at least receive the support of sufficient divisions striking from the north to reduce appreciably the Russian weight against his own troops. Von Moltke rejected Conrad's request for such support on the grounds that the chief German responsibility was to the western front. On August 15, therefore, the Austrian commander appealed directly to General von Prittwitz, head of the German Eighth Army defending East Prussia. Conrad urged Prittwitz to leave German reserve and militia units guarding the Prussian frontiers while the major part of the Eighth Army struck south in the general direction of Siedlice in Russian Poland, a point roughly half-way between Warsaw and Brest Litovsk. While Prittwitz agreed that the plan was a good one, he could hardly accept the proposal because at just this time the major part of his troops faced two entire Russian armies. With a mere nine divisions at his disposal, the suggested attack was out of the question. On August 17 the Russians began their campaign to conquer East Prussia and by August 20 they defeated Prittwitz at Gumbinnen. Conrad's request became impossible to fulfill.[4]

That the German forces in Prussia were in serious trouble apparently made no impression on Conrad von Hötzendorf, because he continued to demand a drive on Siedlice. On August 28, while the Battle of Tannenberg was still without a clear-cut decision, he wrote to Baron Artur Bolfras, head of the Military Chancellery in Vienna, complaining that the Germans had not fulfilled their prewar agreement to send twelve divisions to the east for the purpose of striking at Russian

[3] Bertrand Auerbach, *L'Autriche et la Hongrie pendant la Guerre*, p. 20. The remark quoted was that of General Krauss, who before the war had been commandant of the Austrian War School. C.R.M.F. Cruttwell, *A History of the Great War, 1914–1918*, p. 51; Freytag-Loringhoven, *Menschen und Dinge*, p. 221; Auerbach, *L'Autriche et la Hongrie*, p. 22; Churchill, *Unknown War*, pp. 227–29.

[4] Churchill, *Unknown War*, pp. 229, 134, 138; Conrad, *Aus Meiner Dienstzeit*, 4:203, 391–93, 451–53; Theobald von Schäfer, "Das Militärische Zusammenwirken der Mittelmächte im Herbst, 1914," *Wissen und Wehr Monatshefte* (1926), p. 214.

Poland. Instead they had dispatched only nine, and had sent those in a different direction, toward the Masurian Lakes region. The result, Conrad bitterly declared, was that the Austrians now bore the full brunt of Russian strength in Galicia and were saddled with a superior enemy force. As far as he was concerned they owed Germany no thanks whatsoever.[5]

The Austrian chief rejoiced when on August 30 the new German commander in the east, von Hindenburg, announced the victory at Tannenberg and the crippling of Samsonov's army. Conrad telegraphed to Moltke that now certainly he could count on a German strike against Siedlice. But the Eighth Army still faced the heavy threat of Rennenkampf's troops, still quite intact, and although two new German corps were dispatched to the east, they were not slated for cooperation with the Austrians. Conrad was dismayed because his own situation in Galicia was becoming dangerous; without aid it would be desperate. He now appealed directly to Franz Joseph, requesting that he personally contact the German Kaiser. Von Moltke sent excuses on September 6, declaring that first Rennenkampf would have to be defeated. Once this occurred Germany would send four to five army corps and cavalry into Poland. A week later, when the Russians had been defeated at the Masurian Lakes, Eric von Ludendorff, Hindenburg's chief of staff, finally issued orders directing German forces to come to Austria's relief. It was too late. The Austrian retreat to the Visloka was already in progress. Conrad von Hötzendorf's disgust with Germany was summed up in his dispatch to Captain Moritz Fleischmann, Austrian military representative at Hindenburg's headquarters in Marienburg: "I can only deplore that the situation was not considered from this larger view [Siedlice] but from the secondary standpoint of clearing a province [East Prussia]."[6]

The whole matter of additional German support went beyond the two military chiefs. Conrad took his case to the Ballhausplatz on September 8 where he declared that because the German ally insisted on cleaning up matters in East Prussia, something he saw as a secondary goal, "the great success on the Polish front has been put in question and the heavy weight of the Russian superiority placed on us." He warned of the possibility of a major retreat. Berchtold immediately sent in-

[5] Conrad, *Aus Meiner Dienstzeit*, 4:561, 563. The fullest account of the Austrian offensive is found in Austria, Bundesministerium für Heereswesen, *Österreich-Ungarns Letzter Krieg, 1914–1918*, 1:155–335.

[6] Conrad, *Aus Meiner Dienstzeit*, 4:573–74, 625, 656, 670; Eric von Ludendorff, *My War Memories*, 1:47, 57, 60, 66–67. The fullest account of Tannenberg and the Masurian Lakes campaign is found in Germany, Reichsarchiv, *Der Weltkrieg, 1914–1918* (12 vol. ed.), 2:111–237, 268–317.

structions to Hohenlohe in Berlin, telling him to make much more serious and pressing representations with Zimmermann at the Foreign Office for additional German aid, and to pass along similar instructions to the Austrian military representative at German headquarters, Count Joseph Stürgkh. Stürgkh was to submit the Austrian request for more support to the chief of staff, the chancellor, and Kaiser Wilhelm himself. To impress the German government even further, Hohenlohe was to mention to Zimmermann, though "obviously without authorization," that if the aid was not forthcoming and if Germany continued to propose that Austrian forces cede provinces, then Austria would attempt to conclude a peace "to end a war in which we bleed ourselves uselessly."[7]

Zimmermann's reaction was surprise and concern. Both he and Hohenlohe could agree that they were diplomats and as such had no real understanding of military strategy. But the undersecretary nevertheless drew attention to the fact that German troops in Prussia faced large Russian forces and this alone constituted an indirect unburdening of the Austrian armies. It was unbelievable that the German General Staff would fail to meet its obligations by refusing to send its full strength against Russia, but the first job was to defeat France. The dispute reached Bethmann-Hollweg, who stated that in light of Germany's facing a superiority of 300,000 men in the west and twelve Russian corps in the east, it was simply impossible to send more aid now. But he did promise that as soon as Germany's back was free in Prussia, a general action in Poland would be ordered.[8]

While this exchange was taking place, Conrad continued to assert that the German East Army was operating contrary to agreements reached between the two commands before the fighting began. He made this charge for the first time on August 24, and then on September 6 suggested that because the Germans had withheld their offensive against Siedlice, Austrian troops might not succeed in Poland. In response to these accusations, Berchtold, taking the typical stance of a diplomat, asked General Conrad whether he had specific agreements, in writing, with the German command. If so, Berchtold wanted to know the precise terms of the written accord. It was such a document, he remarked, that would constitute the necessary "substrata for continuing the conversations with the German government."[9] Conrad could not offer a written military agreement, for there was none.

---

[7] Staatsarchiv, PA, box 500, no. 7880, Conrad to Berchtold, 8 September 1914; no. 551, Berchtold to Hohenlohe in Berlin, 8 September.

[8] Staatsarchiv, PA, box 500, no. 508, Hohenlohe to Berchtold, 9 September 1914; no. 4315, Foreign Office report, 9 September.

[9] Ibid., no. 13, Berchtold to Conrad, 11 September 1914.

Berchtold's inquiry was written on the same day that Conrad von Hötzendorf ordered the retreat of his troops. Berchtold had been unable to save the situation. Hohenlohe touched the core of the matter when he wrote to Vienna that the diplomats were not in a position to solve a question that was purely military in nature. Zimmermann was a powerful figure in the German Foreign Office, but neither he nor Jagow nor even the chancellor himself could by themselves make much impression when it came to affairs that were the domain of professional soldiers. This realization did not keep Hohenlohe from bitterly remarking to his German colleagues that it was Germany which had caused the failure of the whole campaign in the east and left Austria-Hungary in the lurch. The Wilhelmstrasse proved much more impressed, however, by Hohenlohe's observation that the Austrian retreat to a position behind the San River meant German Silesia would now lie open to a Russian attack.[10] At German headquarters people were hardly unaware of that problem.

General Prittwitz, unable to cope with the Russians, had been replaced by Hindenburg and Ludendorff on August 23, and von Moltke, having failed at the Marne, was succeeded by Falkenhayn on September 14. By this time Conrad and most of his staff had come to feel, if indeed somewhat unfairly, that Germany had sacrificed thousands of Austrian lives in order to protect its own interests, failing to understand the broader needs of both allies. Nevertheless, the friendship which in the prewar years had flourished between Conrad and von Moltke had thus far provided a certain leaven to the animosities roused by military events. Once Moltke was gone, there developed an ever increasing coldness between the two general staffs. Usually at loggerheads on questions of strategy, Conrad and Falkenhayn also proved to be complete opposites not only in physical appearance but in personality traits.

Falkenhayn has been described as a "pure soldier type"—a man with sharply cut features and piercing eyes, tall, slender, retaining something of the young lieutenant's dash. Conrad was smaller, almost delicate looking, with a slight nervous quiver about the mouth. Snow-white mustachios gave him the rather misleading look of a kindly grandfather. He was often to prove petulant and supersensitive. Unlike the German commander, who often dispatched his affairs orally, Conrad, with

[10] Ibid., no. 520, Hohenlohe to Berchtold, 13 September 1914; report no. Z 78 A/P, Hohenlohe to Berchtold, 14 September; Count Joseph von Stürgkh, *Im Deutschen Grossen Hauptquartier*, p. 41; Conrad, *Aus Meiner Dienstzeit*, 4:733, 737, 810–11; Ludendorff, *War Memories*, 1:71; Freytag-Loringhoven, *Menschen und Dinge*, p. 234.

something of the scholar about him, preferred the written word. Both were well-trained professionals, but the Austrian leaned more toward the theoretical side. He was a superb strategist and certainly his German colleagues did not fail to give him his just deserts on this score. Ludendorff was later to describe him as "a strategist with an unusually fertile mind," and "a clever and distinguished general of great mental adaptability." Coloring his military outlook, and at times detrimental to the immediate military needs of the Central Powers, was Conrad's constant concern for the political future of the Dual Monarchy. For his German counterpart he often proved much too ethereal.

Falkenhayn was a thorough pragmatist who always weighed the potential of a campaign against concrete conditions—manpower, guns, terrain, and the fighting capacities of his own troops as well as those of the enemy. Whatever his involvement in political considerations may have been, and at times it was considerable, his outlook was governed by his more immediate military tasks. Conrad may have been praised for his "grandiose conceptions"; in Falkenhayn's view these did not win wars.[11]

When Falkenhayn took up his new post, it was obvious that something had to be done to help the Austrian ally and to eliminate the threat to Silesia. A successful Russian advance into that area meant the loss of raw materials without which Germany could not long continue the war. Furthermore, if the Czarist armies entered Bohemia, he feared that the Dual Monarchy would experience crippling "internal convulsions," making it impossible to induce the Bulgarians, Rumanians, and Turks to join the conflict against the Entente. When Ludendorff, having gone to Austrian headquarters for talks with Conrad on September 18, reported his findings it became clear that only one decision could be made. The retreat of the Austrians behind the San had resulted in over forty divisions being jammed into a narrow corridor, roughly 150 kilometers wide, between the Carpathians and the Vistula. The troops were dead tired and unless relief came the Austrian army was finished. Falkenhayn therefore acted on the suggestion which had sometime before been made by his eastern commanders. Unable to send contingents from the west because of the failure of the Schlieffen Plan against the French, he left the barest number of troops to guard Prussia

---

[11] Stürgkh, *Im Deutschen Grossen Hauptquartier*, pp. 23, 25; August von Cramon, *Quatre Ans au G.Q.G. Austro-Hongrois pendant la Guerre Mondiale*, pp. 48–49; Ludendorff, *War Memories*, 1:75; Auerbach, *L'Autriche et la Hongrie*, pp. 16, 34; Freytag-Loringhoven, *Menschen und Dinge*, p. 226; Adriano Alberti, *General Falkenhayn: Die Beziehungen zwischen den Generalstabschefs des Dreibundes*, pp. 4, 27.

and rerouted almost the entire Eighth Army to Silesia, massing it in the area of Posen as the Ninth, with Hindenburg in charge.[12]

There now began for the first time a close cooperation in the field between the German and Austrian armies. By September 27 the German Ninth Army was operational and the following day it began an offensive against the Russians. The campaign was not planned as an all-out move, since Falkenhayn was not ready to change his focus from the western front to the eastern. The objective was to force Grand Duke Nicholas to shift large numbers of troops from Galicia to meet the German threat in Poland and thus save Conrad's forces from catastrophe. Along with this, of course, the campaign was intended to secure Silesia from a Russian invasion. On October 4 the Austrians, having by now regrouped behind the Visloka, began their own forward movement toward the San which they hoped would allow them to strike northeast toward Ivangorod, while the Germans aimed at Warsaw. The objective was to force the Russians back across the Vistula.[13]

Unfortunately they did not attain their objective. Hindenburg's army advanced rapidly in spite of roads now a foot thick in mud from autumn rains, but the Austrians did not do well. Although they reached the San, they were unable to go beyond. By the end of the month the Czarist commander had transferred fourteen corps to Poland and part of these swung against the Austrian First Army under Dankle. Unable to hold against the Russian counterattack, Dankle ordered a retreat. Because his army was the connecting link between the Austrian left and Hindenburg's southern flank, the order was crucial to the entire operation. German headquarters in the east was thunderstruck when it heard of Dankle's withdrawal for this meant that the whole German southern wing would be exposed to a Russian envelopment. The only course was to break off the entire engagement, the position of the German Ninth Army having been made completely untenable. On October 27 the order for a general retirement was given and six days later the Central Powers were back where they had started.[14]

[12] Erich von Falkenhayn, *The German General Staff and Its Decisions 1914–1916*, pp. 19–20, 21, 24; Ludendorff, *War Memories*, 1:76; Schäfer, "Militärische Zusammenwirken," pp. 217, 219.

[13] Falkenhayn, *German General Staff*, p. 24; Ludendorff, *War Memories*, 1:76, 79, 81, 84; Churchill, *Unknown War*, pp. 239–40, 244–45.

[14] Ludendorff, *War Memories*, 1:82, 88, 93; Max Hoffmann, *Der Krieg der Versäumten Gelegenheiten*, pp. 54–55, 61, 62; Churchill, *Unknown War*, pp. 242, 243, 245–49; Germany, Reichsarchiv, *Der Weltkrieg*, 5, pt. 1:402–90; Wolfgang Foerster, ed., *Mackensen: Briefe und Aufzeichnungen*, p. 84.

In part, the defeat had been caused by the absence of a unified eastern command, something not achieved in the first two years of the war. Archduke Frederick, commander in chief of the Austrian military forces, had on September 14 contacted Kaiser Wilhelm and suggested that Hindenburg be placed under Austrian control. Wilhelm refused, and therefore each of the armies, while working in conjunction with the other, functioned under the orders of its own General Staff. The refusal of the Germans to accept Austrian supervision in the field raised Conrad's ire and led him to distrust German leaders. Did the Germans, he asked, want to insure their own mastery over the alliance? Were they merely concerned with furthering their own interests? Or, had they rejected the proposal for unified command because they had no faith in the capacities of Austrian military leaders? In October, before the Austrian retreat, the Germans had requested Conrad to put his own First Army under the direct order of Hindenburg. Kaiser Wilhelm had personally written to Franz Joseph asking that such a unified command be established. The Austrian Emperor had answered that his armies would work in the closest cooperation with the Germans, but he had ignored the request for unity and things remained as they had been, separate armies working under separate orders. Franz Joseph's response reflected the categorical refusal of Conrad von Hötzendorf to accept German domination in the field. Conrad not only feared that fragmentation of his armies would eventually result but, further, that Austrian units might be allocated to fronts where only German interests would be served. He saw the Kaiser's request as a personal affront for it seemed to question his own capacities as a commander. When on October 21 the German representative at Neu-Sandec attempted to get Conrad to reverse his position, the latter would not hear of it, and he was supported by Archduke Frederick and the Emperor, as well.[15]

On this particular matter the Austrian Foreign Office disagreed with Conrad's posture. On November 3 Berchtold went so far as to contact the Austrian Emperor to suggest that in light of the present war situation nothing should be neglected that would produce the necessary solidarity between the two allies. He particularly favored a unified command because it would irrevocably commit Germany to a real continuation of operations against the Czar. Berchtold's thinking was colored by Hohenlohe, who had written that a unified command in the east would "provide singularity of purpose." The ambassador had talked with Zimmermann, who strongly supported the idea because

[15] Conrad, *Aus Meiner Dienstzeit*, 4:751, 786; 5:181, 182, 219, 381–82, 383, 393, 408; Germany, Reichsarchiv, *Der Weltkrieg*, 5, pt. 1:467–68, 551; Ludendorff, *War Memories*, 1:78; Schäfer, "Militärische Zusammenwirken," pp. 218–19, 227.

each military headquarters was now blaming the other for the failure of the attempted counterattack against the Russians. The only way to avoid this in the future was to produce a general command over both army groups. More than this, Hohenlohe had received the impression that Germany was much more concerned with bringing England to its knees by a successful operation in the west. If this occurred, Zimmermann had asserted, the Russian opposition would break of itself. Hohenlohe's view was that the destruction of Russia was the chief purpose of the war, and he suggested to Berchtold that this be stressed. A unified command was one way of accomplishing it.[16]

What it all got down to was simply a difference in the degree of emphasis which each allotted to the eastern front at this time. The Wilhelmstrasse fully supported the wishes of the German military, who wanted a unified command in the east to bring about greater cohesion of the war effort, even though the major emphasis of their thinking lay on affairs in the west. Austrian diplomats also desired greater cohesion, though partly for different reasons. Conrad refused, and because he had the full confidence of Franz Joseph, he carried the day.

In spite of the absence of a unified command, the efforts of the Central Powers in the east were not crippled. On November 11, two weeks after the retreat had been sounded, both German and Austrian forces were again on the offensive. Hindenburg's Ninth Army had managed temporarily to relieve the beleaguered Austrians, but the general situation in the east was no better at the beginning of November than it had been at the end of September. Silesia was still in danger of Russian invasion. The Germans had tried an attack from the south and had failed. They now decided to try from the north, and it was absolutely necessary that the new attempt be made. By November 1 the German eastern command had ascertained that the Russians were giving up the all-out pursuit of the Ninth Army, since only cavalry units continued the Russian advance. Fortunately for the Germans, they had cracked the Russian wireless code and discovered that the grand duke was massing his troops for a great attack aimed at a deep invasion of Germany, involving Russian armies from the Baltic to Poland, scheduled for November 14. Hindenburg and Ludendorff had therefore to begin a campaign before this date to make the Czarist operation impossible. A masterful transfer of almost the entire Ninth Army from Cracow north to Thorn was successfully completed within ten days, and on November 11 General Mackensen, now commanding

---

[16] Staatsarchiv, PA, box 500, unnumbered memo, Berchtold to Franz Joseph, 3 November 1914; report no. Z 99 A-G/P, Hohenlohe to Berchtold, 1 November.

the Ninth, began an attack from Thorn in a southward direction along the Vistula, against the Russian right flank. The hole in the Polish salient created by the transfer of the Ninth from the area of Posen was filled by an Austrian army deployed from the Carpathians where, for the moment, it was not needed.[17]

The development of this maneuver had revealed fundamental disparities in strategy not only between Falkenhayn and Conrad, but also between the German High Command and its own generals in the eastern theater. After the retreat of the Central Powers in late October, Falkenhayn had written to Conrad suggesting he come to Berlin on October 30 to discuss future action. The Austrian commander refused to make the trip, in spite of the urging of Archduke Frederick that he comply so as not to produce discord. Conrad answered that considering the military situation on his own front, he could not under any circumstances leave his headquarters. If Falkenhayn wanted to see him, he would have to come to Neu-Sandec. Failing this, Conrad was willing to send his aide-de-camp, Major Rudolf Kundmann, to be his personal representative in the Berlin talks. The German chief smarted under what he saw as a personal slight, but he held back his anger and met with Kundmann on the scheduled date. Conrad himself hardly saw his refusal as insulting. His own ideas on how future campaigns should be conducted had already been expressed in a telegram to German headquarters. Until the Battle of the Marne he had believed the Central Powers had to hold as best they could against Russia and give operations in the west every opportunity. A rapid victory over the French had failed and could not now be achieved. Therefore, it was necessary to shift the emphasis to the east and to go on the defensive on the western front. If Germany shifted some twenty to twenty-four divisions for action against the Russians, a decisive victory would be possible, after which the two allies could devote themselves to winning the war against the French and English. That nothing was now to be expected from a continuation of the offensive in France was obvious from the development of trench warfare with its concomitant war of position. In the east there was still a war of movement, giving the expectation of rapid and significant success if the opportunity to exploit such a situation was not lost.[18]

As far as Conrad was concerned, there was no sense in going to Berlin to rehash what he had already stated in written form. His views

[17] Paul von Hindenburg, *Aus Meinem Leben,* pp. 95, 96, 98; Hoffmann, *Der Krieg,* pp. 62–63, 77; Falkenhayn, *German General Staff,* pp. 33–34; Ludendorff, *War Memories,* 1:96, 99–100, 106.
[18] Conrad, *Aus Meiner Dienstzeit,* 5:312, 313, 323, 324, 309–11, 301; Stürgkh, *Im Deutschen Grossen Hauptquartier,* pp. 102–3.

had been clearly presented. They required only a yes or no answer. In fact, however, the problem was more complex than this. Falkenhayn rightly believed that sweeping successes against the Russians could not now be gained. The Russians' superiority in numbers was great, the area in which they could maneuver was extensive, and winter weather would make fighting difficult. He therefore wanted a limited operation, a delaying action for the present. Falkenhayn had believed up until November that the decision could be obtained on the western front. By November 1 he was willing to shift his emphasis for a while from west to east but not before he had taken Ypres to secure his lines in the west. At the meetings in Berlin on October 30 he found the Austrian plan being supported by Ludendorff. The German eastern command wanted thirty divisions, ten more than Conrad had requested, and completely agreed with Conrad that a decision was now possible against the Russians. Falkenhayn refused the massive transfer, which would have compromised the entire operation on the western front. The most he would commit himself to was six corps to be sent about fourteen days after Ypres had fallen. No specific date for the shipment of these troops was set, however, and the transport of the divisions involved was to be handled piecemeal. In the meantime Hindenburg would have to get along with what he now had available, except for seven divisions of infantry and one of cavalry which could be immediately allocated.[19]

Both Hindenburg and Conrad remained totally convinced that Falkenhayn had misjudged the situation. The Austrian commander went so far as to prevail once again on Franz Joseph to intercede with a direct letter to the Kaiser, but Wilhelm supported his chief of staff.[20]

Without additional troops, Mackensen committed the Ninth Army to combat on November 12, striking in the direction of Lutz. The Russians fell back upon the city and a heavy battle occurred which, though it resulted in a German success, took until December 6 to win. Losses were again extremely high, numbering 35,000 German and 70,000 Russian killed and wounded. Once Lutz had fallen Mackensen was in a position to push forward to Warsaw but his offensive came to a halt some thirty-five miles from the objective. The skillful and

[19] Conrad, *Aus Meiner Dienstzeit*, 5:323–24, 339, 340; Germany, Reichsarchiv, *Der Weltkrieg*, 6, pt. 2:1–3; Falkenhayn, *German General Staff*, pp. 28, 34, 37; Hoffmann, *Der Krieg*, pp. 79–80.

[20] Conrad, *Aus Meiner Dienstzeit*, 5:343, 351. In Kundmann's report of the Berlin meeting he declared that Falkenhayn had said transport of troops from west to east would begin in about six weeks rather than fourteen days. Conrad expressed his general irritation by pointing to the fact that the initial plan to shift emphasis to the east after six weeks had now been extended to nineteen. See Conrad, pp. 340–41. Germany, Reichsarchiv, *Der Weltkrieg*, 5, pt. 1:553–59.

dogged resistance of the Russian forces, the reduction in available German troops through battle casualties, and the intense cold, which Conrad later estimated stood in some sectors at minus 13 degrees centigrade, brought an end to the advance.[21]

Meanwhile the Austrians had also attempted a movement against the Russians in southern Poland and in Galicia. Progress was negligible but Conrad did succeed in stabilizing his front against strong Russian opposition and eliminated the possibility of losing Cracow. By December the Austrian line lay along the Dunajec River, thirty-five miles east of the city, and curved southward and eastward along the Carpathians.[22]

Bogged down by the superiority of Russian numbers, by ice and snow and general fatigue, the German and Austrian attack came to a full halt. For the first time there began in the east a war of position that essentially remained unchanged until the spring of 1915. Surveying the general scene, the military leaders of the Central Powers were not pleased with the situation but at least they had managed to eliminate the threat posed by Russia at the start of October. The attack by the Ninth Army had disrupted the plans of Grand Duke Nicholas to invade Germany, and Silesia had been secured by the time Mackensen paused for breath in December. Although the Austrians had lost the Bukovina and most of Galicia, they had been saved from utter collapse by the help of their German ally, and had themselves managed to stave off a Russian thrust into Hungary.[23]

Disparate German and Austrian Strategies

In December, 1914, while the offensive against the Russians was still in progress, the differences between Conrad von Hötzendorf and Falkenhayn became even more apparent. On December 2 they met for the first time at Breslau, where high-level discussions were held with the German Kaiser, the Austrian Archdukes Frederick and Charles, Hindenburg, Ludendorff, and Conrad's aide-de-camp, Kundmann. Conrad wanted a decisive operation against the Czarist armies. Falkenhayn, however, explained that the western enemy was far superior in fighting ability and constituted the greater danger. Until there was a guarantee against a French breakthrough there could be no thought of transfer-

[21] Cruttwell, *History of the Great War*, pp. 85, 86, 88; Churchill, *Unknown War*, pp. 258, 260, 261, 264; Conrad, *Aus Meiner Dienstzeit*, 5:568.
[22] Cruttwell, *History of the Great War*, pp. 88, 89; Ludendorff, *War Memories*, 1:109, 110.
[23] Hindenburg, *Aus Meinem Leben*, pp. 98–99; Ludendorff, *War Memories*, 1:112; Germany, Reichsarchiv, *Der Weltkrieg*, 6, pt. 2:368.

ring additional forces to the east. In his estimation, if the Central Powers could force the Russians to retreat behind the Vistula and the San, they would have done enough. In the process the Russian armies would be worn down and their offensive capacities appreciably reduced. If the campaign should fail to achieve a Russian retreat, German and Austrian units would have to dig in and establish a stationary line of defense.[24]

Conrad was, of course, disappointed with his German colleague's interpretation, but it was clear that Falkenhayn would not change his opinion and had the support of Kaiser Wilhelm. The Austrian general gave in for the time being. If the offensive in progress against the Russians succeeded, perhaps he could influence the German High Command to change its point of view. But he simmered over the fact that the decision for a limited campaign on the eastern front had obviously been made before his arrival and he had been faced with a take-it-or-leave-it situation. It was a bitter blow to have his own ideas pigeonholed, particularly since he was convinced that a smashing victory against the Russians was now possible, if only he had the men. He could not himself muster troops, and, lacking the means, could only chafe at the frustration of his plans.[25]

The middle of December brought a request from Falkenhayn for another meeting, this time in Oppeln, to plan future operations. Actually he was thinking of reshipping divisions from east to west because he was planning a campaign against the French, to begin in February. At this meeting, Conrad again voiced his opinion that they ought to go beyond the Vistula and the San. He saw Russia as the chief enemy and believed that if they could defeat the Russian armies decisively, their other enemies would fall in due course. Falkenhayn remained adamant. He could not devote major portions of the German army to an eastern campaign which would take perhaps three months to complete while letting operations go on the western front. Some German units in the trenches there had not had a rest in nine weeks and needed relief. If the French were to break through, a victory against Russia would have no value since Germany would then be endangered. The only concession Conrad was able to get was the promise that German troops would not be shipped from the east until the Vistula had been reached.[26]

The opposing views would somehow have to be resolved. The meetings thus far had served to show the basic difference between Germans and Austrians as to how the war should be waged. In Janu-

[24] Conrad, *Aus Meiner Dienstzeit*, 5:649, 650, 651, 456.
[25] Ibid., pp. 652, 654, 660.
[26] Ibid., pp. 809, 817–20.

ary, 1915, for military as well as political reasons, it would be Conrad, backed by Hindenburg, Ludendorff, and Bethmann-Hollweg himself, who would succeed in carrying the day by convincing the German Kaiser that they were correct and Falkenhayn was wrong.

At the turn of 1915 one thing was certainly clear—general hostility between the two high commands had risen, not declined. Count Joseph Stürgkh, the Austrian general, assigned to represent Conrad at German headquarters, had had a difficult job since August. Describing his own feelings over the constant requests for troops and equipment, he said, "I came often as a beggar who must plead for alms." If Stürgkh's pride was somewhat hurt by Falkenhayn's sarcastic manner, this was nothing at all compared with Conrad von Hötzendorf's reaction. When in January Stürgkh returned for conferences with his chief, he found him suffering from a persecution complex. Conrad disliked the German officers attached to his own headquarters; he declared they were spies, accused them of "sniffing into everything," of "ensnaring him in a net." He even thought they influenced the press against him. When he greeted Stürgkh, his first remark was, "Well, how are things with our underhanded enemy, the Germans? And what is that actor, the Kaiser, doing?" In short, he had become a complete Germanophobe.[27]

The Germans, on the other hand, had lost a good deal of respect for their Austrian ally. Falkenhayn referred to Austria as "the weak brother." Hindenburg's attitude was expressed in a letter to Falkenhayn in which he declared, "The Austro-Hungarian Army Command and the Austro-Hungarian troops are no longer factors by which a large scale operation can be put through."[28]

The German attitude was based on more than the failure of Austria to produce concrete results against Russia. The Germans were concerned with the general pessimism of Austrian officers. Following the original Austrian retreat from the eastern areas of Galicia, the atmosphere at Conrad's headquarters was described as "like that of a funeral," and the morale did not improve as losses mounted and successes failed to materialize. German headquarters could not have been more amazed or disgruntled at the abortive attempts of the Austrians to deal with so small an adversary as the Serbs. When, by the end of December, Austrian troops were completely driven from Serbian soil, the German military shook their heads, attributing the defeat to Austrian "sloppiness" and "coffee-house ways." As time went on their negative attitude increased, since the German commanders could never be quite

---

[27] Stürgkh, *Im Deutschen Grossen Hauptquartier*, pp. 9, 11, 25, 60, 115, 116.
[28] Germany, Reichsarchiv, *Der Weltkrieg*, 6, pt. 2:363; Conrad, *Aus Meiner Dienstzeit*, 5:78.

sure the Austrians would not suddenly crumble, making a shambles of their own plans. It is significant that in December Falkenhayn did not present his plan to reduce German divisions in the east until Hugo Freytag-Loringhoven, the German representative at Austrian headquarters, assured him that Austria could hold out.[29]

The Generals and Diplomacy

This lack of confidence in the Austrian ally led Falkenhayn to try another approach to eliminate Russia as an active enemy. What had not been accomplished by military means might possibly be done through diplomatic circles. His reasoning resulted from the failure to secure any decisive victory in the Ypres offensive and from the obvious fact that the attack against Russia in November, 1914, would have limited results. By mid-November Falkenhayn no longer believed it possible to win a smashing victory against the Entente.[30]

Now the chief of the General Staff suggested to Bethmann-Hollweg that the two-front war had to be ended. He could win a conflict against the French and British but to do this Russia had to be eliminated as an opponent. This ought to be done through negotiations with Russia leading to a separate peace. Except for a few minor border rectifications and an indemnity, territorial agreements with Russia ought to be based on the status quo. Finally, no move was to be made unless Austria was in complete accord and shared in the negotiations.[31]

The chancellor was not pleased with Falkenhayn's attempt to fish in diplomatic waters but he went so far as to raise the issue with Zimmermann. Bethmann had no evidence that Russia was ready to accept such overtures and even in the event of greater successes against Russia on the battlefields, he doubted that the Czar's government would entertain the idea. Zimmermann was no less critical of the project and advocated that no action be taken in this direction lest overtures be seen by Russia and its allies as a sign of weakness. If they wanted Russia out of the war they would have to defeat it in the field, regain Galicia and Poland, and support the interest of their Austrian allies.[32]

Falkenhayn's suggestion caused many repercussions. On December 6

[29] Hindenburg, *Aus Meinem Leben*, pp. 129–30; Auerbach, *L'Autriche et la Hongrie*, p. 29; Wilhelm Groener, *Lebenserinnerungen*, p. 206; Ludendorff, *War Memories*, 1:111; Freytag-Loringhoven, *Menschen und Dinge*, pp. 254–55.
[30] Paul Sweet, "Leaders and Policies: Germany in the Winter 1914–1915," *Journal of Central European Affairs* 16 (October 1956):230–31.
[31] Ibid., p. 232.
[32] Ibid., pp. 234, 236–37; Germany, Reichsarchiv, *Der Weltkrieg*, 6, pt. 2:405, 408.

Bethmann went to Posen for talks with Hindenburg and Ludendorff and told them of Falkenhayn's proposal. Both men scoffed at the idea and impressed Bethmann with the fact that the Russians could indeed be defeated if the eastern command was given the necessary troops to finish the job. The chancellor returned to Berlin feeling certain Hindenburg and Ludendorff were correct. When in further discussions with Falkenhayn, the latter showed signs of defeatism by saying the German army was now "a shattered organ," Bethmann was convinced that the chief of the German High Command had to be replaced. The highest echelons of German leadership thus separated into two opposing camps holding widely divergent views.[33]

Conrad von Hötzendorf first got wind of the fact that the Germans were considering a separate peace with Russia when Captain Moritz Fleischmann, Austrian army representative at Hindenburg's headquarters, reported the affairs discussed during Bethmann's visit to Posen. The issue was directly broached by Freytag-Loringhoven in a conversation with Conrad on December 14, and characteristically the latter thought the worst. "They would conclude peace and leave us sitting in the pepper?" he asked, and immediately fired off a telegram to Berchtold in Vienna, concluding, "I should think that Germany, to whom we have proven so selfless an ally and whose territories we have preserved from enemy invasion for four full months under the greatest sacrifices, would not now in this difficult moment leave us in the lurch and thus unilaterally treat with our enemies to our harm."[34]

Berchtold was not upset, since he already knew there was some talk going on in Germany of a separate peace with the Russians. He personally did not believe Germany would initiate negotiations along this line without Austrian concurrence and Hohenlohe's subsequent commentary on the issue proved him right. Conrad was, of course, concerned that negotiations might take place at the expense of Austria's losing Galicia. The Austrian ambassador in Berlin raised the point with Jagow, who remarked without hesitation that any peace negotiations would certainly be based on a complete liberation of East Prussia as well as Galicia from Russian control. This, he declared, was a *"conditio sine qua non."* Apparently this was enough to satisfy Conrad, for he dropped the issue.[35]

[33] Germany, Reichsarchiv, *Der Weltkrieg,* 6, pt. 2:413–15; Sweet, "Leaders and Policies," pp. 243–44, 248.

[34] Conrad, *Aus Meiner Dienstzeit,* 5:752–53, 754, 755; Germany, Reichsarchiv, *Der Weltkrieg,* 6, pt. 2:416.

[35] Staatsarchiv, PA, box 500, no. 381, Conrad to Berchtold, 15 December 1914; no. 5715, Berchtold to Conrad, 19 December; unnumbered report, Hohenlohe to Berchtold, 21 December; Conrad, *Aus Meiner Dienstzeit,* 5:848, 898, 900.

At best, Falkenhayn's suggestion regarding peace in the east had proved unfortunate. It had not only agitated Austria, but had also revealed in sharp relief the widely divergent views within the highest echelons of German leadership on the question of pursuing the war. It produced resentment among German diplomats, who felt their own military were engaging in affairs they did not understand, and it placed in question the desirability of Falkenhayn's continuance as chief of the High Command.

The matter of Russia was not the first instance in which military leaders were led to consider diplomatic problems. The German and Austrian generals had been deeply concerned over the Balkans and Italy since war began. While the military troubled themselves over diplomatic and political questions, they found the diplomats dabbling in military matters. The whole issue of the Balkans and Italy and their relation to the outcome of the war was so important that intrusion of opinion, influence, and pressure by military and diplomatic leaders was scarcely avoidable.

At the start of the war Conrad clearly concerned himself with the Balkan states more than did his German colleague. Moltke was taken up with the western front. A certain victory there in six weeks would obviate the necessity for worrying about Bulgaria and Rumania. Then, too, Moltke had a high regard for the fighting capacities of the Austrian army and believed it capable of dealing with the Russians without the help of Balkan armies. To some extent his telegrams to Conrad expressed a naiveté, for he was unaware of the subtleties involved in Balkan politics. On August 5 he wrote to Conrad emphasizing the need for Austria to direct its major effort against the Russians. He was hardly worried about the Italians because, "Italy could not be such a dog as to fall upon Austria's rear." The Rumanian problem would, he believed, still turn out well and in a few days Bukarest would engage its armies against the Czar. As for the Bulgarians, they were to be loosed against the Serbs: "Let the pack kill each other."[36]

Conrad von Hötzendorf believed the diplomatic problem of the Balkan states to be much more complex and worrisome. On August 2 he had spoken with Berchtold and said he must know for sure what Rumania would do. Would it be neutral, would it join their side, or would it perhaps declare armed neutrality? For him it was an issue of the greatest importance that Rumania mobilize. Then, in writing, he suggested to Berchtold that the Rumanians be guaranteed against their fear of Bulgaria and be given Bessarabia as a war prize. He declared,

[36] Stürgkh, *Im Deutschen Grossen Hauptquartier*, pp. 23, 159; Conrad, *Aus Meiner Dienstzeit*, 4:195.

"This proposal is so urgent it should be made immediately." Once Rumania had joined, Bulgaria would oppose Serbia if given compensations in Macedonia. His concluding remark reflected his general concern: "The war has broken out so suddenly that there is no time for systematic methods."[37]

Conrad also sent Moltke various telegrams explaining the Italian and Balkan situations facing the military men and diplomats. On the Italian frontier the Austrian defenses were extremely limited, and since it could not be ascertained how Italy would decide, he requested German reinforcements to insure against a possible Italian attack on the Tyrol and then on Austria proper. The Bulgarians hesitated in spite of Vienna's doing all it could to bring them in against the Serbs. Conrad thought Bulgaria was waiting for the Austrians "to pull the chestnuts out of the fire alone," and he wanted Moltke to get German assistance in dissipating Bulgaria's caution. The Rumanians, in declaring their neutrality, angered him; they failed, in his opinion, to see that if Rumania wanted to avoid vassalage to Russia, it had to join the Central Powers. Here, too, he asked that Germany do all it could to obtain Rumanian action on their side.[38]

Moltke, peculiarly enough, saw these problems as more the concern of Austria than of Germany. He continued to believe the Italians constituted no immediate threat. He told the Austrian military representative, von Stürgkh, that in an emergency he would send whatever he could, even if it was only a few thousand men, but to Conrad he wrote that no reinforcements were available at this time for the Italian frontier. His views on Rumania and Bulgaria clearly threw the weight of solution on Austrian shoulders. For its cooperation Rumania ought to receive from Austria worthwhile assurances of better treatment for the Rumanians in Hungary. His reference was to the Transylvanian problem and Count Tisza's unbending position regarding concessions. "At such times as this," said Moltke, "one must not be doctrinaire." Moltke had mentioned to the German Foreign Office that pressure must be put on Bulgaria to enter against the Serbs, but here again he felt that the major work rested with Austria. Apparently he was under the impression that negotiations between Austria and Bulgaria leading towards a formal accord had already been completed, for he somewhat impatiently remarked to Conrad, "You want us to instruct Bulgaria how to proceed. Can you not do the same? You have an alliance with the people."[39]

---

[37] Conrad, *Aus Meiner Dienstzeit*, 4:166; Staatsarchiv, PA, box 516, folio 7A, unnumbered letter, Conrad to Berchtold, 2 August 1914.
[38] Conrad, *Aus Meiner Dienstzeit*, 4:194, 195, 209.
[39] Ibid., pp. 203, 204; Stürgkh, *Im Deutschen Grossen Hauptquartier*, p. 23.

The Austrian chief of staff, having got nowhere with his German colleague, went back to exerting influence on Berchtold. By the end of August, Conrad was more concerned than ever, saying that a decisive stage had been reached. Austria was now feeling the weight of the Russian superiority on the eastern front; though Germany concerned itself purely with East Prussia, the Austrian forces still held. It was most urgent that diplomatic action be taken to assure Rumanian entry against the Russian armies. Bulgaria must immediately be brought in to free Austrian troops from their burden in Serbia.[40]

Berchtold was annoyed, for most certainly he did not have to be told of the advisability of winning the Balkan states as allies. He answered the chief of staff that the diplomats, and these included the Germans as well, were doing all they could in Bukarest and Sofia. In fact, both Rumanians and Bulgarians would be influenced by what happened on the war fronts in Russia and Serbia, and without victories there the participation of the two Balkan states was quite "unthinkable." By the opening of September it was clear that the Austrians had suffered a bad defeat at the hands of the Serbs, who had forced the Austrian commander, Oskar Potiorek, to sound the retreat. Berchtold let Conrad know that the setback had seriously compromised the Austrian diplomatic position in Sofia. On September 8 the foreign minister wrote again, declaring that Rumanian cooperation rested on a decisive victory against the Russians. Certainly Berchtold was much dismayed when on September 11 Conrad ordered the retirement of his armies, threatened with disaster at the hands of the Czarist forces. Several months later Franz Joseph was to sum up cogently what Berchtold must now have been thinking: "How on earth can we pursue even a tolerable foreign policy when we fight so badly."[41]

Just as Berchtold needed military victories to give him diplomatic success, Conrad could point to the military's need for allies. He could not win a war without sufficient men and that lack he attributed to Vienna's diplomatic failure in the Balkans. Without Bulgaria he had failed against the Serbs; unless Rumania threw in its lot with the Central Powers he would have no victory against the Russians. This, his position in mid-September, was supported by the German General Staff, which informed Hohenlohe through Jagow that with Rumanian

---

[40] Staatsarchiv, PA, box 499, no. 305, Conrad to Berchtold, 24 August 1914.

[41] Staatsarchiv, PA, box 499, unnumbered telegram, Berchtold to Conrad, 24 August 1914; no. 12, Berchtold to Baron Wladimir von Giesl, Austrian Foreign Office representative at Austrian military headquarters, 21 August; unnumbered secret note, Berchtold to Conrad, 8 September. See also Conrad, *Aus Meiner Dienstzeit*, 4:519, 520; Albert von Margutti, *The Emperor Francis Joseph and His Times*, p. 336. Margutti was an aide-de-camp of Franz Joseph.

aid the Russian campaign would surely be won. The German chiefs saw no sacrifice on the part of Austria as too much when weighed against the price of existence itself. They therefore believed that Austria-Hungary must leave nothing untried to win the participation of Rumanian troops. Kaiser Wilhelm wrote to Franz Joseph that Rumania was the real key to success against the Czar. He believed the burden was Austria's, remarking, "I hope your government succeeds in still winning Rumania for action. Then we can, God willing, expect a successful outcome to this difficult struggle." Berchtold, supported by Tisza, stood his ground and refused far-reaching concessions to the Bukarest government, not only because the latter's policy concerning military participation was highly ambiguous, but also because Czernin had reported that at best the Rumanians would only be able to allocate two army corps for a Russian campaign. Three more were available but those were guarding the Bulgarian border. Thus Rumanian participation at the moment would hardly be decisive.[42]

Conrad came to the conclusion that since diplomacy had not succeeded in obtaining the Balkan states as allies, there was only one way to win them—to defeat Russia by having Germany send reinforcements to the eastern front in large numbers. The Balkan question thus became an additional support to the arguments he presented against the German High Command's unwillingness to relegate the western front to a secondary position. Conrad steadfastly held to this view and since the Austrians failed to repulse the Russian armies in October and November, the Austrian chief of staff convinced Vienna that he was right. On November 13 Berchtold staunchly supported Conrad in a letter to Archduke Frederick. The foreign minister said Rumania would join their side on the basis of results, not promises, and that results depended on Falkenhayn sending enough German divisions to the east to allow for a major decision on this front. His remarks to Frederick were made by way of answering von Hindenburg's assertion that Rumania would join the Central Powers if Austria offered sufficient concessions in Transylvania.[43] Conrad carried the argument further when he went to Oppeln in December for talks with Falkenhayn. With extensive German support in the east they could not only defeat Russia in the field but destroy its pose as protector of the Balkan peoples. If Russia fell, its influence in the Balkans fell with it. The

[42] Staatsarchiv, PA, box 500, no. 4315, Foreign Office memorandum, Berchtold, 9 September 1914; no. 4392, daily report, Berchtold, 15 September; no. 534, Hohenlohe in Berlin to Berchtold, 19 September; Conrad, *Aus Meiner Dienstzeit*, 4:769, 785.

[43] Staatsarchiv, PA, box 499, unnumbered resume of a Berchtold-Conrad meeting, 2 November 1914; Conrad, *Aus Meiner Dienstzeit*, 5:474, 486, 487.

implication for the future of the Central Powers in this area was obvious.[44]

The Balkan question produced further disparity between the two commanders concerning allocation of troops. The entry of Turkey on the side of Germany and Austria, its need for munitions, and the failure of Potiorek's forces to defeat Serbia in order to open the necessary supply route by rail to Constantinople, constituted the basis of the argument. Zimmermann advised Falkenhayn in a long *Denkschrift* on November 14. After considering the fact that Turkey might be forced out of the war if the munitions were not sent, he asserted that another campaign mounted in Serbia, to which Germany would contribute 30,000 troops, would bring Bulgaria in. The fact that Bulgaria had 400,000 men available for combat made it an attractive prize. Furthermore, if the Turks were not supplied, their increasing weakness would mean a possible hostile action by Bulgaria, aimed at seizing Adrianople or even Constantinople. The repercussions of such a move would lead the Rumanians and Greeks to join the Entente. The importance of a campaign in Serbia was therefore clear: without it, the loss of all the Balkan states for the Central Powers was quite possible.[45]

Falkenhayn, who had earlier in the month discussed the issue with Jagow, proved cold to the pressure of the German diplomatic corps. The general had defined the Serbian problem as an Austrian one. But apparently the force and comprehensiveness of Zimmermann's *Denkschrift* was enough to change Falkenhayn's mind, because on November 16 he told Conrad he was ready to support a special undertaking by Austria aimed at freeing the northeast corner of Serbia to open the Turkish transport route.[46]

The Austrian High Command unfortunately could not now consider relegating any more forces to the Serbian front. Conrad was facing a dangerous situation in the east, and at the moment he had all he could do to plug the holes in his line against the Russians. The problem of supplying additional Austrian units for the Serbian theater was nothing new. As early as September 30, in response to Berchtold's suggestion that reinforcements be allocated, Conrad wrote that he had thirty-eight and a half divisions deployed in the east and eleven in Serbia. There simply weren't any more to deploy! If this was the case in September, certainly it was so in November. Besides, Potiorek's campaign seemed to be resulting in a defeat of the Serbs; hence Potiorek could get along

[44] Conrad, *Aus Meiner Dienstzeit*, 5:819.

[45] Carl Mühlmann, *Oberste Heeresleitung und Balkan im Weltkrieg, 1914–1918*, pp. 56–58.

[46] Ibid., pp. 58–59; Germany, Reichsarchiv, *Der Weltkrieg*, 6, pt. 2:417–18.

with what he had. In another two weeks, however, Potiorek's forces were again routed and forced to retreat behind the Save River.[47]

The defeat in Serbia only made for increasing pressure on Conrad to mount a special offensive there. Urged by German leaders, both military and diplomatic, Berchtold had decided by November 24 that Serbia was perhaps more important than Russia. He therefore tried through the German Foreign Office to influence Falkenhayn to send troops to Poland so as to free Austrian units for the special campaign against the northeast corner of Serbia. When Conrad heard of this, he was furious since it meant that Berchtold had indirectly promised Berlin to allocate Austrian troops from the eastern front, and had done so without Conrad's prior approval. Clearly, the Foreign Office had gone over his head. He informed the foreign minister that any such shift of troops was impossible.[48]

Berchtold refused to backwater. He wrote to army headquarters, saying that any decision to allot troops for the southwestern theater would remain the jurisdiction of the High Command. But while he understood things were not very favorable on the Polish front at the moment, they might improve in the near future. Given such a possibility, it was his own duty to inform Conrad of the great political significance attached to a victorious operation in Serbia. It was more than a question of getting munitions to Turkey, or of impressing the Bulgarians sufficiently to win them as active allies. The Rumanian scene was critical and if the Central Powers wished to keep Rumania from joining the Entente, the Rumanians would have to be given the impression that Austria-Hungary was strong. The key was a success against Serbia; this would also free the armies fighting there and allow for their transport to the east. Then Rumania would decide not to take hostile action. The strengthening of forces in the Carpathians would convince Bukarest that a war against the Monarchy would be no promenade.[49]

The argument between the two men continued into December. To Conrad von Hötzendorf the matter was elementary, and on December 21 he laid out the whole picture for the foreign minister, hoping the latter would finally obtain a "true" perspective on military affairs. The chief of staff simply could not understand why the Ballhausplatz was so fascinated by Serbia when there was no question in his own mind that a defeat of Russia would decide the entire war. Berchtold talked of

[47] Staatsarchiv, PA, box 499, unnumbered resume of Berchtold-Conrad meeting, 2 November 1914; Conrad, *Aus Meiner Dienstzeit*, 5:27; Churchill, *Unknown War*, pp. 264–69.

[48] Conrad, *Aus Meiner Dienstzeit*, 5:596, 597.

[49] Staatsarchiv, PA, box 499, no. 5389, Berchtold to von Giesl, 26 November 1914.

a decision against the Russians in the immediate future but Conrad had no expectation of this. A few days later, when Czernin visited army headquarters and warned that both Rumania and Italy would declare war against the Monarchy by spring if a great success had not occurred in the field, Conrad threw up his hands. As a soldier he knew only that he could not win a war simultaneously against the Russians, the Serbs, Rumania, and Italy. It had long been his impression that the problems he faced were caused by the failure of the diplomats. On December 30, meeting Berchtold for personal discussions, he considered military campaigns rather than diplomacy. He refused to budge on the question of Serbia. Falkenhayn could talk of being willing to send troops for such an operation but if the Germans had troops to spare, they ought to send them to Poland. It was there that the decision would come. On this note the matter ended, at least temporarily. Berchtold and the Germans had to be content with Conrad's forecast in late December—a campaign in Serbia could not be mounted until March, 1915, at the earliest.[50]

In retrospect it would seem that the first five months of the war had produced only conflict and hostility within the camp of the Central Powers: conflict and hostility between Falkenhayn and his eastern command, Falkenhayn and the Wilhelmstrasse, Falkenhayn and Conrad, and Conrad and the Austrian Foreign Office. It would seem, too, that such conflict could only demoralize the German and Austrian war effort. Yet, this did not occur, for while various government and military leaders disagreed in their interpretations of the best diplomatic and military measures to be pursued, the disagreement was not permitted to obscure the chief goal—to win the war. Squabblings might be bitter but they were not allowed to paralyze military endeavors.

[50] Conrad, *Aus Meiner Dienstzeit*, 5:851, 854, 910, 911, 520, 956.

Chapter 12

A Year
of Success, 1915

Nineteen fourteen closed with Germany and Austria doing little more than holding their own in the east. In Serbia successive Austrian offensives had been destroyed by the determined and clever counter-thrusts of the Serb commander, Putnik. In contradistinction to the preceding five months, 1915 was to be the best year of the war for the Central Powers. By August the entire Russian line was shattered and the Czar's armies sent reeling in a great retreat. By December, Serbian resistance was destroyed and the country conquered. These victories were not easily achieved.

Pless, Teschen, and the Foreign Offices

In early January, 1915, several meetings took place in Berlin and at German headquarters. Those who emphasized the eastern war theater emerged supreme. Conrad had met with Falkenhayn on January 1, seeking to impress upon him the need for a new eastern offensive, but he had failed. Behind Conrad's insistence were several sound reasons. The Russians had continued to press their attacks in the Carpathians and their siege of the key Galician fortress city of Przemysl appeared to be on the verge of succeeding. The Austrians therefore wished to mount a campaign which would clear the Carpathians once and for all, believing that with luck they would turn an advance into a decision. It was not merely the threat to Hungary or the desire to relieve Przemysl that preoccupied Conrad. Reports filtering in from his military attaché in Rome told him of the continued preparations of the Italians, whose first- and second-line troops now numbered 800,000. All signs pointed to Italy's being ready for war by the end of March. The Austrian High Command did not doubt that the Italian action would be directed against the Central Powers. There were also reports of an open accord between Italy and Rumania and this meant an attack by two new enemies that would make Austria's position hopeless. The only way to prepare for this threat was to attack the Russians and rapidly succeed against them. The Serbian front could be kept quiescent; no offensive

275

could be mounted here by either side for the next two months because of the ice on the Save and Danube rivers. The forces there were more than enough for adequate defense; Conrad felt so sure of this he was ready to transfer three divisions to the Carpathians.[1]

The Austrian chief of staff was not alone in his unshakeable conviction that the crucial action lay in the east. Hindenburg and Ludendorff not only supported his request but supplemented it with their own idea. Aside from sending replacements to the Carpathians they wanted to mount an additional and simultaneous attack from the north, from Prussia. The complete plan envisaged a huge pincers, the prongs of which would close from a distance of 600 kilometers. As Conrad put it, it was an offensive planned in the "grand manner."[2]

General Falkenhayn weighed the possibilities of the venture and decided against it. He had been carefully massing and training four new corps of men and he envisaged using them in the west against the English and French either in January or February. The situation of the Austrians was not particularly good in the Carpathians but in his own view there was really no emergency there. The relief of Przemysl was desirable but since in the final analysis it would mean nothing for the general war situation it was not worth the expenditure of the troops it would require. The giant pincers movement as conceived by Hindenburg and Ludendorff was enough to fire the imagination of any professional soldier, but Falkenhayn's cold analysis discarded the idea as impracticable. The distances to be covered and the limited troops available made success highly questionable. While the eastern commanders had their eye on the four new corps, Falkenhayn refused to give them up. The only result of such an offensive would be local successes and the exhaustion of all the troops he now had available. He therefore rejected the whole maneuver.[3]

Hindenburg now reached the end of his patience. Supported by Ludendorff, Bethmann-Hollweg, and the Austrian chief of staff, he appealed directly to the Kaiser to rescind Falkenhayn's decision. Wilhelm, impressed by the arguments of his eastern commanders and by the political implications of a Russian offensive as it had been outlined

[1] Austria, Kriegsarchiv, Conrad-Falkenhayn Korrespondenz (hereafter cited as C.-F. K.), Russische Front, 1915, no. 5999, Conrad to Foreign Ministry, 5 January; Max Hoffmann, *Der Krieg der Versäumten Gelegenheiten*, pp. 89–90; Eric von Ludendorff, *My War Memories*, 1:113; Erich von Falkenhayn, *The German General Staff and Its Decisions 1914-1916*, p. 58; Winston S. Churchill, *The Unknown War: The Eastern Front*, p. 277.

[2] Wilhelm Groener, *Lebenserinnerungen*, p. 212; Paul von Hindenburg, *Aus Meinem Leben*, pp. 104–5; Churchill, *Unknown War*, p. 289; Staatsarchiv, PA, box 499, no. 372, Conrad to Berchtold, 15 January 1915.

[3] Falkenhayn, *German General Staff*, pp. 59–61.

by Bethmann and the Wilhelmstrasse, decided against Falkenhayn.[4] The westerners had lost.

Conrad had originally asked that four to five divisions be sent from the German Ninth Army to reinforce his attack in the Carpathians. On January 8 he received word from Falkenhayn that his general plan had been approved but that only three and a half divisions could be allocated and these would operate under a German general, Alexander von Linsingen, who would have equal authority with his Austrian colleagues. It is significant that while the bitter argument between the German military leaders had been solved by the Kaiser's decision on January 9, they had not aired their family squabbles before their Austrian ally. A full week later Conrad was still writing telegrams to Falkenhayn trying to convince him that *all* available German reinforcements should be sent to Prussia for a simultaneous attack from the north. Falkenhayn now graciously consented and Conrad graciously accepted.[5]

It took several weeks for the Austrians to make their necessary troop dispersements and for von Linsingen, with what was now called the German Southern Army, to take up his position. On January 23 the attack in the Carpathians began. Seemingly successful at first when the enemy was driven from the whole Carpathian ridge, the offensive ground to a halt before Russian counterattacks launched in mountain snows throat-deep. Although the Russians were outweighed by the Austrian and German supremacy of ten divisions, they continued to frustrate Conrad's attempts to gather real momentum. The Austrian general repeatedly called for still more support from the German High Command, and while Falkenhayn did send an additional division he refused the subsequent requests.[6]

The Germans' reluctance to pour their limited strength into a doubtful venture was quite understandable, considering the attack they had themselves begun from East Prussia on February 7, the Winter Battle of Masuria. The immediate objective of the strike was to cut the

[4] Churchill, *Unknown War*, pp. 273, 276, 278, 280.

[5] C.-F. K., Russische Front, 1915, no. 6005, Conrad to Hindenburg, 5 January; no. 480, Falkenhayn to Conrad, 8 January; no. 6347, Conrad to Falkenhayn, 16 January; no. 490, Falkenhayn to Conrad, 17 January; no. 6395, Conrad to Falkenhayn, 18 January.

[6] Germany, Reichsarchiv, *Der Weltkrieg, 1914–18*, 7:89; for a detailed description of the Carpathian battles at this time see ibid., pp. 89–116; C.-F. K., Russische Front, 1915, no. 7071, Conrad to Falkenhayn, 11 February; no. 7151, Conrad to Falkenhayn, 14 February; no. 7191, Conrad to General Alexander von Linsingen, 15 February; no. 7479, Conrad to Falkenhayn, 24 February; no. 7508, copy of Falkenhayn's refusal to send further troops, 25 February; A. A. Brussilov, *A Soldier's Notebook, 1914–1918*, pp. 72–139.

Russian communication lines to Kovno. Then the new German Tenth Army in conjunction with the Eighth was to wheel south upon the Russians entrenched before the Augustow Forest, slightly northeast of Lyck. The thrust went well and by February 25 Lyck had been taken, Kovno and Grodno were threatened, and the entire Russian Tenth Army had been surrounded and annihilated in the forest region. The attack had been mounted in the course of blizzards and frightful cold, but the sufferings were, in the eyes of the commanders, worth the result. In the blood-red snows of northern Poland the Russian dead totalled 100,000 and aside from 11 captured generals, 110,000 enemy troops had been taken prisoner. The victory notwithstanding, eastern commanders could not declare that they had succeeded from a strategic point of view. The results had been favorable but limited, and Falkenhayn's analysis of what would happen had proved correct. The jaws of the gigantic pincers had failed to shut. Falkenhayn must have thought about Hindenburg something similar to what Emperor Franz Joseph had earlier remarked about Conrad: "We cannot find any suitable sphere of activity for a chief of staff with such soaring plans. We would be far better off with a man who doesn't want to bridge the ocean."[7]

The next attempt to defeat Russia would not be made until the end of April but in the early months of 1915 diplomatic problems continued to concern the military. The increasing alienation of the Italians had led the Wilhelmstrasse to send von Bülow to Rome as early as December of 1914 in the hope that he might somehow satisfy Italian territorial aspirations. Such satisfaction could be achieved only at the expense of the Austrians. Bülow talked blithely about the cession of the Trentino but Austria refused to consider such an amputation. In January Berchtold was replaced by Burian, who proved immovable on the issue. In late January the new Austrian foreign minister visited German headquarters where he personally conversed with the Kaiser, Bethmann, and Jagow. In his report of this meeting he wrote, "I had once again to suffer all the complaints about our threatened collapse should Italy and Rumania attack us, since we, as well as Germany, could not counter them. This danger stood directly at our door if we did not buy Italian neutrality with a sacrifice."[8]

But Burian was not to be moved by such pleas. The Austrians had decided they could afford to wait and see how events developed.

[7] Ludendorff, *War Memories*, 1:117, 118, 123–27; Churchill, *Unknown War*, pp. 291, 293–300; Albert von Margutti, *The Emperor Francis Joseph and His Times*, p. 334. See map, p. 285.

[8] Staatsarchiv, PA, box 503, no. 686, report of conference by Burian, 27 January 1915.

Vienna had very few illusions about the Italians and believed they would declare war when they were ready. At the turn of 1915 they were not ready and Burian summed up his attitude by saying, "When someone points an unloaded pistol at my chest, I will not immediately give up my pocketbook. I wait until the pistol is loaded and until a decision is thus to be made." Falkenhayn was to observe cogently that if the Monarchy waited until the danger was imminent, it might very well be unable to meet that danger.[9]

Unsuccessful through direct contact with the Austrian foreign minister, the Germans had Falkenhayn try to prevail upon Conrad to use his influence. It was not difficult for the Wilhelmstrasse to push the German general in this direction, for indeed he had already talked with Burian, and so strongly that the latter had judged Falkenhayn "the source of the whole great alarm on the issue of Italy and Rumania." Falkenhayn had told him flatly that the Central Powers would break if faced with a million Italian troops. To make matters worse, he underscored the fact that Germany had no additional units to spare for an Italian campaign.[10]

When approached by his German colleague, the Austrian chief of staff proved as intractable as the foreign minister. On January 20 Conrad wrote that the purchase of Italian neutrality was "entirely impossible." He requested Germany to demonstrate the solidarity of the Central Powers by sending a small contingent of troops to the Italian border. Such a demonstration would prove that any attack on Austria-Hungary meant a war with Germany, too. Falkenhayn immediately rejected the suggestion, stating that such a move would be seen by the Italians as a definite German threat and would cause the negotiations in Rome to break down. Conrad's answer to this was the assertion that if the German government thought it could pacify the Italians through territorial concessions at the Dual Monarchy's expense, it was quite wrong. Austria saw the negotiations as totally worthless. Conrad and Burian were agreed that in the matter of Italy the eleventh hour was not at hand and therefore things could be allowed to swing on the hinge of military successes.[11] This last remark was made a few days before the Austrian attack commenced in the Carpathians. The

[9] Margutti, *Emperor Francis Joseph*, p. 343; Count Joseph von Stürgkh, *Im Deutschen Grossen Hauptquartier*, pp. 113, 118; W. W. Gottlieb, *Studies in Secret Diplomacy in the First World War*, pp. 240, 284, 286, 300–301; Austria, Kriegsarchiv, Conrad Archiv, Folio B-7, report of conference at Teschen, 20 February 1915.

[10] Staatsarchiv, PA, box 503, no. 686, report of Burian, 27 January 1915.

[11] C.-F. K., Russische Front, 1915, no. 6474, Conrad to Falkenhayn, 20 January; no. 502, Falkenhayn to Conrad, 21 January; no. 6509, Conrad to Falkenhayn, 22 January.

failure of that offensive, the subsequent counterthrusts of the Russians in March aimed at breaking through into Transylvania, and the bombardment of the Dardanelles in the middle of that month made the Austrians change their tone. These events produced a negative reaction in Rumania and Bulgaria and brought into sharper focus the need for a Serbian campaign to supply the Turks. It was therefore necessary for Burian to soften his approach concerning Italy and to discuss less reluctantly concrete territorial concessions with the Italian government, something he had already started on March 9.[12]

From the time he took office Burian staunchly agreed with the Austrian chief of staff that the general struggle could be decided in the east. But by March, Burian believed the decision against Russia could not be obtained in the near future and he strongly urged Conrad to turn to the Serbian theater once again. In the foreign minister's opinion, such a campaign would not only solve the munitions transport problem for the Turks but would also have a very favorable effect on the Balkan states—particularly Bulgaria and Rumania. Burian took an extremely tactful approach, telling Conrad he had no desire to meddle in military affairs which were obviously not his forte, but he did feel strongly that it was his duty as foreign minister to point out why the proposed Serbian action was essential from a political standpoint. He was acutely aware of the safety factors without which a new operation in Serbia would be impossible. He realized that the eastern front had to be so strongly fortified that Hungary would be completely safe from a Russian breakthrough into Transylvania. And he knew that a Serbian campaign would depend on his own diplomacy being successful in Italy. Without an accord there to eliminate the threat of a sudden Italian attack, a Serbian offensive could not be executed.[13]

General von Falkenhayn, if somewhat less tactfully, also wrote to Conrad advocating an offensive against the Serbs. This he believed could be a successful and quick campaign. Spurred on by the worries of the Wilhelmstrasse concerning Italy and the Balkans, he began in March to press his Austrian colleague more strongly on the two questions of Italy and Serbia—an exertion which continued for months. In his opinion there was nothing to be realized from a continued operation in the Carpathians; he therefore advocated going on the defensive against the Russians and transferring attention to the

---

[12] Gottlieb, *Secret Diplomacy*, pp. 309–11.

[13] Staatsarchiv, PA, box 499, unnumbered instruction, Burian to Count Douglas Thurn, Foreign Office representative at Austrian army headquarters, 28 March 1915. Here Burian summarizes his whole point of view from the time he entered his post.

southwest. Reports in his possession showed that the attacks by the Entente on the Dardanelles might succeed in winning Bulgaria and Rumania for the enemy, to say nothing of what those attacks meant to Turkish continuance in the war. The Central Powers, therefore, had to mount a Serbian offensive to get munitions to Constantinople and to impress the Balkan peoples with German and Austrian strength. A rapid shift of focus from the Carpathians to the Danube was in order. While Bulgarian participation was desirable from the standpoint of available troops, it was hardly essential. Germany and Austria could do the job alone. And if they found it impossible to defeat Serbia completely, an occupation of the vital northeast corner of the country would be quite enough to solve their problems regarding Turkey and to break the communication line between the Serbs and Russia, and the Serbs and Rumania.[14]

Falkenhayn hammered away at the Italian problem. During March, he refused Conrad's request for additional troops in the Carpathians. This was not the important issue, he said. What was really necessary was the success of political negotiations going on with Rome. Germany and Austria had to win Italy and Rumania, too, so that they would either join the Central Powers or would at least be seen by the Entente as "unsalvageable." Both states could be won if "our political leaders are conscious of what is at stake," and that consciousness was something which both he and Conrad must work to bring about. What he really wanted was to have Conrad bring his own influence into play with Vienna for purposes of winning the Italians.[15]

Conrad's reaction to all of this was largely negative. To Burian and Falkenhayn both, he wrote that an Austrian offensive against Serbia was now simply out of the question. The Russians were continually attacking on the Carpathian wall and the Austrians could not hope to hold them without German aid. No one wanted a Serbian offensive more than he but it would require eight to ten fresh divisions, and unless Germany was willing to assign replacements to the eastern front, he could not transfer such a group to the Serbian theater. Moreover, he saw Bulgarian participation in the campaign as essential, since "under no condition can we begin alone again." Conrad rejected the idea that his armies could go on the defensive in the Carpathians with impunity; his front there was weakened and the Russians persistently threatened to break through into Transylvania. Suppose he withdrew troops from the east and began an attack on the Serbs, and suppose also the Serbian

[14] C.-F. K., Balkan, no. 617-01-b, Falkenhayn to Conrad, 21 March 1915.
[15] C.-F. K., Italien, no. 571, Falkenhayn to Conrad, 10 March 1915; Russische Front, 1915, no. 587, Falkenhayn to Conrad, 15 March.

front stagnated. Then certainly the Russian armies would sweep into Hungary and in the wake of their success lead the Rumanians and Bulgarians to join the Entente. As far as the Italians were concerned, he had begun early in March to back Falkenhayn in working for positive negotiations, but by the beginning of April he was convinced that the Italians would break off their talks and make war against the Monarchy. He had reached this conclusion because he knew that Italy was continuing to build its armed strength and was sending its troops to the Austrian borders. He therefore began to think in terms of minimum numbers of units necessary to guard Austria against an Italian invasion. Since Austria had no reserves to spare, he asked Falkenhayn if seven German divisions could be sent there.[16]

Falkenhayn replied that he had no troops available to send against Italy. The solution, he said, lay exclusively in the hands of Vienna, which ought to give the Italians what they wanted without any argument and settle with them later after the major enemies of the Central Powers had been shattered. Conrad was quick to point out that he himself desired a peaceful solution of the Italian affair. Unfortunately, the Italians wanted war. And if the Monarchy gave Rome the territorial concessions it demanded, that is, the Tyrol and Trentino, this would not prevent a conflict. It was clear to him that Italy would attempt to drive into the heart of the Monarchy itself. Concessions would only serve to put Italian troops on the doorstep of Austria's heartland. It was certainly true that a war with the Italians at the present time was highly undesirable, in fact impossible, given the overall military situation, but Conrad warned that they had to beware of "Italian perfidy." There was one thing which in his estimation would hold back the Italians—a rapid and victorious military campaign. Serbia was out because Bulgaria would not commit itself to help. The western front offered no possibilities. There was only one chance for success—another offensive against the Russians.[17]

Falkenhayn had at his disposal some fourteen new divisions which he had developed as reserves, hoping again to use them in the west. But conditions on the western front were not now favorable for producing any great victory; Falkenhayn could employ his reserves more profit-

[16] C.-F. K., Balkan, no. 8273, Conrad to Falkenhayn, 22 March 1915; Italien, no. 7957, Conrad to Falkenhayn, 11 March; no. 8625, Conrad to Falkenhayn, 1 April; no. 8657, Conrad to Burian, 1 April; no. 8786, Conrad to Falkenhayn, 5 April; Staatsarchiv, PA, box 499, no. 8557, Conrad to Burian, 30 March.

[17] C.-F. K., Italien, no. 675, Falkenhayn to Conrad, 6 April 1915; no. 667, Falkenhayn to Conrad, 1 April; no. 8657, Conrad to Falkenhayn, 1 April; no. 8822, Conrad to Falkenhayn, 6 April.

ably elsewhere. The reports coming from the Austrians spoke of an ever-blackening picture in the Carpathians, where a successful Russian offensive was expected more every day. Although Conrad suggested on April 6 another outflanking movement against the Czar's armies, the German chief went back to an idea which Conrad had presented earlier: a thrust directly through the Russian line, to be delivered between Gorlice and Tarnow, two points located just north of the Carpathians in western Galicia. If the attack was to have any effect on the general war situation it would have to be planned as a major offensive, not simply to relieve the hard pressed Austrians but to cripple permanently the striking power of the Russian army. Falkenhayn decided on just this and wired Conrad he was sending at least eight divisions.[18]

By May 1 the new German Eleventh Army and the Austrian Fourth, totalling eighteen divisions in all, were ready for the strike. The greatest care had been taken to keep the concentration of the Eleventh Army a secret from the enemy. Hindenburg had provided diversionary action in the north and in the west a gas attack was made on Ypres. After a tremendous artillery barrage, the German and Austrian troops under the unified command of von Mackensen began the battle on May 2. Forty-eight hours later the Russians, staggering under the blow, broke and fell back. The retreat produced an untenable situation; along a 100-mile front three Russian armies retired between Gorlice and the Upper Vistula, and those further north and south followed suit. In short, the whole Russian line had been unhinged. After long months of frustration German and Austrian generals had the break they wanted. Throughout the spring and summer of 1915 they kept the machine moving, kept the Russians off balance, and maintained the advance. On May 15 Mackensen's forces reached the San. Przemysl was retaken at the beginning of June and on June 22 Lemberg fell, to be followed by Rava Ruska, causing a further retreat of the enemy behind the Bug River. Further north the decision was made to clear all of Poland, and Hindenburg's forces took Lublin and Kholm in July, and Warsaw in August, and forced the exhausted Russians to retire upon Vilna. By the time the offensive halted in September the battlefront of the Central Powers in the east ran in an almost straight line from Dvinsk in the north to Czernowitz in the south—an accomplishment which had been

---

[18] Falkenhayn, *German General Staff*, pp. 80, 82, 87–88, 92; Hoffmann, *Der Krieg*, p. 103; Churchill, *Unknown War*, pp. 306–8; C.-F. K., Russische Front, 1915, no. 716–0–1b, Falkenhayn to Conrad, 13 April; August von Cramon, *Quatre Ans au G.Q.G. Austro-Hongrois pendant la Guerre Mondiale*, pp. 30–33.

Conrad's fondest dream. A victory against the enemy had indeed been achieved in the "grand manner."[19]

Military and Diplomatic Interplay—Italy and Rumania

The victory in the east took months, and while it was being achieved there were many problems and issues to be discussed, fought over, and solved.

Once Falkenhayn had decided on the Gorlice-Tarnow offensive, he redoubled his efforts to influence the Austrians to make concessions to Italy. On April 19 he wrote to Conrad pointing out that since the planned campaign in the east would require every trooper they had, any decision by Italy to begin action in the field would be an "almost insufferable burden." Open hostilities must therefore be avoided "by all means."[20]

The Ballhausplatz and Austrian headquarters at Teschen were, however, already in agreement that the Italian negotiations would probably fail. Burian had written to Conrad on April 17, saying that while he would continue to treat with Rome, the military preparations being made by Italy gave evidence of an eventual attack. On this basis he believed Conrad had the right to ask their German ally for forces to help oppose a belligerent Italy. It is significant that the foreign minister now talked not of concrete success in his negotiations but of being able to delay Italian war participation until the Central Powers had disposed of their enemies on other fronts. It was now a question of winning as much time as they could. Nor did Conrad let Vienna forget just how important this was. He repeatedly wrote to Burian in these April days stressing that the coming operation in the east would permit no diversion of forces if it was to succeed. He realized that Austrian interests were much at stake in the Italian question, but the only path available was to try to reduce the extent of concessions and somehow pacify Rome, at least temporarily. As late as May 5 he was still writing to Burian along these lines, declaring: "If the war is to end victoriously for us, war with Italy must be unconditionally avoided."[21]

[19] Groener, *Lebenserinnerungen*, pp. 227, 229; Falkenhayn, *German General Staff*, pp. 96, 94, 100; Churchill, *Unknown War*, pp. 309–15; C.-F. K., Russische Front, 1915, no. 754, Falkenhayn to Conrad, 22 April; Ludendorff, *War Memories*, 1:145, 146, 156, 160–61, 166, 170; Hoffmann, *Der Krieg*, pp. 106, 109–10. For the military details of the eastern campaign in the spring and summer of 1915, see Germany, Reichsarchiv, *Der Weltkrieg*, vol. 8; Austria, Bundesministerium für Heereswesen, *Österreich-Ungarns Letzter Krieg*, vols. 2 and 3. See map, p. 285.

[20] C.-F. K., Italien, no. 741–0–1b, Falkenhayn to Conrad, 19 April 1915.

[21] C.-F. K., Italien, no. 150, Burian to Conrad, 17 April 1915; no. 9229, Conrad

RIGA

DVINSK

BALTIC SEA

KÖNIGSBERG

KOVNO

VILNA

DANZIG

GERMANY

GRODNO

RUSSIA

THORN

Bug R.

WARSAW

BREST LITOVSK

PINSK

LINE OF FARTHEST ADVANCE

Vistula R.

LUBLIN

KHOLM

San R.

DUBNO

CRACOW

TARNOW

RAVA-RUSKA

GORLICE

LEMBERG

PRZEMYSL

HUNGARY

CZERNOWITZ

THE GORLICE-TARNOW
BREAKTHROUGH

— — — — Line of April 1915
-·-·-·-·-·- Line of August 1915
————— Line of September 1915
————➤ Hindenburg's Pincers Plan

Conrad, realizing the shaky ground upon which peace with Italy still existed, continued to press the German chief of staff for a precise commitment of troops for the Italian border, and Falkenhayn just as persistently continued to decline. By so doing, the Germans intended to keep before the Austrians the specter of an indefensible border, something which would force them to conclude their negotiations with the Italians on a positive level. To assure Conrad that Germany was not ignoring the Monarchy, Falkenhayn tried to smooth over his refusal of troops by writing, "Your Excellency knows from experience how I stand with regard to you and your situation, which in my view is also ours." And on May 1 he reiterated the appeal that Conrad von Hötzendorf "as a comrade in this struggle and as a German" use his influence on the Emperor and Burian to conclude with Italy immediately. The Austrian commander was just as single-minded and while Falkenhayn's urging had its effect, Conrad nevertheless answered on May 4 that he still wanted to know "if, when, and in what strength Germany will provide military forces against Italy." It was not until May 7, when talks between the two were held at Teschen, that the Germans finally agreed to contribute forces for a possible conflict, though the number of troops was made to depend on the general situation.[22] In light of the fact that Italy had signed the Secret Treaty of London with the Entente on April 26, Conrad's insistence that they prepare against Italy reflected the Austrians' keener awareness of what could and what could not be expected from that quarter.

The Austrians were not greatly surprised when Italy declared war against the Dual Monarchy on May 23. Burian had earlier told Conrad he thought he could hold off the Italians until approximately mid-May and his estimate proved correct. In spite of the declaration of war, the Austrians were saved from catastrophe by two facts: the breakthrough at Gorlice-Tarnow had freed Hungary from imminent invasion, and the Italians took considerable time to begin an offensive. The successes in the east allowed Conrad to transfer five divisions from the Russian front which, along with two from Serbia and one from Germany, provided a minimal defense. Against the eight divisions of the Central Powers there were massed eighteen Italian. In spite of superior numbers, the forces of General Luigi Cadorna got nowhere; they were so

to Falkenhayn, 18 April; enclosure to no. 9229, Conrad to Burian, 18 April; no. 9883, Conrad to Burian, 5 May.

[22] C.-F. K., Italien, no. 714-0-1b, Falkenhayn to Conrad, 10 April 1915; Russische Front, 1915, no. 7720, Falkenhayn to Conrad, 1 May; Italien, no. 9763, Conrad to Falkenhayn, 4 May; no. 9970, Conrad to General Artur Bolfras, Military Chancellery in Vienna, 9 May.

hampered by mountainous terrain and the persistent opposition of the Austrians that the Italian front remained stabilized until the following year.[23]

That Italy and Germany did not immediately declare war on each other was of great significance. Germany depended on Italy for the importing of needed raw materials from foreign countries, so that it was expedient for the Germans to maintain the Italian entryway if they possibly could. The German-Italian break did not come for fifteen months. This situation was not calculated to make for amicable relations between the Austrian and German chiefs of staff, because Conrad felt the Germans were shirking their responsibility. When in June, Conrad heard that German troops were ordered not to cross the Italian border and that in any fight occurring between German and Italian units in the Tyrol, the latter must first provoke a conflict, he sent a telegram to Falkenhayn: "Your Excellency would incur special thanks from me if future direct orders to German commanders under Austro-Hungarian Supreme Command were as infrequently sent as they are from here to Austro-Hungarian commanders fighting with the German armies."[24]

The rebuke reflected the irritation he had felt for a month over the situation on the eastern front where, because of German insistence, General Mackensen had been given control of the Galician operation. Mackensen was made subject not to Teschen but to the German High Command, a condition which put Conrad in the shadow, but about which he could do nothing if the Germans were to take up an offensive against Russia. Austrian army commanders in the east found themselves subject to German orders and Conrad agreed because he had to. Now, with the Austrian Archduke Eugene as commander of the Italian front, Conrad wanted the same authority for Austria in the southwest as existed for the Germans in the east. In the case of the Italian theater the issue was clearly much more than a question of command. If Eugene was given complete control of German troops there, he would commit them, creating an official war situation between Germany and Italy. Falkenhayn answered that he quite agreed with the Austrian chief of staff when it came to purely military matters; he had no desire to bypass Conrad, for he had personally told him of the orders which had gone out to the German units from Pless. On the other hand the

[23] C.-F. K., Italien, no. 9229, Conrad to Falkenhayn, 18 April 1915; Falkenhayn, *German General Staff*, pp. 106, 108, 109; Germany, Reichsarchiv, *Der Weltkrieg*, 8:31.
[24] C.-F. K., Italien, no. 2076, Falkenhayn to Conrad, 4 June 1915; no. 11170, Conrad to Falkenhayn, 4 June.

political situation was of such great importance that he himself "was directly responsible for the transmission of these orders at the correct time."[25] Once again, Conrad could do nothing but accept the situation.

The one instance where Conrad's wishes proved crucial was that of Serbia. In May, a few days before Italy declared war on Austria, Bethmann-Hollweg contacted Falkenhayn, stating that if the Italians attacked and if the projected campaign against the Serbs was given up, the Bulgarians and Rumanians would probably join the Entente. The Turks had to be relieved, for the attack on Gallipoli had begun in April and Turkish munitions were extremely low. If the Turks fell, the Bulgarians and Rumanians would turn upon Turkey to satisfy their territorial ambitions. Falkenhayn agreed that the situation was dangerous and again pressed Conrad to mount a campaign against the Serbs. The Austrian general had talked of releasing ten Austrian and ten German divisions from the eastern front, where things at the moment were going well, but he wanted them sent to the Italian theater. Falkenhayn, calculating that it would take the Italians four weeks to complete their preparations after a war declaration and another four weeks to fight their way to a point where they really threatened the Monarchy, suggested a lightning-fast offensive against Serbia. If they used seventeen divisions the whole thing would be over by the first of July, before Italy really posed a problem, and then most of these divisions could be turned against the new enemy.[26]

The plan was bold and if Falkenhayn's calculations proved correct and the action was successful, the problem of the Balkans and Turkey would be solved within sixty days. But Austrian headquarters refused to go along. Conrad still saw Bulgarian troops as a vital component for any Serbian offensive, but Bulgaria consistently refused to participate. Now, at a time when Austria was threatened by full-scale war with Italy, Falkenhayn was suggesting they go it alone. A Serb campaign would require at least four weeks to prepare, the Serbian army would fight ferociously as it had in the past, and while the Central Powers bogged down there, the Italians would strike into inner Austria because of the weakened defenses on the frontier. The Italian advance would mean Rumania's joining in against the Central Powers. Bulgaria would

[25] C.-F. K., Russische Front, 1915, no. 716-o-1b, Falkenhayn to Conrad, 13 April 1915. At this time Falkenhayn in a peremptory fashion laid down his wishes, declaring that the Eleventh German and the Fourth Austrian armies on the Gorlice-Tarnow line would be under a unified command and "in this case naturally a German one." Churchill, *Unknown War*, p. 313; C.-F. K., Italien, also numbered as 2076, Falkenhayn to Conrad, 5 June 1915.

[26] Carl Mühlmann, *Oberste Heeresleitung und Balkan im Weltkrieg, 1914–1918*, pp. 107–8; C.-F. K., Italien, no. 1355, Falkenhayn to Conrad, 19 May 1915.

have no choice but to go along, and Germany and Austria would be faced with new defeats rather than victories. On these bases he wished to remain on the defensive in Serbia, to push on in the east, and to allocate forces from the Russian front when the Italians threatened Austria's "inner zone." Conrad's interpretation prevailed and the Germans were forced to delay their Serbian plan.[27] They could not go it alone.

Once the Italians had declared war, the Central Powers feared the entry of Rumania more than they previously had. Falkenhayn and Conrad agreed on one thing—that the entry of Rumania as an enemy would constitute an intolerable military situation. Both men would have been delighted with Rumanian cooperation, since a sudden addition of 400,000 fresh troops would have allowed for great freedom in reallocation of the divisions now fighting the Russians. Apparently, they assumed that once Rumania had joined in, its chief of staff would shunt about his troops as he was told. Falkenhayn, hearing that Burian was taking a cool attitude toward Bukarest at a moment when things were going well on the eastern front, warned that a sudden reverse might occur. If, he reasoned, the Rumanians believed that they would be courted only in the case of extreme emergency, their price would immeasurably increase. Thus he wanted Burian to act now and concluded that "Our situation is really too serious to leave any chance unused." Conrad concurred and in writing to the Ballhausplatz stressed the urgency of avoiding a Rumanian attack. Should this happen, he warned Burian, "The war is lost for us." If an actual Rumanian commitment did not materialize, Vienna must at least obtain benevolent neutrality by offering territorial concessions.[28]

Militarily, the one thing that kept Rumania from joining the enemy was the great success of the Central Powers after the Gorlice-Tarnow breakthrough. It was Falkenhayn who sought to exploit these victories. Since he was unable to mount a Serbian attack because of the Austrian chief's refusal, and since he seemed to get nowhere on the question of enticing Rumania to ally itself against the Entente, he now suggested that Vienna persuade Bratianu at least to reopen the Rumanian railroad route and in this way solve the Turkish munitions problem. Conrad

[27] C.-F. K., Italien, no. 10450, Conrad to Falkenhayn, 20 May 1915; no. 10635, Conrad to Falkenhayn, 23 May.

[28] Austria, Kriegsarchiv, Armee Oberkommando, Operationen (hereafter cited as AOK Op.), folio 551, unnumbered telegram, Falkenhayn to Conrad, 2 June 1915; no. 11051, Conrad to Falkenhayn, 2 June; no. 11784, Conrad to Burian, 19 June; no. 67, secret, Conrad to Burian, 20 June; C.-F. K., Balkan, no. 10618, Conrad to Burian, 23 May; no. 11784 and attachments, Falkenhayn to Conrad, 18 June.

proved amenable and did what he could with Burian. Falkenhayn, meanwhile, talked directly with Count Tisza in Berlin on June 17, attempting to change the Hungarian prime minister's attitude on concessions being offered for Rumanian aid. The general believed that Rumanian aspirations to Transylvania and the Bukovina should be satisfied. If the Central Powers won the war, the Dual Monarchy would be so strong that it would not matter what had been granted to the Rumanian government.[29] He failed to win his point.

Both Burian and Tisza continued to hold their ground, stating that concessions would be a sign of weakness. Falkenhayn responded by writing Conrad that this position was so invalid as to be unworthy of an opposing view. He urged the Austrian chief to convince his own people that "we cannot lose a day" in resolving the matter. Conrad did continue to write to Burian but his own arguments were colored by his being an Austrian patriot as well as a general. He therefore did not in the final analysis approve of his German colleague's largesse when it came to territorial grants. The previous March Conrad had suggested that concessions be offered to Bratianu in Bessarabia and in small sections of Transylvania in return for Rumania's joining against the enemy. Falkenhayn now urged that the Bukovina be given up simply for Rumanian neutrality. The Bukovina in exchange for mere transit of Turkish munitions Conrad saw as much too high a price, nor could he accept sweeping grants of territory in Hungary, even for participation. The general need not have worried, because this was precisely the point of view taken by the Ballhausplatz. On July 11 Burian replied, agreeing with Conrad's opinion in no uncertain terms.[30]

The Rumanian problem remained unresolved. Falkenhayn failed in what he had hoped to accomplish by working through Austrian military headquarters, a through passage to Turkey. On the other hand, Rumania made no move to join the Entente and for the moment the German and Austrian military could breathe a bit more easily.

The Bulgarian Military Convention and the Serbian Campaign

It was in that same month of July, 1915, that serious arrangements finally began for what was to be a highly successful Serbian campaign. In the east, although the Central Powers had rolled forward from

[29] C.-F. K., Balkan, Falkenhayn to Conrad, 2 June 1915; the telegram is attached to no. 11051, Conrad to Burian, 2 June; no. 11784, Falkenhayn to Conrad, 18 June.
[30] AOK Op., folio 551, no. 11890, Falkenhayn to Conrad, 21 June 1915; no. 8577, Conrad to Burian, 30 March; C.-F. K., Balkan, no. 11890, Falkenhayn to Conrad, 21 June; no. 11890/1, Conrad to Falkenhayn, 21 June; no. 12364, Conrad to Burian, 4 July; no. 236, Burian to Conrad, 11 July.

victory to victory, Russia was still far from collapse. Falkenhayn had never believed that a Russian collapse would occur, but he did believe it quite possible to nullify the offensive capacities of the Russian armies. By the end of July, the reports from the front and the location of the battle line on the map told him his goal had essentially been achieved. At various stages of the offensive he had suggested that the eastern front be stabilized, but on the insistence of Conrad, Hindenburg, and Ludendorff, and influenced by success, he had agreed to let the campaign go on. As July drew to a close he decided the Russian front must definitely be closed down in deference to other theaters.[31]

Falkenhayn's thinking was based on the fact that if they were going to relieve the Turks by taking the Serbian railroad connection, they would have to do so by September at the latest. The attack there would have to be completed by November, because after that time, the rains in Serbia would make operations impossible. A report from Michahelles in Sofia on July 24 clinched his decision. The negotiations of the Central Powers with the Bulgarian government had finally borne fruit and King Ferdinand was now ready to send a Bulgarian staff officer to Pless to sign a military convention. Falkenhayn immediately got off a wire to Conrad, informing him of the Bulgarian officer's visit and of the need to begin an attack on Serbia within four to six weeks—the time it would take to complete their operations in eastern Poland. In the negotiations which were to take place Germany and Austria must obligate themselves to contribute six divisions each and must require the same number from the Bulgarians. The command of the operation must be in the hands of a German general.[32]

Conrad, who by now saw the situation in the east as highly favorable, was ready to consider activating the Serbian front as long as the Bulgarians committed themselves. He therefore agreed to Falkenhayn's suggestions but declared that while the campaign would be commanded by von Mackensen, the latter must be under the direction of Austrian headquarters.[33]

The negotiations for a military convention with Bulgaria were the signal for another outbreak of hostility between the two commanders. The Austrian chief's anger at the proceedings was justified, since Falkenhayn did not invite Conrad to take direct part in the conversa-

---

[31] Hoffmann, *Der Krieg*, p. 110; Falkenhayn, *German General Staff*, pp. 141–42.

[32] Falkenhayn, *German General Staff*, pp. 117–20; Mühlmann, *Oberste Heeresleitung*, p. 123; C.-F. K., Balkan, no. 4670R, Falkenhayn to Conrad, 27 July 1915.

[33] C.-F. K., Balkan, no. 13384, Conrad to Falkenhayn, 28 July 1915. In this telegram, while Conrad gave his consent to the signing of a military convention, he mentioned that if "the Italian dam broke" he would be unable to send six Austrian divisions to Serbia.

tion which now took place at Pless. The German general explained that the negotiations in the first days of August were only preliminary talks, and that as soon as Colonel Gantscheff had full powers to conclude something concrete, Conrad's personal participation would be requested. Without waiting for Conrad's suggestions, Falkenhayn put together a draft of a convention, which he sent to Teschen for Austrian approval. He furthermore said Gantscheff had requested that von Mackensen take his orders directly from the German High Command; and since the whole operation had been developed by the German military, Falkenhayn was quite in agreement with this request.[34]

Conrad was angered at not being invited to Pless, but he boiled at the idea of losing control over the military operations in Serbia. He was perfectly willing to have von Mackensen as a field commander but he insisted that the directives, modifications, and supplements under which von Mackensen would operate must emanate from Austrian headquarters. After all, it was on Austrian soil that the striking forces would be assembled. It was on Austrian railroads that they would travel, and since the armies of the Monarchy fought on three different fronts, he certainly could not turn over the control of the Austrian railway net to the Germans. More than this was at stake: the prestige of the Monarchy must be considered. If Germany was allowed to command the campaign the effect on the Monarchy's position in the eyes of the Balkan peoples would be extremely adverse. Any military convention with Bulgaria needed the approval of Conrad's Emperor, and Franz Joseph would give no approval unless Mackensen was made subject to the Austrian High Command. As August wore on, Conrad remained adamant on the matter.[35]

The German military representative at Teschen attempted to change Conrad's viewpoint. When von Cramon suggested that the Austrian position might result in the failure to win Bulgarian participation, the chief of staff said he would be sorry if this was the outcome, but he had had enough humiliation at the hands of the German ally. Cramon, in an attempt to solve the problem, went to Pless and spoke with Gantscheff. He pointed out that it would really make no difference who sent Mackensen his orders, since the people behind those orders would be the same men who had handled the Gorlice-Tarnow breakthrough, the German High Command. Gantscheff refused to

---

[34] C.-F. K., Balkan, no. 8414 P, Falkenhayn to Conrad, 4 August 1915.
[35] C.-F. K. Balkan, no. 13740, Conrad to Falkenhayn, 6 August 1915; no. 13830, Conrad to Falkenhayn, 7 August; no. 13990, Conrad to Falkenhayn, 13 August.

accept the argument. Von Cramon then suggested that the question of issuing orders be left out of the discussions and not written into the convention. The wording would stipulate only that a German general would command in the field. Gantscheff and Falkenhayn agreed but Conrad refused.[36]

The German chief had, of course, become extremely irritated by Conrad von Hötzendorf's implacable position on what was really a minor point in the major project before them. But irritation or no, it took a personal trip by Falkenhayn on September 5 and an hour's discussion at Austrian headquarters before Conrad gave way. His capitulation was made only after Falkenhayn had agreed that both chiefs of staff would jointly decide on what orders were to be issued and that the Austrians would handle the distribution of those orders.[37]

On the following day, September 6, the military convention was signed at Pless. Except for the question of command, the stipulations had not been difficult to formulate. Gantscheff had negotiated with Falkenhayn for over a month, but these protracted conversations were necessary because the military agreement was made to hinge on the signing of an actual alliance with a secret annex. The provisions of the alliance and annex were the province of the respective foreign offices and the diplomatic maneuvering took time. Once the diplomats formulated the clauses on which all three powers agreed, the signatures of the alliance and military convention followed simultaneously.

Colonel Gantscheff was quite persistent in his demands, but Falkenhayn readily agreed and obtained Conrad's approval. The Bulgarian did what he could to reduce the risks his country would run in the military campaign. He reduced Falkenhayn's original request for six Bulgarian divisions to four on the grounds that Bulgaria had to guard its own borders. Gantscheff even demanded that the Central Powers guarantee in the convention that Rumania would remain neutral. This guarantee, he felt, could be made certain if the Germans and Austrians would send sufficient troops to the Hungarian-Rumanian border, where they could serve as a deterrent. Conrad refused, and properly so, because there was no way of guaranteeing Rumanian neutrality. The Bulgarians nevertheless got the military protection they wanted. A special clause in the convention allowed Turkey to make itself part of the agreement, and, if it did, it was obligated to send troops to Bulgaria upon request. To protect the ports of Varna and Burgas on the Black Sea, Germany and Austria agreed to send the necessary troops, and if the port of

[36] Cramon, *Quatre Ans au G.Q.G.*, pp. 63–64.
[37] Ibid., pp. 64–65.

Dedeagatch on the Aegean should be endangered by enemy attack, the Germans obligated themselves to make sure that Turkey sent forces to defend the area.[38]

The agreement was not by any means one-sided. The Central Powers got a firm commitment for four Bulgarian divisions, and a guarantee that Bulgaria would permit through transit of war materials on their way to Turkey. Conrad's worry that Bulgaria might provoke a conflict with Greece and Rumania was stilled; an article of the convention committed the Bulgarians to unconditional neutrality regarding the Greeks and Rumanians for the duration of the campaign in Serbia, assuming that those states themselves remained neutral.[39] Preparations for the Serbian offensive could now begin in earnest.

The campaign commenced on October 7, a month after the signing of the alliance and military convention. The thirty-day lapse between signature and action was due to the need for concentration of troops, a job that was masterfully executed by General Wilhelm Groener. By using six railroads and 12 to 16 troop trains a day, along with a total of 140 to 160 trains to handle heavy artillery and equipment, Groener put a total of twelve German and Austrian divisions into the battle areas in a little over three weeks. With the Austrian Third Army on his right flank, Mackensen struck directly over the Danube and Save rivers. The crossings had been studied for months by a group of German staff officers working under Colonel Hentsch, and the result of the careful planning was that the German Eleventh Army negotiated the passage of these rivers with no trouble, occupying Belgrade two days later.[40]

If the strike against Serbia was initiated with no difficulty, there had nevertheless been a good deal of friction in the higher echelons over the question of troop disposition. Hindenburg and Ludendorff had protested Falkenhayn's withdrawal of troops from the eastern front. The German command in the east resented the way Falkenhayn had handled the offensive against the Russians. At Posen on July 1 they had it out in the presence of the Kaiser. Hindenburg and Ludendorff wanted a grand flanking attack mounted on the Russians from the

[38] C.-F. K., Balkan, no. 8635, Falkenhayn to Conrad, 24 August 1915; no. 14484, Conrad to Falkenhayn, 25 August. The suggestion that the Central Powers guarantee the neutrality of Rumania must have seemed ridiculous to Conrad. He read reports of feeling against Austria running so high in the Rumanian army that targets on the training ranges were represented as Austrian soldiers. Vasil Radoslavov, *Bulgarien und die Weltkrise*, pp. 190–93. A copy of the military convention is presented here.

[39] C.-F. K., Balkan, no. 14810/1, Conrad to Burian, 2 September 1915; Radoslavov, *Bulgarien und die Weltkrise*, pp. 190–93.

[40] Groener, *Lebenserinnerungen*, p. 254; Churchill, *Unknown War*, pp. 339, 340, 341.

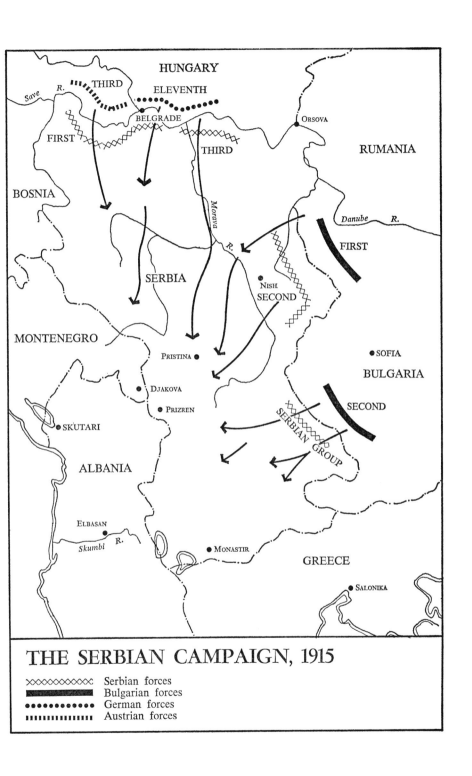

THE SERBIAN CAMPAIGN, 1915

×××××××××× Serbian forces
▬▬▬▬▬▬ Bulgarian forces
•••••••••••• German forces
⫿⫿⫿⫿⫿⫿⫿⫿ Austrian forces

north, which would carry the German troops behind the Russian lines and lead, they hoped, to a decisive defeat. The chief of staff saw the plan as much too grandiose, the Kaiser agreed with him, and Hindenburg and Ludendorff were forced to give way. In August, Hindenburg again argued for a strong push from the north, for only in this manner could the Russians be annihilated. Falkenhayn's answer was that annihilation had never been contemplated. The High Command had wanted "a simple and decisive victory" and this was what had been achieved. When Falkenhayn began pulling out units in September for the coming offensive on Serbia, Hindenburg attempted opposition. He was now east of Vilna and he sought to take Riga, something he could not do if his forces were reduced. He asked that the matter be brought to the attention of the Kaiser in the hope that the High Command would decide in his favor. The German chief of staff refused to continue the discussion—and that was that.[41]

Falkenhayn also had his difficulties with Conrad on the matter. Conrad was much more interested in continuing action in the east than in starting another attack on Serbia. He had begun a further offensive on Volhynia, the northwest province of the Ukraine, in late August, an action which Falkenhayn strongly opposed now that negotiations with the Bulgarians were coming to a close. When the offensive failed, the Germans had to send troops to buttress their ally, and the condition Falkenhayn imposed before he sent support was that Conrad call off the campaign there and stabilize his line. It is interesting, too, that Conrad supported Hindenburg in his desire for a further attack on the Russians from the north. Falkenhayn reminded the Austrian general that if they were to seek victory on other fronts, the forces in the east would have to be reduced to a minimal group fighting a minimal action. It is noteworthy that Conrad did not specifically agree to a holding action in East Galicia and in Volhynia until his wire of October 2, some five days before the Serbian action began. Nor did he immediately send the six divisions he had promised. It is true that eventually this number took part but when the attack began there were only two entirely Austrian divisions on the Serbian front. The deficit was made up by Germany.[42]

There was no question of the outcome of the Serbian offensive once

---

[41] Hoffmann, *Der Krieg*, p. 112; Falkenhayn, *German General Staff*, pp. 126–27, 141–42, 147, 149, 152, 157, 160–67.

[42] Falkenhayn, *German General Staff*, pp. 168–69; C.-F. K., Balkan, no. 14655, Conrad to Falkenhayn, 29 August 1915; no. 6589R, Falkenhayn to Conrad, 2 September; Russische Front, 1915, nos. 16154 and 16206, Conrad to Falkenhayn, 1 and 2 October; Groener, *Lebenserinnerungen*, p. 255.

it actually started. The Serbian armies, totalling roughly 200,000, faced an enemy superiority of 100,000 men. While the Germans and Austrians struck from the north, two Bulgarian armies advanced from the east. The First, under General Kliment Bodjadjieff, hammered its way toward Nish and a rendezvous with the German Eleventh Army, while the Second, under Georgi Todoroff, fought to the south and west to cut off the Serbian escape route to Greece.[43]

By the end of October the allied armies were deep into central Serbia and Todoroff's divisions had cut the rail line leading to Salonika. Nish fell on November 5 and the Serbian armies began to disintegrate. Pushed south and west, they had only one avenue of retreat, which led through the wild Albanian mountains already covered with snow. At the end of the month Conrad wired Vienna that the action against the Serbs could now be seen as essentially concluded. The Serbian troops who had not been killed, wounded, or captured, floundered through the mountain passes and emerged exhausted on the Albanian coast where the Entente assembled them and shipped them to Corfu.[44]

In the course of the campaign Falkenhayn and Conrad worried about the diplomatic scene. There was, to be sure, the continuing question of Rumania. Would it remain neutral, now that Serbia was under attack? Would it allow Russia through passage of troops to attack the weakened eastern front? These were the questions confronting the two chiefs of staff, leading to persistent inquiries and suggestions at the Wilhelmstrasse and Ballhausplatz.

Conrad, before he signed the military convention with the Bulgarians, had asked Burian for a full orientation on the Rumanian position, though his concern here did not preclude his signature of the document. The answer he wanted came on September 10 from the Austrian military attaché in Bukarest, who wrote that both the German and Austrian ministers were quite certain there was nothing to fear from Rumania, considering the favorable situation on the Russian front. On the same day Conrad was informed that Bratianu had given positive assurances to Czernin that Rumania would remain quiet if the Central

---

[43] Falkenhayn, *German General Staff*, p. 183; Margutti, *Emperor Francis Joseph*, p. 350.
[44] Churchill, *Unknown War*, pp. 342, 346, 347; Falkenhayn, *German General Staff*, pp. 198, 203; C.-F. K., Balkan, no. 18400, Conrad to Burian, 26 November 1915; no. 18557, Conrad to Burian, 29 November. Detailed examinations of the Serbian campaign are found in Max von Gallwitz, *Meine Führertätigkeit im Weltkriege, 1914-16*, pp. 379-465; Wolfgang Foerster, ed., *Mackensen: Briefe und Aufzeichnungen*, pp. 210-79; Germany, Reichsarchiv, *Der Weltkrieg*, vol. 9; Austria, Bundesministerium für Heereswesen, *Österreich-Ungarns Letzter Krieg*, vol. 3.

Powers attacked the Serbs. Conrad felt somewhat better after receiving this news, but in the course of the Serbian campaign the Austrian general kept a wary eye on the Rumanian scene.[45]

Falkenhayn was in close touch with German diplomatic officials on the question. Although he came to the conclusion that Rumania would probably undertake nothing against the Central Powers, he asked the German diplomats to make certain.[46]

The concern in German and Austrian military circles led the diplomats to attempt a more precise definition of Rumania's position, particularly on the question of prohibiting through transport of Russian troops after the Serbian campaign got under way. Rumania gave the desired assurances.

A much larger problem than Rumania was that which originated when the English and French landed two divisions at Salonika between October 2 and October 5. Their obvious intention was to support the Serbs in the coming battle. Conrad immediately wrote to Falkenhayn and Burian saying that he interpreted the presence of Entente troops at the Greek port as a sign of open Greek hostility. Athens had permitted the enemy to debark troops on Greek soil. The Greek government must be informed that its action was that of an enemy and not a neutral.[47]

Conrad von Hötzendorf was nervous, for he was thinking of 200,000 Greek soldiers available for combat. Falkenhayn and Burian reacted in a much calmer fashion. Falkenhayn agreed that Greece *ought* to turn back the Entente forces, but the Central Powers could not expect the Greeks to risk war with the Entente simply to fulfill the demands of international law when neither Germany nor Austria had sufficient forces to come to their aid. There was no sense in taking a strong position with Athens and running the risk of having Greece really join the enemy, particularly when the German Foreign Office had told him the position of the Greeks *vis-à-vis* the Central Powers was rather

[45] C.-F. K., Balkan, no. 14901, Conrad to Burian, 3 September 1915; Russische Front, 1915, no. 2384, Lt. Col. Maximillian Randa, Austrian military attaché in Bukarest, to Conrad, 10 September; no. 2380, Austrian military attaché in Bukarest to Conrad, 10 September; no. 15659, Conrad to Burian, 20 September; unnumbered Denkschrift by Conrad on the general war situation, 22 October; no. 18076/1, Conrad to Falkenhayn, 18 November.

[46] C.-F. K., Balkan, no. 16693, Conrad to Falkenhayn, 13 October 1915. Conrad recapitulates here a conversation he had had with Falkenhayn on the Rumanian issue in which the German chief said that they were probably safe from Rumanian attack. The diplomacy concerning this point is discussed in chapter 9 above.

[47] C.-F. K., Russische Front, 1915, no. 16542, Conrad to Falkenhayn and Burian, 9 October.

favorable. Burian concurred with this point of view and instructed Szilassy, the Austrian minister, to deliver a carefully worded protest speaking only of "future dangers" that might arise from Greece's ignoring its responsibilities as a neutral state.[48]

No matter what was said to Conrad, he continued to be uneasy over the situation. In the opening days of November it was agreed that German, Austrian, and Bulgarian troops would take action against the Entente divisions that had now moved into Serbian territory. But such action, involving an offensive against Salonika, would come only after the present campaign was brought to an end. Conrad, therefore, repeatedly stressed the necessity of a rapid conclusion to the Serbian offensive. He continued to believe they might otherwise find themselves facing Greece and perhaps Rumania as well. When he heard in mid-November that Falkenhayn had pulled eight German divisions out of the Serbian theater before victory was complete, he asked for an explanation. If the German High Command was giving up the joint attack, then Conrad wanted to know, so that he could judge what he himself ought to do. Falkenhayn's answer was prompt and angry. He replied that he had not changed his intentions on the joint operation, but the troops he had withdrawn were no longer needed to carry through the battle. Nor would he expose German soldiers to hunger or to spotted typhus any longer than he had to. Insofar as any move against the Entente forces to the south was concerned, the troops available outnumbered the French and British by two to one. There was therefore nothing to worry about.[49]

Events proved Falkenhayn correct. There were plenty of troops to defeat the Serbs, the Greeks did not enter the war, and on December 5 the Bulgarians easily forced the French and British back across the Greek border.

The Germans now decided there was no need for an attack on Salonika. First of all, Falkenhayn needed the men elsewhere. Second, he had no desire to become further involved in a Balkan venture, for he had always seen that area as a secondary theater. Third, because of supply problems connected with such an attack, Mackensen believed a fully prepared action against Salonika would not be possible before

[48] C.-F. K., Russische Front, 1915, no. 15876, Falkenhayn to Conrad, 10 October; no. 354, Burian to Szilassy in Athens, 8 October. A copy of the instruction to Szilassy was sent to Conrad.

[49] Falkenhayn, *German General Staff*, p. 206; C.-F. K., Russische Front, 1915, unnumbered resume of the situation by Conrad, 22 October; no. 18076, Conrad to Falkenhayn, 17 November; no. 18076/1, Conrad to Falkenhayn, 18 November; no. 18076/2, Conrad to Falkenhayn, 20 November; no. 18555, Falkenhayn to Conrad, 22 November.

April. On the basis of these considerations German headquarters refused to order further action.[50]

The result of this decision was an open break between the German and Austrian chiefs of staff. Conrad, hearing that the Salonika action was no longer contemplated, decided this meant that Mackensen's command over all forces in Serbia was now at an end and Austrian units were again directly under Teschen's orders. On this basis, Conrad ordered General Hermann Kövess to march on Montenegro and Albania. This new offensive had been decided through correspondence between Conrad and Burian. Conrad believed that occupation of these two countries was to the benefit of Austria-Hungary and that if the Austrian army did not occupy these states and secure the Adriatic coast for the Monarchy, certainly the Bulgarians would. He had not liked the extensive increases in territory granted to the Bulgarians in September when the alliance was signed. The further extension of Bulgaria to the Adriatic was in his estimation against Austrian interests. A telegram sent to him by Burian on Christmas Day showed that Vienna agreed with his position.[51]

Now that the commander had the backing of Vienna, he could go ahead with the project in spite of Falkenhayn's firm disapproval. The German chief, hearing of Conrad's orders to Kövess, asked that they be rescinded. Conrad refused and Falkenhayn, feeling that Austria was putting its own interests before those of the general war effort—he believed those troops should be sent back again to the eastern front—declared that he no longer had any trust in the Austrians. As far as he was concerned, Conrad had broken his word on the issue of joint command in Serbia. Not until Skutari fell on January 23, 1916, were ties reestablished between the two men. A relationship between them was patched together at the behest of von Cramon, the German representative at Teschen, but it was scarcely animated. The new year began on a sour note.[52]

Whatever the animosities between the two chiefs of staff, the turn of 1916 saw them riding the wave of victory. Galicia was theirs. Poland and the Duchy of Courland were theirs. Serbia, Montenegro, and Albania were theirs. The Italian and the western fronts held, and the Dardanelles had been saved. But Germany and Austria-Hungary had paid a frightful cost for their successes. Over 800,000 men had died

---

[50] Falkenhayn, *German General Staff*, pp. 207, 214, 215, 216.

[51] Cramon, *Quatre Ans au G.Q.G.*, p. 71; C.-F. K., Balkan, no. 18400, Conrad to Burian, 20 November 1915; no. 18266, Burian to Conrad, 22 November; Russische Front, 1915, no. 5892, Burian to Conrad, 25 December; Staatsarchiv, PA, box 499, no. 19948, Conrad to Burian, 26 December.

[52] Cramon, *Quatre Ans au G.Q.G.*, pp. 82–87.

since the start of the war, and when all was said and done the Central Powers could not look forward with optimism to ending the holocaust in the near future. In a telegram to Count Tisza, General Conrad was forced to conclude, "In spite of the military successes of 1915 we are not in a position to entirely force our will upon the enemy powers and make peace necessary for them."[53]

The remark might not have been apt had the German and Austrian diplomats successfully achieved their aims in the early months of the war. This, of course, had not occurred, and as the war went on Conrad and Falkenhayn by necessity became more and more involved in diplomatic considerations. At times this involvement was due to the diplomats themselves, particularly on the German side. Falkenhayn did all he could to convince the Austrians of the necessity of mounting a Serbian campaign, not only because he realized its military importance with regard to aiding the Turks, but also because the Wilhelmstrasse had impressed upon him the repercussions of the successful completion of the desired Balkan coalition. In the case of Italy, the pressures Falkenhayn brought to bear on Conrad von Hötzendorf for a peaceful settlement were certainly prompted by military considerations, but they also reflected the desires of German diplomats to make Vienna change its policies on territorial concessions. Falkenhayn took the same position as the Wilhelmstrasse in the case of Rumania—that its participation against the Entente was worth the price of the concessions it demanded. He went so far as to carry on conversations with the main figure involved, Count Tisza, and his attempts failed as thoroughly as did those of Bethmann-Hollweg.

Conrad von Hötzendorf was even more concerned with the diplomatic scene. As an Austrian, however, he was much more aware of the repercussions that diplomatic measures could have for the future position of his own country. He understood the importance of successful diplomacy for military victory as well as his German counterpart and perhaps understood it better. Aside from his strong disagreements with Falkenhayn on military strategy, his constant awareness of maintaining Austria-Hungary's interests made him much less willing to put pressure on the Ballhausplatz than Falkenhayn would have liked.

[53] Falkenhayn, *German General Staff*, p. 142; Groener, *Lebenserinnerungen*, p. 259; Fritz Franek, *Die Entwicklung der Österreich-Ungarns Wehrmacht in die Ersten Zwei Kriegsjahren*, Table 1; C.-F. K., Russische Front, 1916, no. 19830, Conrad to Count Tisza, 3 January.

Chapter 13

The Setbacks
of 1916

The victories of 1915 were to be followed by a year of uncertainty, animosity, and disagreement. When it became apparent that the campaign against Serbia was succeeding, the Wilhelmstrasse concerned itself with Austria's war aims in the Balkans. As early as October, 1915, von Jagow asked Tschirschky in Vienna to find out just how far Austria intended to occupy Serbia and what the Monarchy's intentions were there. Burian's answer was that his government would demand unconditional surrender by the Serbian army and the immediate cession of all lands requested. The foreign minister also spoke of the possibilities of establishing an independent Albanian state, of Austrian control of the Sanjak, and of eliminating the chances of Italy's controlling the eastern coast of the Adriatic.[1]

The Germans were not pleased with Austria's insistence on a harsh treatment of Serbia, since unconditional surrender meant the Serbs would fight bitterly and to the end; such terms gave the Entente a moral justification for landing troops at Salonika to support the Serbian army. Berlin was also skeptical of the wisdom of an independent Albania though it accepted Burian's views on the Sanjak and on coastal control. The Wilhelmstrasse may not have liked the Monarchy's plans but it decided against further embroilment in the Serbian question. The two powers had been at loggerheads on the disposition of Poland, and Bethmann-Hollweg wished to avoid additional tension between the two allies. Germany not only accepted the plan for Serbia's unconditional surrender but also, in order to quiet Austrian fears of possible German incursion, said that it had no interest whatsoever in administering any part of Serbia unless this was demanded by purely military considerations.[2]

Problems of Disposition: Serbia, Montenegro, Albania

The problem of war goals and the future disposition of Serbia, Montenegro, and Albania was to produce a debate of major proportions in Austro-Hungarian circles. The debate was not to be resolved in

1916 and the issue of what to do with the conquered Balkan states was in early January relegated to a limbo classified as "tentative plans." On the basis of his military victories, Conrad took high ground on what the government's Balkan goals ought to be. A few days before Christmas, 1915, he wrote Burian a testy dispatch complaining that Austria seemed to lack any positive or clear goals. At any rate, he had not received them from the foreign minister. For him, as a military leader, precise orientation on these goals was extremely significant; while he did not offer specifics, he charged that the lack of such information had produced difficulties for the army. He now wanted that information.[3]

Burian's answer was defensive in tone but precise. There were certain questions, he said, which had not yet been answered, but there was a war on and these would have to wait. In general the goal of the Monarchy was "to win the greatest possible growth in power and security." More specifically, Serbia and Montenegro were to be under the Monarchy's political, military, and economic jurisdiction, while Albania would become an effective protectorate. Before all this could be realized it would be necessary for the military to do several things: hold fast on the Russian front, continue with operations in the Balkans until Montenegro was completely overrun, drive the Entente troops from Salonika, and go on the offensive against Italy. Diplomatic goals, he concluded, were tied to the success of military operations.[4]

Count Tisza and Burian also engaged in an exchange of views on Balkan war aims. In answer to Burian's suggested formula for a solution to the Serbian or South Slav question "within the framework" of the Monarchy, Tisza declared that if Burian meant by this an opposition to a Serbian policy that was against the integrity of the Monarchy, he could certainly agree. If Burian meant annexation of Serbia, he was definitely opposed, since it would endanger the future interests of the Monarchy as a whole. To assert that annexation of Serbia was the only real solution to the Serbian danger was based, said Tisza, on the erroneous assumption that an independent Serbian state could not be rendered harmless and pulled "within the gravitational sphere of the Monarchy." Tisza warned that to annex the country would only increase Serbian national consciousness and agitation within the Monarchy, which would find itself with a few million additional Serbs

[1] Austria, Kriegsarchiv, Conrad Archiv, folio B-7, no. 712, Burian to Hohenlohe, 30 October 1915; no. 718, Burian to Hohenlohe, 2 November.
[2] Ibid., no. 470, Hohenlohe to Burian, 31 October; no. 7025, Friedrich von Wiesner, Foreign Office representative at Teschen, to Conrad, 23 November; Gerhard Ritter, *Staatskunst und Kriegshandwerk*, 3:105–6. For extensive coverage of the Polish problem see Ritter's chapters 5 and 7.
[3] C.-F. K., Russische Front, 1915, no. 19380, Conrad to Burian, 22 December.
[4] Ibid., no. 5892, Burian to Conrad, 25 December.

living inside its borders. Tisza offered what was to him a simple solution. Austria-Hungary need only annex the northwest corner of Serbia and make sure that Serbia and Montenegro were cut off from the coast. These two states would then be entirely dependent economically on the Empire, and political dependence would follow as a natural result.[5]

Conrad showed just how contrary his opinions were to Tisza's views when on January 4 he wrote the Hungarian minister-president a long explanation of his own position. He could in no way accept the idea of continued Serbian independence. Even though it might become an Austrian protectorate, the only result would be new crises and new difficulties. Serbia could never be anything, he believed, except "the friend of our enemies." Conrad also rejected the idea supported by both Tisza and Burian, that an independent Albania could be successfully dominated inasmuch as the state would necessarily become a protectorate. He doubted that an independent Albania could for long manage to exist. On the other hand, he was not in favor of annexing the whole country, for that would be a burden the Monarchy could not handle. Conrad advocated annexation of northern Albania with the rest to be divided between Bulgaria and Greece.[6]

A Ministerial Council meeting took place on January 7 to try to resolve these strong disparities. Present were Karl Stürgkh, the minister-president of Austria, Tisza, Burian, Conrad, Alexander von Krobatin, the minister of war, and Ernest von Körber, the finance minister. Burian, presiding as chairman, prefaced his remarks by suggesting that any decisions reached by the council would necessarily be tentative since all would depend on the outcome of the war. Having said that much he then got down to cases. He began with Serbia, attempting to win over Tisza by showing him that annexation would not be so bad after all. In the first place, Bulgaria would obtain a sizable portion of the country on the basis of the German-Austrian-Bulgarian Alliance signed in September, 1915. The sections of Serbia which had previously belonged to Albania would be returned. What remained would be only a small mountain country with one and a half million people. Its incorporation would not mean any really significant increase in the Monarchy's population, but if it remained independent it would once again become a center for anti-Austrian agitation. Insofar as Montenegro was concerned, he was not opposed to its remaining independent for it could never be a danger to Austria equal to its Serbian neighbor.

[5] Austria, Kriegsarchiv, Conrad Archiv, folio B-7, unnumbered confidential letter, Tisza to Burian, 30 December 1915.
[6] C.-F. K., Russische Front, 1916, no. 19830, Conrad to Tisza, 4 January.

So long as the sea coast as far as the Albanian border was ceded, Montenegro could be left autonomous. It could not be allowed to join Serbia, however, since this would create a Piedmont of the Balkans. He wanted to leave Albania independent, with those lands restored which had been taken by Serbia and Montenegro during the Balkan Wars. Albania would, nevertheless, become an Austrian protectorate, which would serve the Monarchy's Balkan interests.

Tisza's chief disagreement was with Burian's proposed annexation of Serbia, for which he flatly refused to take any responsibility. The fact that Stürgkh, Krobatin, Körber, and Conrad supported Burian on annexation did not dismay him. He unequivocally opposed such a move, and reminded the council that on July 19, 1914, a guarantee against far-reaching control of Serbia had been given him in a ministerial meeting. To placate him the council agreed, in principle, to the idea that any annexations in Serbia would be incorporated by Hungary rather than by Austria. Thus Tisza, who had stood alone on the question, emerged from the conference with the assurance that although parts of Serbia might be annexed, in the future Hungary would hold the whip-hand there.[7]

Austria-Hungary's intention to annex part of Serbia emerged, but no precise decision was reached on what to do with Montenegro and Albania. Nor could it have been otherwise. When the meeting took place Austrian forces were still in the process of crushing Montenegro, which had not yet sued for peace, and there was fighting in Albania as well. Indeed, Conrad's strong annexationist views were to lead to friction with Bulgaria over the occupation of certain areas in Albania and western Serbia. A bitter feud was finally resolved only by the intercession of Falkenhayn.

Austrian insistence on a special Montenegrin campaign had, by mid-January, resulted in the complete subduing of that state. The Montenegrin government requested that peace be concluded and on January 25 signed the documents of surrender, placing Austrian forces in full control of the country. While the fighting was still in progress, Bulgarian troops, operating in conjunction with Mackensen's German divisions, struck south to the Greek border, occupying the strategically important towns of Pristina, Prizren, and Debra in western Serbia, as well as Djakova in Montenegro. By February, Bulgarian troops held Elbasan, having thrust into Albania. Conrad had been watching these developments with great concern since late December, when he wrote

[7] Austria, Kriegsarchiv, Conrad Archiv, folio B-8, unnumbered copy of Ministerial Council minutes, 7 January 1916. See also Ritter, *Staatskunst und Kriegshandwerk*, 3:109–10.

to Burian that Bulgaria was going to make its own further military participation dependent on territorial concessions beyond those promised by Germany and Austria in the Bulgarian alliance. On January 7 he went to Vienna to speak with the foreign minister and warned that if Bulgaria was permitted to continue administering these newly occupied areas, the question of Bulgarian control would soon arise. He therefore urged that Bulgarian forces be removed from Pristina, Prizren, and Djakova, that Bulgaria be barred from "accompanying us in Albania," and that Austria declare that northern and middle Albania, Montenegro, and the sections of Serbia west of the line drawn in the Bulgarian alliance be clearly set forth as territories which were Austria's "exclusive sphere of interest."[8]

By February Conrad and Burian were in disagreement, not on whether Bulgaria ought to control the towns in question—both believed they should not—but on how to deal with the situation effectively. Conrad took the position that the Bulgarians must be told "hands off"; otherwise they would simply set up housekeeping and remain. Should that occur, Austrian war aims in the Balkans would emerge badly crippled. Burian refused to become quite so excited. He intended Prizren and Pristina to go to post-war Albania, but this allocation was a purely political matter and would have to be handled as such. The fact that Bulgarian troops occupied these towns did not mean that significant political consequences would necessarily result, since military administration of an area need not be prejudicial to its future. Conrad thought Burian's attitude naive, and remarked, "The Bulgarians are realpolitikers. They know that we now need them. . . . They know that we live in a time when the force of facts negates all diplomatic chess moves, all disinterested and solitary plans. This they use and handle to their own advantage." Where Bulgarians occupied territory, there they stayed, he concluded.[9]

Burian defined the Austrian position when he met with King Ferdinand, Radoslavov, and the Bulgarian chief of staff, Nikolaus Zekoff, on February 15 in Vienna. He told them that the area west of the boundary delineated in the existing alliance was an Austrian sphere of interest. The Bulgarians pretended to agree, but insisted that the evacuation of Bulgarian troops was a matter to be decided between the

---

[8] Austria, Kriegsarchiv, B-Group, Montenegro, AOK Op., folio 553, no. 20877, report on the Montenegrin surrender terms, Lt. Field Marshal Joseph Metzger, 25 January 1916; folio 551, no. 20476, Conrad to Burian, 13 January.

[9] AOK Op., folio 538, no. 22234, Conrad to Falkenhayn, 3 February; folio 551, no. 19448, Conrad to Burian, 23 December 1915; Austria, Kriegsarchiv, Conrad Archiv, folio B-8, no. 9053, Burian to Conrad, 16 February; no. 21717, Conrad to Burian, 18 February 1916.

respective Austrian and Bulgarian high commands. An explosive situation existed, for by this time both Bulgarian and Austrian units were occupying the disputed areas without attempting any cooperative policies on administration. Burian urged Conrad to avoid conflict with the Bulgarian forces because good relations simply had to be maintained. Conrad suggested to Zekoff that the Bulgarians evacuate, but Zekoff refused. To avoid a possible break Burian was prepared to have Austrian troops clear the disputed areas, leaving them to the Bulgarians until the end of the war. Any claim to the territories, he reasoned, would depend entirely on the strength of the Monarchy at that time. But Conrad would not budge.[10]

To break the impasse the Germans now took a hand. The Bulgarians had expressed to Berlin their true position: anything west of the line delineated by the existing alliance was really a no-man's land; the terms of the alliance had not stipulated otherwise. Hence, the ally occupying it had a legitimate claim. From a strictly legal point of view they were correct and the Germans accepted their right to administer areas occupied by their troops.[11]

Jagow at the Wilhelmstrasse talked with Hohenlohe, saying that things could not be allowed to reach a breaking point between Austria and Bulgaria. Falkenhayn was upset by reports reaching him that Conrad had demanded that Zekoff evacuate Prizren and Pristina. Zekoff had utterly refused and declared he would bring in additional Bulgarian divisions to maintain control if necessary. On March 22 Falkenhayn offered a compromise plan. Bulgarian troops would evacuate Djakova and Elbasan, and Austrian units would be cleared from Prizren and Pristina, which would be controlled by the Bulgarians until Sofia and Vienna could reach a formal accord on the issue.[12]

Neither Conrad nor Burian was very happy over Falkenhayn's solution, but they accepted it for the moment. On April 1 the Bulgarian and Austrian high commands agreed to a series of stipulations, though the agreement, significantly, was oral and was never signed. It went into effect when the Germans notified each party of the other's verbal approval. What the stipulations resulted in was this: the Bulgarians

[10] Austria, Kriegsarchiv, Conrad Archiv, folio B-8, no. 776, Burian to Conrad, 19 February 1916; AOK Op., folio 551, no. 9288, Count Thurn to Conrad, 23 February; folio 538, no. 22234, Conrad to Falkenhayn, 3 February; no. 21587, Conrad to Burian, 14 February; Austria, Kriegsarchiv, Conrad Archiv, folio B-8, no. 1403, Lt. Col. Wladimir Laxa, Austrian military attaché in Sofia, to Conrad, 3 March; no. 9372, Burian to Conrad, 28 February.

[11] AOK Op., folio 539, no. 23140, Conrad to Burian, 25 March 1916.

[12] Austria, Kriegsarchiv, Conrad Archiv, folio B-8, no. 9420, Burian to Conrad, 1 March 1916; AOK Op., folio 539, no. 12012 P, Falkenhayn to Conrad, 22 March.

succeeded in moving their control of southern Serbia to the west as far as the existing Albanian border. With German support they had won their point, and they kept Prizren and Pristina. On the other hand, the Austrians insisted on the inclusion of several clauses which made the Bulgarian occupation valid only for the duration of the war, obligated the Bulgarians to withdraw from Prizren and Pristina in case these areas were not promised to Bulgaria in a future accord, and because Conrad had insisted on a border being set, established clear-cut Austrian control in northern and central Serbia, in Montenegro, and in northern and middle Albania. Although the Austrians were still in disagreement among themselves as to the precise extent of their future annexations in the conquered Balkan states, they had made clear the boundaries of their sphere of interest. The final reckoning with Bulgaria was postponed, and Germany, while its compromise plan did not please the Austrians, had at least averted an open break between Austria and Bulgaria and made it possible for these two to turn to other pressing matters.[13]

Repercussions of the Brussilov Offensive

While all this was going on Falkenhayn was taken up with his plans for an attack on the western front at Verdun. Beginning on February 21 the battle for Verdun became a furnace which eventually consumed close to 300,000 German troops. In order to concentrate on this key French fortress, Falkenhayn refused the suggestions of Hindenburg and Ludendorff, who were interested in further offensives against the Russians and who asked for additional German divisions. The eastern commanders fumed but there was nothing they could do. Falkenhayn had the support of the Kaiser.[14]

Conrad was not averse to keeping things quiescent on the eastern front because he himself had a great project in mind: a campaign in the Tyrol that would bring about the collapse of Italy. The two chiefs of staff had talked about Conrad's projected offensive as early as December 10, 1915. In that conversation their disagreement on the advisability of such an attack was already quite clear. Conrad believed that only after Italy was defeated would there be sufficient troops available to force the French to capitulate. He proposed a Tyrolian offensive using sixteen divisions and ninety batteries of heavy guns. For this action he

---

[13] AOK Op., folio 539, no. 149, Burian to Conrad, 25 March 1916; no. 23083, Conrad to Burian, 23 March; no. 10199, Burian to Conrad, 29 March; no. 23374, Conrad to Burian, 1 April; no. 23701, copy of the agreement, 1 April.

[14] Walter Goerlitz, *History of the German General Staff, 1657–1945*, pp. 176–77; Germany, Reichsarchiv, *Der Weltkrieg, 1914–1918*, 10:426.

requested four German divisions and a third of the necessary artillery. But Falkenhayn would not go along. In the first place, Falkenhayn had no confidence in the capacity of such an offensive to force Italy to sue for peace. Second, he wanted Conrad to remain on the defensive in this theater and to ship all available forces to the Russian front so as to make additional German divisions available for the west. Then, too, he believed the Austrian estimates of necessary men inadequate. He pointed out that at least twenty-five divisions and much more artillery would be needed. From any practical point of view he did not see the Italian campaign as well conceived. To Falkenhayn it seemed that the offensive would be mounted to satisfy Conrad's desire for revenge against a hated enemy rather than to meet the greater needs of the combined war effort.[15]

In spite of these arguments Conrad was not dissuaded; if he could not mount his campaign with German help, he would do it alone. By February he was making preparations. Unfortunately, he was held up by the continuation of snows and bad weather in general which repeatedly forced him to postpone action. The day was set for April 10, was moved up to April 20, then to May 1 and finally to May 15. By this time he had massed two full armies consisting of ninety battalions of men with over forty batteries of artillery. These preparations notwithstanding, as late as May 3 Falkenhayn was still trying to convince his Austrian colleague to cancel the offensive. He wrote to Cramon, saying that the campaign would not amount to much "unless by some great surprise." Cramon was to tell Teschen that "together we can finish the Italians later." Conrad only snorted at such a suggestion. He could not stop now, now when his heavy artillery had already been in place for long weeks, the combat sectors allotted, the troops ready, and his finger poised "to push the button." Cramon wrote to Pless that the whole matter seemed to be a question of Conrad's honor and there was no stopping the attack. At first, the whole thing went very well—Ludendorff was later to call the offensive "brilliant"—but by the end of the month the Austrian forward movement had lost its initial punch. When the Russian front suddenly erupted on the Austrian sector, Conrad was forced to go on the defensive against Italy. His armies soon faced decimation in the east.[16]

[15] Germany, Reichsarchiv, *Der Weltkrieg*, 10:4-7, 571; AOK Op., folio 551, no. 19974, Falkenhayn to Conrad, 11 December 1915; Ritter, *Staatskunst und Kriegshandwerk*, 3:223-24.

[16] August von Cramon, *Quatre Ans au G.Q.G. Austro-Hongrois pendant la Guerre Mondiale*, pp. 98, 100, 102-3, 104; Austria, Kriegsarchiv, Berichte Cramon, folio 607, no. 27475, Falkenhayn to Cramon, 3 May; no. 1484, Cramon to Falkenhayn, 4 May; no. 1520, Cramon to Falkenhayn, 10 May; Germany, Reichsarchiv, *Der Weltkrieg*, 10:460.

On June 4 Field Marshal Archduke Frederick was celebrating his sixtieth birthday at Austrian headquarters when reports began arriving that the Austrian Fourth Army under General von Linsingen was under attack by Russian forces. In March, the Russians had responded to their allies' request that the German pressure on Verdun be reduced by a Russian thrust on the eastern front against the German-held sector in the north. That attempt had been successfully beaten off. The Russians then began plans for a major spring offensive to start approximately in mid-June and to be synchronized with a British-French operation on the Somme. Again, the Russians focused their attention on the German segment of the front, more specifically, against Hindenburg's army group. To keep the Central Powers from transferring reinforcements from the south, General Brussilov was to prepare a subsidiary attack there. When Conrad began his campaign against the Italians in mid-May, the Russians were not yet ready to begin their full-scale operation, but they were asked if a diversionary action could be put into effect to help reduce the danger now threatening the Italians. Brussilov, having four full armies under his command, was prepared to take the offensive.[17]

Beginning at dawn on June 4, Russian artillery pounded the Austrian line west of Rovno for six hours and the infantry advance began. The action did not come as a surprise to Austrian headquarters, because Intelligence had captured a message from Brussilov to his troops on June 3: "The hour has come to expel the enemy! All armies on our front will attack. I am convinced our army will win a complete victory." It would not be a complete victory but it would be a great one. The Russians sliced through Linsingen's Fourth Army with great ease, punching a hole twenty-five kilometers wide and six deep in the first twenty-four hours. By June 6 the bulge was seventy-five kilometers wide and twenty deep. By June 7 the depth had reached forty, and the Austrian Fourth Army had been shattered, with 40,000 men taken prisoner. Before Brussilov was finally contained and the line essentially stabilized, his armies had regained an area sixty miles to the west of the original battle line along a 200-mile front. Approximately 300,000 Austrians had been captured, along with hundreds of guns.[18]

By the end of August faith in Conrad's abilities as chief of staff had been badly crippled within the Monarchy and in Germany, and Falkenhayn had been forced to resign. Rumania was now actively in

[17] Cramon, *Quatre Ans au G.Q.G.*, pp. 104–6; Churchill, *Unknown War*, pp. 359–61; Germany, Reichsarchiv, *Der Weltkrieg*, 10:433, 435, 436, 445–47.

[18] Winston S. Churchill, *The Unknown War: The Eastern Front*, pp. 362–63; Germany, Reichsarchiv, *Der Weltkrieg*, 10:448, 449, 453, 456, 457; Oskar Regele, *Feldmarschall Conrad*, pp. 365–66. See map, p. 311. The Austrian Fourth was part of Linsingen's German Army Group.

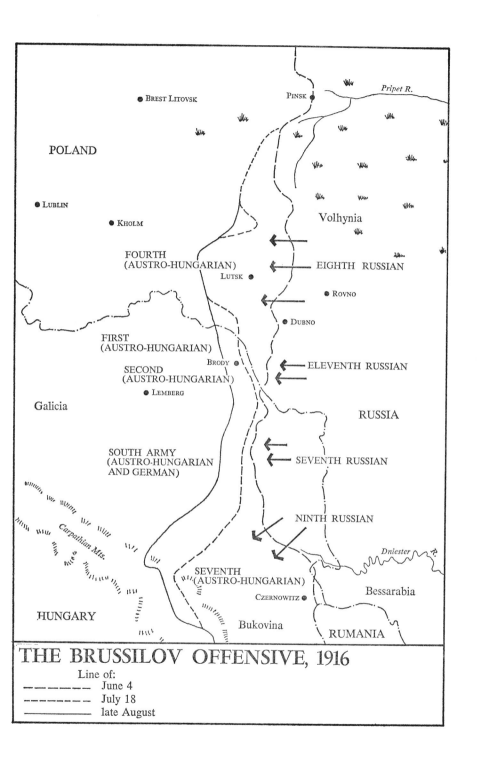

BREST LITOVSK

PINSK

Pripet R.

POLAND

LUBLIN

KHOLM

Volhynia

FOURTH
(AUSTRO-HUNGARIAN)

LUTSK

EIGHTH RUSSIAN

ROVNO

DUBNO

FIRST
(AUSTRO-HUNGARIAN)

BRODY

SECOND
(AUSTRO-HUNGARIAN)

LEMBERG

Galicia

ELEVENTH RUSSIAN

RUSSIA

SOUTH ARMY
(AUSTRO-HUNGARIAN
AND GERMAN)

SEVENTH RUSSIAN

NINTH RUSSIAN

Carpathian Mts.

Dniester R.

SEVENTH
(AUSTRO-HUNGARIAN)

CZERNOWITZ

Bessarabia

HUNGARY

Bukovina

RUMANIA

THE BRUSSILOV OFFENSIVE, 1916

Line of:
–––––––– June 4
– – – – – July 18
————— late August

the war on the side of the Entente and the military condition of the Central Powers had deteriorated considerably from what it had been at the beginning of the year.

Basic to the original decisions by Falkenhayn and Conrad to go ahead with their individual plans for Verdun and the Tyrol was the contention that the eastern front must retain sufficient forces to hold defensively. Although by May Falkenhayn had considerably thinned the German-held portions there, this did not prove disastrous for him, since Brussilov's main weight fell upon the Austrians. But Conrad had extracted six divisions of crack soldiers from the east and sent them against the Italians. Archduke Frederick had confided to Cramon that he was much concerned over the weakening of the Austrian positions against four Russian armies, and Franz Joseph had personally discussed it with Conrad four days before Brussilov gave the signal for his advance. Conrad assured the Emperor there was nothing to worry about. Unfortunately, he miscalculated the ability of his eastern armies to hold.[19]

No sooner did the Austrian Fourth Army begin to retreat than Conrad requested aid from Pless. Falkenhayn answered on June 6 that reserves were not available now and Austria would have to handle the matter by itself. The refusal was perfectly reasonable because on May 23 both chiefs of staff had agreed that reinforcements would be sent south from the German-held sector only when Russia shifted major strength from the north to Galicia. At the moment, wrote Falkenhayn, not one Russian soldier had been transferred. In any event, he could not spare any divisions from the north where Hindenburg's and Prince Leopold's army groups were outweighed by a three to one Russian superiority. Nor, as he told Cramon, could he send forces from the western front where he momentarily awaited an English offensive. Conrad would have to send reserves from Italy. "This is bitter," he noted, "but I see no other way out."[20]

On June 10 the Russian forces broke through the Austrian Seventh Army in the south and Conrad again pressed for German reinforcements. If the Russians could continue their lunge there, Austria would lose the whole Bukovina and Hungary would stand threatened. It was now more probable that Rumania would submit to Entente pressure

---

[19] Max Hoffmann, *Der Krieg der Versäumten Gelegenheiten*, p. 133; Germany, Reichsarchiv, *Der Weltkrieg*, 10:441, 445; Joseph Redlich, *Schicksalsjahre Österreichs, 1908–1919*, 2:123.

[20] C.-F. K., Russische Front, 1916, folio 512, no. 28852, Falkenhayn to Conrad, 6 June; Austria, Kriegsarchiv, Berichte Cramon, folio 607, no. 28849, Falkenhayn to Cramon, 5 June.

and join in against the Central Powers. He saw the general picture as so serious that it far transcended Austrian interests per se; it was now decisive for the general outcome of the war. Falkenhayn was not very worried about the Rumanians as long as the Bulgarians remained poised on their borders, but there was no escaping the need for drastic action to save the Austrian army from collapse. He wired to Cramon that he was sending four divisions of infantry, with heavy artillery and two additional cavalry brigades. By the end of August, Pless had routed to the Austrian sector some fourteen divisions from Hindenburg's and Prince Leopold's army groups in the north, twelve divisions from the western front, and one from the Balkans. By comparison the Austrian contribution was pitifully small: three infantry divisions in June and three more in July from Italy, plus one additional division scraped together from here and there. Conrad was not shirking his responsibility; he was unable to muster more. He constantly feared an offensive on the part of Italian troops and so he could not strip the various segments of the Italian front without running the risk of engulfment. Indeed, the Italians counterattacked in mid-June in the Tyrol and by mid-July were preparing the sixth battle of the Isonzo. Both attacks were successfully contained.[21]

If Germany faced the necessity of sending sizable numbers of its own replacements into the Austrian line to support the sagging ally like so many corset-stays, then Falkenhayn felt he had the right to ask that the entire Austrian front, from the Pripet River to the Dniester, be placed in the hands of a German to serve as the joint commander. He first proposed this on June 12, choosing von Mackensen for the job on the basis of his military capacities and previous successes. Cramon had informed Falkenhayn that the fighting spirit of the Austrian troops, who were now reeling from retreat to retreat, was almost nonexistent. It was obvious that what was needed to boost morale was a man "whose name meant something." But Conrad reacted coldly to the suggestion; he saw here a threat to Austria's control of its own forces, in spite of the fact that Mackensen would be subject to Teschen and his staff would be filled out with Austrian officers. The most Conrad was willing to concede was Mackensen's command of the Southern and Seventh armies. He agreed that Mackensen was a commander of great worth but he did not see a unified command as essential now. What

---

[21] Germany, Reichsarchiv, *Der Weltkrieg*, 10:481; Austria, Kriegsarchiv, Berichte Cramon, folio 607, unnumbered report, Cramon to Falkenhayn, 11 June 1916; no. 1680, Cramon to Falkenhayn, 11 June; no. 29079, Falkenhayn to Conrad, 11 June.

would be meaningful was sending as many troops as possible to the Russian front to meet the crisis.[22]

Falkenhayn could not accept such a reduction of Mackensen's authority and he wrote to Cramon that only by establishing a unified command for the whole front would any significant change be produced. His proposal, he asserted, was the only thing that could settle "the dragging disputations between Conrad and myself over the leadership of operations and division of forces." Again Conrad was sounded but he sidestepped the issue. What Falkenhayn envisaged was "an extraordinary measure." Conrad could only entertain the possibility of such a command after he had talked with Franz Joseph, a conversation which, in turn, would rest on evidence being presented that a strong German army had been designated for the fight against Brussilov. Falkenhayn responded on June 19 with the reminder that there were now eight and a half German infantry divisions, one cavalry division, and supporting heavy artillery serving on the Austrian line. Two additional divisions were on the way. If this was not a strong German army, what was? But Conrad refused to consider the matter further and Mackensen stayed in the Balkans.[23]

The military repercussions of the Brussilov offensive had a profound effect upon Conrad's reputation within the Monarchy. Public spirit plummeted once news of the extensive reversals was published. In Vienna people were depressed and worried when casualty reports failed to appear by June 20. The government's reticence was understandable in light of the tremendous damage that had been done. In the first twelve days of battle the Austrian Fourth Army had lost 54 percent of its effectives and the Seventh Army, 57 percent. If Conrad at the start of 1916 could afford to take a rather cavalier attitude toward Burian and other ranking officials, he now found himself on the receiving end. Confidence in his capacities was now much shaken and lack of respect for his judgment was reflected in the communications between Teschen and Vienna during the second half of June. It was now that Burian first demanded "a full and clear insight" into the new military situation. He wanted answers to three precise questions: Had a satisfactory agreement been reached with the Germans on military

[22] Austria, Kriegsarchiv, Berichte Cramon, folio 607, no. 29196, Falkenhayn to Cramon, 12 June 1916; unnumbered report, Cramon to Falkenhayn, 11 June; no. 1687, Cramon to Falkenhayn, 12 June; no. 1688, Cramon to Falkenhayn, 13 June.

[23] Austria, Kriegsarchiv, Berichte Cramon, folio 607, no. 29236, Falkenhayn to Cramon, 13 June; C.-F. K., Russische Front, 1916, no. 2, secret, Conrad to Falkenhayn, 19 June; no. 29546, Falkenhayn to Conrad, 19 June; Germany, Reichsarchiv, *Der Weltkrieg*, 10:484–85, 490.

help to meet the present situation? Could the government expect that Russia would be stopped in Volhynia and that an advance in northeast Galicia could be successfully opposed? Was the Russian advance against the Seventh Army to be halted and were additional forces being sent in the near future to strengthen this army? Conrad's answers were promptly forthcoming though they were not entirely as frank as they should have been. He asserted that clear agreements existed with the German High Command, "as always." In truth, "as always," there was little agreement. He then understated the help which Pless was sending by remarking that Germany was not in a position to do much but was offering what it could spare. With unwarranted optimism he declared that in Volhynia the Russians would not only be stopped but the previous situation would be reestablished. It was common knowledge in military circles that the generals would be glad if they could merely bring the Russians to a halt. In reference to northeastern Galicia and the Bukovina Conrad was perfectly candid. He could not be sure of the future in Galicia and he could not guarantee sufficient reinforcements to stop the Russian advance through the Bukovina.[24]

In the last week of June, Burian, Tisza, and Stürgkh met to orient themselves on the military situation, particularly in the Bukovina and Galicia. They found Conrad's information insufficiently precise. What they wanted was numbers of divisions, their location, and the exact conditions on the various sectors of the front. Colonel Oskar Slameczka attended that meeting as Teschen's representative. He could only be surprised at the strong demand for this kind of information, which would not be of much help to these gentlemen, but he was told they could not transact their affairs without the precise data. His answer was that he was not authorized to offer such materials without instructions from the highest war chiefs. Tisza took the matter to the commander in chief, Archduke Frederick, and Frederick, rather at sea on how to proceed, asked Franz Joseph.[25]

The old Emperor was as much upset about Conrad's military reversals as were other government officials, but to this had been added an additional irritation with the way in which the general was conducting his personal life of late. Conrad had always been a most proper type of man. He did not smoke, drank little, ate sparingly and preferred

---

[24] Redlich, *Schicksalsjahre Österreichs*, 2:122, 123, 126–27; Cramon, *Quatre Ans au G.Q.G.*, pp. 116, 117; AOK Op., secret, folio 475, no. 12294, Burian to Conrad, 23 June 1916; no. 9, Conrad to Burian, 24 June.

[25] AOK Op., secret, folio 475, no. 10, enclosure A, Slameczka to Conrad, 25 June 1916; no. 24, Tisza to Archduke Frederick, 7 July (see also attached report).

walking alone to conversing at dinner with his staff. He was also a widower. Suddenly he decided to remarry and, of all people, a divorcee. Not only was the marriage carried out, but the bride now set up residence at army headquarters with her new husband. Franz Joseph saw the whole affair as rather undignified and an unpardonable frivolity during wartime. So when he was approached by Archduke Frederick, he was in no mood to stand by his chief of staff, and gave orders that Tisza and Burian were to be sent whatever detailed information they wanted.[26]

In this way Conrad was placed in tow to the civilian authorities and lost a good deal of his previous autonomy. To underscore the point Burian sent him a stinging telegram stating that, "At the present moment when the war has reached its high point, or at least appears to be reaching it, and the development of military events can possibly lead to a decision, the directors of foreign policy need a continual and detailed orientation on the war situation more urgently than before." He went on to say that Conrad's reports were not sufficient, that favorable and unfavorable events were merely offered without conclusions and evaluations of their significance, while topographical information remained spotty. He considered all of this detail essential if he was properly to correlate foreign policy with military happenings so that his decisions would be neither too optimistic nor too pessimistic. From now on he wanted full apprisals.[27]

Conrad replied that he was astounded at such words, for Burian had always been free, since he became foreign minister, to ask concrete questions, which had been given concrete answers. In fact, Burian had never asked for such precise data though he had had plenty of opportunity to do so in their personal meetings in Vienna. And when it came to Conrad's failure to interpret the military facts, he was a general and not a prophet. There was no place where prophecy was less possible than in the art of war. Nor was it needed. For example, Burian knew of the Russian superiority in men and could draw his own conclusions. The exchange ended there but the documents demonstrate that in succeeding months Conrad was much more careful to supply copious information than he had previously been. That exacting reports on the multifarious shifting of divisions, regiments, and battalions were not of much use in foreign policy decisions was not the point. A lack of confidence in Conrad was.[28]

[26] Cramon, *Quatre Ans au G.Q.G.*, pp. 181–82; Churchill, *Unknown War*, p. 357; AOK Op., secret, folio 475, no. 238, Franz Joseph to the High Command, 8 July 1916.
[27] AOK Op., secret, folio 475, no. 313, Burian to Conrad, 7 July 1916.
[28] Ibid., no. 25, Conrad to Burian, 8 July 1916.

Unified Command

Conrad von Hötzendorf was now to find himself at bay from two directions—Vienna and Pless. Falkenhayn was determined to push through a workable solution to the question of a unified command on the eastern front. A few weeks after Conrad had rejected the idea of Mackensen taking control of most of the Austrian sector, Falkenhayn wired Cramon instructions to suggest the appointment of Hindenburg as commander of the whole front from the Bukovina to the Baltic Sea. Hindenburg would remain, "naturally," under the control of German headquarters in the west, but Pless would send him his orders only after agreement had been reached with the Austrian High Command. Hindenburg's proposals for the use of Austrian units would be sent to Teschen but only through Falkenhayn's headquarters. Conrad refused the scheme because people in the Monarchy would not understand such a bypassing of the Austrian commander in chief, Archduke Frederick, and they would see in the acceptance of the plan the complete stripping of Austrian power to handle its own military operations. With Hindenburg in such thorough control the enemy would conclude that Austria had reached the end of its strength and that its troops could only be inspired by a famous German general. The enemy would then be assured that "we had played our last trump."[29]

The matter of unified command was hardly laid to rest, for it came up for much additional discussion in July and until the first days of September, when it was resolved. Conrad did all he could to frustrate Falkenhayn on this question, but he found himself fighting Burian and Franz Joseph as well, and he was eventually defeated. On July 18 Burian informed him that the problem had been discussed during a conference with the Emperor. Unification was seen as desirable to centralize the disposition of allied troops and thus reduce the time involved in negotiations between German and Austrian headquarters. Burian was now asking what measures Conrad had taken to eliminate the obstacles to such a command.[30]

Conrad's answer was impatient and angry. He would not send Burian any information; the matter was one to be handled exclusively by high military echelons and the decision was theirs. Furthermore, he requested that Burian abstain from further interference and that third parties not be brought into the issue. But the next day, Conrad received a communication from Franz Joseph himself saying that he had seen

---

[29] Austria, Kriegsarchiv, Berichte Cramon, folio 607, no. 30349, Falkenhayn to Cramon, 3 July 1916; no. 1803, Cramon to Falkenhayn, undated.
[30] AOK Op., secret, folio 475, no. 332, Burian to Conrad, 18 July 1916.

dispatches between Hohenlohe in Berlin and Burian demonstrating that the German plan for Hindenburg's takeover had been rejected by Teschen, though Teschen had not bothered to report this to him. Conrad immediately sent him a summary of what had occurred as well as the reasons for his refusal to concur with Falkenhayn's wishes. The German chief of staff had made various suggestions since June which, taken together, were aimed at serving only German interests, German influence and prestige. It seemed to Conrad that the system used over the past two years, involving direct communications between the two headquarters staffs, was the only proper one. The current suggestion that Hindenburg control the eastern front could not possibly involve anything but Hindenburg's complete subservience to Pless. The idea of Hindenburg's mustering any independence from German headquarters could only be entertained by "unreliable diplomats dealing in things military in the exchange of their dispatches." He had personally gone to Berlin and talked with Falkenhayn, who had said that Hindenburg's name would be meaningful to Austrian troops as well as to the enemy, and that he knew "certain circles" in Vienna would be inclined to accept him. Conrad von Hötzendorf had again refused because the name of Hindenburg would "strike no fire" with Austrian forces and the experiment would be worthless. If, Conrad warned the Emperor, the whole eastern command fell into German hands, it would mean that Russian areas occupied by German divisions would be secured even at the cost of further invasion of Austro-Hungarian possessions. And at the end of the war Germany would retain its own conquests of Russian territory even if it meant parts of the Monarchy must go to Russia as compensation. Fully aware of his duty, he had refused the scheme, and he asked that the diplomats be kept out of what were purely military matters so as not to ruin all his endeavors at getting what was needed: the greatest possible German aid to meet the Monarchy's needs.[31]

Conrad's opposition to Hindenburg's control of the eastern front was shortly to weaken as a result of several things. Additional defeats in the area around Brody meant the Russians might succeed in taking the key city of Lemberg in Galicia. The deteriorating situation with Rumania indicated that Austria would need still more help and would now have to cooperate with German desires. With the battles of the Somme and the Isonzo in progress, the eastern front was on its own for replacements, a condition clearly necessitating every bit of efficiency in

[31] Ibid., no. 40, Conrad to Burian, 19 July 1916; no. 242, Franz Joseph to Conrad through Bolfras, 19 July; no. 41, Conrad to Franz Joseph, 19 July.

troop displacement that could be mustered. And, finally, there was the apparent inclination of Franz Joseph to accept some sort of unified command.[32]

Falkenhayn now made a new offer which was supported by Wilhelm II, who, in turn, personally requested Franz Joseph to concur and asked that Archduke Frederick and Conrad be sent to Pless to arrange the settlement. Wilhelm, in his telegram to Franz Joseph, said that "The situation in the east seems to me so serious that one must consider corresponding measures." Franz Joseph agreed with him, and on July 27 Conrad and Archduke Frederick met with Falkenhayn, Hindenburg, and the Kaiser at German headquarters. Out of this meeting came an agreement giving Hindenburg limited control of the eastern front. This involved direct mastery over the Austrian Fourth, First, and Second armies so that Hindenburg was now at liberty to supervise the Austrian sector from the Pripet Marshes to a point somewhat south of Lemberg. He was to be subject to the German High Command but in military matters south of the Pripet River, Pless would issue him no orders unless Austrian headquarters had first given full consent. Furthermore, concerning the area north of the Pripet, the Germans obligated themselves to give prior consideration to operations of the Austrian Southern, Third, and Seventh armies, and Conrad agreed to reciprocate. While both allies accepted the shift of troops from one front to another as might be necessary, Conrad was so suspicious of Austrian troops being used to serve purely German interests that he insisted on incorporating into the formal agreement a statement which declared that Hindenburg's job was solely to stop the Russian advance on the front he commanded. In his communications with Falkenhayn prior to the meeting at Pless, he had been even more specific, stating that the duty of Hindenburg would be limited to repulsing the Russians in Volhynia and eastern Galicia. Falkenhayn had agreed.[33]

Thus on July 28 Hindenburg took over his new duties. Falkenhayn had not obtained all he wanted but at least he had achieved a partial solution. Conrad did not care for the deal at all, but was really forced into it by circumstances over which he had no power. He came away from the Pless conference comforting himself with the fact that at least the Austrian armies responsible for defending southern Galicia, the

---

[32] Germany, Reichsarchiv, *Der Weltkrieg*, 10:529–30; Eric von Ludendorff, *My War Memories*, 1:229.

[33] AOK Op., secret, folio 475, no. 30, Falkenhayn to Conrad, 23 July 1916; no. 361, Franz Joseph to Archduke Frederick, 24 July; no. 52, draft of the agreement between German and Austrian headquarters, 28 July; no. 53, Franz Joseph to Conrad, 29 July; no. 44, Conrad to Falkenhayn, 24 July.

approaches to Hungary east of the Carpathians, the Bukovina, and the Italian theater were still in his hands.

Five weeks later the Austrian chief found his freedom of action still more restricted. Toward the end of August Falkenhayn approached him with a scheme aimed at producing a unified command for the whole war effort on all fronts—one that would place under a single roof the military campaigns and activities of Germany, Austria-Hungary, Bulgaria, and Turkey. This was not entirely Falkenhayn's brainchild, since Enver Pasha, King Ferdinand, and even certain officers of the Austrian army who were not under Conrad's immediate control at Teschen, had expressed a desire to see something like this emerge. In part the German chief of staff wanted such a structure in order to control more thoroughly the Bulgarian army, whose importance increased in direct ratio to the uncertainty of continued Rumanian neutrality during August. In part he wanted it to end the interminable haggling between himself and Conrad over questions of which front ought to be emphasized at any given time. Moreover, the shortage of replacements had become so severe and the pressure of the Entente so all-pervasive—attacks on the Somme, on the Isonzo, against the Austrian Fourth and Seventh armies, against the Bulgarians facing Sarrail's Salonika force—that something approximating a central military agency was patently called for.[34]

Falkenhayn went to Teschen on August 24 for conversations, but after Conrad had thought it over he wired his characteristic "no." He did not think such an all-engrossing unified command would work, because if one of the allies disagreed with any particular order there would be no unity. Falkenhayn's idea was to have the Kaiser sit as the supreme chief of the allied armies, using the German chief of staff as his implementing organ. But, objected Conrad, the Germans could not deal effectively with what was his own specific duty, that is, the solution of special problems having to do with the Empire and its particular military interests. And as far as Bulgaria was concerned, any general agreement on command would mean nothing because Bulgaria took military action to meet its own political aspirations. Furthermore, how could Germany hope to lead the allies effectively when, as in the case of Italy, it was not itself yet at war with one of Austria's enemies?[35]

Conrad's reasoning was sound enough on each of these points but

---

[34] Cramon, *Quatre Ans au G.Q.G.*, pp. 116, 124–25; AOK Op., secret, folio 475, no. 85, Conrad to Franz Joseph, 23 August 1916.

[35] AOK Op., secret, folio 475, no. 88, Conrad to Falkenhayn, 26 August 1916.

Falkenhayn must have read with amazement the Austrian chief's bland assertion that he could not remember a case where Austrian and German headquarters had not been able to reach agreement. True, he had attacked the Montenegrins on his own initiative, but he had been successful. True, they had not agreed on Italy but he had *tried* for an agreement. But it was precisely because of the bitterness engendered in the case of Montenegro and the numerous warnings of Falkenhayn to remain on the defensive in Italy, to say nothing of the exhausting feuds in 1915 concerning Russia and Serbia, that Pless now sought to unify the direction of the conflict.[36]

Conrad von Hötzendorf got to the basis of his rejection when he stated that in his opinion a German-led command of this sort would mean that the whole Austrian army would be under foreign domination and such domination would have an effect on much more than simply the conduct of Austrian military affairs. The repercussions would be felt on the political level because the whole future relationship between the German Reich and the Monarchy would be affected. Austro-Hungarian independence, power, and prestige would be at stake. Beyond the question of the Monarchy and its future, there was that of Bulgaria and Turkey and their continued loyalty to the Central Powers. In each of these two countries there were powerful pro-Entente forces who would use German supremacy in a unified command as a basis for agitating against men like Radoslavov, Zekoff, and Enver Pasha, and would possibly cause their political overthrow. In the end the men who supported German influence would no longer hold power and a situation would have developed quite contrary to Falkenhayn's expectations.[37]

Conrad became so upset over the possibilities of the project's implementation that he threatened to resign if it went through. While Franz Joseph had lost a certain amount of confidence in his chief of staff, he was not prepared to replace him. Besides, he did not like the proposal any more than did his general. Nevertheless, the Emperor believed that the issue of unified command should be further pursued so that in the future Germany and Austria would not work tangentially. Conrad now made a countersuggestion. To develop a unified leadership the four allied commands would come to agreement in each single instance on operational goals and forces to be used. Where troops of more than one ally were involved, agreement would be reached between the parties concerned as to who would issue the orders. The stimulus for

[36] Ibid.
[37] Ibid.

strengthening the ties between the commands would rest with each of the individual allies. While the German High Command would lead the negotiations between the allies, each would control the shifting of its own forces from one war theater to another. Where agreement proved impossible among the four, the vote of Germany *and* Austria-Hungary would be decisive.[38]

What Conrad envisaged here was not really a unified command at all but rather something that constituted a supreme war council in which each of the four allies maintained a great deal of independence. His proposal was a much-watered-down version of what the Germans had in mind.

An answer from Pless was not immediately forthcoming, since on August 29 Falkenhayn was forced to resign and was replaced by Hindenburg and Ludendorff, the latter holding the position of first quartermaster general. The title was rather misleading since in reality Ludendorff's duties made him the equivalent of a vice chief of staff. The partners were to work hand in glove in running Germany's war. Falkenhayn had fallen victim to Bethmann-Hollweg's behind-the-scenes agitation. Reversals on the eastern front, setbacks at Verdun in June and July, and the declaration of war by Rumania on August 27 (something which Falkenhayn had not expected), were all elements in the decision by Wilhelm II to replace him. Conrad was delighted with the change, having always gotten on rather well with Hindenburg and Ludendorff. The three had consistently seen eye-to-eye on emphasizing operations in the east. In spite of this, Conrad was not to take a more charitable view of the Germans. On the contrary, he came to distrust Ludendorff, for whom he saw Hindenburg as only a cover, more than he had Falkenhayn. He later labeled the new commander a second Bismarck whose intention was to put the Monarchy completely under German leadership in political as well as military affairs. Yet, in spite of his uneasiness concerning future German-Austrian relations, Conrad was able to work with Pless more smoothly than heretofore on immediate military needs.[39]

Pless wasted no time in again taking up the question of a unified command. Ludendorff, having been filled in on the extent of the negotiations with Teschen, made a detailed compromise proposal,

[38] Cramon, *Quatre Ans au G.Q.G.*, pp. 125–26; AOK Op., secret, folio 475, no. 88, Conrad to Falkenhayn, 26 August 1916.

[39] C.-F. K., Russische Front, 1916, no. 6518, copies of the Kaiser's official appointment of Hindenburg and Ludendorff and his acceptance of Falkenhayn's resignation, 29 August 1916; Ritter, *Staatskunst und Kriegshandwerk*, 3:225, 226, 227; Austria, Kriegsarchiv, Conrad Archiv, folio B-8, unnumbered letter, Conrad to Bolfras in Vienna, 14 October.

which he sent to Conrad on September 2. It was clear, he said, that there must be understanding and amity among the allies, but on the other hand it was necessary that orders originate from one place so as to provide a crucial cohesion. That place of origin should be the German crown. Because the war had shown that Germany had constantly striven to support its allies, no fear should exist that Germany would make decisions prejudicial to the interests of those allies. The fate of each of the four nations was so closely bound to that of the others that only a unified command could meet the obligation imposed. That fate had to be met on the basis of purely military considerations. If the German Kaiser commanded the operations of the allies, the rights of each chief of staff would, nevertheless, remain unimpaired. The Supreme Command would be concerned only with the general situation, with the unity necessary to put through operations placed in a larger context, with basic goals. It would deal with forces to be committed to the various fronts, with the makeup of orders where more than one ally was committed, with the judgment of reports on military plans which each ally would be asked to submit, and with each ally's power and capacity. All decisions would go through German headquarters, but the relationship presently existing between each ally's chief of staff and his own field commanders would remain untouched. Such an arrangement was to come into effect only if all agreed.[40]

Franz Joseph, Burian, and Conrad were willing to accept the new organization, but Conrad proposed to Vienna that Germany first commit itself to a special secret clause, which Vienna readily approved. The clause stated that when the Kaiser took over the general command of operations he would agree to view the territorial integrity of the Monarchy as the equivalent of that of the Reich. When this integrity was affected by a decision the unified command might make, the Austrian army chief was not bound to give his consent to that decision. Any operation involving that integrity must first have the approval of Franz Joseph before the Kaiser could implement it. In this manner Conrad successfully hedged the power of the supreme commander since the word integrity allowed for wide interpretation. Conrad and Hindenburg signed the agreement on September 6 and Bulgaria and Turkey somewhat later in the same month.[41] A unified command had finally been born, but too late to be of any striking significance.

[40] AOK Op., secret, folio 475, no. 33982, Ludendorff to Conrad, 2 September 1916.
[41] AOK Op., secret, folio 475, no. 107, Burian to Conrad, 3 September 1916. See attachments for Conrad's suggested secret clause; no. 112, Conrad to Burian, 7 September; no. 181, Conrad to Burian, 11 November.

The Rumanian Campaign

The question of command had proved difficult enough to solve but the problem of what to do about Rumania was much worse. From the time Brussilov's offensive began Conrad was distraught over the possibility of Rumania's attacking the Monarchy by invading Transylvania. Rumania's longtime fear of having to fight the Bulgarians on its southern border while at the same time trying to deal with the Austrians was progressively minimized the more Brussilov's offensive succeeded and the more the Entente entertained the idea of a thrust at the Bulgarians from Salonika. In mid-June, 1916, Conrad wrote to Falkenhayn that the Russians and Italians were trying for a decision by attacking simultaneously, and if Russian advances continued there was no doubt in his own mind that the Rumanians would declare war. The grim fact was that he had no available troops to stop the Rumanian army should it begin an offensive across the Transylvanian border. And he again warned Pless in early July that if the Russians succeeded in getting over the Carpathians there was nothing to stop them. A Russian strike in combination with a Rumanian would finish Austrian resistance. To preclude a Rumanian attack, German reinforcements must be sent to aid Austrian forces, which might then stop Brussilov in the south. A Russian failure to advance would cause the Rumanians to hold off. Falkenhayn agreed that the situation was serious and he promised reinforcements for the southern theater as soon as they became available.[42]

One of the factors involved in the forced resignation of Falkenhayn at the end of August was that he misjudged the Rumanians and the imminence of their war participation on the side of the Entente. In spite of Conrad's telegrams and in spite of awareness in the German Foreign Office of the rapid deterioration in relations between Bukarest and the Central Powers, Falkenhayn could still wire Conrad as late as mid-August that from all reports he had, the Rumanian attack would be a long time in developing. It was not that he believed the Rumanians would remain neutral but rather that he judged their decision would be withheld until October, well after the harvests had been gathered.[43]

Falkenhayn's mistake was poor judgment, not carelessness. In June,

---

[42] Austria, Kriegsarchiv, Berichte Cramon, folio 607, no. 1680, 11 June 1916; C.-F. K., Russische Front, 1916, no. 7, Conrad to Falkenhayn, 2 June; AOK Op., secret, folio 475, no. 26, Conrad to Falkenhayn, 9 July; no. 30747, Falkenhayn to Conrad, 10 July.

[43] Carl Mühlmann, Oberste Heeresleitung und Balkan im Weltkrieg, 1914–1918, p. 170; Germany, Reichsarchiv, Der Weltkrieg, 10:602, 559; C.-F. K., Russische Front, 1916, no. 32893, Falkenhayn to Conrad, 13 August.

July, and August a good deal of negotiation took place between Germans and the Bulgarian chief of staff, and as much preparation was made as was practically possible against future hostilities with Rumanian troops. In June, Falkenhayn called for and got a strengthening of Bulgarian troops on the southern Rumanian border. By the end of the month he had asked for a commitment by the Turks for additional strength. The difficulty was that the exact number of divisions needed to take care of the Rumanian threat could not be fixed because the situation on the Russian front continued to be fluid. In late July, however, a military convention among the four allies was agreed to, which left Bukarest in no doubt that it would face all of them in case of war. Germany pledged one division, the Bulgarians pledged four, the Turks two, the Austrians their Danubian flotilla. And in August, Conrad scraped together five divisions to defend Transylvania. It was not much, considering that Rumania could throw in over twenty divisions for an initial campaign, but the replacement and reinforcement problem had by now become critical. The Germans on the eastern front were responsible for a battle line of over 1,000 kilometers, and Hindenburg and Ludendorff, to support the Austrians, had stretched that line as thin and taut as a bow string. Falkenhayn could not pull units from the west because of fighting at Verdun and the Somme. Conrad was concerned with holding against the Italians, and the Bulgarian and small German forces in Macedonia had to deal with the Salonika army. The situation could not have been worse.[44]

In trying to develop the best possible defense against a future Rumanian offensive Conrad found himself once again at swordspoint with Burian and with German military leaders. When in July, Burian asked him how much of a Bulgarian force could be counted on to go against Rumania, he answered that Bulgaria had approximately 300,000 men. Two-thirds of these were in Macedonia and of the remainder only 70,000 would be available to move against Rumania in the Dobrudja. And even if additional Bulgarian troops became available, they would not be of appreciable aid to the weak Austrian forces in Transylvania since the Bulgarian railroads could transport only a single division in a two-week period. Burian, Tisza, and Stürgkh met again with Col. Slameczka on July 13, very much disturbed by Conrad's information. Tisza was especially concerned, saying he had been led to believe the Bulgarians had 500,000 or 600,000 men available. Now he was being told they had half that figure. Slameczka pointed out that Bulgaria did

---

[44] Mühlmann, *Oberste Heeresleitung*, pp. 166–67; Germany, Reichsarchiv, *Der Weltkrieg*, 10:599–601, 603.

have such a pool of men but the shortage of commissioned and non-commissioned officers and the lack of necessary artillery made formation of additional units impossible. Well then, asked the Hungarian president, in case of a Rumanian invasion of Transylvania was he to assume that there would be no capacity to oppose it? Slameczka could only answer weakly that this would "not entirely" be the case. Conrad candidly told Burian that if Rumania attacked Transylvania a border defense would be effectively impossible and that forces there would have to retreat and surrender Transylvanian territory until additional reinforcements could be brought in. He nevertheless had some ideas on how the Rumanian strike might be vitiated or perhaps avoided altogether. So it was that in August he suggested a demarche by the four allies which would involve an open declaration to Bukarest that an attack on one would constitute an attack on all. Such a declaration would end Bratianu's attempts to avoid war with the Monarchy's three allies and would give him pause. The idea was rejected by Burian as too risky because it would be seen as a bellicose threat and would only irritate, not pacify, the Rumanians.[45]

Distrusting the Bulgarians thoroughly, Conrad attempted to obtain a precise commitment from them that they would indeed take the field against Rumania. That Bulgaria had already made such a commitment through the military convention signed on July 28 did not impress him because shortly thereafter Colonel Rudolf Nowak, now the Austrian military attaché in Sofia, reported a conversation in which he had sounded General Zostoff of the Bulgarian staff. Zostoff had stated that Bulgaria was not obligated to any offensive against Rumania even if Rumania attacked the Monarchy first. And since the Salonika forces were soon going to undertake a serious campaign against Bulgarian troops, Bulgaria would be unable to send any additional units to the Rumanian border. To the Austrian military this meant that the Bulgarians might well renege on their obligations stated in the 1915 alliance, that is, that Bulgaria would move against Rumania should the latter attack the Monarchy without provocation.[46]

Conrad reported this conversation to Falkenhayn and Burian. Falkenhayn dismissed it by saying that Zostoff's opinions were not very important. The men who controlled Bulgaria's war effort were King Ferdinand and Zekoff, and of these two the Central Powers could be certain. Burian was very impatient with Teschen because of the at-

[45] AOK Op., secret, folio 475, no. 27, Conrad to Burian, 11 July 1916; no. 35, minutes of ministerial meeting, 13 July; no. 58, Conrad to Burian, 5 August; no. 3907, Burian to Conrad, 10 August. See also chapter 10 above, pp. 226–47.

[46] AOK Op., secret, folio 475, no. 66, Conrad to Falkenhayn, 11 August 1916.

taché's interference. Radoslavov had talked with Tarnowski about Zostoff's statement and had agreed with it. No commitment concerning a specific attack could now be made, noted Radoslavov, for if Rumania heard of it, provocation would have been established, and this would then run contrary to the wording of the alliance. And why, queried Radoslavov, had such an important consideration been discussed with Zostoff when it should have been discussed with him? Burian had a question of his own: Why had Conrad not given him foreknowledge of a matter pertaining to alliance obligations? The business should have gone through Minister Tarnowski and not through a military attaché. Conrad had acted rashly and by so doing had given the impression that Austria was trying to strong-arm Bulgaria—an impression which had produced a very negative reaction in Sofia.[47]

In the meantime, Nowak had seen Radoslavov and had vehemently denied he was trying to manipulate Zostoff into anything. Radoslavov regally dismissed the whole issue as a misunderstanding. The confusion ended there but not before Conrad got off a counterblast to Burian, protesting that he had never instructed Nowak to apply pressure and that Burian himself had said that a Bulgarian operation against Rumanian troops was strictly the province of army leadership. On that basis, he, Conrad, had negotiated with the Bulgarian High Command.[48]

The source of the difficulty had been Conrad's nervousness, so intense that he found it impossible to leave well enough alone. In reality there was nothing to worry about since the Bulgarians had no intention of avoiding a fight with the Rumanian army; they had been looking forward to it since the end of the Balkan Wars. This soon became apparent when Mackensen was placed in charge of what would be a combined operation against Rumania (something foreseen by the military convention of July) but which in the end evidenced a predominance of Bulgarian soldiers. Conrad von Hötzendorf was still dissatisfied, though now his dissatisfaction centered around differences of opinion as to what strategy could best be applied to a belligerent Rumania. Conrad strongly advocated an attack by Mackensen's army over the Danube and directly into Rumania toward Bukarest. By early August he was sending the Bulgarians both light and heavy bridging materials to be used for crossing the river. On the other hand, the Germans favored first driving into the Dobrudja, which would clear

---

[47] Ibid., no. 32796, Falkenhayn to Conrad, 12 August 1916; no. 365, Burian to Conrad, 14 August.

[48] Ibid., no. 3741, Nowak to Conrad, 12 August 1916; no. 79, Conrad to Burian, 16 August.

their flank of a combined Rumanian and Russian offensive. They could not see how a Danube crossing could be successful when they would have to defend the rest of the Bulgarian border against a Rumanian enemy supported by Russian units. They had insufficient troops to handle both tasks. Conrad brushed all this aside, asserting that a move into the Dobrudja would not succeed once it ran up against Russian opposition. And even if it did succeed it would have no effect on the Rumanian push into Transylvania. By comparison, a quick strike over the Danube toward the Rumanian capital would not only disturb the Rumanian march into Hungary but would have a decisive result. It could be supported by Austrian troops in Transylvania and would end the threat to that area.[49]

Mackensen now tried to convince Conrad that the Dobrudja move was initially the best. He assured him that it was not intended to satisfy Bulgarian territorial ambitions there but to give his forces greater freedom and security and to shorten the existing southern border in the Dobrudja by half, assuming that they could take Silistria. Crossing the Danube was just not feasible. There were insufficient infantry and artillery. In principle, responded Conrad, he could agree; from a practical point of view, he could not. This was followed by a blast against the Bulgarians, which Conrad sent to Burian on August 19. The Bulgarians were apparently influenced by two considerations in their military negotiations. They sought to avoid fighting the Russians and, as had been witnessed the previous winter, they committed their troops only where there was an opportunity of extending control. It was because of this that the emphasis was being placed on the Dobrudja. There was, of course, some truth in Conrad's view, for certainly the Bulgarian king was interested in obtaining that territory. But Conrad's logic was faulty, since it was known that the Rumanians were to be supported in the Dobrudja by Russian units. Perhaps more important, Conrad refused, as in various past instances, to deal realistically with what could and could not be accomplished militarily at the moment. In the end Hindenburg ruled out the Danube crossing and Mackensen went ahead with the Dobrudja plan.[50] The decision proved a wise one.

When Cramon called Falkenhayn by phone on August 27 to tell him Rumania had declared war, the German chief of staff at first refused to

[49] Ibid., no. 39, Conrad to Nowak in Sofia, 19 July 1916; no. 55, Conrad to Burian, 3 August; no. 63, Conrad to Falkenhayn, 8 August; no. 73, Conrad to Mackensen in Uskub, 15 August.
[50] Ibid., no. 475, Mackensen to Conrad, 17 August 1916; no. 81, Conrad to Mackensen, Falkenhayn, and Burian, 18 August; unnumbered, Conrad to Burian, 19 August; no. 33918, Hindenburg to Conrad, 1 September.

believe it, notwithstanding the signs, the telegrams, the plans and discussions of the past two months. But if he was surprised, the Kaiser was shattered. Wilhelm was now convinced that the war was conclusively lost and that further bloodletting would be meaningless. He bitterly—and quite unfairly—reproached Falkenhayn for having done nothing to prevent the Rumanian decision. Falkenhayn was guilty of an unwarranted optimism as to the date when Rumania would make its decision, but to have kept the Rumanians neutral would have required at least the retaking of the Bukovina. In light of the continued Russian weight on the southeastern front, the reoccupation had been impossible to achieve. The commanders were glad they had managed by late August to bring the Russians to a halt at the Carpathian wall. Hindenburg had a very positive effect on Wilhelm's attitude and a few days after the new chief of staff was in office the royal opinion had changed at least to the point of seeing things as better than hopeless.[51]

That by December the Rumanians were to be completely defeated and their country occupied by the Central Powers was a condition which in August would have seemed almost miraculous. The Rumanians began their drive into Transylvania with a ten to one numerical superiority over an Austrian army hastily gathered together by Conrad, consisting of approximately 25,000 tired men. Conrad had already prepared Vienna for the fact that there was no chance of an effective border defense and that southeastern Transylvania would have to be given up at least temporarily. But he held out hope that troops being shifted to the Transylvanian front would be in position in about two weeks and would then blunt the Rumanian campaign. Burian asked him caustically if it was not to be feared that within two weeks Rumania's energetic attack would overrun Transylvania in its entirety. Conrad's answer was that concrete promises were never possible in wartime but the Austrian High Command would not permit extensive loss of territory within the Empire. In spite of this bravado Teschen knew it had little field strength to offer. It was the Germans who took the burden and ended by defeating the Rumanians.[52]

As soon as Hindenburg and Ludendorff took over command at Pless, they decided that every available man from the western and eastern fronts must be sent to meet the new enemy. In both theaters German units went on the defensive and Pless cut every corner it could, even to

[51] Cramon, *Quatre Ans au G.Q.G.*, p. 135; Staatsarchiv, PA, box 520, Count Thurn to Burian, 31 August 1916.

[52] AOK Op., secret, folio 475, no. 93, Conrad to Falkenhayn, 28 August 1916; no. 390, Burian to Conrad, 31 August; no. 104, Conrad to Burian through Wiesner, 1 September.

the point of using garrison troops in Belgium. Troops in rest areas were shipped out. Training of new recruits was cut short. New divisions that had been slated for the west were rerouted. While the Austrian First Army was positioned to defend Transylvania from Rumanian forces attacking from Moldavia in the northeast, a new German army, the Ninth, was created and Falkenhayn given command. In spite of efforts to give him an effective force, all he had to work with when he took over on September 6 was four divisions; they opposed two full Rumanian armies. Mackensen had one German division to guard the Danube against eight Rumanian on the other side. Facing the Dobrudja there were approximately four and a half divisions to deal with five Rumanian backed by Russian support. The strain on nerves at Pless and Teschen was enormous. Ignoring the odds, Mackensen boldly crossed the Dobrudja frontier on September 1 and five days later took Turtukai. On September 9 he entered Silistria. By the end of the month he was nearing the port of Constanza, which he secured in October. His attack had been a brilliant stroke and had done what it was intended to do—worry and divert the enemy.[53]

While Mackensen was on the attack, there was little that Falkenhayn could do initially but hold as best he could. The Rumanians had very quickly taken Kronstadt and then Hermannstadt, but they proved to be very slow in pushing their advantage. The Austrian First Army held its ground in the north, the Russians were thwarted in their attempt to pass over the Carpathians, and Falkenhayn received additional divisions to increase his power. He now gradually became able to take the initiative and by September 30 had reoccupied Hermannstadt. At the same time the Austrians proved capable of beginning forward movement in the north. In October Falkenhayn retook Kronstadt but he needed more troops if he was to get through the mountains and into Rumania itself. Seven new divisions were now allotted to him, and since Mackensen had done so well in the Dobrudja, he was able to break off his offensive there and reroute his troops to the Danube. The Danube crossing at Sistova, which Conrad had originally desired, was now readied though it was not begun until November 23. Once the crossing was accomplished the Central Powers were on their way to a smashing victory. The Rumanians pulled back large numbers of their armies in the north to face Mackensen's threat to their capital city. Once this happened, Falkenhayn could successfully thread his way

[53] Mühlmann, *Oberste Heeresleitung*, p. 171; Ludendorff, *War Memories*, 1:248, 280, 286; Churchill, *The World Crisis*, 3:209, 210; Wolfgang Foerster, ed., *Mackensen: Briefe und Aufzeichnungen*, p. 284. For greater detail on his Dobrudja campaign see *Mackensen, Briefe*, pp. 285–321.

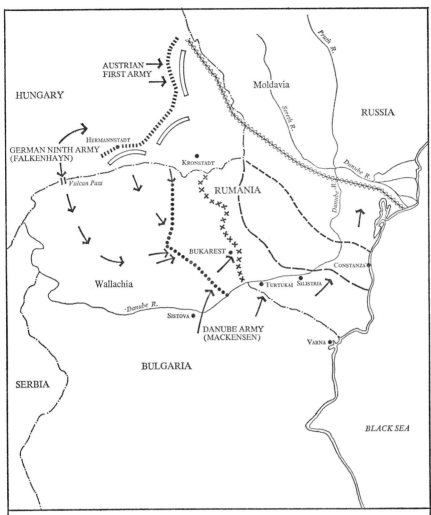

THE CAMPAIGN OF THE CENTRAL POWERS
AGAINST RUMANIA, 1916-1917

	Rumanian armies
	German and Austrian thrusts
‖‖‖‖‖‖‖‖‖	Line of farthest Rumanian advance

Lines of German progress:

●●●●●●●●●●●●	November 3, 1916
✕✕✕✕✕✕✕✕✕✕	December 6, 1916
	December 10, 1916
– – – – – – –	December 17, 1916
∞∞∞∞∞∞∞∞∞∞	January 8, 1917

through the mountain passes of the Transylvanian Alps leading to the Rumanian plain. He had probed those passes earlier but they were two to three thousand feet deep and very difficult to take when defended by the Rumanian armies at their full strength. Once reduced to take care of Mackensen's attack in the south, the Rumanian forces could not hold against Falkenhayn, who plunged through the Vulcan Pass, a real gateway, to link up with Mackensen's group. The Germans were now fifteen divisions strong. On December 6 Mackensen celebrated his sixty-fourth birthday by occupying Bukarest. And by January 8, 1917, the Rumanian army had been pushed to the Sereth River in Moldavia. Rumania was out of the war as an effective belligerent.[54]

Though the year had ended on a note of triumph, there was little optimism. Both Germany and Austria had paid a staggering price in lives but had little to show for it in concrete military achievements. Falkenhayn had failed at Verdun and Conrad in the Tyrol. Combined forces in the east had fallen back before the Russian onslaught and the entire Austrian army was near collapse. Disaster at the hands of the Rumanians had narrowly been averted. In January, 1916, the military thinking of both allies had been offensive in nature. As the year wore on their orientation shifted to defense and containment. By Christmas they derived comfort only from the fact that their defense against the concerted efforts of the Entente had been successful. The one bright star in a rather gray military sky was the defeat of Rumania.

The relationship between the two Central Powers had proved as disappointing as the military events themselves. Cooperation between the German and Austro-Hungarian high commands had, since the start of the war, always been less than it should have been. But 1916 demonstrated an increase in the divergencies between the two headquarters. A supreme unified command was brought into existence, but this did not herald the lessening of animosities.

To make matters worse strife existed within high-echelon circles in both countries. Falkenhayn, fallen victim to Bethmann-Hollweg's dislike, had been forced to resign. Von Jagow was also to resign his post by the end of the year, to be replaced by Zimmermann. More dramatic, and perhaps more meaningful in terms of continued war effort, were the changes in Austria-Hungary. In November, Franz Joseph died and was succeeded by Archduke Karl, who did not agree with Conrad's

[54] Ludendorff, *War Memories*, 1:280, 281, 282, 284, 285–86, 296, 298, 299, 300, 303; Churchill, *World Crisis*, 3:211; Ernst Kabisch, *Der Rumänien Krieg, 1916*, p. 147. For details concerning the German Ninth Army, see Erich von Falkenhayn, *Der Feldzug der 9. Armee.*

views. The chief of staff was made a field marshal and then, ninety days later, was relieved of his post and transferred to Italy as a field commander. Emperor Karl took over the direction of the war himself, replaced Burian with Czernin as foreign minister in December, and advocated an end to the war. Wilhelm II still had stomach for continuing the fight. Karl did not.

Chapter 14

Conclusions

The relations between Germany and Austria-Hungary from 1914 to 1917 do not allow for easy characterization. These relations were neither consistently disparate nor consistently cooperative and demonstrate no continuous domination by one partner or the other. The alliance between the two was a troubled and sometimes tortured one. At its best it was held together by agreement on general goals; at its worst, by the recognition that the war was one of survival for the two empires. It worked because of the necessities of wartime. Cooperation was often achieved because of expediency, not because of genuine and carefully reasoned conviction that brought the two allies to a common meeting ground.

The disparities arising between the two foreign offices were not based on differences of goal. The goal was obvious and easy to define: victory in the field against the Entente powers. There was unity of means—to gain that victory through the establishment of a strong Balkan coalition which, once committed to the Central Powers, would give them a very large fighting force against the Russians and eliminate any possible threat of attack from the Balkan area. The disagreement between Vienna and Berlin came in the approach to be taken in attempting to establish that coalition. This disagreement was based on two quite different points of view, which to any disinterested observer were, peculiarly enough, equally valid.

The German attitude was based on necessity, on the understanding that war is an extremely pragmatic condition allowing for little in the way of subtlety and requiring immediate solutions as problems arise. Germany disliked the idea of signing an alliance with Turkey because of all the concomitant obligations such an accord involved or implied. It disliked the idea of an alliance with Bulgaria, which it distrusted. Nor did it particularly enjoy the prospect of territorial concessions to Rumania at the direct expense of its Austrian ally. But for Berlin it was not a question of like or dislike. In the eyes of German leaders no sacrifice was too great if it served the war effort.

That was not the position taken by the Dual Monarchy. By the very nature of its makeup and its geographical position, Austria was deeply concerned with Balkan affairs. What happened in the Balkans could have a direct bearing on the well-being of the Empire. The Ballhausplatz therefore approached its diplomatic policy with the constant awareness that any commitment might directly affect the interests of the Monarchy either immediately or in the future. Austria understood as well as Germany that the war was a life-or-death struggle and was willing to make sacrifices to win that struggle. But its leaders often looked further into what would be the postwar world than did Berlin, and they refused sacrifices which would clearly compromise the postwar power status of Austria-Hungary. When no such compromise was involved, Vienna cooperated with the Wilhelmstrasse. When Austrian interests were endangered it balked at measures suggested by Berlin. And when territory of the Monarchy proper was at stake, it flatly rejected the remonstrations of its ally. These three approaches are clearly demonstrated by the negotiations which occurred with Turkey, Bulgaria, and Rumania.

World War I Austria has sometimes been classified as Germany's "brilliant second." It is manifest that such a title is a misnomer. It was the Austrians who first interested Berlin in alliances with Turkey and Bulgaria and then convinced the Germans of the necessity of such alliances. And it was Austria, too, that first recognized the extent to which the old alliance with Rumania had deteriorated by August, 1914. As the war proceeded, the Ballhausplatz proved scarcely docile as an ally, hardly willing to follow where Germany might try to lead.

In Turkey the Austrians, aware that Germany held there a much stronger economic and military position than the Monarchy, were perfectly willing to let the Wilhelmstrasse initially dominate, first in establishing an accord and then in obtaining direct participation in the war. Although as late as July, 1914, Germany hesitated to establish a direct diplomatic connection with the Turks, once Berlin decided to accept a commitment the German policy regarding Constantinople remained consistent. Thus in November, 1914, when the Turkish government suggested an alliance of much greater scope than that signed the previous August, Bethmann-Hollweg accepted the Turkish request. He did so unwillingly, but he agreed with the reasoning of Ambassador Wangenheim that the war had to be won by *all* means.

It was at this point that the Austrians took issue, because the commitments desired by the Turks involved a responsibility to protect Turkey against possible attacks by any future hostile coalition of Balkan states. Austria-Hungary bordered on three of these states and therefore moved cautiously in formulating any such accord. Burian sought to make sure Turkey could not cause Austria undue trouble in the future.

If the Ballhausplatz was loathe to accept a new and far-reaching alliance with the Turks, it nevertheless concurred because the war effort demanded this. It cannot be denied that Berlin produced this concurrence by working patiently to smooth away Austria's objections. The Austrians often saw more clearly the subtleties of a situation, but German thinking was superior in its consistent recognition of the demands of the moment.

What applied in the case of Turkey applied even more strongly in the case of Bulgaria. Once convinced by Vienna that it was necessary to obtain Bulgaria as an ally, the German diplomats went at the affair with hammer and tongs. If it meant giving Bulgaria large territorial concessions, then this had to be done. If it meant signing a precise alliance, then one must be signed. Berlin did not negotiate recklessly nor with anything even approaching abandon, but as 1915 wore on, the need for Bulgarian aid became increasingly greater and German attempts to persuade King Ferdinand and Radoslavov to join the Central Powers became correspondingly stronger. These attempts ended in a firm concurrence of German diplomats with the Bulgarian wish for an alliance and an apparent willingness to accept whatever demands the Bulgarians thought necessary.

In Austrian diplomatic circles the negotiations with Sofia caused considerable resentment against the Wilhelmstrasse. When Burian took over at the Foreign Office he declared that he would be satisfied with Bulgarian neutrality. For this neutrality he was willing to pay a price, but the written guarantees of wider concessions desired by the Bulgarians were something which he hardly approved since these "involved the further destinies of Austria-Hungary." Again, by consistent pressure Berlin convinced Austria it ought to give way, and the written guarantees were offered. When Sofia later sought to realize its territorial ambitions through a formal alliance, the Germans eagerly took the initiative and brought the matter to a rapid conclusion in spite of Austria, which would have preferred to pick its way more carefully. Burian saw this German initiative, this German determination to "close the deal," as extremely high-handed and indeed as a demonstration of German rudeness toward his government. He nevertheless agreed once again for the sake of the war. This overriding consideration in no way obviated the fact that Austrian statesmen understood the Balkan mind better than most of their German counterparts. Necessarily, they had had more experience in dealing with the Balkans. Bismarck had lumped together the Balkan states, referring to them as "those people down there." For the Austrians they were immediate neighbors whose ambitions had to be carefully weighed in terms of possible impingement on the Monarchy's welfare. In the case of Bulgaria, Vienna went along with the necessary concessions because the Monarchy would not, in any direct sense, be territorially marred thereby.

In the final analysis, Bulgaria was won by the Central Powers simply because they could bid higher at the bargaining tables than could the Entente. The Radoslavov government had its eye primarily on Serbia and Serbian Macedonia, and, since Serbia was an ally of the Entente, the latter could not make its offers sufficiently enticing. Germany, of course, could give away the areas desired with impunity, the Kaiser's suspicions of King Ferdinand's slyness notwithstanding. Austria was much more concerned with its own postwar relationship to Serbia, though that concern did not prove an insurmountable barrier to satisfying Bulgarian ambitions there if the satisfaction was crucial to the outcome of the general conflagration. Austrian caution during the final negotiations in Sofia leading to the alliance proved warranted when in 1916 Bulgarian troops took over the control of territories further to the west than had been contemplated. The Austro-Bulgarian crisis that ensued was based on the fact that a further Bulgarian extension endangered the full realization of Austrian war goals. Austria envisaged either annexation or a political protectorate over Serbia, Montenegro, and Albania, all three being seen as a strategic unit. The Germans managed to find a compromise. The Austrians accepted it rather than openly break with a wartime ally. But Austria allowed no illusions; if the Central Powers were victorious, it would insist on the containment of Bulgarian ambitions where they encroached on Austrian well-being. The Ballhausplatz was willing to meet the necessities of war on a minimal basis but no more. It did not entirely agree with the German view that the two Central Powers, if victorious, could override wartime contractual obligations. And because of this disagreement German-Austrian relations were often less smooth than Berlin believed they could and should be.

While the Dual Monarchy was elastic to some extent on the Bulgarian issue, it was unbending in regard to Rumania. In the first place, Vienna was more thoroughly aware, at the start of the war, how far the existing alliance with Rumania had deteriorated. Czernin evaluated it as hardly worth the paper on which it was written. Germany was much more optimistic. Even when it became clear that the Rumanians would not participate on the side of the Central Powers, the German government was quite willing to make offers of territory in the Bukovina and whatever concessions were necessary in Transylvania to insure a permanent Rumanian neutrality. War or no war, the Ballhausplatz turned a deaf ear to German representations to grant land which was an integral part of the Empire. Even so, Austrian leaders would have offered Bessarabia and part of the Bukovina had Bukarest displayed any intention of actively joining the Central Powers against the Entente. The absence of this intention convinced Burian that offers made to Rumania were of no value and could only result in an immediate loss of prestige for Austria-Hungary. Unable to obtain Rumanian participation, Burian was most certainly unwilling to make any territorial sacrifices in return for mere neutrality. Even if there had been no Rumanian vagaries, Count Tisza would hardly have agreed to sufficient concessions in Transylvania to satisfy Bukarest's ambitions there.

The Austrians were not so shortsighted as the Wilhelmstrasse believed. Once they had analyzed the Rumanian scene—and they did so perhaps with more astuteness than the Germans—they reacted correctly. It became painfully clear that Bukarest was involved in heavy negotiations with the Entente and that Rumania was strongly inclined in that direction. Because of their military successes against Russia after April, 1915, the Central Powers could virtually count on the continued neutrality of Bratianu's government. What made the situation so nerve-wracking was the uncertainty as to whether this neutrality would last in the face of military reversals. Nervous though he was, there was one thing Burian steadfastly refused to do—amputate large sections of the Monarchy. German-Austrian diplomacy was therefore much hampered in Bukarest from the beginning. Even so, it cannot be said to have entirely failed, since the Rumanians were at least kept neutral for two years.

What brought the Rumanians into the war was not so much the failure of the Central Powers' diplomacy as events on the battlefield. The Entente made Bratianu very attractive offers, but he waited until it seemed to him that the military situation was decidedly favorable. Conditions seemed right when Brussilov succeeded in smashing the Austrian battle line. Once the Central Powers began losing on the eastern front, the fear of their military threat to Rumania's existence disappeared and with it went the foundation on which Czernin and Bussche had rested their diplomatic endeavors since late 1915. Those endeavors were limited by the steadfast refusal of Vienna to change its policy on concessions to Bukarest and nothing the Germans could say was sufficient to override the Austrian decision on this question.

The German and Austrian ministers in the various Balkan capitals, while individually acting in accordance with the often divergent policies of Berlin and Vienna, managed a surprising degree of cooperation between themselves. It is interesting to note that as on-the-scene observers they were often in agreement that their governments were acting unwisely. This was particularly evident in Constantinople where neither Wangenheim nor Pallavicini was convinced that Turkish participation was necessarily the best of all conditions. On the contrary, both saw many advantages to Turkish benevolent neutrality. But faced with explicit instructions to obtain Turkey's active war participation, both ambassadors put aside their reservations and followed their orders. In the case of Bussche and Czernin in Bukarest, each disapproved of Vienna's refusal to consider making larger concessions to Bratianu's government. But Czernin's point of contention with Bussche was that the trump card of concessions must be played at just the right time and not before. It was Bussche's lack of subtlety and his irregular shifts in diplomatic posture that led Czernin to bemoan having to work with his German colleague. Nevertheless, the two diplomats did what they could to present a solid phalanx: Bukarest was a particularly difficult ministerial post considering the Rumanian hostility toward the Central Powers, and certainly any open dissension would have been most harmful.

The one case of serious discord was found in Sofia. The German minister, Michahelles, possessed a strong personality that sometimes made things difficult for Tarnowski, especially in the last months of negotiations leading to alliance with Bulgaria. The Ballhausplatz instructed Tarnowski to let Radoslavov make the overtures for the alliance in order to increase Austrian bargaining power and reduce concessions. But he found himself helpless before the barrage of hints by his German colleague that the Central Powers were most willing to sign an accord. Tarnowski reacted with great bitterness at having the ground cut from under him by the German's lack of finesse. But even in this case, the dissonant notes were kept to a minimum. There was a war to be won.

Aside from the differences between the German and the Austrian approach, the job of establishing the desired Balkan coalition was difficult because the Balkan situation was so complex. The Central Powers had to cope not only with the ambitions of Turkish, Bulgarian, and Rumanian leaders, but also with deep-seated fears, distrust, and animosities among the three states. Turkey was hostile toward Bulgaria. Bulgaria feared Rumania and Greece and distrusted Turkey. Rumania feared Bulgaria and was pro-Russian and pro-French. Out of this unhealthy situation Germany and Austria had to construct somehow a favorable climate in which the desired coalition could be realized. This would have been a formidable problem in peacetime. The uncertainties of war and the risks involved for any state making binding arrangements under such conditions made the task infinitely more demanding. The diplomacy of the Central Powers faced greater obstacles as the war progressed, because the longer the conflict went on, the more valuable became the participation of the Balkan states, and as their value went up so did their demands. The Central Powers actually did quite well considering that they unravelled two-thirds of the diplomatic knot. Separate accords were signed with Turkey and Bulgaria and, while the frictions between the two were not obliterated, a Turkish-Bulgarian accord permitted at least a temporary wartime arrangement which proved workable.

German-Austrian relations on the military level demonstrate that the clash of opinion between the two high commands was strong and often bitter. Here again discord arose because of differences in viewpoint— differences between Falkenhayn's insistence that the major decision of the war would come in the west and Conrad's unshakeable conviction the victory would be decided in the east against Russia. As in diplomacy, so in military affairs, one can make a good case for the validity of either viewpoint.

Certainly Conrad's skill at the planning board was great, but he was often carried away by his own strategy. His offensives usually failed to develop fully because he lacked the war machine to give them the decisive punch they needed to succeed. It was, of course, on just the question of increasing the striking power of forces in the east that Conrad, Hindenburg, and Ludendorff clashed with German Headquarters West. Falkenhayn's one great talent was that he never allowed himself to be carried away by a grandiose scheme. He always weighed strategy against the limitations imposed by the facts of the situation and these facts were often the simple arithmetic of just how many divisions were available for any given action. The German chief was always wary of endangering the western front, even for a decisive victory against the Russians. The Russian armies had a great deal of striking power and the conflict in the east involved a large front and great distances. Falkenhayn recognized more clearly than his German and Austrian opponents the sizable demands that would be made on the military resources of the Central Powers by a large and sustained offensive there. When he decided to attempt a breakthrough at Gorlice-Tarnow in the spring of 1915, he held off until he could muster the necessary divisions to handle the offensive effectively. It is significant that he never believed the Central Powers could bring about the total collapse of Russia on the battlefield and it was this belief which kept him from viewing the eastern campaign as more than a limited action.

The personality clash between Falkenhayn and Conrad von Hötzendorf can only be considered most unfortunate, for it compounded what would in any case have been a difficult military situation. Unquestionably, Conrad was often unfair and parochial. As time went on his attitude grew progressively worse. While it was not always justifiable it was at least understandable in light of the often tactless remarks by German military leaders on the fighting capacities of the Austrian forces. Conrad's armies did not do well in the field and this only increased his sensitivity to German criticism. That Falkenhayn was almost invariably correct when he warned against Conrad's plans to undertake offensives against the Russians or the Italians, and that the Serbian and Rumanian campaigns were great successes under German leadership, made Conrad's humiliation unbearable. The German High Command's seemingly constant quest for control of operations, which involved the subordination of Austrian generals and divisions, produced in him a resentment that knew no bounds. To a large degree his disappointments explain his loss of perspective, which, all things considered, Falkenhayn handled with great patience. The two were simply miles apart in the way they approached matters. One wrote long explanations of how and why things ought to be done, and was often influenced by long-range political considerations. The other penned terse, tightly-reasoned messages based on immediate military needs and conditions.

In spite of all the disagreements and hostilities, the military leaders reacted in much the same way as their diplomatic counterparts. The war had to be won and in deference to this end the animosities were glossed over, though barely, and cooperation was maintained.

An examination of the relations between the military and the diplomatic corps does not show a predominance of influence by either. Each concerned itself with the other's sphere of activity, not because one or the other sought alone to control the direction of the war, but rather because the events of the war demanded mutual intrusion and dependence.

Falkenhayn became an advocate of a special campaign against the Serbs as early as November, 1914. While he realized that the Turks needed munitions, it was Jagow and Zimmermann who brought to his attention the heavy repercussions that any fall of Turkey would have on the position of the Balkan states. Foreseeing the effect on the outcome of the war, Falkenhayn attempted to convince Conrad to mount another Serbian attack. In the spring of 1915, the Entente landing at the Dardanelles made the Serbian campaign crucial to Turkey's continued participation in the war. Conrad's refusal to commence such an action was based initially on his preoccupation with Russia, but once the Czar's armies began their retreat, he agreed to mount an offensive against the Serbs if Bulgaria participated. To obtain this participation was the business of the diplomats and Falkenhayn ended by reversing the coin. Initially the Wilhelmstrasse had pressed him for a Serbian campaign. He now pressed the diplomats to win the Bulgarians. In actuality the German general and the Foreign Office ended by working hand-in-glove on the issue. While the latter negotiated with Sofia, Falkenhayn smoothed the way for a military convention with the Bulgarian representative sent to Pless.

One of the most striking examples of cooperation between the German military and the diplomatic corps was the issue of Italian-Austrian negotiations. In an attempt to bring every influence to bear on Vienna to make those concessions which would have placated Rome, Bethmann-Hollweg and Jagow had Falkenhayn repeatedly raise the issue with Conrad von Hötzendorf. Because of the military threat Italy would pose as a hostile belligerent, they hoped that the Austrian general would in turn use all his influence to sway his government. The maneuver failed, but Falkenhayn had made every effort to aid German diplomacy in achieving its goal.

It would be misleading to assert that such cooperation was constant. There were times when Falkenhayn made unsolicited suggestions to the Foreign Office, such as when he mentioned to Bethmann-Hollweg in late 1914 that Germany ought to negotiate a peace with the Russians. The Wilhelmstrasse resented his meddling in affairs that were not his province and did not attempt to hide its displeasure. When he suggested economic pressure to force Rumania into the war against the Entente, the reaction again was irritation. The tone of the various communications between Falkenhayn and the men concerned with German diplomacy was definitely most formal and at various times quite cool. But most important, whenever German diplomats and generals needed each other's assistance, it was forthcoming.

The relationship between Conrad von Hötzendorf and the Ballhausplatz was much more intimate. Conrad was extremely conscious of preserving the interests and prestige of the Monarchy, and by the time the war broke he had already established a close tie with Austrian diplomatic policy makers. The Austrian documents show that he was kept well informed on policies after the war began, in spite of his occasional protests to the contrary. Conrad felt no great elation over the diplomacy of the Ballhausplatz. He believed Austrian policy in the

Balkans had failed to achieve its goal. Yet, strangely enough, though this was his conviction he supported Vienna on precisely those points that made the winning of Rumania and, therefore, the completion of the desired Balkan coalition, impossible. When it came to offering concessions which would have sacrificed Austro-Hungarian soil, he was every bit as adamant as Burian. In April and May, 1915, he was much more concerned than Falkenhayn over the Italian threat, because an Italian action would be aimed at Austria. He agreed that Italy had to be kept from participating in the war but he also thought concessions had to be minimal in order to preserve Austrian interests. And in 1916 he struck the same pose with respect to Rumania.

Conrad found himself on the horns of a dilemma. He was a military chief who was aware of what concessions were needed to win the war. He was also an Austrian; his job was to preserve the Monarchy and he never once forgot it. The Germans understood the dilemma but would not accept it as valid in light of the war situation. From a purely military point of view they were right, and Conrad might have been a lot more successful if he had devoted himself entirely to the hard facts of combat rather than spending long hours formulating written political think-pieces with which to bombard his government.

In January, 1917, the Central Powers could hardly look with satisfaction at the general war picture. On the western front they had managed to hold against the enemy offensives but that was all. In the east the Russians had been halted, but the German-Austrian line was shaky and prospects of any great Russian reversal in the immediate future were dim. Nor could the two allies look to the Balkans with equanimity. The Rumanian threat had been eliminated, but the now sizable Entente army at Salonika meant a continued threat to Macedonia. There was no hope, as the new year began, that the war would soon end, much less that the Entente would be defeated. The cost in lives had been dreadful but it had not brought victory any closer. Military leaders must have looked wistfully back to the beginning of the war when they had hoped and expected that Turkey, Bulgaria, and Rumania would all quickly enter as their allies. Had that occurred the war might have had a strikingly different outcome. As it was, Turkey and Bulgaria were won piecemeal, vitiating the impact of their participation, and by the opening of 1917 the war machinery of both was already heavily strained. No matter where the military might look there was little reason for optimism.

There is no doubt that the German-Austrian combination was an unhealthy one. Yet, one cannot escape the fact that the two powers were faced with extreme difficulties. The differences in diplomatic and military points of view, the ambitions of the Balkan states, the conflicts between personalities which were only magnified by the tensions of the war—all these make not for the conclusion that the alliance was bound to fail, but rather for wonder that it managed to hold together effectively as long as it did.

Selected
Bibliography

Bibliographies and Indexes

American Historical Association. *A Catalogue of Files and Microfilm of the German Foreign Ministry Archives, 1867–1920.* Oxford: Oxford University Press, 1959.
Dutcher, G. M., et al. *A Guide to Historical Literature.* New York: Macmillan Co., 1936.
Langer, W. L., and others. *Foreign Affairs Bibliography.* 3 vols. New York: Harper and Bros., 1933, 1945, 1955.
Spann, Othmar. *Bibliographie der Wirtschafts und Socialgeschichte des Welkriegs.* Vienna: Holder-Pichler-Tempsky, 1924.
Stropp, R. *Aufstellungsverzeichnis des Politischen Archivs des Ministeriums des Äussern, 1848–1918.* Vienna: Österreichisches Staatsarchiv, 1956.
Weltkriegsbücherei. *Bibliographie zur Geschichte Österreich-Ungarns im Weltkrieg, 1914–1918.* Stuttgart: Deutschen Verlagsanstalt, 1934.

Unpublished Documents

Austria. Haus-Hof-und Staatsarchiv, Politisches Archiv. (Cited in the notes as Staatsarchiv, PA.)
Bulgarien Geheim, boxes 512–14.
Bulgarien Allgemeines, boxes 872, 873.
Rumänien Geheim, boxes 503, 516–20.
Rumänien Allgemeines, boxes 881–83.
Türkei Geheim, boxes 521, 522.
Türkei Allgemeines, boxes 873, 941, 948, 968.
Varia, boxes 78, 190, 312, 313, 346, 372, 496, 499, 500, 536, 820.
———. Kriegsarchiv. Conrad-Falkenhayn Korrespondenz. (Cited in the notes as C.-F. K.)
Balkan.
Italien.
Russische Front, 1915, 1916.
———. Kriegsarchiv. Conrad Archiv. Folios B-7, B-8.
———. Kriegsarchiv. Armee Oberkommando, Operationen. (Cited in the notes as AOK Op.) Folios 475, 503, 538, 539, 551, 553.
———. Kriegsarchiv. Folio 607, Berichte Cramon.
———. Kriegsarchiv. Evidenzbureau. Folio 5629, "B" Akten.
Germany. Foreign Ministry Archives. University of California Microfilm Series. (Cited in the notes as GFMA.)
Bulgarien. Series 2, reels 12–15.
Rumänien. Series 1, reels 18–26.
Türkei. Series 1, reels 13, 17, 393, 394; series 2, reel 29.
———. Foreign Ministry Archives. St. Anthony's College Collection. (Cited in the notes as GFMA, St. Anthony's Collection.) Türkei, reels 46, 77, 93.

Published Documents and Official Collections

Austria. Königlicher und Kaiserlicher Handelsministerium. *Wirtschaftliche Verhältnisse Rumänien, 1913.* Vienna: Hof-und Staatsdruckerei, 1915.
Wirtschaftliche Verhältnisse Griechenland. Vienna: Verlag des Königlicher und Kaiserlicher Österreichisches Handelsmuseums, 1916.
———. *Österreich-Ungarns Aussenpolitik von der Bosnischen Krise 1908 bis zum Kriegsausbruch 1914: Diplomatische Aktenstücke der Österreichisch-Ungarischen Ministeriums des Äussern.* Edited by Ludwig Bittner and Hans Übersberger. 9 vols. Vienna: Österreichischer Bundes Verlag, 1930. (Cited in the notes as *Ö-U Aussenpolitik.*)
———. Ministerium des Äussern. *Österreichisch-Ungarns Rotbuch. Diplomatische Aktenstücke betreffend die Beziehungen Österreich-Ungarns zu Rumänien, Juli 22, 1914, bis August 27, 1916.* Vienna: Königlicher und Kaiserlicher Hof-Verlags, 1916. (Cited in the notes as Austria, *Rotbuch.*)
Bulgaria. *Statistique du Royaume de Bulgarie, 1913–1922.* Sofia: State Publication, 1924.
France. Ministère des Affaires Étrangères. *Documents Diplomatiques: Affaires d'Orient, Mai-Décembre 1897.* Paris: Imprimerie Nationale, 1898.
Germany. *Die Grosse Politik der Europäischen Kabinette, 1871–1914.* Edited by Johannes Lepsius and others. 40 vols. Berlin: Deutsche Verlagsgesellschaft für Politik und Geschichte, 1922–1927. (Cited in the notes as *G.P.*)
———. Kaiserlichen Statistischen Amte. *Statistik des Deutschen Reichs. Auswärtigen Handel im Jahr 1913. Rumänien.* Vol. 4. Berlin: C. Heymanns Verlag, 1914.
———. Kautsky, Karl, ed. *Die Deutschen Dokumente zum Kriegsausbruch.* 4 vols. Charlottenburg: Verlags Gesellschaft für Politik, 1919.
Greece. "Diplomatic Documents, 1913–1917." Translated by T. P. Ion. *American Journal of International Law,* supplement to vol. 12, pp. 86–195. New York, 1918.
Tirpitz, Alfred von. *Politische Dokumente: Deutsche Ohnmachtspolitik im Weltkriege.* Hamburg: Hanseatische Verlagsanstalt, 1926.

Official Military Histories

Austria. Bundesministerium für Heereswesen. *Österreich-Ungarns Letzter Krieg, 1914–1918.* 7 vols. Vienna: Verlag der Militärwissenschaftlichen Mitteilungen, 1930.
Germany. Reichsarchiv. *Der Weltkrieg, 1914–1918.* 12 vols. Berlin: Mittler und Sohn, 1925–1931.
———. *Der Weltkrieg, 1914–1918: Kriegsrüstung und Kriegswirtschaft.* 2 vols. Berlin: Mittler und Sohn, 1930.

Memoirs and Diaries

Bethmann-Hollweg, Theobald von. *Reflections on the World War.* 2 vols. London: Thornton Butterworth, 1920.

Brussilov, A. A. *A Soldier's Notebook, 1914–1918*. London: Macmillan and Co., 1930.

Burian, Stephan, Count. *Drei Jahre*. Berlin: Ullstein Verlag, 1923.

Conrad von Hötzendorf, Franz. *Aus Meiner Dientstzeit, 1906–1918*. 5 vols. Vienna: Rikola Verlag, 1921–1925.

Cramon, August von. *Quatre Ans au G.Q.G. Austro-Hongrois pendant la Guerre Mondiale*. Paris: Payot et Cie, 1922.

Czernin, Ottokar. *Im Weltkrieg*. Vienna: Ullstein Verlag, 1919.

Djemal Pasha. *Memories of a Turkish Statesman, 1913–1919*. New York: G. H. Doran Co., 1922.

Einstein, Lewis. *Inside Constantinople*. London: John Murray, 1917.

Falkenhayn, Erich von. *The German General Staff and Its Decisions, 1914–1916*. New York: Dodd, Mead and Co., 1920.

Foerster, Wolfgang, ed. *Mackensen: Briefe und Aufzeichnungen*. Leipzig: Bibliographisches Institut AG, 1938.

Freytag-Loringhoven, Freiherr Hugo von. *Menschen und Dinge*. Berlin: Mittler und Sohn, 1923.

Gallwitz, Max von. *Meine Führertätigkeit im Weltkriege, 1914–16*. Berlin: E. S. Mittler und Sohn, 1929.

Grey, Sir Edward, Viscount of Fallodon. *Twenty-five Years*. 2 vols. New York: Frederick A. Stokes Co., 1925.

Groener, Wilhelm. *Lebenserinnerungen*. Gottingen: Vandenhoeck und Ruprecht, 1957.

Hindenburg, Paul von. *Aus Meinem Leben*. Leipzig: Hirzel Verlag, 1934.

Hoffmann, Max. *Der Krieg der Versäumten Gelegenheiten*. Munich: Verlag für Kulturpolitik, 1924.

Ionescu, Take. *Souvenirs*. Paris: Payot et Cie, 1919.

Izzet Pasha. *Denkwurdigkeiten*. Leipzig: K. F. Koehler, 1927.

Liman von Sanders, Otto. *Five Years in Turkey*. Berlin: August Scherl, 1920.

Ludendorff, Eric von. *My War Memories*. 2 vols. London: Hutchinson and Co., 1924.

Margutti, Albert von. *The Emperor Francis Joseph and His Times*. London: Hutchinson and Co., 1921.

Marie, Queen of Rumania. *The Story of My Life*. New York: Charles Scribner's Sons, 1934.

Morgenthau, Henry. *Ambassador Morgenthau's Story*. New York: Doubleday, Page and Co., 1918.

Napier, H. D. *The Experiences of a Military Attaché in the Balkans*. London: Dranes, 1924.

Nekludoff, Anatole. *Diplomatic Reminiscences before and during the World War, 1911–1917*. New York: E. P. Dutton and Co., 1920.

Nicholas, Prince of Greece. *My Fifty Years*. London: Hutchinson and Co., 1926.

Redlich, Joseph. *Schicksalsjahre Österreichs, 1908–1919: Das Politische Tagebuch Joseph Redlichs*. Edited by Fritz Fellner. 2 vols. Graz: Verlag Hermann Böhlaus, 1954.

Stürgkh, Count Joseph von. *Im Deutschen Grossen Hauptquartier*. Leipzig: Paul List Verlag, 1921.

Tirpitz, Grand Admiral Alfred von. *My Memoirs*. 2 vols. New York: Dodd, Mead and Co., 1919.

Tisza, Stephan, Count. *Briefe, 1914–1918.* 2 vols. Berlin: Verlag von Reimar Hobbing, 1928.

Secondary Accounts

Alberti, Adriano. *General Falkenhayn: Die Beziehungen zwischen den Generalstabschefs des Dreibundes.* Berlin: E. S. Mittler und Sohn, 1924.
Albertini, Luigi. *Origins of the War of 1914.* 3 vols. London: Oxford University Press, 1957.
Ancel, Jacques. *L'Unité de la Politique Bulgare, 1870–1919.* Paris: Editions Bossard, 1919.
Andreades, André M. *Oeuvres Études sur les Finances Publiques de la Grèce Moderne.* Athens: Faculté de Droit de l'Université d'Athènes, 1939.
Antonescu, C. G. *Die Rumänische Handelspolitik von 1875–1910.* Leipzig: Wilhelm Schunka Verlag, 1915.
Auerback, Bertrand. *L'Autriche et la Hongrie pendant la Guerre.* Paris: Librairie Felix Alcan, 1925.
Auffenberg-Komarów, Moritz von. *Aus Österreich-Ungarns Teilnahme am Weltkriege.* Berlin: Ullstein Verlag, 1920.
Basilesco, Nicholas. *La Roumanie dans la Guerre et dans la Paix.* 2 vols. Paris: Librairie Felix Alcan, 1919.
Bujac, J. L. *Premières Contributions à l'Histoire de la Grande Guerre. La Roumanie.* Paris: L. Fournier, 1916.
Burian, Stephan, Count. *Austria in Dissolution.* London: Ernest Benn, 1925.
Chambers, F. P. *The War behind the War, 1914–1918.* New York: Harcourt, Brace and Co., 1939.
Churchill, Winston S. *The World Crisis.* 6 vols. New York: Charles Scribner's Sons, 1927–1931.
————. *The Unknown War: The Eastern Front.* New York: Charles Scribner's Sons, 1931.
Cioriceanu, George D. *La Roumanie Économique et ses Rapports avec l'Étranger de 1860 à 1915.* Paris: Marcel Giard, 1928.
Collenberg, L. R. von. *Die Deutsche Armee von 1871 bis 1914.* Berlin: Mittler und Sohn, 1922.
Craig, G. A. *The Politics of the Prussian Army, 1640–1945.* Oxford: Clarendon Press, 1955.
Cruttwell, C.R.M.F. *A History of the Great War, 1914–1918.* Oxford: Clarendon Press, 1934.
Dejanova, Milka. *Die Warenausfuhr Bulgariens und Ihre Organisation seit dem Jahr 1900.* Sofia: Herman Pohle, 1930.
Djuvara, Mircea. *La Guerre Roumaine, 1916–1918.* Paris: Berger-Levrault, 1919.
Dorizas, Michail. *The Foreign Trade of Greece.* Philadelphia: University of Pennsylvania Press, 1925.
Driault, Edouard. *Le Roi Constantin.* Versailles: L'Imprimerie Moderne de Versailles, 1930.
————, and L'Heritier, Michel. *Histoire Diplomatique de la Grèce de 1821 à nos Jours.* 6 vols. Paris: Les Presses Universitaires de France, 1926.
Dunan, Marcel. *L'Été Bulgare.* Paris: Librairie Chapelot, 1917.
Earle, E. M. *Makers of Modern Strategy.* Princeton: Princeton University Press, 1948.

Edmonds, J. E. *A Short History of World War I.* London: Oxford University Press, 1951.

Emin, Ahmed. *Turkey in the World War.* New Haven: Yale University Press, 1930.

Falkenhayn, Erich von. *Der Feldzug der 9. Armee.* 2 vols. Berlin: Mittler und Sohn, 1921.

Fay, Sidney B. *The Origins of the World War.* 2 vols. New York: Macmillan Co., 1930.

Feis, Herbert. *Europe, the World's Banker, 1870–1914.* New Haven: Yale University Press, 1930.

Fischer, Fritz. *Griff Nach Der Weltmacht.* Düsseldorf: Droste Verlag und Druckerei, 1961.

Franek, Fritz. *Die Entwicklung der Österreich-Ungarns Wehrmacht in die Ersten Zwei Kriegsjahren.* Vienna: Verlag der Militärwissenschaftlichen Mitteilungen, 1933.

Frangulis, A. F. *La Grèce et la Crise Mondiale.* Paris: F. Alcan, 1926.

Gibbons, Herbert. *Venizelos.* 2d ed. Boston: Houghton Mifflin, 1923.

Goerlitz, Walter. *History of the German General Staff, 1657–1945.* New York: Frederick A. Praeger, 1953.

Golovine, Nicholas N. *The Russian Campaign of 1914.* London: Hugh Rees, 1933.

———. *The Russian Army in the World War.* New Haven: Yale University Press, 1931.

Gottlieb, W. W. *Studies in Secret Diplomacy During the First World War.* London: George Allen and Unwin, 1957.

Gourko, Basil. *War and Revolution in Russia, 1914–1917.* New York: Macmillan Co., 1919.

Gratz, Gustav, and Schüller, Richard. *Der Wirtschaftliche Zusammenbruch Österreich-Ungarns.* Vienna: Holder, Pichler, Tempsky, 1930.

Great Britain. Historical Section of the Foreign Office (cited in the notes as HSFO).

    Bulgaria. London: H.M. Stationery Office, 1920.

    Greece with the Cyclades and Northern Sporades. London: H.M. Stationery Office, 1924.

    Rumania. London: H.M. Stationery Office, 1918.

Great Britain. Naval Intelligence Division. *A Handbook of Greece.* London: H.M. Stationery Office, 1918.

Grebler, Leo, and Winkler, Wilhelm. *The Cost of the War to Germany and Austria-Hungary.* New Haven: Yale University Press, 1940.

Hantsch, Hugo. *Leopold Graf Berchtold.* 2 vols. Vienna: Verlag Styria, 1963.

Hauser, Henry. *Germany's Commercial Grip on the World.* New York: Charles Scribner's Sons, 1917.

Helmreich, E. C. *The Diplomacy of the Balkan Wars, 1912–1913.* Cambridge: Harvard University Press, 1938.

Howard, Harry. *The Partition of Turkey, 1913–23.* Norman: University of Oklahoma Press, 1931.

Ionescu-Sisesti, George. *L'Agriculture de la Roumanie pendant la Guerre.* Paris: Les Presses Universitaires de France, 1929.

Jotzoff, Dimitri. *Zar Ferdinand von Bulgarien: Sein Lebenswerk im Orient.* Berlin: P. J. Oestergaard Verlag, 1927.

Kabisch, Ernst. *Der Rumänien Krieg, 1916.* Berlin: Verlag Otto Schlegel, 1938.

Kann, R. A. *The Multinational Empire.* 2 vols. New York: Columbia University Press, 1950.

Kaptcheff, G. I. *La Debâcle Nationale Bulgare devant la Haute-Cour.* Paris: Voltaire, 1925.

Konstantinoff, Panayott. *Der Aussenhandel Bulgariens.* Leipzig: Rascher et Cie, 1914.

Lanyi, Ladislas. *Le Comte Étienne Tisza et la Guerre de 1914-18.* Paris: L. Lagny, 1946.

Larcher, Maurice. *La Guerre Turque dans la Guerre Mondiale.* Paris: Berger-Levrault, 1926.

Lee, Arthur. *The Royal House of Greece.* London: Ward, Lock and Co., 1948.

Leschtoff, Lübomir G. *Die Staatsschulden und Reparationen Bulgariens, 1878-1927.* Sofia: Verlag T. F. Tschipeff, 1933.

Levandis, John. *The Greek Foreign Debt and the Great Powers, 1821-1898.* New York: Columbia University Press, 1944.

Lewis, Bernard. *The Emergence of Modern Turkey.* New York: Oxford University Press, 1961.

Loewenfeld-Russ, Hans. *Die Regelung der Volksernährung im Krieg.* Vienna: Holder, Pichler, Tempsky, 1926.

Lukacs, Geza. *Die Handelspolitische Interessengemeinschaft Zwischen dem Deutschen Reiche und Österreich-Ungarn.* Göttingen: O. Hanke, 1913.

Lupu, Nicholas. *Rumania and the War.* Boston: R. G. Badger, Gorham Press, 1919.

Mach, Richard von. *Aus Bewegter Balkanzeit, 1879-1918.* Berlin: E. S. Mittler und Sohn, 1928.

Madol, Hans. *Ferdinand von Bulgarien.* Berlin: Universitas Deutsche Verlags, 1931.

Magnus, Leonard A. *Rumania's Cause and Ideals.* New York: E. P. Dutton and Co., 1917.

Mandelstam, André. *Le Sort de l'Empire Ottoman.* Paris: Librairie Payot et Cie, 1917.

Martin, Percy. *Greece of the Twentieth Century.* London: T. Fisher Unwin, 1913.

Mazard, Jean. *Le Régime des Capitulations.* Algiers: Jean Gaudet, 1923.

Meyer, Henry Cord. *Mitteleuropa in German Thought and Action, 1815-1945.* The Hague: M. Nijhoff, 1955.

Minesco, Constantin. *L'Action Diplomatique de la Roumanie pendant la Guerre.* Paris: Societé Generale de l'Imprimerie, 1922.

Moukhtar Pasha. *La Turquie, l'Allemagne et l'Europe.* Paris: Berger-Levrault, 1924.

Mühlmann, Carl. *Das Deutsch-Türkische Waffenbündnis im Weltkriege.* Leipzig: Verlag Koehler und Amelang, 1940.

———. *Deutschland und die Türkei, 1913-1914.* Berlin: W. Rothchild, 1929.

———. *Oberste Heeresleitung und Balkan im Weltkrieg, 1914-1918.* Berlin: Wilhelm Limpert, 1942.

Naumann, Victor. *Profile.* Munich: Duncker und Humblot, 1925.

Nogales, Rafael de. *Four Years Beneath the Crescent.* New York: Charles Scribner's Sons, 1926.

Nossig, Alfred. *Die Neue Türkei und Ihre Führer.* Halle: Otto Hendel Verlag, 1916.

Politis, Nicholas. *La Guerre Grèco-Turque.* Paris: A Pedone, 1898.

Pomiankowski, Joseph. *Der Zusammenbruch des Ottomanischen Reiches.* Vienna: Amalthea Verlag, 1928.

Pribram, Alfred F. *Austria-Hungary and Great Britain, 1908-1914.* London: Oxford University Press, 1951.

Price, Crawford. *Venizelos and the War.* London: Simpkin, Marshall, Hamilton, Kent and Co., 1917.

Prost, Henri. *LaBulgarie de 1912 à 1930.* Paris: Éditions Pierre Roger, 1932.

————. *La Liquidation Financière de la Guerre en Bulgarie.* Paris: Marcel Giard, 1925.

Protić, Stojan [Balkanicus]. *The Aspirations of Bulgaria.* London: Simpkin, Marshall, Hamilton, Kent and Co., 1915.

Radoslavov, Vasil. *Bulgarien und die Weltkrise.* Berlin: Ullstein Verlag, 1923.

Raffalovich, Arthur. *Le Marché Financier, 1913-14.* Paris: Librairie Felix Alcan, 1915.

Redlich, Joseph. *Austrian War Government.* New Haven: Yale University Press, 1929.

Regele, Oskar. *Feldmarschall Conrad.* Vienna: Verlag Herold, 1955.

Resmiritza, N. *Essai d'Économie Roumaine Moderne, 1831-1931.* Paris: Librairie Générale de Droit et de Jurisprudence, 1931.

Rieber, Alfred J. "Russian Diplomacy and Rumania," in *Russian Diplomacy and Eastern Europe, 1914-1917,* edited by Alexander Dallin. New York: King's Crown Press, 1963.

Ritter, Gerhard. *Staatskunst und Kriegshandwerk.* 4 vols. Munich: Verlag R. Oldenbourg, 1954-1968.

Rosenberg, Arthur. *The Birth of the German Republic.* London: Humphrey Milford, 1931.

Sakazov, Ivan. *Bulgarische Wirtschaftsgeschichte.* Berlin: Walter de Gruyter and Co., 1929.

Sarrail, Maurice. *Mon Commandement en Orient, 1916-1918.* Paris: Ernest Flammarion, 1920.

Seignobosc, Henri. *Turcs et Turquie.* Paris: Payot et Cie, 1920.

Serbesco, Sebastien. *La Roumanie et la Guerre.* Paris: Librairie Armand Colin, 1918.

Seton-Watson, Robert W. *A History of the Roumanians.* Cambridge, England: Cambridge University Press, 1934.

————. *Roumania and the Great War.* London: Constable and Co., 1915.

Seyfert, Gerhard. *Die Militärischen Beziehungen und Vereinbarungen zwischen dem Deutschen und dem Österreichischen Generalstab vor und bei Beginn des Weltkrieges.* Leipzig: J. Moltzen, 1934.

Slivensky, Ivan. *La Bulgarie depuis le Traité de Berlin.* Paris: Jouve et Cie, 1927.

Smith, C. Jay, Jr. *The Russian Struggle for Power, 1914-1917.* New York: Philosophical Library, 1956.

Soteriadis, George. *An Ethnological Map Illustrating Hellenism in the*

Balkan Peninsula and Asia Minor. London: Edward Stanford, 1918.
Stickney, Edith. *Southern Albania or Northern Epirus in European International Affairs, 1912–1913*. Stanford: Stanford University Press, 1926.
Strupp, Karl. *Die Beziehungen Zwischen Griechenland und der Türkei von 1820–1930*. Breslau: J. U. Korn Verlag, 1932.
Toynbee, Arnold. *Greek Policy Since 1882*. Oxford: Oxford University Press, 1914.
Trumpener, Ulrich. *Germany and the Ottoman Empire, 1914–1918*. Princeton: Princeton University Press, 1968.
Tsouderos, E. J. *Le Relèvement Économique de la Grèce*. Paris: Berger-Levrault, 1919.
Tuchman, Barbara W. *The Guns of August*. New York: Macmillan Co., 1962.
Wedel, Oswald H. *Austro-German Diplomatic Relations, 1908–1914*. Stanford: Stanford University Press, 1932.
Whitman, Sidney. *Reminiscences of the King of Rumania*. New York: Harper, 1899.

Periodicals

Bliss, Frederick. "Djemal Pasha: A Portrait." *The Nineteenth Century and After*, no. 514 (December 1919) pp. 1151–61.
Bompard, Maurice, "L'Entrée en Guerre de la Turquie." *La Revue de Paris* 13 (1 July 1921): 61–85; 14 (15 July 1921): 261–88.
Diamandy, Constantin. "Ma Mission en Russie, Octobre 1914–Mai 1915." *Revue des Deux Mondes* 60 (November–December 1930): 421–32.
"Enemy Portraits: Count Adam Tarnowski." *New Europe* 2 (15 February 1917): 151–54.
"Enemy Portraits: Enver Pasha." *New Europe* 1, no. 5 (16 November 1916): 149–52.
Franek, Fritz. "Probleme des Organisation im Ersten Kriegsjahre." *Militärwissenschaftlich Mitteilungen*, 1930, pp. 977–90.
Hegemann, Margot. "Zum Plan der Abdankung Carols I von Rumänien in September, 1914." *Zeitschrift für Geschichtswissenschaft* 4 (1957): 823–26.
Kerner, Robert J. "Mission of Liman von Sanders." *Slavonic Review* 6 (June 1927): 12–27.
Mehlan, Arno. "Das Deutsch-Bulgarische Weltkriegsbündnis." *Historische Viertelsjahrschrift* 30 (1935): 771–806.
Near East 8, no. 197 (12 February 1915): 424.
Pears, Edwin. "Turkey and the War." *Living Age*, no. 3674 (5 December 1914), pp. 579–89.
Pinon, René. "La Rivalité des Grandes Puissance dans l'Empire Ottoman." *Revue des Deux Mondes* 42 (1907): 338–75.
Schäfer, Theobald von. "Das Militärische Zusammenwirken der Mittelmächte in Herbst, 1914." *Wissen und Wehr Monatshefte* 7 (1926): 213–34.
Seton-Watson, Robert W. "Wilhelm II's Balkan Policy." *Slavonic Review* 7 (June 1928): 1–29.
Silberstein, Gerard. "The Serbian Campaign of 1915: Its Diplomatic Background." *American Historical Review* 73 (October 1967): 51–69.

———. "The Central Powers and the Second Turkish Alliance, 1915." *Slavic Review* 24 (March 1965): 77–89.

———. "The Serbian Campaign of 1915: Its Military Implications." *International Review of History and Political Science* 3 (December 1966): 115–32.

Sokolovich, P. P. de. "Le Mirage Bulgare et la Guerre Européenne." *Revue d'Histoire Diplomatique* 31 (1917): 7–36.

Sweet, Paul. "Leaders and Policies: Germany in the Winter 1914–1915." *Journal of Central European Affairs* 16 (October 1956): 229–52.

Talaat Pasha. "Posthumous Memoirs of Talaat Pasha." *New York Times Current History* 15, no. 2 (November 1921): 287–95.

Trumpener, Ulrich. "German Military Aid to Turkey in 1914: An Historical Re-evaluation." *Journal of Modern History* 32, no. 2 (June 1960): 145–49.

"Tsar Ferdinand: A French Silhouette." *New Europe* 3, no. 33 (31 May 1917): 219–21.

Viner, Jacob. "International Finance and Balance of Power Diplomacy." *Southwestern Political and Social Science Quarterly* 9 (March 1929): 407–51.

Wank, Solomon. "The Appointment of Count Berchtold As Austro-Hungarian Foreign Minister." *Journal of Central European Affairs* 23 (July 1963): 143–51.

Wiener Zeitung. 1913–17.

Reference Works

Danchov, N. G., and Danchov, I. G., eds. *Bulgarian Encyclopaedia.* Sofia: St. Atanasov, 1936. 4 vols.

Christern, Herman, ed. *Deutsches Biographisches Jahrbuch.* Berlin: Deutsche Verlags Anstalt, 1925.

Meyer's Lexikon. Leipzig: Bibliographisches Institut, 1928.

Santifaller, Leo, ed. *Österreichisches Biographisches Lexikon, 1815–1950.* Graz: Verlag Hermann Böhlaus, 1957.

Stahl, Wilhelm, ed. Schulthess' *Europaischer Geschichtskalender.* Munich: C. H. Beck, 1914–1918.

Statesmen's Yearbook. London: Macmillan and Co., 1914–1916.

Wer Ist's. Leipzig: H.A.L. Degener, 1911.

Index

Aegean Islands, 50–51, 53
Albania: Austrian position on, 46, 172; and Austrian war aims, 302–08 passim
alliances: German-Turkish, 13, 108–09; Austro-Turkish, 15–16, 109–10 (*see also* Second Turkish Alliance); Austro-Rumanian, 31, 35, 36, 138; German-Rumanian, 31, 36, 138; Rumanian-Serbian, 38; Greco-Serbian, 48, 57; Bulgarian-Turkish (1914), 134; Bulgarian-Turkish (1915), 124–26; Austro-Bulgarian, 173–74; German-Bulgarian, 173–74
army: retreat of Austrian, 252–53, 254, 256, 257, 258, 265, 270, 273, 279–80, 310–13; failure of Italian, 286–87; Austrian, on Italian front, 309; Rumanian, attacks Transylvania, 329. *See also* German Ninth Army; military preparations
—casualties of: Turkish, 112, 126–27; Austrian, 253, 310, 314; Russian, 278; Serbian, 297; Central Powers, 300–301
—strength of: Austrian, 59–61; German, 59, 62; Russian, 67; Rumanian, 67; Bulgarian, 68; Turkish, 68–69
—successes of: Russian, 252–53, 310–13; German, 258, 260, 262–63; Hindenburg and Ludendorff, 277–78; Mackensen, 283–94, 330–32; Austrian-Bulgarian-German, 297; German, against Rumania, 330–32
Austria-Hungary: and Bulgarian alliance, 17, 18, 26–27, 157, 170, 173–74, 337; and Turco-Bulgarian accord, 28–29; Transylvanian factions in, 34; and Greek ambitions, 46; control of Epirus by, 46; and Greek-Turkish accord, 58; Balkan policy of, 58, 335; military problems of, 59–61; war preparations in, 61–62; war supplies of, 63; and Second Turkish Alliance, 102–10 passim; Serbian campaign of, 117; and Bulgarian troops, 131; Bulgarian policy of, summarized, 174, 176; on Rumanian concessions, 188, 204, 233; and Italian problem, 205–06; Russian offensive by, 252; military situation of, 253; Balkan war aims of, 302–08; public opinion in, 314; Turkish posture of, 335–36; and German

policy on Bulgaria, 336; and Rumanian aspirations, 337–38. *See also* alliances; army; Berchtold; Burian; Conrad von Hötzendorf; Franz Joseph; Tisza; Triple Alliance
—commercial relations of: with Turkey, 5; with Bulgaria, 21–24; with Rumania, 32; with Greece, 41
Averescu, Alexander (Rumanian chief of staff, 1912–1913), 67

Balkan coalition: German policy on, 8, 11, 33, 45–46, 47–49, 52, 58, 196; Austrian policy on, 9, 10, 17, 33, 45–46, 47–49, 58; and Balkan states, 195
Bassewitz, Rudolf von (German chargé d'affaires in Athens), 47
Beck, Friedrich von (Austro-Hungarian chief of staff, 1881–1906), 64
Beldiman, Alexander (Rumanian minister to Germany), 204, 220, 246
Berchtold, Count Leopold von (Austro-Hungarian foreign minister, 1912–1915): on Turkish alliance, 15; on Balkan coalition, 17; on Bulgarian-Rumanian tie, 18, 46; on German view of Bulgaria, 20; on Bulgarian alliance, 25–27 passim, 48, 130, 134–35, 137, 141–42; and Austro-Rumanian alliance, 35; analyzes Rumania, 37; on Greece, 46, 57–58; on Kavalla, 49–50; on Turkish-Bulgarian accord, 83; rejects Rumanian dreibund, 84; on Pan Turanism, 99; on Holy War, 99; on Second Turkish Alliance, 102, 105, 106; background and capacity of, 129–30; on Bulgarian alliance and Rumania, 131; on Entente offers to Bulgaria, 138, 139; on Bulgarian maneuvers, 143, 144, 147, 149; resignation of, 150; Rumanian policy of, 181, 184, 187, 188, 190, 193, 199; and Rumanian fear of Bulgaria, 197; and German military aid, 255; and separate peace, 255, 267; on diplomatic success, 270; on military campaigns, 271, 273
Bessarabia: Jagow on, 38, 192, 233; Franz Joseph on, 182; and Rumania, 190, 219; Carp on, 203; Bussche on, 204; Czernin on, 206; Burian on, 215;

Conrad on, 268, 290; Falkenhayn on, 290

Bethmann-Hollweg, Theobald von (German chancellor, 1909–1917): on Turkish alliance, 12–14 passim; on *Goeben* and *Breslau*, 78; on Balkan coalition, 84; on financial support of Turkey, 93; on Turkish alliance extension, 102–03; urges Serbian campaign, 117; on Bulgarian loan, 148; on Rumanian concessions, 182–84, 185, 193–94, 208, 214; on Trentino, 201; on Tisza, 207; on Turkish supply, 215; on German-Rumanian war, 235; and military aid to Austria, 255; on separate Russian peace, 266; on Falkenhayn, 267; on Serbia, 288, 302

Bieberstein, Marschall von (German ambassador to Turkey, 1897–1912), 4

Black Sea, attack on: and Turkish leaders, 89, 90, 92, 97; and Dardanelles, 89; and Germany, 90, 92, 95; and Austria, 92; and Entente, 97

Bratianu, Ion (Rumanian prime minister, 1914–1918): 180; appointed prime minister, 36; and support of Austria, 38; on Rumanian commitments, 135, 213, 235; Entente negotiations by, 180, 207, 234, 237; and neutrality, 180, 239; and accord with Russia, 191; and Italy, 191, 205, 208; and Bulgaria, 195, 220, 230, 240; on Turkish munitions, 206–07, 216; on Bukovina, 211–12, 239; on Serbia, 220; on Rumanian troops, 220, 226, 229; and military events, 232, 338; and intervention, 234; and war preparations, 234; bolder stand of, 236; military demands of, 237; and fait accompli by, 237; deceptions of, 237–38, 240, 243; on Austro-Bulgarian troops, 239; war intentions of, 239

Breslau, 78, 79, 96–97

Bronsart von Schellendorff, Gunther (German military attaché in Bukarest), 198, 200

Brussilov offensive: influence of, on Rumania, 232; and Austrian leaders, 233, 312–13, 314–15, 317; Rumanian reaction to, 234, 324; against Austrian armies, 310, 312, 314; and Falkenhayn, 313

Bukovina: desired by Rumania, 180; Russia on, 182, 191, 203, 208, 237; Bethmann on, 184; Berchtold on, 184, 187, 191; Tisza on, 185, 191; Ru-

manian occupation of, 189–90; Italy on, 192; Austrian war threat over, 192; Austrian troops in, 202; Carp on, 203; Rumanian king on, 203; Germany on, 208, 212; Burian on, 209, 211, 212, 215, 223; Bratianu on, 211, 212, 213, 239; Marghiloman on, 218, 232; Czernin on, 218, 232–33; Austrian offer of, 219; Russian advance in, 233; Falkenhayn on, 290; Conrad on, 290, 312, 315

Bulgaria: anti-Russian, 16; turns to Central Powers, 17; commerce, 20–21; economy, 20–21; loans by, 21, 22–23, 147–49, 155; neutrality of, 28, 56; refuses Turkish alliance, 29; and Greece, 45, 138; relations with Turkey, 83, 84, 120, 138, 142; and German-Austrian alliance draft, 130–31; diplomatic situation of, 133, 150; public opinion in, 137, 144, 150; and Entente alliance, 138–39, 165; and Austro-German offers, 142; effects of battles on, 146; and declaration of guarantees, 161; bargaining skill of, 177; declares war on Serbia, 178; and Rumanian neutrality, 195–96; Rumanian fear of, 196–97; and Rumanian troops, 229; troop movements of, 230, 297, 305, 307–08; and threat of war, 307; attack on Rumania, 326–27. *See also* army; Triple Alliance; individual statesmen; military men; countries

—alliance with Central Powers: negotiations for, 129, 130, 167–68; and Macedonia, 129, 130, 136, 139, 141, 142, 143, 144–45, 152, 157, 162–63, 171, 173; and Pirot-Nish area, 139, 141, 143; and neutrality, 153–54, 155–56, 157; and contested zone for, 162; and German concessions for, 162; decision on, 166–67, 169; and military convention with, 169–70, 174–76, 293–94; final form of, 170–71, 173–74; significance of, 176–78

—alliance with Turkey (1914): original negotiations for, 28–29; Austrian attempts at, 82, 83, 85; German attempts at, 82, 83; role of Thrace in, 83; and Rumania, 85–86; conclusion of, 85, 134; nature of, 85, 134; Bulgarian guarantees in, 134, 135; and Rumanian accord, 135

—alliance with Turkey (1915): demands for, 120, 123; Austrian attempts at, 120–23 passim; German attempts at, 120–24 passim; Radoslavov on, 120–21, 122, 123; Turkish posture on, 121, 123, 124; terms and signing of, 124–26

Bülow, Bernhard, Prince von (German special ambassador in Rome, 1914–1915), 278

Burian, Stephan, Baron von (Austro-Hungarian foreign minister, 1915–1916), 150–51; and Bulgarian-Turkish alliance, 120; succeeds Berchtold, 150; views of, on Bulgaria, 151, 152, 153, 157, 158, 161; and Toscheff, 152; on Serbian campaign and Italy, 154–55; on Bulgarian mobilization and Italy, 155; on Bulgarian loan, 155; on von der Goltz, 162; on Bulgarian commitment, 164; on Bulgaria and the Entente, 165; on Bulgarian alliance terms, 168, 169, 171; on Michahelles, 169; on Serbian attack, 169, 280; on German offers to Bulgaria, 172; refuses Carp plan, 203–04; and Rumanian cooperation, 209–15 passim, 218; and Rumanian neutrality, 209, 212–15, 230; on Rumanian terms, 210–13 passim; and Tisza, 211; and German views on Rumania, 215; and Marghiloman plan, 219; on Rumanian army, 229–30; on Bulgarian threat, 231; on Brussilov offensive, 233; on German-Rumanian war, 235; on Rumanian king, 236; on Rumanian collective demarche, 241; and attack on Rumania, 242; Italian policy of, 280; and Italian belligerency, 284, 286; on Austrian war aims, 302, 303–08 passim; on Bulgarian troop occupations, 306, 307; demands military information, 314–15; relieved of post, 333; Bulgarian policy of, summarized, 336; Rumanian policy of, summarized, 338

—and concessions: on Macedonia, 153; on contested zone, 166; on Trentino, 201, 205; to Rumania, 210, 212, 223; for Turkish supply, 214, 215; to Italy, 278–79

Bussche, Hilmar von dem (German minister to Rumania, 1914–1916), 186–87; and Tisza, 187, 192; on concessions, 187, 189; on Transylvanian reforms, 188; and Czernin, 190, 210, 216, 222, 227, 231, 233, 339; and Austrian strategy, 194; on Rumanian

neutrality, 200; on Carp plan, 203; and Bratianu, 205, 216, 220, 226, 239–40; and King Ferdinand of Rumania, 205, 206, 222, 235, 236, 242–43; on military events, 205; on Turkish supply, 206, 217, 224; and Czernin independent action, 212; and Rumanian military accord, 222; and Falkenhayn, 226; on Rumanian troops, 229; on Bulgarian menace, 231; and Rumanian decision, 233; on German support of Austria, 234, 235; on Rumanian commitment, 235; on military preparations, 240

Cadorna, General Luigi (Italian chief of staff), 286–87

Carol (king of Rumania, 1881–1914): loyal to Triplice, 31; on Transylvania, 34; attitudes of, 35–36; and Rumanian belligerency, 38; and Franz Joseph, 38; and Wilhelm, 38; and Crown Council decision, 39; and aid to Central Powers, 67; on neutrality, 135; political control by, 179; on violation of Rumania, 181; on public opinion, 182

Carp, Petru (Rumanian prime minister, 1912): pro-German, 36; plan of, for Rumanian aid, 203; ambitions of, 204; on Crown Council, 245

Carpathian mountains: Russian campaigns in, 208, 275, 283; and Austrian army, 253, 257, 261, 263, 276, 277, 279, 280, 329, 330; Conrad on defense of, 273, 281; Falkenhayn on, 280, 281; and Gorlice-Tarnow breakthrough, 283

Caucasus campaign, 94, 111–13

Central Powers: diplomatic goal of, 3; Bulgarian policy of, 16, 24; and Bulgarian economy, 20, 21–24; and Greek finance, 42, 43; disagree on Greece, 45–46, 49; and Kavalla, 49; initial frustration of, 58; war supplies of, 62; and economic coordination, 63; and military cooperation, 64, 65; military isolation of, 69; and Turkish capitulations, 80–81; and Turkish participation, 82; and Turkish financing, 93; and Bulgarian alliance, 130–31, 145, 173–74; and Balkan accords, 133; on Bulgaria attacking Serbia, 165; sign Bulgarian military convention, 174–76; mount Serbian attack, 178; and Rumanian neutrality, 181,

207; Rumanian policy of, 181, 191–92, 216, 221–22, 240–42; and Rumanian-Bulgarian accord, 195; Rumania and welfare of, 199–200; and Italy, 200–201; and Rumanian hostility, 200; and Rumanian grain, 223–24, 225; and Rumanian cabinet, 228; and Rumanian politics, 232, 242; unanimity between, 234–35; and Bratianu, 237; and Entente concessions, 237; military cooperation between, 258; disparity between, 334, 339; and Balkan complexities, 339–40; military condition of, 343; problems of, 344. *See also* Triple Alliance

—commerce of. *See* Bulgaria; Greece; Rumania; Turkey

—military high commands of: hostility between, 251–60 passim, 265, 340; disparity between, on Balkans, 272; and dispute on Italian campaign, 287; and Bulgaria, 291–93; and Serbia, 299; open break between, 300. *See also* German High Command; inter-allied hostilities; individual military men

Conrad von Hötzendorf, General Franz (Austro-Hungarian chief of staff, 1906–1917): and Moltke, 8, 65; prewar plans of, 65–66; on Schlieffen plan, 65; on Rumania, 67–68, 211, 221, 241, 242, 269, 270, 289, 290, 297–98, 324–28 passim; on Turkish relief, 86; on Serbian campaign, 117–19, 154, 252, 272–74, 281–82, 288, 291; on Italy, 205, 279, 282, 284, 286, 308–09; on Russian march through Rumania, 221; and eastern front, 252, 253, 254, 261–62, 263, 296, 312–13, 314; on prewar agreements, 253–54, 255; character of, 256–57; and Falkenhayn, 261; frustrations of, 264, 341; Germanophobia of, 265; on Russia, 267, 271–72; Balkan concerns of, 268–69; on Bulgaria, 269, 270, 291–93, 306, 326; on command of German troops, 287; on Turkish munitions, 289–90; on Salonika campaign, 298, 299; and attack on Montenegro, 300; and Austrian war aims, 303–08 passim; optimism of, 315; loss of confidence in, 316; relieved of post, 333; dilemma and weaknesses of, 340, 343; and foreign office, 342–43. *See also* Carpathian mountains; Falkenhayn; inter-allied hostilities; unified command

Constantine (king of Greece, 1913–1917): pro-German views of, 47; and Dreibund connection, 47; seeks German support, 48; on war preparations, 54; on neutrality, 55

Costinescu, Emil (Rumanian finance minister), 207, 224

Council of Ambassadors, 45, 51

Crajniceanu, General Gregor (Rumanian chief of staff, 1908–1912), 67

Cramon, General August von (German liaison officer at Austrian army headquarters, 1915–1918): on Bulgarian military convention, 292–93; and Conrad-Falkenhayn dispute, 300; and Italian campaign, 309; and Austrian forces, 312; on Austrian armies, 313; and unified command, 314

Crown Council. *See* Rumania

Czernin, Ottokar von (Austro-Hungarian minister to Rumania, 1913–1916): posted to Bukarest, 33; analyzes Rumania, 33–34, 37; on Carol, 35, 189, 190; on Bulgaria, 36, 230–31; and Berchtold, 181, 188, 190; on Rumanian situation, 181; pessimism of, 186; on Transylvania, 188, 189, 213; and Ferdinand, 201, 230, 236, 237; and Bratianu, 202, 211, 213, 216, 218, 220, 230, 234, 237, 238, 239; and Stirbey, 202; and Queen Marie, 202; and Burian, 203–04, 209, 211, 213, 215, 218, 219, 222–23, 227, 228, 230, 231, 236; and Carp, 203; strong tactics of, 206; and Rumanian mobilization, 220; on Rumanian commitments, 222; on Russian march through Rumania, 222, 230; and Rumanian cabinet, 227–28; on Rumanian neutrality, 227; on diplomatic threats, 227; and dislike of Bussche, 231; on bribes, 233; on Brussilov offensive, 233; on Rumanian decision for war, 233; on Rumanian preparations, 239; appointed foreign minister, 333

—and Rumanian concessions: on granting of, 186; on timing of, 189; on publication of, 193; on offers of, 209, 222; and Bussche on, 339

Danev, Stojan (Bulgarian prime minister, 1913), 17

Dankle, Viktor (Austrian general), 258

Dardanelles: defense of, 88; German naval commanders on, 88; and Black Sea attack, 89; closure of, 91; and English fleet, 91; and Sir Edward

Grey, 91; Wangenheim on, 91; British attack on, 114, 118, 124; German defense of, 114, 118; Usedom on, 117; Entente landings at, 118; saved, 126; Turkish losses at, 126; and Bulgarian neutrality, 152; and Gallipoli, 217

Debra, 305

Derussi, George (Rumanian minister to Bulgaria), 196, 197

Djakova: Bulgarian occupation of, 305–07 passim

Djavid Bey (Turkish finance minister): alliance disclosed to, 73; and army reduction, 93; anti-German views of, 101; resignation of, 101

Djemal Pasha (Turkish minister of marine): alliance disclosed to, 73; background of, 75–76; Machiavellianism of, 75–76; accepts intervention, 92, 96; and Egypt, 94–95, 112–13; requests alliance extension, 101. See also Turkey

Dobrudja campaign, 327–28

Dreibund. See Triple Alliance

Dual Monarchy. See Austria-Hungary

Elbasan: Bulgarian occupation of, 305–07 passim

Emperor. See Franz Joseph

Empire. See Austria-Hungary

England, 225, 226. See also Dardanelles; Entente Powers

Enos-Midia line: and Bulgaria, 121–22; and Turkey, 121; Entente offers of, 153, 156

Entente Powers: rapprochement with Rumania by, 36; and Capitulations, 80; disagree over Bulgaria, 138–39; lose Bulgaria, 139; offers of, to Bulgaria, 165; ultimatum of, to Bulgaria, 178; and Salonika landing, 298

Enver Pasha (Turkish minister of war): pro-German, 6; approaches Wangenheim, 10; and Greco-Turkish war, 51; and army reforms, 69; clashes with Liman, 69; rise of, 74; attitude of, 74; calculations of, 75; Wangenheim on, 75; on Black Sea attack, 89; and intervention, 92, 96; military plans of, 94; instructs Souchon, 96; sealed orders of, 96; ends Turkish neutrality, 98; impatience of, 98; Pan-Turanism of, 99; on alliance extension, 101; military campaign of, 111–12; and munitions, 114; on Serbian campaign, 117; and Falkenhayn, 127. See also Bulgarian-Turkish alliance

Erzberger, Matthias (German politician): meets with Tisza, 213–14; and Transylvanian reforms, 214

Falkenhayn, Erich von (German minister of war, 1913–1914; chief of staff, 1914–1916): and aid to Turkey, 114; Zimmermann to, on Turkey, 116; on Serbia, 117, 119, 154, 160, 280–81, 288, 291, 341; and Bulgarian-Turkish alliance, 122, 124; and plans of Enver, 127; on Italian entry, 205, 279; on Rumania, 211, 216, 222, 223, 226, 229, 242, 289, 290, 298, 324, 330; succeeds Moltke, 256; character of, 256–57; and relief of Austria, 257–58; Conrad meets with, 261; on western front, 261, 263, 264; on Russian campaign, 262, 276, 282–83, 296; and Wilhelm, 262; on Austrian weakness, 265–66; on Russian peace, 266; on Italian concessions, 279, 281, 282, 284, 286; on Turkish munitions, 289; and Tisza, 290; and Bulgarian military convention, 291–93; closes Russian front, 291; on Volhynia, 296; on Salonika, 298, 299–300; on Montenegro, 300; on Bulgarian occupations, 307; on Italian offensive, 309; and Brussilov offensive, 313; resignation of, 322; pragmatism of, 340; strategy of, 340; and Foreign Office, 341–42; patience of, 341. See also Conrad von Hötzendorf; inter-allied hostilities; meetings, military; unified command

Ferdinand (king of Bulgaria): 19–20; and Franz Joseph, 18; politics of, 19; caution of, 26; approves alliance, 27; and Bulgarian interests, 30; and diplomatic initiative, 30, 135; on signing of alliance, 132–33; anti-Russian views of, 136; refuses commitment, 146–47; and Bulgarian military, 154; refuses war entry, 163; and military convention, 166; decides on alliance, 166–67

Ferdinand (king of Rumania): 198; and Bratianu, 196, 237, 242; pro-German, 198; on neutrality, 198, 213, 228; dilemma of, 199; on success of Central Powers, 201; on Bukovina, 202–03; caution of, 207; on Turkish supply, 217; on Serbia, 220; opposes cabinet change, 227; denies Entente alliance, 236

Fethi Bey (Turkish minister to Bulgaria), 142

Filipescu, Nicholas (leader of Rumanian Conservative Party faction): nationalism of, 179; pro-Entente, 198; pro-French, 207; demands mobilization, 220; desires war, 234

finances. See Bethmann-Hollweg; Burian; Central Powers; loans by Central Powers; Michahelles; Tarnowski

Fitschev, General (Bulgarian chief of staff, 1914–1915), 146

Fleischmann, Moritz von (Austrian liaison officer at German headquarters east), 254

Forgach, Johann von (section chief, Austrian Foreign Office): on Rumanian occupation of Transylvania, 188

Franz Joseph (emperor of Austria-Hungary): on Bulgarian alliance, 24; and Tisza, 34; and Carol, 38; requests Rumanian support, 182; on Conrad, 315–16, 321; and unified command, 317, 319, 321, 323; death of, 332

Frederick, Archduke (commander in chief of Austrian armies): requests unified command, 259

Freytag-Loringhoven, General Hugo von (German liaison officer at Austrian army headquarters, 1914–1915), 266, 267

Fürstenberg, Prince Emil von (German legation secretary in Athens), 50

Gantscheff, Peter (Bulgarian colonel): ordered to Pless, 123; negotiations of, 167, 168; and Bulgarian military convention, 291–93 passim

George (king of Greece), 44, 47

German High Command: and Turkish military action, 86; disagreement in, 261, 262, 267, 275, 276, 277, 294–96; controls Austrian generals, 287. See also Central Powers; Falkenhayn; Hindenburg; Ludendorff; inter-allied hostility; Wilhelm II

German Ninth Army: southern attack by, 258; northern attack by, 260–61; under Mackensen, 260–61; advance of, 262–63

Germany: on Bulgaria, 18, 19, 26, 28, 136, 140, 149, 150, 153–54, 157, 162, 171, 173, 174, 176, 307–08, 336; on Rumania, 18, 19, 32, 84, 194, 208, 212, 221, 235, 238, 246, 337; on Greek loan commission, 43; efforts by, to align Greece, 47; caution of, on Greece, 48; on Kavalla, 49; on Greco-Turkish accord, 50; Greek policy of, 53; on Turkish-Bulgarian accord, 53; military strength of, 59; military cohesiveness of, 62; war supplies of, 62–63; ships of, 77, 78; and Turkish navy, 79; Turkish loan from, 81; and Second Turkish Alliance, 102–10 passim; and Turkish supply, 118; and Bulgarian-Turkish alliance, 120; supports Austria in Bukarest, 201; favors Carp plan, 204; on Rumanian-Russian talks, 208; and Tisza, 208; and Marghiloman plan, 219; on Austrian armies, 265; and Italian belligerency, 287; and Austrian war aims, 302; and Dobrudja campaign, 327–28; and war sacrifices, 334; consistency of, 335; Turkish posture of, 335–36; expediency of, 336. See also army; German High Command; German Ninth Army; Triple Alliance; individual statesmen; military men

Geshov, Ivan (Bulgarian prime minister, 1911–1913), 17

Ghenadiev, Nicoll (leader of Bulgarian Stambulovist Party), 143, 150

Goeben, 78, 79, 96–97

Goltz, General Colmar von der (German advisor to Turkish army), 4; work of, 69; on English loan to Bulgaria, 148; on loan by Central Powers, 148; tension created by, 162

Gorlice-Tarnow attack, 283–84

Grand Vizier. See Said Halim Pasha

Greece: favors Entente, 39–40; economy of, 40–43; finances of, 41–43 passim; Entente proponderance in, 43; hostile to Bulgaria and Turkey, 44–45; and Bulgarian alliance, 45; Albanian ambitions of, 46; and conflict with Turkey, 50, 52, 84, 85, 86, 94; neutrality of, 58, 177; islands of, 79; and Serbia, 83, 133, 177; and Rumanian dreibund, 84; Berchtold on, 84, 138–39; Germany and ambiguity of, 84; guaranteed Kavalla, 129; and Bulgaria, 133, 139, 151, 167, 168, 170, 174; Entente position on, 138–39; cooperation of, with Rumania, 140; and casus foederis, 151; and concessions, 156; coastal areas of, 158; Rumanian ties with, 158; king of, and neutrality, 177; Zimmermann on, 272; Conrad on, 298–99; Falkenhayn on, 298–99

Grey, Sir Edward (British foreign secretary): on Dardanelles, 91; and offers to Bulgaria, 138; on Balkan league, 138

Groener, General Wilhelm von, 294

Halil Bey (Turkish minister of foreign affairs): on intervention, 92, 96; wavering of, 96; on alliance extension, 100–101, 106, 107

Hilmi Pasha (Turkish ambassador to Austria-Hungary), 50

Hindenburg, General Paul von (German chief of staff, 1916–1919): made eastern commander, 254; and Ninth Army, 258; retreat of, 258; relief of Austria by, 260; supports Conrad strategy, 262; and Bethmann-Hollweg, 267; on concessions to Rumania, 271; on Russian offensive, 276; and Wilhelm, 276; attack by, 278; opposes Falkenhayn, 296; and unified command, 317–18, 319, 323; succeeds Falkenhayn, 322; and Rumania, 329–30

Hohenlohe, Prince Gottfried zu (Austro-Hungarian ambassador to Germany, 1914–1918): and Turkish alliance, 102; on Bulgaria, 143, 144, 151, 156, 307; and Totschkoff, 156; and Michahelles, 169; on Austrian interests, 172; on German rudeness, 176; and Wilhelm on Rumania, 188; on Tisza, 192–93; and Rumanian belligerency, 193; on German-Rumanian war, 235; and Russian march through Rumania, 241; and military aid, 255; on Austrian retreat, 256; on military problems, 256; on unified command, 259–60; on peace with Russia, 267; and Rumanian aid, 270–71

Holy War, 99–100

Hötzendorf. See Conrad von Hötzendorf

Humann, Hans (German naval attaché in Constantinople), 4–5

Hungary. See Austria-Hungary

Iliescu, Dimitri (Rumanian general), 193

inter-allied hostilities: between diplomats, 20, 160–62 passim, 168, 169, 176, 182, 194–95, 214, 215, 227, 235; between military chiefs, 261, 264, 265, 267, 274, 291–95 passim, 300, 321

Ionescu, Take (leader of Rumanian Conservative Democrat Party): supports Bratianu, 179; pro-British, 207; demands mobilization, 220

Italy: opposes Greece, 47; and Second Turkish Alliance, 104, 109–10; declares war, 163, 286; and Rumania, 187, 206, 275; German fear of, 205; and outcome of war, 268; military preparations of, 275; and concessions to, 278; Conrad on, 284, 286; Falkenhayn on, 284; Austrian attack on, 308, 309; attacks by, 313. See also army; Triple Alliance; individual statesmen; military men

Izzet Pasha (Turkish minister of war), 69

Jagow, Gottlieb von (German secretary of state for foreign affairs, 1913–1916): on Turkish negotiations, 9, 76, 105; distrust of Bulgaria by, 19; on Greek aspirations, 47; on Kavalla, 49; urges Serbian attack, 117; on Turkish strength, 119; on Bulgarian negotiations, 136, 140, 144, 148, 154, 155, 166; on von der Goltz, 162; on Serbian attack, 163; on Bulgaria and Entente, 165; and Bulgarian alliance terms, 168, 171–72; on Michahelles, 169; ignores Austria, 172; and Trentino concession, 201; and promises to Rumania, 210; advises Czernin, 212; and Marghiloman plan, 219; rejects force in Rumania, 223; and war with Rumania, 229, 235; on Bessarabia, 233; on Rumanian collective demarche, 241; on Russian peace, 267; resignation of, 332

Kaiser. See Wilhelm II

Karl, Archduke (successor to Franz Joseph), 332

Kavalla, 49, 53, 138, 142

Körber, Ernest von (Austrian finance minister), 304, 305

Kress von Kressenstein, Colonel Friedrich (staff officer, German military mission to Turkey), 95, 112

Krobatin, Alexander von (Austrian minister of war), 304, 305

Kundmann, Rudolf (aide-de-camp to Conrad von Hötzendorf), 261, 263

Leipzig, Colonel von (German military attaché in Constantinople), 154, 155–56

Liman von Sanders, General Otto (head of German military mission to Turkey): military reforms of, 4; on Turkish army, 8, 13; work of, 69; and Enver, 69, 95; and German ships, 77; and Berlin, 95; and Wangenheim, 95; on Egypt, 95

loans by Central Powers: to Bulgaria, 22–24, 147–49, 167–68, 171–72, 174, 177; to Turkey, 81–82, 93, 94. See also Bethmann-Hollweg; Burian; Central Powers; Michahelles; Tarnowski

Ludendorff, General Erich (chief of staff to Hindenburg, 1914–1916; German first quartermaster-general, 1916–1919): and relief of Austria, 254; and Conrad, 262, 276; and Bethmann, 267; and strategy, 276; and Rumanian attack, 329–30. See also unified command

Macedonia: Bulgarian claims in, 26, 27, 129, 136, 168; Greek view of, 44; and Venizelos, 44; Greek-Serbian division of, 45; Constantine on, 55; and Central Powers, 123, 136, 141; Russia and Bulgaria in, 133, 139; and Entente, 138, 139, 156, 165, 180; Bulgarian action in, 141; note of guarantee on, 143–45; and Bulgarian neutrality, 152, 170; Bulgarian declaration on, 157, 161; German concessions on, 171; and Bulgarian alliance, 173–74; Conrad on, 269; Bulgarian troops in, 325

Mach, Richard von (German correspondent for Kölnische Zeitung): urges Bulgarian concessions, 153

Mackensen, August von (German general): and Serbian campaign, 176, 291–92; command of Ninth Army, 260–61; on Salonika campaign, 299; and Rumanian campaign, 327–32 passim

Majorescu, Titu (Rumanian prime minister, 1912–1914): cabinet of, replaced, 36; pro-German, 218; and lack of majority, 227, 228; and Rumanian king, 242

Mallet, Sir Louis (British ambassador to Turkey): supports Capitulations, 80

Marghiloman, Alexander (leader of Rumanian Conservative Party faction): pro-German, 179; and concessions to Rumania, 182, 232–33; political plan of, 218

Marie (queen of Rumania), 186, 198, 202, 221

Maritza line: Bulgarian-Turkish negotiations on, 120–26 passim

meetings, diplomatic: in Vienna, 18, 215, 306; at Konipischt, 35; at Constanza, 36; at Pless, 140, 195, 200, 205, 210, 278; in Budapest, 187; in Berlin, 214, 290

meetings, military: in Berlin, 261, 275; in Breslau, 263–64; in Oppeln, 264; in Posen, 267, 294–95; at Pless, 275–77, 292–93, 319; at Teschen, 285, 293, 320; in Vienna, 315, 325

Metianu, Archbishop (Rumanian metropolitan), 194

Metternich, Otto von (German prince): mission to Bukarest, 221

Midia. See Enos-Midia line

Michahelles, Gustav (German minister to Bulgaria): on Bulgarian loan, 22, 24, 155; on Bulgarian guarantees, 85; and Radoslavov, 85, 138, 139, 144, 155, 157, 165, 172; and signing of Bulgarian alliance, 129; and King Ferdinand of Bulgaria, 132, 135, 154, 162; and Tarnowski, 132, 133, 144, 161, 165–66; on Bulgarian-Turkish Alliance, 134; Bulgaria distrusted by, 140; on written guarantees, 144, 158; and Jagow, 147, 155, 158, 165, 171, 173; on Bulgarian demands, 154; on Entente, 166; and lack of subtlety, 169, 339; submits alliance terms, 172

military preparations: of Austria, 64–66 passim; of Germany, 64–66 passim; of Russia, 66; of Rumania, 67; of Turkey, 69

Ministerial Council (Austrian): and Bulgaria, 26; on Austrian war aims, 304–05

Moltke, General Helmuth von (German chief of staff, 1906–1914): on Turkish army, 8; and Conrad, 64; misunderstanding of, 64; distrust of Bulgarians by, 68; approves Enver plan, 95; and Austrian relief, 253, 254; on Italy and Balkans, 268–69; on Bulgaria, 269; on Rumania, 269

Monarchy. See Austria-Hungary

Montenegro: Austrian march on, 300; disposition of, 302–05; dispute over, 305–07 passim; surrender of, 305

Mortzun, Vasil (Rumanian minister of interior): on neutrality, 189; and concessions, 209

Nicholas, Grand Duke (Russian commander in chief): plans of, disrupted, 263

Nish. See Pirot-Nish area

Nowak, Rudolf (Austrian military attaché in Sofia): and Bulgarian attack on Rumania, 326, 327

Ottoman Empire. See Turkey

Pallavicini, Johann von (Austrian ambassador to Turkey, 1906–1918): stature of, 5; on Turkish alliance, 13–14, 15–16; and Wangenheim, 14, 15, 80, 81, 86–87, 92, 98, 99, 102, 108; on Turkish-Bulgarian alliance, 29, 83, 120, 123; on Greek-Turkish accord, 57; and Turkish concessions, 79; and Said Halim, 85; on Turkish commitment, 87; on Black Sea attack, 90, 92; and Holy War, 99–100; and Turkish alliance extension, 101–02; on Turkish vierbund, 104; on Second Turkish Alliance, 106–08 passim

Pan-Turanism, 7, 99

Pirot-Nish area, 139, 141, 143

Pless. See meetings, diplomatic; meetings, military

Pohl, Admiral Hugo von (chief of German Admiralty staff), 88

Porumbaru, Emanuel (Rumanian foreign minister), 230

Potiorek, General Oskar (Austrian commander in Serbia), 252, 270, 272

Pristina: Bulgarian occupation of, 305–07 passim

Prittwitz, General Maximilian (commander in East Prussia, 1914): and Austrian strategy, 253; defeat of, 253; replaced by Hindenburg, 254

Prizren: Bulgarian occupation of, 305–07 passim

public opinion: Rumanian, 36, 38, 194, 199, 207, 233; Turkish, 100; Bulgarian, 137, 144, 150; Austrian, 314

Quadt, Albert (German minister to Greece), 47, 54

Radeff, Simon (Bulgarian minister to Rumania), 197

Radoslavov, Vasil (Bulgarian prime minister, 1914–1918): Pro-German and -Austrian, 17; background and capacities of, 131–32; political strength of, 132, 137; refuses commitment, 132, 138; on Rumanian accord, 135; territories desired by, 136; Entente negotiations with, 139–40; on written declaration, 143; on note of guarantee, 144, 145, 157, 163; on Bulgarian neutrality, 152, 164; on military convention, 170; opposition to, 178; and Bulgarian-Rumanian guarantees, 196; and Derussi, 197; and Bratianu, 230; and Bulgarian troops, 231–32; on alliance obligations, 327

Rumania: declares neutrality, 31, 56; population of, 31; economy of, 31–32; attitude toward Central Powers, 33, 179, 180, 202, 229; and Transylvania, 34; public opinion in, 36, 38, 194, 199, 207, 233; and Austrian ultimatum to Serbia, 37; Crown Council of, 38, 39, 190, 243; and Russia, 38, 182, 190–91, 221; and Serbia, 38; army of, 67; refuses military aid, 68; seeks dreibund, 84; assures neutrality, 135; and Bulgaria, 135, 195, 196; political parties in, 179; and Italy, 187, 206; military opinion in, 198; effect on, by war events, 199, 200, 201, 202, 204–05, 208, 209, 217, 219, 229, 232, 234; and Turkish supply, 206–07, 210, 212–16 passim; political leaders in, 207; and Entente agreements, 220; and grain supply, 223–24, 225, 229; war spirit in, 234; war preparations of, 238, 240; ultimatum to, 241; declaration of war by, 243–44, 328; position of, summarized, 246–47; military convention against, 325; attacks Central Powers, 329; defeat of, 332. See also army; Triple Alliance; individual statesmen; military men; countries

Russia: and Rumania, 38, 182, 190–91, 221; military condition of, 66; mobilization of, 66–67; and Bulgaria, 133, 139; attacks Prussia, 253. See also army; individual statesmen; military men; countries

—decisive campaign against: Conrad on, 261, 262, 264, 271, 273–74, 275, 276, 282; Falkenhayn on, 262, 263–64, 276, 294–96; Hindenburg and Ludendorff on, 262, 276, 294–96; Berchtold on, 271; and Wilhelm, 276–77; limited success of, 278; second attempt at, 283–84, 291

Said Halim Pasha (Turkish grand vizier): pro-German, 6; alliance offers of, 12; and Venizelos, 52; on neutrality, 73–74; background of, 74; on German ships, 77; on Black Sea attack, 89; threatens resignation, 97; and Second Turkish Alliance, 104; and Pallavicini, 107. See also Bulgaria, alliance with Turkey (1915)

Salonika: and Greece, 45, 298; and Entente, 229, 298, 324, 343; German-Austrian campaign against, 299, 300; and Bulgarian troops, 297, 325, 326; and Serbia, 302

Sanders, Liman von. See Liman von Sanders

Sazanov, Serge (Russian foreign minister, 1910–1916), 38

Schellendorff, Bronsart von. See Bronsart von Schellendorff

Schlieffen, General Alfred von (German chief of staff, 1891–1906), 64

Second Turkish Alliance: initial form of, 100–102; and Austria, 102–03, 105, 108–09; and Germany, 102–03, 105, 107, 108–09; changes in, 104; and Italy, 104; articles of, 105; and explicative note, 105, 109; and military convention, 106; final terms of, 108–09; significance of, 110

Serbia: and Turkish supply, 126; quiescent front in, 275–76; Bulgarian occupations in, 305–08 passim
—campaign against: and Potiorek, 252, 270, 272; Conrad on, 272, 273, 274, 288; Balkan significance of, 272, 273–74, 288; Falkenhayn on, 272; Zimmermann on, 272; start of, 294; troop dispositions for, 294–96; success of, 296–97

Slameczka, Oskar (Austrian military representative for Conrad): interrogation of, 315, 325–26

Sofia (queen of Greece), 47

Souchon, Admiral Wilhelm (commander-in-chief, Turkish navy): and Tirpitz, 77; command of cruisers by, 77; and Turkish navy, 79, 93; and Black Sea attack, 89, 90, 96; and Enver, 96

Stirbey, Prince (Rumanian statesman), 202

Stürgkh, Joseph (Austrian military representative at German headquarters): 255, 265

Stürgkh, Karl (prime minister of Austria, 1911–1916): at Ministerial Council, 304; on war aims, 305; military orientation of, 315, 325

Szögyény, Ladislaus (Austrian ambassador to Germany): and Jagow on Turkey, 9; and Bulgarian loan, 147

Talaat Bey (Turkish minister of interior): pro-German, 6–7; talents and duties of, 75; temporizing by, 75; and Bulgaria, 85; and Black Sea attack, 89; and intervention, 92, 96; on alliance extension, 101, 107. See also Bulgaria, alliances with Turkey

Tannenberg, 254

Tarnow attack, 283–84

Tarnowski, Adam (Austrian minister to Bulgaria, 1911–1917): on Bulgarian Russophobia, 17; and Bulgarian alliance, 26–27, 130, 134, 176; and Bulgarian neutrality, 27; on Bulgarian-Turkish alliance, 29, 85, 121, 134; and Berchtold, 130, 138, 141, 142, 143, 145; and Radoslavov, 131–32, 138, 139, 141, 143, 152, 162–65 passim, 167; and Michahelles, 132, 133, 169, 339; background and capacities of, 135–36; on Bulgarian concessions, 139; on Bulgarian hesitations, 140–41; on Entente offers, 141, 165; and Ghenadiev, 143; and Radoslavov declaration, 143; on Bulgarian loan, 147; and Burian, 152, 161, 164, 165, 168; on written guarantee, 158; on von der Goltz, 162; on Bulgarian commitment, 164

Teschen. See meetings, military

Theotoky, Nicholas (Greek minister to Germany), 47, 56, 78

Thrace, 83

Tirpitz, Admiral Alfred von (German navy minister), 77, 78, 88

Tisza, Stephan (prime minister of Hungary): personality and goals of, 185; and concessions to Rumania, 185, 187, 188–89, 193, 194, 211, 213; visits German headquarters, 195; Bethmann on, 207; on Italy, 211; and Turkish supply, 214; Moltke on, 269; war goals of, 303–05 passim; military orientation of, 315, 325. *See also* individual statesmen; military men

Tonchev, Andreas (Bulgarian finance minister): 17, 148, 149

Toscheff, Andrew (Bulgarian minister to Turkey; later to Austria-Hungary): and Turkish treaty, 82–83; on Serbian campaign, 150; on concessions, 153

Totschkoff (Bulgarian leader of Macedonian Committee): and Bulgarian-Turkish alliance, 123; on written guarantees, 156; on Macedonia, 162–63

Transylvania: Carol on, 34; Czernin on, 34, 193; Franz Ferdinand on, 34; Tisza on, 34, 187, 188–89, 193; Magyar domination in, 35; Rumanian Liberal Party on, 35; and Rumania, 180, 329; and Bussche, 187, 188, 192–93, 194; and Tschirschky, 188; timing of reforms in, 188–89; and Bethmann, 193–94, 214; publication of reforms in, 194; result of reforms in, 194; Austro-German conflict over, 194–95; and Erzberger, 213–14; Austrian defense of, 325, 330

Trentino, 201, 205

Triple Alliance (Triplice): and Turkey, 5–7 passim, 9–14 passim, 50, 53, 54; and Bulgaria, 17–20 passim, 22, 24, 25, 26, 29, 30, 53; and Rumania, 28, 31, 33, 35, 38, 68; and Balkan combination, 33, 45; and Greece, 47–50 passim, 54, 55; and Italy, 104

Tschirschky, Heinrich von (German ambassador to Austria-Hungary): and Turkish negotiations, 15; and German policy change, 25–26; and Berchtold on Greece, 48; and Turkish alliance, 106; and Bulgarian alliance, 129; and Toscheff, 150; on Bulgarian concessions, 153; and Rumanian concessions, 182–85 passim, 188, 190, 193, 208; and Austrian army, 193; on Carp plan, 204; on Tisza-Bethmann meeting, 215; and Marghiloman proposal, 218–19

Turkey: German predominance in, 3–4, 98; Austrian interests in, 5; cabinet of, 6, 7, 73; German views on, 8, 10; and alliance with Central Powers, 9–16; and Bulgarian alliance, 29, 82; and Greece, 45, 50, 51, 52; and neutrality, 56, 73; military condition of, 68–69; and alliance obligations, 73; and Entente attack, 73; and England, 76; and German ships, 77–78; and Capitulations, 79–81; treasury deficit of, 81; German loan to, 81; and Bulgarian war entry, 83, 119, 142; fleet of, 87–88; and war with Italy, 96; declaration of war by, 97; liability of, 98; Holy War by, 99; public opinion in, 100; and alliance extension, 100–101; military action of, 111–14; munitions problem of, 114, 116–19 passim, 122, 124, 126, 127–28; supply routes to, 114, 116; and Bratianu, 116; worth of, as ally, 127. *See also* army; Second Turkish Alliance; Triple Alliance; individual statesmen; military men; countries

—war participation of: and Turkish leaders, 73–74; and German-Austrian concessions, 79–81 passim; and Bulgaria, 82–85; and Conrad, 86; and Enver, 89, 94, 96; and Turkish cabinet crisis, 97. *See also* Berchtold; Bethmann-Hollweg; Pallavicini; Wangenheim; Wilhelm II

unified command: Archduke Frederick on, 259; Austrian control of, 259; Conrad on, 259, 313, 314, 317–23 passim; Franz Joseph on, 259, 317–23 passim; Hohenlohe on, 259–60; Wilhelm II on, 259, 319; Zimmermann on, 259–60; Falkenhayn on, 313, 314, 317–21 passim; Ludendorff plan for, 323; creation of, 323

Usedom, Guido (German admiral, commander of Dardanelles), 88, 116

Venizelos, Eleutherios (Prime minister of Greece): advent of, 44; expansionism of, 44; and grand vizier, 52; on Bulgaria, 56–57; on aid to Turks, 56–57; and Entente Powers, 57

Waldburg, Heinrich von (German chargé d'affaires in Bukarest), 38

Waldersee, Alfred von (German chief of staff, 1888–1891), 64

Waldthausen, Julius von (German minister to Rumania, 1912–1914), 37, 181, 182, 186

Wangenheim, Hans von (German ambassador to Turkey, 1912–1915): capabilities of, 4; and Turkish alliance, 9, 10, 11, 13; and Pallavicini, 14–15, 80, 81, 86–87, 92, 98, 99, 102, 108; on

Greco-Turkish alliance, 51; and Enver, 75; and Turkish action, 76, 96; ships desired by, 77; and *Goeben* and *Breslau*, 78, 88, 89; and Turkish concessions, 79; and Turkish Capitulations, 80; and Turkish loans, 81–82, 93, 94; on Bulgarian-Turkish alliance, 82, 83, 84, 120–21, 133–34; on Turkish commitment, 87, 98; on Black Sea attack, 88, 90, 91, 92; and Liman von Sanders, 95; and Holy War, 99; and Turkish alliance extension, 101–02, 103, 105, 107; and signing of Turkish alliance, 106, 108; on Serbian offensive, 116; on Turkish endurance, 116, 119

Weitz, Paul (German correspondent for *Frankfurter Zeitung*), 5

Wilhelm II (German kaiser): on Turkish alliance, 11, 12; royal connections of, 18–19; and King Ferdinand of Bulgaria, 19, 47; and Michahelles, 28; on Bulgarian-Turkish alliance, 30, 83; and Tisza, 35; and King Carol, 38, 182; and King Constantine, 47, 53, 54, 56; on Greece, 48; on Black Sea attack, 89; and Liman von Sanders, 95; on Rumanian concessions, 187, 271; and Burian, 201; and King Ferdinand of Rumania, 202–03, 217; on Turkish supply, 217; on Russian campaign, 276–77; and unified command, 319, 323; and Rumanian declaration of war, 329

Young Turks: pro-German, 5; and cabinet factions, 6; and Balkan coalition, 6; and diplomatic isolation, 6; and Pan-Turanism, 7, 99; control of, by triumvirate, 101

Zekoff, Nikolaus (Bulgarian chief of staff): 306–07, 321, 326

Zimmermann, Arthur (German undersecretary of state for foreign affairs, 1911–1916): and Wilhelm II, 25; and Black Sea attack, 90; on Wangenheim, 92; on Holy War, 99; on Turkish alliance extension, 102, 103; on Serbian offensive, 116, 117; and ultimatum to Bulgaria, 137; on Bulgarian loan, 147, 148; and von Mach, 152; and Transylvania, 188; on Bussche, 195; on German meddling, 195; on German military aid, 255, 256; on unified command, 259–60; on Russian peace, 266; on Turkish supply, 272; replaces Jagow, 332

Zostoff (Bulgarian general), 326–27

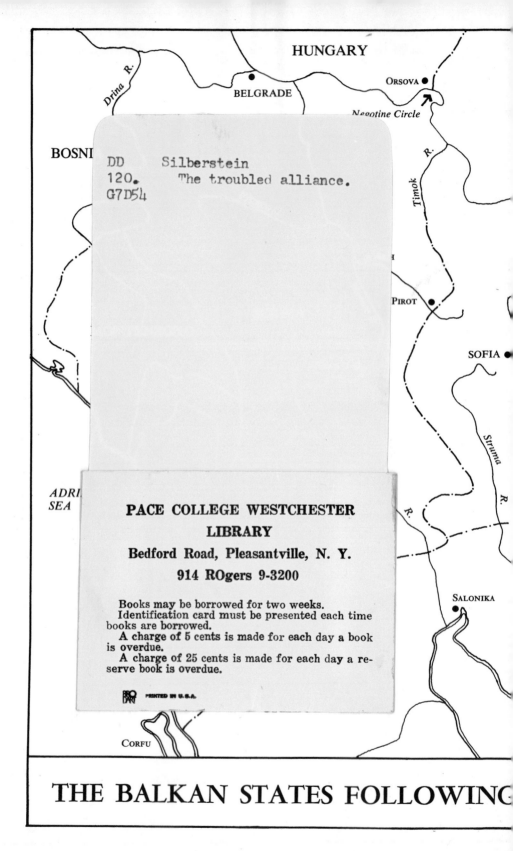